WAR TIME

*Providing new perspectives and
knowledge on an increasingly complex,
uncertain, and interconnected world.*

The Chatham House Insights Series
Series Editor: Caroline Soper

The Insights series provides new perspectives on and knowledge about an increasingly complex, uncertain, and interconnected world. Concise, lively, and authoritative, these books explore, through different modes of interpretation, a wide range of country, regional, and international developments, all within a global context. Focusing on topical issues in key policy areas, such as health, security, economics, law, and the environment, volumes in the series will be written accessibly by leading experts—both academic and practitioner—to anticipate trends and illuminate new ideas and thinking. Insights books will be of great interest to all those seeking to develop a deeper understanding of the policy challenges and choices facing decision-makers, including academics, practitioners, and general readers.

Published or forthcoming titles:

Amitai Etzioni, *Foreign Policy: Thinking Outside the Box* (2016)

David Lubin, *Dance of the Trillions: Developing Countries and Global Finance* (2018)

Keir Giles, *Moscow Rules: What Drives Russia to Confront the West* (2019)

Nigel Gould-Davies, *Tectonic Politics: Global Political
Risk in an Age of Transformation* (2019)

Jamie Gaskarth, *Secrets and Spies: UK Intelligence
Accountability after Iraq and Snowden* (2020)

Chatham House, the Royal Institute of International Affairs, is a world-leading policy institute based in London. Its mission is to help governments and societies build a sustainably secure, prosperous, and just world.

Chatham House does not express opinions of its own. The opinions expressed in this publication are the responsibility of the author(s).

WAR TIME

Temporality and
the Decline
of Western Military Power

Edited by

STEN RYNNING

OLIVIER SCHMITT

AMELIE THEUSSEN

BROOKINGS INSTITUTION PRESS
Washington, D.C.

CHATHAM HOUSE
The Royal Institute of International Affairs
London

The Brookings Institution is a private nonprofit organization devoted to research,
education, and publication on important issues of domestic and foreign policy. Its
principal purpose is to bring the highest quality independent research and analysis
to bear on current and emerging policy problems. Interpretations or conclusions in
Brookings publications should be understood to be solely those of the authors.

Library of Congress Control Number: 2020952573
ISBN 9780815738947 (pbk)
ISBN 9780815738954 (ebook)

9 8 7 6 5 4 3 2 1

Typeset in Adobe Garamond

Composition by Elliott Beard

Contents

Foreword   xi

Acknowledgments   xv

Introduction
STEN RYNNING | OLIVIER SCHMITT | AMELIE THEUSSEN
1

PART I
"CIVIC MILITARISM" AND THE TRAJECTORY OF WESTERN POWER

The Western Experience in Balancing Liberal and Military Virtues
STEN RYNNING
19

ONE
The Modern State
Rise and Decline of Civic Militarism
SARAH KREPS | ADI RAO
25

TWO
Making Time an Ally
Uncovering the Perils of Tactical Military Speed
PAUL BRISTER
42

THREE
Benefit or Burden?
NATO-led Military Missions and Western Cohesion
REBECCA R. MOORE
58

FOUR

The Future of the West

What If the United States Pulls Out of NATO?

TOBIAS BUNDE

85

PART II

WESTERN PERCEPTIONS OF TIME AND
THE INTERNATIONAL NORMATIVE ORDER

A Normative Order under Pressure

AMELIE THEUSSEN

109

FIVE

Civilian Casualties and Contemporary Coalition Operations

The Case of Afghanistan

KATHLEEN J. MCINNIS

115

SIX

Conflicting Norms of Intervention

When and How to Use Military Force?

NATASHA KUHRT

138

SEVEN

In the Shadows

The Challenge of Russian and Chinese Gray Zone Conflict for the West

AMELIE THEUSSEN | PETER VIGGO JAKOBSEN

161

EIGHT

Competing Norms

What If China Takes Control of Djibouti to Protect Its People?

ERNST DIJXHOORN

184

PART III
MILITARY OPERATIONS AND TEMPORALITY

Speed, Time, and Western Military Power
OLIVIER SCHMITT
207

NINE
Fighting, Fast and Slow?
Speed and Western Ways of War
PASCAL VENNESSON
211

TEN
War at Information Speed
Multi-Domain Warfighting Visions
NINA A. KOLLARS
230

ELEVEN
The Limits of Technology
The Impact of Speed and Innovation on Western Military Primacy
HEATHER WILLIAMS
253

TWELVE
Military Operations
What If Digital Technologies Fail on the Battlefield?
JOSEPH HENROTIN | STÉPHANE TAILLAT
275

Conclusion
STEN RYNNING | OLIVIER SCHMITT | AMELIE THEUSSEN
291

Contributors 303

Index 305

Foreword

There was a time not so long ago when the West hoped that it could stop worrying about its military power, and its ability to project it globally. The Cold War had come to an end with no Armageddon being necessary to determine its outcome. The peace dividend was being richly harvested at home. The citizens of the Western democracies, largely freed of the burdens of conscription and civil defense, came to believe that the residual security threats could be safely dealt with by the small professional armies that remained. If anything, the difficulties of peacekeeping and reconstruction in places like the Balkans, Afghanistan, and Iraq seemed to point to the limitations of military power rather than its utility. Could not development agencies, police trainers, NGOs, and diplomats do a better job? With declining budgets and a fraying link to civil society, armed forces in the Western democracies began to question their purpose and mission.

Yet, as so often in history, predictions of a more peaceful international order have been upended in a quick succession of strategic turning points. Russia has annexed Crimea and deployed its forces and personnel in Ukraine, Syria, Libya, and the Sahel. NATO is back to territorial collective defense. China has flexed its muscles in the East and South China Seas, Iran has spread its military tentacles across the Middle East, Turkey has intervened in Syria and now the eastern Mediterranean and Libya, nuclear modernization is proceeding apace, and it took a massive military coalition led by the United States to defeat a single terrorist group in Syria and Iraq. This year's annual report by the Stockholm International Peace Research Institute puts global military spending at just short of US$1.7 trillion, its highest-ever figure. Across the board military innovation is accelerating, from hypersonic missiles to space competition to cyber and autonomous weapons. Whatever the Western democracies may think about the usefulness of military power, their adversaries need no such persuasion when it comes to deploying their armies, navies, and air forces to advance their interests and influence in twenty-first-century geopolitics. As Trotsky famously put it: "You may not like war, but war likes you."

This shift has forced Western policymakers to face some unpleasant questions. How much military power do we need today to counter the threats and uphold our interests? What does this mean in terms of budgets, capabilities, technology, and organization? Are we as far behind our potential adversaries as is often claimed (especially by them) and if so, how can we best catch up, identifying our strengths and exploiting their weaknesses? How can we optimize our military power for deterrence so that we can transit the current turbulence in global geopolitics without lapsing into catastrophic war, particularly between the great powers?

These are tough questions and it is easy for policymakers to become overwhelmed by too many security challenges hitting them simultaneously from too many directions. Likewise pundits disagree over whether the response lies in more tanks or more cyber weapons, more soldiers or more intelligence analysts, engagement abroad, or pulling up the drawbridge at home. The choices range from grand strategy at the top, and how to merge military power with the other instruments of state influence, to the contract for the next field radio at the bottom. So where can the busy policymaker and the interested general reader turn for an accessible and authoritative guide through this maze of interrelated challenges, presented in a single volume rather than in scores of books and hundreds of think-tank reports? The answer is here, in *War Time: Temporality and the Decline of Western Military Power.*

The merit of this study lies first and foremost in the expertise of the authors who have contributed to it. Their judgments are grounded in deep research and their proposals have been carefully thought through. Yet their chapters have also been subjected to an exceptionally rigorous peer review process to ensure the accuracy and the quality of every paragraph. I myself had the opportunity to participate in this peer review process on one of the two days of workshop sessions at Chatham House and to see how thorough and far-reaching it was. Consequently the reader has the benefit of the best knowledge and most balanced assessments currently available. The second merit is the comprehensive nature of the study. It explores every aspect of security and defense policy, both domestic and international. It looks at alliances such as NATO and the transatlantic defense relationship, the role of the major military powers such China and Russia, the future of interventions based on the lessons learned from past experience, and the prospects for new norms and agreements to constrain dangerous military activity and aggression. Finally a very useful section puts the vital element of technology in the valuable context of speed, process, and military doctrine and organization. This helps to clarify many complex issues and to bring technology and strategy together, when so often they are addressed separately.

For all these reasons I am pleased to endorse this book and am honored to have participated, however modestly, in its elaboration. It is a work that deserves a wide and serious readership, and I am confident it will achieve it.

Jamie Shea
Professor of Strategy and Security, University of Exeter
Former NATO Deputy Assistant Secretary General for Emerging
    Security Challenges

Acknowledgments

Not just war, but also this book, is a product of its time. It has been shaped by a long war studies tradition that invites different disciplines to come together in a quest to produce relevant knowledge about the character of contemporary wars and the West's alleged decline. These are complex phenomena shaped by a multitude of factors, yet all are, as we argue in this book, connected by a certain understanding of temporality in the form of trajectories, perceptions, and pace. This project has brought together an outstanding group of experts to contribute their assessments of the role of time in Western concepts of military power and the West's ability to win wars. Without their willingness to draw on their professional experience, this book would not exist. The excellent Center for War Studies at the University of Southern Denmark, where we, the editors, are located, provided the necessary networks, connections, and expertise to make this book a reality, and we thank all of our colleagues for their ideas, comments, and support.

For organizing a workshop dedicated to the book at Yale University in August 2019, we would especially like to thank our colleague James Rogers. We are grateful for the support of Paul Kennedy, head of Yale's International Security Studies, and to workshop presenters and discussants—Shama Ams, Bach Avezdjanov, Jean-Francois Bélanger, Michael Brenes, Agnes Callamard,

Neil Cooper, Michael Franczak, Carolyn Horn, Wes Hutto, Jens Ringsmose, Jean-Baptiste Jeangene Vilmer, Emily Whalen, Michael John Williams, and Claire Yorke—for immensely helpful feedback.

We are indebted to David Dunn, Sibylle Scheipers, and Jamie Shea for constructive and insightful comments offered during and after a further study group workshop at Chatham House in September 2019. This workshop was co-funded by Chatham House and the Carlsberg Foundation, and we are grateful for their support. Finally, we gratefully acknowledge the anonymous reviewers who in early 2020 commented on the full manuscript. All remaining errors or inconsistencies in the book are solely our own responsibility.

We would like to thank our editors at Chatham House, Caroline Soper, Amanda Moss, and Margaret May, for believing in this project from the outset, for their outstanding help with and organization of the entire process, and for truly excellent editing. We also thank our partner in the United States, William Finan of the Brookings Institution Press, for sharing Chatham House's belief in the book and agreeing to publish it.

As the saying goes, all good things take time. The initial conversation with Caroline Soper and William Finan about what was then just an idea for a book took place in San Francisco in April 2018. The rest is a history of engagement and preoccupation that has come at a cost to our families. For their unfailing support we are beyond grateful.

Sten Rynning, Olivier Schmitt, and Amelie Theussen

WAR TIME

Introduction

STEN RYNNING

OLIVIER SCHMITT

AMELIE THEUSSEN

Why do Western countries lose wars? Military interventions in Iraq, Afghanistan and Libya, as well as the recent assertive behaviors of countries such as Russia and China, have shattered the image of a dominating West whose superior politics and military forces would almost inevitably overwhelm its opponents. Western military superiority is not a new idea, but it was given particular credence by the Western "victory" in the Cold War, followed by the successfully fought Gulf War of 1991, and then the liturgy of a Revolution in Military Affairs that the West supposedly mastered. Military exhaustion and defeat have since challenged the West, feeding waves of debate, first on whether it was and indeed should be vanishing as a force of international order,[1] then on whether liberal order could survive without it,[2] and, finally, on whether the West might still prove able to reconfigure its tools of war to a new age of forever wars in zones of contested power and insurgency.[3]

With this book we wish to take a fresh look at why "the West" is overwhelmingly powerful on the battlefield and yet also strategically fragile. We acknowledge that "the West" is a contentious term, whose definition has been changing over time. For example, Philippe Nemo establishes a morphogenesis of the West based on five foundational stages of equal importance.[4] The first is the "Greek miracle" at the end of the eighth century B.C., which generated ideas of societies based on law, reason, and education. The second stage is the Roman cosmopolis, which transformed law into an abstract set of rules determining and guaranteeing individuals' private property, thus establishing the subjects of law as autonomous moral agents. The third stage is the advent of Christianity, which introduced a new relationship with time, substituting an eschatological, linear perception of time (with a beginning and an end) to a cyclical perception for which time is an eternal revolving. The fourth stage is the Gregorian Reform and the "Papal Revolution" of the eleventh to thirteenth centuries, during which the Catholic Church replaced the Augustinian theology of the original sin with Anselm's doctrine of free will (which would influence St. Thomas Aquinas and Jean Calvin). This theological innovation emphasized that individuals' efforts matter in the process of their salvation. Finally, the fifth stage is the creation and promotion of modern liberalism, beginning with the English revolution in the seventeenth century. Of course, all these stages have been mixed, accepted, and respected to various degrees by specific political communities, but taken together they form the basis of a relatively shared self-perception and worldview among several societies. Building on this description, and for the purpose of this book, we understand "the West" as an institutional practice of military power directed by primarily liberal governments and societies.

We recognize the profound changes in the security environment of the West, from the rise of transnational terrorism to the return of great power conflict, and we contribute to the discussion on the Western way of war by using temporality as an anchoring concept. Temporality is here understood in the broad sense of how the past, the present, and the future relate to one another: it is thus a form of experience and thought among actors. Historians know well that time is not a neutral phenomenon experienced by all individuals equally, but a construct whose shape and texture vary:[5] already in 1889, philosopher Henri Bergson observed that time was "qualitatively multiple." In the context of this book, we understand temporality as composed of three interrelated dimensions: *trajectories, perceptions,* and *pace,* all of them shaping the actors' experiences and understanding.

Trajectories relate to the classical metaphysical discussion about the flow of time and its contested linearity and determinism. Actors thus tend to make sense of their experience through narratives implying a specific understanding of the flow of time. Since Edward T. Hall's classic *The Silent Language* (published in 1959), it has been well documented that Western actors tend to think of time as linear (or "monochronic"), and thus within the frame of the Aristotelian narrative structure (stories with a beginning, middle, and end);[6]

this in turn shapes how they perceive their own trajectories. This understanding has several consequences when it comes to the study of war. First, there is a relation between trajectories and identities: war narratives always involve the notion of extracting the individual from the present in order to protect the future of the political community. Traditional societies usually focus on a warrior gaining "eternal glory" though courage on the battlefield, but modern discourses of patriotism add a temporal dimension by emphasizing the nation's survival in the future. More importantly in the context of this book, the linear understanding of time places the trajectory of the West within a framework story of rise enabled by a "military revolution" (beginning), dominance (middle), and eventual fall (end), with numerous attempts by authors to discern whether the inevitable fall has already happened, is underway, or has not yet begun.

The second dimension of temporality explored in this book is the importance of perceptions of time. It is only logical that the multiple ways through which time is perceived across cultures and periods shape socio-political activities, including war and warfare.[7] Those perceptions shape, for example, the definition of the enemy, who can be presented as belonging to another temporality ("backward" or "barbarian"). It is telling that, when reacting to Russia's aggression against Ukraine in 2014, former US Secretary of State John Kerry declared: "You just don't, in the twenty-first century, behave in nineteenth-century fashion by invading another country on a completely trumped up pretext."[8] Political objectives thus define a clash of temporalities. Another example relates to the understanding of war: if war is perceived as cyclical, and thus inevitable, decisionmakers can have a higher tolerance of violence, feeding greater belligerency on the battlefield. Thus perceptions of time constitute a critical dimension in assessing the evolution of Western military power.

The third dimension of temporality is related to how humans experience the pace of life, defined as "the race, speed and relative rapidity or density of experiences, meanings, perceptions and activities."[9] Here again, research has shown that different cultures and historical periods experience pace differently. For example, historian Jean-Claude Schmitt has studied in detail how Western medieval societies from the eighth to the fourteenth century were profoundly shaped by specific "rhythms" that regulated the entire pace of life, from walking and praying to all forms of social intercourse.[10] When it comes to studying the pace of contemporary societies, Robert Levine and his colleagues have pioneered a number of comparative studies of indicators such as walking speed in downtown areas, postal clerk efficiency, public clock accuracy, and work speed.[11] They find that the pace of life is significantly faster in most Western countries than in other parts of the world. Extrapolating from these findings, it is no stretch to imagine that speed, as the defining feature of how Western societies experience the pace of life, also shapes the way they wage war in fundamental ways.

In this book we dissect this Western condition as a distinctive Western temporality composed of the combination of trajectories, perceptions, and pace, as defined here, shedding a new light on the debate about the past and future of Western military power.

The aim is not to engage the grand and politicized debate on whether the West is doomed or bound to lead. Rather, it is to argue that its historically contingent superiority in war has come with an inbuilt fracture that the West has only begun to understand. For the better part of two centuries this condition was underappreciated because the West generated the industrialized muscle that allowed it not only to win wars but to fight in the overwhelming ways that held its liberal and martial communities—citizens and soldiers—together in the belief that war must be fought only for progressive purposes. The West thus posed as the master of war. Today it is adjusting to the reality that, even when Western network-centric firepower is applied with precision from over the horizon, the inner pace and vagaries of war will dominate. This suggests that for the martial communities within the West, war was all along a recurrent phenomenon that not even liberal society could escape, while for liberal communities control must be regained by new means. As current strategies can no longer reconcile these communities, the West must look anew at its political, normative, and military understandings of war on the basis of a renewed understanding of temporality.

Writing in the shadow of the world wars of the early twentieth century, J. F. C. Fuller argued that "there is no reason why the world of today should be in its present mess."[12] If only governments and analysts had diagnosed with greater accuracy the forces that recast civilization through the nineteenth century, and their impact on warfare, he wrote, then it would have been within their powers to avert upheaval. Perhaps such diagnostic perception of unfolding tectonic shifts is a tall order, but it remains a key challenge for our era too. With this book we hope to contribute to meeting this challenge.

The following sections develop these three dimensions of trajectories, perceptions, and pace in more detail, before a discussion of the structure of the book explains the ways in which they are interrelated.

Trajectories: The Fate of the West

The first dimension of temporality addressed in this book is the trajectory of Western military power. The roots of Western military superiority and their durability define a great debate in the field, namely over the importance of the so-called military revolution in shaping the West's trajectory in the international system and the extent to which it depended on certain institutional practices, as opposed to brute material power.

Michael Roberts broke new ground in 1955 by introducing arguments about a "military revolution."[13] In his view, a combination of changes in tactics (volley fire, artillery, and cavalry charges) and strategies (related to the conduct of the Thirty Years' War) led to an increase in the size of armed forces, leading in turn to the emergence of the modern state, which had to establish the bureaucratic apparatus for extracting the resources required to wage wars. This self-reinforcing feedback loop of more resources leading to more military power and even more resources was famously summarized by Charles Tilly: "war made the State and the State made war."[14] Geoffrey Parker subsequently connected military revolution to the rise of the West in the international system. His causal paths differed slightly from those identified by Roberts (seeing guns and fortifications rather than tactical innovation as the drivers of change), but more significantly Parker explicitly linked the military revolution to the rise of Western domination in the international system: "the key to the Westerners' success in creating the first truly global empires between 1500 and 1750 depended upon precisely those improvements in the ability to wage war which have been termed 'the military revolution.' "[15] In this perspective, the gain in military effectiveness granted by the military revolution allowed Western countries to dominate, and thus subjugate, the empires they encountered in the Americas, Asia, and Africa: Western domination was established at gunpoint, thanks to the military revolution.

This argument has triggered an important debate among military historians,[16] with recent works questioning the logic of the revolution and Europe's expansion. First, the "military revolution" was not limited to Europe, since elements of it are found in many other empires at the time: the Chinese, for example, had already invented gunpowder and reached the key milestones of military and administrative modernity by 1200.[17]

Second, the "revolution" did not give any kind of military edge to the Europeans, since Western expansion until the nineteenth century was not conducted by mass armies of musketeers and pikesmen but instead by tiny expeditionary forces, essentially supported by private entrepreneurs. Those forces were often in awe of the massive empires they encountered in Africa, Asia, and the Americas: European expansion is better explained by a combination of deference to local polities in Asia and Africa, and disease propagation in the Americas, undermining the idea of any Western military superiority.[18]

Third, true Western global domination can only be observed with the creation of colonial empires in the nineteenth century. This domination was enabled by a combination of the economic and technological advantages granted by the industrial revolution[19] and an imperial ideology triggering competition between European powers.[20] However, this period was virtually over by the 1960s with the decolonization process, and Western countries have failed to use military power effectively in the Global South since then. While this critical engagement with Roberts and Parker is diverse and builds on a variety of factors, it does tend to minimize politico-military factors in favor of momentary industrial might and thus to portray Western preeminence as an accident rather than a systemic characteristic.[21] Most starkly, perhaps, Western hegemony could be reduced to its superior access to foodstuffs and coal.[22]

This literature thus downplays the role of political institutions and principles. Where a material reading of the West's rise and decline is confined to the past couple of centuries, a political reading extends across millennia and is unsure of whether decline has even set in. There may be a sense of erosion, but the conviction that competing political institutions and principles, which harness and direct military power, have proven superior is simply not there.

Borrowing from Clausewitz, one might venture that the literature on institutions and principles recognizes that Western political institutions change in *character* over time while contending that their *nature* remains intact: they were established in ancient Greece and Rome and concern ideas such as civic engagement, blind justice, scientific aptitude, and the instrumental use of military force for political purpose.[23] In a strong version, the implication is that as long as Western governments and societies remain wedded to these principles, they can also remain on at least a continuing, if not rising, trajectory, and not one of decline. Thus Victor Davis Hanson, a strong advocate of the idea of a continuous tradition of Western warfare since the classical era, sees a connection between self-government, the steadfast ability to endure battle and deliver fatal blows, and an enduring Western advantage in warfare.[24] However, most analysts take a bleaker view of the ability of Western governments and societies to stick to lasting principles. They see a precipitous decline from vibrant liberal democracy toward hollowed-out democracy, marked by less freedom and civic engagement, and therefore declining power.[25]

A critical issue in this debate over (political) principle and (material) power in the Western experience concerns the fracture in Western political communities between liberal and bourgeois society and military society. The principle of civilian control and instrumental use of military force for political purposes is enduring but in practice revelatory of a contested and difficult civil–military relationship, and military power and fortune are made at the point where this relationship is forged. The early modern European state as conceived by Roberts and Parker became "strong" because it wedded royal authority, uniformed aristocracy, and organizational muscle, but it remained weak in terms of civic engagement. In the young American republic, the attempt to mimic this type of "strong" state (the Hamiltonian option) lost out to a "light" and deliberately weaker state option (the Jeffersonian option) that favored civic engagement. The outcome was a society of riches but a challenge of politico-strategic leadership at the helm of a state that was supposed to be weak.[26]

This concern with civil–military relations as embedded within political institutions, and the resulting ability of the state to offer strategic leadership and the superior control of military force for political objectives, is central to the contemporary debate on the West and war. There is a strong argument that Western state institutions have atrophied and become irrelevant to war.[27] However, research in the field is more generally focused on adaptions within them, including changes to the civil–military balance, asking time and again whether Western governments in practice possess the requisite experience, training, and habit for politico-military strategy.[28] In terms of "military revolution," this literature suggests that Western decline, if such is the case, is due to a loss not of material muscle but of an institutionalized balance between civil and military communities as practiced by Western leadership.

In analyzing the trajectory of time we follow in these footsteps and understand "the West" as an institutional practice of military power directed by primarily liberal governments and societies. We take note of the debate raging over whether the West remains as a frail but active political force;[29] whether its energy has been transplanted to its Soviet/Russian and American peripheries, which have become competing inheritors of the Western tradition;[30] or whether the Western aberration in history has ended as the outsized economies of China and India herald an Asia-centric future.[31] We do not offer a fixed viewed of the geography and boundaries of "the West." Instead, we suggest that the Western practice of bringing military and liberal communities into balance and governing on this basis—and conducting war on this basis—is fragile, contingent, and difficult. We speak of the West but caution that its historical trajectory in terms of war and order is a matter of enquiry.

Perceptions: Western Thought and International Norms

The second dimension of temporality that we explore is the perception of time. As outlined above, this varies depending on the epoch or the culture. Different perceptions of time can have stark political consequences, including for the international institutions that by way of their normative stature today regulate the onset and conduct of war.

State history and context greatly shape changing perceptions of time. For example, as Christopher Clark has demonstrated, different understandings of the role of time had a significant impact on the political stance of different German leaders. In the seventeenth century the Great Elector perceived the present as a precarious condition between a terrible past and an uncertain future, and conceived his leadership role as breaking from entangling traditions in order to maximize choices between multiple possible futures. In contrast, in the following century Frederick II conceived of time as cyclical and aimed at establishing a sort of political stasis that could only benefit the state, while in the nineteenth century Bismarck was caught in a tension between his perception of the political leader as a decisionmaker navigating the torrent of history to the best of his abilities, and a sense of the state's nature as being eternal.[32] Remarkably, from the perspective of International Relations scholarship, the importance of perceptions of time has only rarely been applied to the study of war, although this topic is of increasing interest to scholars.[33] For example, David Edelstein has explored how different time perceptions between states (which he calls "time horizons") can cause strategic frictions: depending on their time horizons, states may favor short-term cooperation and thus inadvertently empower rivals who will challenge them in the long run.[34] Similarly, strategic surprises may often result from conflicting time horizons between policymakers.

Perceptions of time sometimes converge and achieve durability as they become institutionalized, notably in the international arena, where governance by law and custom is notoriously subject to the vagaries of sovereign disputes. Today's international law and customs as they relate to war are greatly indebted to Western thought, carried into the international domain by Western power and its vestiges. Perceptions of time directly shape the ways in which states generate military power. This has important consequences for the West's ability to balance military power and liberal principles, notably pacing itself in the conduct of war.

Pace: Imposing Speed on War

If the West is associated with a certain set of liberal institutionalized practices, and perceptions of time layered into these institutions shape its use of military power, it remains to engage the final dimension of temporality, and notably the pace of war.

Clausewitz distinguishes between abstract war—war in theory—which will escalate to absolute war without breaks in the fighting, and war in reality, in which such breaks are common for a wide variety of reasons, including the imbalance between offense and defense, and imperfect knowledge.[35] In the Clausewitzian tradition war is thus fought at a variable pace but has a culminating point defined by battle. Despite the historical inaccuracy of this battle-centric understanding of war, it nevertheless powerfully shapes Western perceptions of the pace of war.[36] It stands in contrast to supposedly Oriental conceptions of war, in which warfare is an activity not to seek battle but to deceive and conquer the mentality of the opponent—an approach commonly traced to Chinese strategist Sun Tzu but first introduced by the Greek poet Homer, who contrasted it to strategies of physical victory.[37] The Romans, especially, recognized the occasional "profit" in trickery but maintained—and thus shaped a stubborn idea in Western thought—that the enemy could only be truly conquered by "open hand-to-hand combat," namely battle.[38] This opened a tension within Western thinking on war between the idea that the path to such decisive battles involved patience and improvisation, and thus an ability to work with *the pace of war as imposed by circumstance*, and the contrasting idea that Western governments had tools at their disposal to cut through such circumstances and *impose speed on war*, thereby steering it toward the decisive battle.

The question is thus whether the West must be subjected to the pace of war or can be its master. The impact of the Enlightenment and the rise of liberal society within the West has tended to shift Western military thought in the latter direction: one where the West can and must direct the pace of war. This is not because liberal society got involved in military affairs and sought to direct them. Quite to the contrary: because liberal society was set apart from the military domain, and because liberal society privileges human life over communal values such as national prestige or glory, military communities of Western states have come to embrace accelerated wars of maneuver that promise an end to attrition and hence quick victory. Tension and mistrust between Western liberal and military communities have thus since the late nineteenth century caused the military to explore the operational level of war, where one encounters the *blitzkrieg* idea that superior generalship and bold military dashes can deliver the intense but short-lived military effort that liberal society is willing to tolerate, as well as the justice it craves. Regrettably, as Freedman notes, such liberal–military compromises tend to produce problematic strategies of forced warfare that run afoul of complex realities and tragically generate the attritional warfare they were designed to avert.[39]

Relief was offered by the Revolution in Military Affairs (RMA) that was in vogue in the 1990s as the Cold War ended and Western concepts of maneuver warfare prevailed in the 1991 Gulf War. The RMA promised that, with advanced electronic means of intelligence gathering and communication, new weapons and networked forces, along with robust doctrines targeting vulnerable nodes in enemy networks, Western forces would lift the fog of war and allow Western governments to direct the enemy to the point where it would be decisively defeated. The RMA embedded not only the idea of battle as the decisive element in war but also the idea that Western governments could control and accelerate the pace of war at will. In so doing it further embedded a long-esteemed tradition of premising Western international influence on operational mastery in war.

To conceptualize how such perceptions of time and war come together to shape the preparation and conduct of war, Olivier Schmitt has coined the term "wartime paradigms." Schmitt argues that these "emerge at the intersection between socio-technological and security-political imaginaries,"[40] and that a specific wartime paradigm can be identified in Western warfare after the Cold War. Specifically, this wartime paradigm is geared toward optimizing the armed forces for speed while treating war as a form of risk management. The concept of "network-centric warfare" is related to the RMA and remains, under different names, an operational ambition. It encapsulates this perception of speed as critical to achieving battlefield superiority: network-centric warfare is fundamentally the vision of "an emerging, information superiority-driven, information technology-enabled conception of warfare, one in which the ability to gather, process, distribute, and act on information *faster* than the enemy is seen as the key to victory."[41] Moreover, and critically, this emphasis on speed is combined with a conception of war as risk management, meaning the definition of the security agenda in terms of *risks* (to be managed) instead of *threats* (to be deterred). The result is never-ending military operations: "cyclical open-ended approaches remain necessary since risks cannot be completely eliminated and require constant management."[42]

This combination led to a distinctive shape of Western warfare after the Cold War, combining a preference for military interventions (used as a tool of international policing in a risk management perspective) and a force structure favoring expeditionary capabilities.[43] Consequently "the post-Cold War wartime paradigm has . . . shaped a particular way of using force for western warfare. On the one hand, the conception of war as risk management led to a strategic posture in which armed forces have to be able to react quickly to whatever emergency may arise, while also being able to manage such risks in the long run. . . . On the other hand, the operational and doctrinal concepts guiding the transformation of western armed forces emphasized achieving military superiority by disrupting the adversary's system through superior speed (in intelligence-gathering and processing, decision-making, targeting, etc.)."[44]

Recent Western military interventions in Afghanistan, Iraq, and other countries and regions have demonstrated how difficult it is for the West to translate its preponderance and its proclivity toward speed into swift victories.

The Structure of the Book

How Western political and military institutions carry certain perceptions of time; how perceptions of time shape the Western conduct in war; and what it means for the future of Western military power—these are questions we examine in this book. We do so in three parts that investigate the three distinct dimensions of Western power outlined above: its political trajectory and import, its conflicted perceptions of time depending on normative context, and its ingrained habit of seeking to control the pace of war.

The political trajectory section zooms in on the political and military institutions that lie at the heart of Western liberal government and, supposedly, offer a unique path to the strategically controlled mobilization of societal power for military policy. Thus part I is concerned with the underlying question, as we have seen, of whether the rise of the West must be confined to a short and largely accidental burst of nineteenth-century imperial energy, or whether it is more intimately tied to a type of government whose principles were articulated millennia ago. The chapters of this section trace and question Western institutional foundations in three distinct timespans, and from three distinct angles.

The first chapter covers the last 600–700 years of modern state development and investigates the implications of changing models of war finances for the liberal-military balance within Western states. Its conclusion, pessimistic from the point of view of enduring Western power, is that war finances for most of this time have tended to erode rather than reinforce this balancing act at the heart of Western government.

Chapter 2 covers 200 years of strategic thinking, tracing how Napoleonic warfare favored a certain type of politico-military thinking that rubbed against civilian or liberal communities within the West and thus exacerbated civil–military unease. The effort to solve tensions by moving further into the paradigm of Napoleonic warfare, the chapter concludes, is tempting but also futile.

Chapter 3 covers the thirty post–Cold War years, analyzing the trajectory of NATO partnerships and the match between liberally inspired collective action and complex modern military operations. It concludes that NATO has repeatedly fallen for the temptation to shape partnership policy to expedient military needs, in turn eroding its long-term capacity to integrate liberal principle and military power in its partnership structure.

Scenario chapters conclude each section and while the stories they tell are fictive, they illustrate how the tensions identified in the previous sections could come together to diminish Western military power in the future. The scenario in chapter 4 that concludes part I envisages the end of the US participation in NATO and asks the reader to ponder whether NATO is the face of the West, as it is often thought to be, or merely a façade for US leadership. In other words, should we effectively cease to think of "the West" as a force of international order—and has its trajectory come to an end?

Part II focuses on the normative context as a foundation of Western military power. It zooms in on how existing norms represent dominant actors' perceptions of politics, identity, and war, and how contemporary challenges to the normative order are thus based on diverging perceptions of time. Western countries and Western institutions have long regarded themselves as guardians of the international normative order, but norms are not static; they emerge, change, and fall away over time because of invested actors (so-called norm entrepreneurs) and changing circumstances.[45] Part II investigates the significance of these changes for fundamental norms of war and warfare.

Chapter 5 analyzes how different perceptions of time among allies and between the tactical and strategic levels exacerbated the potential for civilian casualties in NATO's engagement in Afghanistan, despite a strong and increasing focus on norms of civilian protection. It cautions that focus on the minimization of civilian casualties can distract from fundamental questions such as campaign strategy and management; a distraction such as this increases campaign duration, which in turn increases the potential for civilian casualties.

Chapter 6 considers how the erosion of the norm of non-intervention enshrined in the United Nations Charter has created indeterminacy and disagreement among Western actors. The West is torn between two temporalities—a need for swift intervention to protect civilians on the one hand, and a wish to avoid protracted armed conflict on the other. This allows competitors such as Russia and China to justify their own actions by reference to these norms and create their own interpretations of them, using the West's own legal argumentation.

Chapter 7 analyzes new forms of conflict in the gray zone between war and peace. It argues that these forms of conflict exploit the Western self-binding obligation to respect international norms based on a clear distinction between *wartime* and *peacetime*, consequently slowing down a possible Western response. Nevertheless, the chapter concludes, there is strength in the Western perception of war- and peacetime as separate, allowing for a more appropriate, comprehensive reaction to challenges in the gray zone.

Finally, the scenario in chapter 8 envisions China taking control over parts of Djibouti as a *fait accompli* and asks the reader to consider how the West could respond in light of these developments of the normative order.

Part III looks at the changing character of war, and its impact on the Western ability to generate military power, addressing the issue of pace in modern warfare. Battlefields in Ukraine, Afghanistan, Syria, and the Sahel have demonstrated that non-state actors were able to employ cheap technological solutions to drastically maximize their fighting power, thereby partly catching up with Western forces.[46] Simultaneously, strategic competitors such as Russia and China are adopting military policies specifically designed to counter Western advantages.[47] These policies include investment in emerging technologies (including hypervelocity missiles, cyber, and artificial intelligence), anti-access/anti-denial strategies designed to negate Western military advantages, and competition below the threshold of open conflict through subversion and sabotage in order to paralyze Western strategic decision-making mechanisms. The pace of modern warfare is therefore paradoxical for Western forces: adversaries are attempting to slow it down at the operational and strategic levels, while it is accelerating at the tactical level.

This section looks at such challenges, highlighting the tension caused by the desire to optimize for speed and the battlefield challenges encountered by Western forces (chapter 9) and the civil-military and operational problems raised by an undue focus on speed through superior information (chapter 10). Chapter 11 dispels some preconceptions about the (negative) consequences of speed (through the banalization of artificial intelligence or hypervelocity glide vehicles) for strategic stability, while the scenario (chapter 12) asks whether Western armed forces would still be able to fight if they were denied one of the key enablers of their speed of operations: digital communications. By questioning this perception of time favoring speed on the battlefield, this section therefore raises uncomfortable questions about the sustainability of Western military power.

NOTES

1. Jeffrey J. Anderson, G. John Ikenberry, and Thomas Risse-Kappen, *The End of the West?: Crisis and Change in the Atlantic Order* (Cornell University Press, 2008); Kishore Mahbubani, "The Case Against the West," *Foreign Affairs,* (May/June 2008).

2. Trine Flockhart, "Is This the End? Resilience, Ontological Security, and the Crisis of the Liberal International Order," *Contemporary Security Policy* (2020), pp. 1–26; G. John Ikenberry, "The End of Liberal International Order?," *International Affairs*, vol. 94, no. 1 (2018), pp. 7–23; Hans W. Maull, *The Rise and Decline of the Post-Cold War International Order* (Oxford University Press, 2018).

3. Jakub J. Grygiel, *Return of the Barbarians: Confronting Non-state Actors from Ancient Rome to the Present* (Cambridge University Press, 2018); David Kilcullen, *The Dragons and the Snakes: How the Rest Learned to Fight the West* (Oxford University Press, 2020); Sean McFate, *The New Rules of War: Victory in the Age of Durable Disorder* (New York: HarperCollins, 2019).

4. Philippe Nemo, *What is the West?* (Pittsburg: Duquesne University Press, 2005).

5. Vyvyan Evans, *The Structure of Time: Language, Meaning and Temporal Cognition* (Amsterdam: John Benjamins, 2005).

6. Patrick Dawson and Christopher Sykes, "Concepts of Time and Temporality in the Storytelling and Sensemaking Literatures: A Review and Critique," *International Journal of Management Reviews*, vol. 21, no. 1 (2019), pp. 97–114.

7. Thomas Lindemann and Jens Thoemmes, "Épistémès temporelles et conflits armés," *Temporalités*, vol. 21, no. 1 (2015), online.

8. Will Dunham, "Kerry condemns Russia's 'incredible act of aggression' in Ukraine," Reuters (March 2, 2014).

9. Carol M. Werner and others, "Temporal Aspects of Homes," *Home Environments*, vol. 8, no. 1 (1985), p. 14.

10. Jean-Claude Schmitt, *Les Rythmes au Moyen Âge* (Paris: Gallimard, 2016).

11. Robert Levine, *A Geography of Time: The Temporal Misadventures of a Social Psychologist* (New York: Basic Books, 1997).

12. John Frederick Charles Fuller, *The Conduct of War, 1789–1961: A Study of the Impact of the French, Industrial, and Russian Revolutions on War and Its Conduct*, reprint (Methuen, 1975), p. 12.

13. Michael Roberts, "The Military Revolution, 1560–1660," in *The Military*

Revolution Debate: Readings in the Military Transformation of Early Modern Europe, edited by Clifford J. Rogers (Boulder, CO: Westview, 1995), pp. 1–12.

14. Charles Tilly, *Coercion, Capital, and European States, AD 990–1992* (Oxford: Basil Blackwell, 1990).

15. Geoffrey Parker, *The Military Revolution: Military Innovation and the Rise of the West, 1500–1800* (Cambridge University Press, 1988), p. 4.

16. McGregor Knox and Williamson Murray, eds., *The Dynamics of Military Revolution, 1300–2050* (Cambridge University Press, 2001).

17. Tonio Andrade, *The Gunpowder Age: China, Military Innovation and the Rise of the West in World History* (Princeton University Press, 2016).

18. J. C. Sharman, *Empires of the Weak: The Real Story of European Expansion and the Creation of the New World Order* (Princeton University Press, 2019).

19. Priya Satia, *Empire of Guns: The Violent Making of the Industrial Revolution* (London: Allen Lane, 2018).

20. Robert Gildea, *Empires of the Mind: The Colonial Past and the Politics of the Present* (Cambridge University Press, 2019).

21. John France, *Perilous Glory: The Rise of Western Military Power* (Yale University Press, 2011); Frédéric Mérand, ed., *Coping with Geopolitical Decline: The United States in European Perspective* (Montreal: McGill-Queen's University Press, 2020).

22. Jared M. Diamond, *Guns, Germs, and Steel* (Spark Pub, 2003); Kenneth Pomeranz, *The Great Divergence: China, Europe, and the Making of the Modern World Economy* (Princeton University Press, 2000).

23. Doyne Dawson, *The Origins of Western Warfare: Militarism and Morality in the Ancient World* (Boulder, CO: Westview Press, 1996); Victor Davis Hanson, *The Western Way of War: Infantry Battle in Classical Greece* (University of California Press, 2000); Victor Davis Hanson, *Carnage and Culture: Landmark Battles in the Rise of Western Power* (New York: Doubleday, 2001).

24. Hanson, *The Western Way of War.*

25. Niall Ferguson, *The Great Degeneration: How Institutions Decay and Economies Die* (Penguin Books, 2012); Farid Zakaria, *The Future of Freedom: Illiberal Democracy at Home and Abroad* (New York: W. W. Norton, 2004).

26. Gordon S. Wood, *Empire of Liberty: A History of the Early Republic, 1789–1815* (Oxford University Press, 2009).

27. Martin Van Creveld, *The Transformation of War* (New York: Free Press, 1991; Collier Macmillan Canada; Maxwell Macmillan International); Martin Van Creveld, *The Rise and Decline of the State* (Cambridge University Press, 1999).

28. Hew Strachan, "Strategy in the Twenty-First Century," in *The Changing Character of War,* edited by Hew Strachan and Sibylle Scheipers (Oxford University Press, 2014), pp. 503–21; Harlan Ullman, *Anatomy of Failure: Why America Loses Every War It Starts* (Annapolis, MD: Naval Institute Press, 2017).

29. Anderson, Ikenberry, and Risse-Kappen, *The End of the West?*

30. Greg Castillo, "East as True West: Redeeming Bourgeois Culture from Socialist Realism to *Ostalgie,*" in *Imagining the West in Eastern Europe and the Soviet*

Union, edited by Gyorgy Peteri (University of Pittsburgh Press, 2010), pp. 87–104; Alina Polyakova, "Strange Bedfellows: Putin and Europe's Far Right," *World Affairs,* vol. 177, no. 3 (2014), pp. 36–40.

31. Kishore Mahbubani, *Has the West Lost It? A Provocation* (London: Allen Lane, 2018).

32. Christopher Clark, *Time and Power: Visions of History in German Politics, from the Thirty Years' War to the Third Reich* (Princeton University Press, 2019).

33. Andrew R. Hom, "Timing is Everything: Toward a Better Understanding of Time and International Politics," *International Studies Quarterly*, vol. 62, no. 1 (2018), pp. 69–79; Sarah Bertrand, Kerry Goettlich, and Christopher Murray, "Special Issue: The Politics of Time in International Relations," *Millennium*, vol. 46, no. 3 (2018), pp. 251–52.

34. David Edelstein, *Over the Horizon: Time Uncertainty, and the Rise of Great Powers* (Cornell University Press, 2017).

35. Carl von Clausewitz, *On War*, edited and translated by Michael Howard and Peter Paret (Princeton University Press, 1976).

36. Cathal J. Nolan, *The Allure of Battle: A History of How Wars Have Been Won and Lost* (Oxford University Press, 2017).

37. Lawrence Freedman, *Strategy: A History* (Oxford University Press, 2013), p. 42; Jean-Vincent Holeindre, *La Ruse et la Force: Une Autre Histoire de la Stratégie* (Paris: Perrin, 2015).

38. Freedman, *Strategy*, p. 45.

39. Lawrence Freedman, "Can There Be a Liberal Military Strategy?," in *Liberal Wars: Anglo-American Strategy, Ideology and Practice*, edited by Alan Cromartie (Abingdon, UK: Routledge, 2015), pp. 70–85.

40. Olivier Schmitt, "Wartime Paradigms and the Future of Western Military Power," *International Affairs*, vol. 96, no. 2 (2020), p. 401.

41. Sean Lawson, *Non-Linear Science and Warfare: Chaos, Complexity and the US Military in the Information Age* (Abingdon, UK: Routledge, 2013), pp. 4–5.

42. Yee-Kuang Heng, "The Continuing Resonance of the War as Risk Management Perspective for Understanding Military Interventions," *Contemporary Security Policy*, vol. 39, no. 4 (2018), p. 547.

43. Anthony King, *The Transformation of Europe's Armed Forces: From the Rhine to Afghanistan* (Cambridge University Press, 2011).

44. Schmitt, "Wartime Paradigms," p. 30.

45. Martha Finnemore and Kathryn Sikkink, "International Norm Dynamics and Political Change," *International Organization,* vol. 52, no. 4 (Autumn 1998), pp. 887–917.

46. Joseph Henrotin, *Techno-Guerrilla et Guerre Hybride* (Paris: NUVIS, 2015); Ahmed S. Hashim, *The Caliphate at War. The Ideological, Organizational and Military Innovations of Islamic State* (London: Hurst, 2018).

47. Bettina Renz, *Russia's Military Revival* (London: Polity, 2018); You Ji, *China's Military Transformation* (London: Wiley, 2016).

PART I

"Civic Militarism" and the Trajectory of Western Power

The Western Experience in Balancing Liberal and Military Virtues

STEN RYNNING

The argument that the power of Western government has a pedigree going back to Graeco-Roman civilization ultimately rests on the case that such power is derived from the inspiration and restraint offered by particular values embedded in political and military institutions.[1] Politically the power of Western government arose from the social environment of a free city, or the freedom of citizens to elect their governments and hold them accountable. Militarily this power emerged from the ability of civic engagement to mobilize society into coherent, tightly organized, and determined combat formations that sought rather than shied away from battle. The face of this power was first the Greek phalanx and later the Roman legion, both superior in shock combat.

If Western military power thus builds on a unique combination of political and military institutional development, it raises the question of whether "civic militarism"—defined as self-governing citizens committed to both martial values and the defense of their republic—is uniquely Western. As noted in the introduction to this volume, this question has engendered vigorous debate. The enduring reference point concerns liberal (or republican) government and military power and not least the question of how to keep one from corrupting the other. Ancient Greek thinkers such as Plato and Aristotle strove to separate the just from the advantageous, which rulers tended to conflate. War among civilized people (the Greeks) must be just, these thinkers argued, whereas it can be unrestrained against barbarians. If we are not able to keep justice and advantage in balance, Thucydides argued in his realist theory of history, we corrupt our own purpose and court defeat. Later, as Western thinking advanced, the limited circle of restrained warfare (Greeks, Romans, Christians . . .) was enlarged to all of humanity. Unrestrained warfare itself then became seen by the West as barbaric, and the human right to life increasingly became the bedrock on which modern ideas of states' rights and duties in war developed—be it for going to war (*jus ad bellum*) or conducting it (*jus in bello*). In its latest garbs, Western thinking is asking whether human rights, as opposed to states' rights, should not be the bedrock for justice in armed conflict; this would represent a leap in the constraints imposed by liberal thought on the Western conduct of war.

Emerging from this history is the critical question of whether the West has lost its balance in terms of "civic militarism"—whether liberal doctrine has grown so large and principled that it can no longer form a partnership with martial virtue within Western institutions. Is it possible that recent Western difficulties in winning wars are symptomatic of a larger and potentially catastrophic disconnect within Western institutions between a military cult of moving fast to destroy things and a political cult of denying war any role in the realm of justice? David Rodin likens this challenge to one of "contingent pacifism," whereby war in theory is permissible but in practice is so constrained by doctrinal liberal and human rights claims that it can never be fought.[2] This first section of the book inquiries into this issue. In particular, it examines whether the conceptions of time embedded in liberal ideals and martial virtue—transcendent and progressive versus cyclical and pragmatic—have become fundamentally disconnected inside Western institutions, eroding the "civic militarism" balancing act that allegedly lay at the heart of Western military power.

Four aspects of this issue are investigated: first, the nature of the modern state and the longevity of a heralded compromise between liberal and military communities within the state; second, whether the type of strategic thought that the liberal state has tended to engender continues to be relevant; third, whether the proclivity of the modern liberal state to act in collective, alliance format according to the liberal principle of multilateralism translates into effective military operations; and finally, whether the West is in fact a mirage behind which not much beside US hegemony is to be found.

The first chapter enters the debate that took off with Michael Roberts's by-now classic argument that European-style modern war represented a revolution in military affairs. The revolution was evident, Roberts argued, in the large-scale deployment of drilled and disciplined troops commanded by a rationalized government capable of mass organization, taxation, logistics, and command.[3] Critics counter that Roberts exaggerated the revolutionary break between a medieval past and modern present and that the modern (Western) state only thrived for a brief period from the early nineteenth to the mid-twentieth century.[4] Today the Western state has reverted to early modern practices of contracting out and privatizing war, and one might even cease to think of the modern state as relevant to war.[5]

In chapter 1 Sarah Kreps and Adi Rao take a long view of these questions, tracing a decline of civic militarism that means fewer large-scale wars but also less civic engagement with conflict, and a corresponding decreasing political ability to control the pace of wars. Kreps and Rao focus on the modern state's financial extraction capacity, which, because it involves taxation for war purposes, involves the citizenry directly in war.[6] Unlike borrowing, taxation offers the state both financial muscle and future freedom of maneuver, but the price to pay for this freedom is the consent of the citizenry and thus a "civic militarism" compact. Kreps and Rao are not able to trace such a capacity over the centuries through which we encounter the "modern" state. Rather, they align with Roberts's critics in arguing for a short-lived modern state. There was indeed a compromise between liberal and military communities within the West, but it was fragile and impermanent. Balanced civic militarism was, they conclude, a historical blip.

Kreps and Rao thus raise concerns about the institutional foundation of Western strategy and the ability of Western governments to close wars. As the control of war is left in the hands of unchecked governments with easy access to borrowed funds, political vagaries move to the forefront at the expense of strategic control. The second chapter zooms in further on such issues of strategy and the Western experience since the Napoleonic wars. Prominent scholars have questioned the ability of the West to produce solid strategy with reference to the balance between the liberal and military communities: Lawrence Freedman has argued that the underlying antagonism of these communities produces dysfunctional strategy; Michael Howard observed disjointed strategy resulting from disconnected liberal thought, which became possible when bourgeois citizens were freed of military engagement as long as they paid for it; and Hew Strachan finds that liberal society increasingly tends to conflate strategy with policy.[7]

Paul Brister enters into this fray in chapter 2, drawing particular attention to the lure of new military technologies that follow from information technology and industry 4.0 developments. Where Western governments tend to focus on "revolutions" and "transformations" in war, Brister points not only to the accelerating pace of modern tactical operations but also to the simultaneous deceleration of strategic pace. War, Brister finds, has two paces and therefore multiple, parallel trajectories. This makes it even harder to maintain the compromise between liberal progressive thought and the tragic vision of politics inherent in the military domain. Brister argues that the West must "slow down to succeed," by which he means favoring defensive strategies adapted not merely to the battlefield but also to the trajectory of political power. Building on the conclusions drawn by Kreps and Rao, Brister also questions whether this *longue durée* mindset will come to dominate, given the lure of fast-paced action inherent in emerging technologies. He raises issues that are discussed in detail in the third section of this book.

Chapter 3 turns to Clausewitz. One of the attractions of his work was his balancing act between the idea that time can be mastered by those educated to understand the principles of war and the idea that time is but a complex framework within which humans grapple with emotions, impulses, and culture. Put differently, in the clash between the science of military precision and the romanticism of martial virtue, Clausewitz refused to choose sides.[8] In war, he contended, one-sided efforts will fail: if war is to serve political objectives, governments must allow representatives of both strains of thought to influence policy and the conduct of war.

If Kreps and Rao and Brister caution that Western governments may not be predisposed by institutional design and strategic culture to work both sides of the equation, the question is whether enhanced international cooperation and partnering—so prevalent in modern war—offers a corrective to or rather exacerbates the West's inclination to lose its balance in always seeking to impose speed on war. The literature on NATO and modern war indicates on the one hand that NATO is experiencing distinct difficulties in coping with the exigencies of connected, complex, and contested international military operations,[9] but on the other hand that NATO and Western militaries more generally are able to learn and adapt, albeit mostly in ad hoc fashion.[10]

Rebecca R. Moore cuts into this debate in chapter 3 with an assessment of NATO, focusing on the role of NATO partners in Alliance operations, and ultimately NATO's ability to leverage partnerships for the good of strategy—and thus to reject the temptation to go for speed. NATO has been engaged in a balancing act, Moore writes, between its liberal impulse to build broad security institutions and its military need to zoom in on only those partners that serve operational needs. Moore is critical of NATO's effort to maintain its "civic military" balance in this respect, especially as it has been tempted time and again to work with partners that were illiberal but effective on the ground. Moore here detects a flaw in NATO's armor—a fracture between its liberal order within Europe and its operational practice beyond Europe. She cautions that the Alliance setting might exacerbate the tendency of Western governments to confuse time and commitment, or to opt for illiberal partnerships in the belief that, in war, time is not on their side.

Finally, in chapter 4, Tobias Bunde considers an overarching question: is the strength of the Western community a mere mirage hiding a reality of American power and hegemony? If this power is subtracted from NATO, does the West disappears entirely? If that is the case, then perhaps the West was powerful only in the long nineteenth century when the modern state ruled, or it may have been powerful in a longer historical perspective stretching back to the ancient world, which just no longer applies. Bunde starts by presenting a key scenario that might result from a US departure from NATO, before addressing this intriguing question of institutional legacy and power. Building on the observations of Kreps and Rao, Brister, and Moore, Bunde identifies a crisis in the balanced civic militarism in the West and provokes the reader to ponder its causes.

NOTES

1. Doyne Dawson, *The Origins of Western Warfare: Militarism and Morality in the Ancient World* (Boulder, CO: Westview Press, 1996); Victor Davis Hanson, *The Western Way of War: Infantry Battle in Classical Greece* (University of California Press, 2000).

2. David Rodin, "Morality and Law in War," in *The Changing Character of War*, edited by Hew Strachan and Sibylle Scheipers (Oxford University Press, 2014), pp. 446–63.

3. Michael Roberts, *Essays in Swedish History* (London: Weidenfeld and Nicolson, 1967).

4. David Parrott, "Had a Distinct Template for a 'Western Way of War' Been Established before 1800?," in *The Changing Character of War*, edited by Strachan and Scheipers, pp. 48–63.

5. Martin van Creveld, *The Rise and Decline of the State* (Cambridge University Press, 1999).

6. Sarah E. Kreps, *Taxing Wars: The American Way of War Finance and the Decline of Democracy* (Oxford University Press, 2018).

7. Lawrence Freedman, "Can There Be a Liberal Military Strategy?," in *Liberal Wars: Anglo-American Strategy, Ideology, and Practice*, edited by Alan Cromartie (Abingdon, UK: Routledge, 2015), pp. 70–85; Michael Howard, *War in European History*, updated ed. (New York: Oxford University Press, 2009); Michael Howard, *The Invention of Peace: Reflections on War and International Order* (Yale Univer-

sity Press, 2000); Hew Strachan, "Strategy in the Twenty-First Century," in *The Changing Character of War*, edited by Strachan and Scheipers, pp. 503–21.

8. Azar Gat, *A History of Military Thought: From the Enlightenment to the Cold War* (Oxford University Press, 2001).

9. Patricia A. Weitsman, *Waging War: Alliances, Coalitions, and Institutions of Interstate Violence* (Stanford University Press, 2014); Sten Rynning, *NATO in Afghanistan: The Liberal Disconnect* (Stanford University Press, 2012); Emile Simpson, *War from the Ground Up: Twenty-First Century Combat as Politics* (Oxford University Press, 2013).

10. Theo Farrell, Frans P. B. Osinga, and James A. Russell, eds., *Military Adaptation in Afghanistan* (Stanford University Press, 2013); Heidi Hardt, *NATO's Lessons in Failure: Institutional Memory in International Organizations* (Oxford University Press, 2018).

ONE

The Modern State

Rise and Decline of Civic Militarism

SARAH KREPS

ADI RAO

In the January 2020 crisis between the United States and Iran, President Donald Trump took to his favorite medium, Twitter, to warn that "if Iran strikes any Americans, or American assets, we have . . . targeted 52 Iranian sites . . . some at a very high level & important to Iran & the Iranian culture, and those targets, and Iran itself, WILL BE HIT VERY FAST AND VERY HARD."[1] Pentagon officials swiftly walked back the threat, saying that "the laws of armed conflict" ruled out attacking cultural sites.[2] It was not the first time President Trump had threatened aggressive measures with the promise of inflicting decisive and quick victory on an adversary. In 2017, he threatened North Korea with "a rain of ruin from the air, the likes of which has never been seen on this earth."[3]

Although Trump has found the allure of the prospect of massive force and quick victory, the modern-day laws of wars have insinuated themselves as a veto player. And so it is that the United States has not actually "won" a war since World War II despite spending more on its military than the next nine countries combined. The changes are all for the good, since civilians have become more protected during wartime than they were during the strategic bombing campaigns of the 1940s, when indiscriminate bombing killed hundreds of thousands of civilians in Germany and Japan. In the Korean War,

Army commander Matthew Ridgway observed that "Americans are not inclined by temperament to fight limited wars. As in the boxing ring, they want nothing less than a knockout. What red-blooded American could oppose so shining a concept as victory? It would be like standing up for sin against virtue."[4]

Today, limited war is the norm. However, since states in the West are still uncomfortable with even this, leaders have reconciled the limited appetite for limited wars by shrouding the appearance of war altogether. One way they have done that is by limiting the sacrifice in both blood and treasure—by moving away from conscription and war taxes and removing the visible signs of war. In so doing, they have also moved away from "civic militarism," in which a democracy draws in all of the resources available to it in the service of victory,[5] with the public offering a check on the longevity of conflict precisely because of its investment in it.

This chapter focuses on the relationship between the public's fiscal sacrifice in war and the conduct of that conflict. Using Charles Tilly's focus on extraction and the development of the state as a point of departure,[6] it suggests an endogenous relationship between the cost of war, the institutional shape of the state, and the war's outcome. It examines the rise of the extractive state to its peak period from about 1850 to 1950, and then traces its decline. Taken together, this suggests that the notion of civic militarism, far from being a permanent feature of Western states, was more of an anomaly. Victor Davis Hanson's notion of free peoples fighting wars by consensus takes the form of a quid pro quo starting in the nineteenth century, before it seemingly dissipates in the following century.[7] During the period when civic militarism manifested itself, countries such as the United States sought to impose pace on war through large-scale and close-ended wars to advance desired outcomes. The decline of civic militarism may mean fewer large-scale wars, but also less civic engagement with conflict and a correspondingly diminished political ability to control the pace of wars.

To make these points, the chapter is organized according to three periods of war and state development. The first section considers the early history of war finance (c. 1200–1850) and details the most crucial developments for understanding what followed. In this early period, technological limits to extraction increasingly forced sovereigns to resort to debt to finance their military ventures. In other words, it was militarism without the civic underpinnings.

The second section considers the period between about 1850 and 1950 when the extractive state took center stage. Large-scale war meant large-scale revenue needs and large-scale commitment from domestic audiences. The extraction-coercion cycle referred to a dynamic in which a more powerful central state could coerce more revenue from the public; this in turn made it even more powerful, creating a link between the military and political development of the state.[8] Although—or possibly *because*—extraction was coercive, the public whose resources were central to warfighting also took on a restraining function with respect to war, leading to the most visible manifestation of civic militarism.

That period, however, ultimately gave way to contemporary developments. The onset of limited war triggered limited appetite for what was perceived as unnecessary public sacrifice, which in turn created incentives for leaders to limit fiscal extraction. In this way the civic militarism apparent in the previous period unraveled.

The focus in this chapter is on the United States as a Western state that has been involved in and indeed led numerous large and small-scale wars, making it a worthy case study for understanding the relationship between war and the state. Examining state development in the context of extraction, we conclude that both the early state and the late state could be characterized as militaristic, and that civic militarism occurred during a comparatively brief interlude between them.

War and State Development

The Western way of war and state-making is unidirectional: war creates resource needs, which leads to extraction, which strengthens the central institutions of the state. Although scholars have observed variations in that relationship, for example, depending on whether the war is intrastate, interstate, or global,[9] the prospect of variation over time has not been given serious consideration.[10] And yet the nature of that longer-term relationship is important because of the impact and role of the public in a democracy as determined by its degree of sacrifice in the service of conflict. Since extraction—in other words, taxation—exerts pressures on the public, leaders who have turned to such fiscal coercion have provided accountability, whether through increased suffrage or veterans' benefits after the war,[11] or through responsiveness to public preferences in terms of the duration and conduct of the conflict itself. Conversely, the absence of extraction would mean no such reciprocal need to provide accountability.

Despite the typical characterization of a fairly simple relationship in which war creates revenue needs that give rise to extraction, its evolution has been far less linear. One view suggests that in earlier periods of conflict, revenue needs were limited by the nature of conflict and rudimentary technological innovation. Instead of relying on costly innovation, infantry units emphasized drill and de-emphasized battlefield heroics. Military units were, in a sense, "commodified" in that forces could be quickly raised and readily deployed so long as the soldiers were trained. As Hanson observes, militaries are ultimately a matter of economics, with states trying to achieve the most military power for the least cost.[12] Infantry was far more efficient than cavalry, especially once the emergence of gunpowder allowed shooters to eviscerate horses.

Cicero famously noted that "the sinews of war are infinite money." Money is never infinite, of course, and it certainly was more finite without significant extraction from the populace. Conquest and tribute—the protection money that a conquered land would pay to the conquerer—could only go so far; self-sustaining warfare required domestic revenue. Early states did engage in some degree of taxation but primarily indirect taxes such as on tea, salt, and linens.[13] As Gerald Harriss remarks, "although the [British] Crown was actively exploiting its feudal and traditional taxes, and was extending them to meet the requirements of new military demands, none of these taxes adequately met its needs."[14] The limits to money therefore meant limits to war and militarism more broadly.

Another consequence was increasingly large piles of debt, which led to inefficiency, insofar as a dependence on credit meant servicing the debt through interest payments. The costs of war, as Geoffrey Parker notes, continued to mount dramatically without a concomitant rise in extraction.[15] By the end of the American War of Independence, 66 percent of total tax revenues went toward servicing the debt. As debt increased, buying on credit became harder and more expensive. Yet the government had to generate additional revenues, which it did from additional indirect taxes such as customs, excise, or stamp duties.[16]

Debt and indirect duties, however, did not meaningfully engage the public. Writing around the time of high British debt in the eighteenth century, Adam Smith noted: "In great empires the people who live in the capital, and in the provinces remote from the scene of action, feel, many of them scarce any inconveniency from the war; but enjoy, at their ease, the amusement of reading in the newspapers the exploits of their own fleets and armies."[17] He advocated more visible costs of war—taxes rather than simply debt—to give people an incentive to want peace. Otherwise, the public would be "commonly dissatisfied with the return of peace, which puts an end to their amusement." Public amusement is the antithesis of civic militarism, an apathy directly challenging the picture of citizen killers who ruthlessly killed and won wars.

Yet some early antecedents of public buy-in emerged. The poll tax in

Europe was as brutally simple as it was ancient; hearth-tax equivalents, similarly, were common and had their own long history; land taxes were a routine tool in the hands of even pre-modern courts. However, increases in the "extensive" margin (that is, new taxes being enacted or brand new entrants added to the tax net) only occur at a glacial pace and are usually spurred by costly wars. States created parliaments to help collect these very taxes with some degree of consent.

Nonetheless, even these financing tools were inadequate in paying for war. Even the *de jure* elegance of poll taxes and hearth taxes often were in practice *de facto* "sub-national taxes"—taxes simply collected by cities, say, within a territory. By the time of the Early Modern era, Western states were usually characterized by rising costs, rising debts, and the resort to militarism on credit. Limits to money meant that, as David Parrott concludes, "the problem was above all of inadequate financial resources to pay or supply the armies . . . this served only to reveal the inherent technological and bureaucratic weaknesses of early modern states confronted with the burden of supporting armies 200–300,000 strong."[18] Financial technologies such as remittance banking, bonds, and currency exchanges emerged to finance involvement in conflict, but it took until the eighteenth century for central banks and bonds to emerge as viable sovereign financing tools, and whether expensive or cheap, debt had now "accelerated" into a situation of being ubiquitous, sophisticated, and crucial to war financing, yet ultimately limiting in terms of the militaristic reach.

The Rise of the Extractive State

Max Boot has written that the wars "celebrated in countless books, movies, and documentaries" are typically large-scale wars like World War II, total wars in which the country invested all of its blood and treasure and an unconditional enemy surrender was achieved. Those, he notes, are the "American way of war"—the reliance on advanced technology and commitment from the public to achieve total victory. It turns out that such wars are more the exception than the norm, even in American history; in the first part of the 1800s the United States engaged in dozens of small-scale military ventures, sometimes for debt repayment, sometimes to stabilize insurrections, at other times to protect American citizens or property.[19] These small wars were in the backdrop of the political landscape for decades, and the public would have been forgiven for not knowing that the US had carried out another incursion against the American Indians, or even a marine landing in North Africa (the Barbary Wars).

Yet as technology changed, the scale and costs of war grew, bringing an increasing need for extraction as an efficient and indeed equitable—since taxation could be done progressively as a function of economic means—way to finance conflict. The great utility of an income tax was that the government could now extract the fruits of most production in the society. Earlier forms of taxation were either greatly regressive (such as sales taxes) or susceptible to evasion (like most extant forms of direct taxation).

This section describes how these revenue needs produced the first income tax in the Civil War, steeply progressive tax rates in both world wars, and a nod in the same direction at the outset of the Korean War. With its fiscal resources invested in the conflict, the public scrutinized the conduct of these wars in ways that percolated to the leadership and imposed a particular pace on the war. As Bruce Bueno de Mesquita shows, the decision to tax a democratic body meant that the state needed to be more selective, to wage wars where the odds of victory were higher and the speed of victory was swifter, in order to provide the public good of security for the state and its populace.[20] In fact this period produced the empirical finding that democracies picked their wars and fought harder during them, consequently winning in the vast majority of cases.[21]

This finding is consistent with the civic militarism and triumphalism outlined by Hanson. He cites "the idea of a free citizenry voting to craft the conditions of its own military service through consensual government."[22] Indeed, the reciprocal nature of foisting the burdens of war onto the backs of a democratic citizenry through extraction while providing compensation by way of greater liberalism and rights in the wake of war, in a system enabling democratic voting for the leaders who made decisions about war and peace, appeared to be a recipe for fighting harder and more successfully, if sometimes over-zealously.

A significant enabler of this cycle was the move from indirect to direct taxes. As the name suggests, indirect taxes are applied to the sale of items. Direct taxes are those that individuals pay directly to the government, the most obvious of these being the income tax. An indirect tax, though a small percentage of each item, can add up in ways that have prompted revolts, including the one that started the American Revolution as well as the later Whiskey Rebellion in the 1790s. Direct taxes are far more visible, in part because the amounts add up far more quickly but also because they cannot be shifted to others—for example by opting out of buying tea, whiskey, luxury goods, or whatever other item is being taxed.

The British were the first to successfully implement an income tax, in preparation for the Napoleonic Wars. During the government of William

Pitt the Younger at the dawn of the nineteenth century, the tax brought in a respectable amount of revenue. Only incomes above £60 were taxed, starting at a mere 1/120th of taxable income; this rate progressively increased to 10 percent for incomes above £200. Self-disclosure of incomes was only required at the tax commissioner's discretion. After a brief period of wavering between imposition and suspension, the tax had become a permanent feature of British society by 1842, under the prime ministership of Robert Peel. It must be noted that most individuals were exempt, as only wealthier households were taxed, a feature of the system throughout the West at the time.[23] War taxes were seen as efficient and equitable, as William Gladstone put it in his role as Chancellor: "an engine of gigantic power for great national purposes."[24] With the coming of the Second Industrial Revolution in the later nineteenth century, both the amount of wealth and the ease with which wealth could be identified, assessed, and extracted had all increased markedly. Factories—the mainstay of industrialization in the West—established consistent payroll records; accounting practices that were developed for private entities would then serve for government auditors and tax commissions. Income taxes become a significant and necessary tool that was already widespread by the time of the two world wars. (Indeed, World War I would force the British government to increase its top rates from 8 to 50 percent.)

In the United States too, one of the key features of the period between the Civil War and the Vietnam War is the significant increase of extraction in wartime via an increasingly bureaucratized state, redistribution of wealth through war, and a tendency to maintain the wartime tax levels in the postwar period. Bureaucracies developed during wartime to collect and implement the taxes remained in place in peacetime, creating a so-called "ratchet effect" linking spending and institutions.[25]

One of the notable features of the Civil War is that the North resorted to direct taxes relatively early on, legislating the first American income tax in 1861. This provided confidence to the financial community, including those providing loans, with regard to the government's solvency. Property taxes were direct taxes, which were at that time a violation of the US Constitution. However, since an income tax did not tax property, it could technically be considered indirect and thus not subject to constitutional prohibitions. The first income tax was 3 percent on incomes over $800, which in fact excluded many wage earners. The Revenue Act of 1862 was also progressive but included more citizens in its net; it exempted the first $600 and became steeper as income increased. This was further reinforced by the 1864 Internal Revenue Act. The Union created a national banking system and a revenue service to collect these taxes. By contrast, the Confederacy relied far more on printing money and debt, creating enormous levels of inflation—9,000 percent by the end of the war—that eroded the value of its currency and financial solvency.[26]

The two world wars followed a similar extractive strategy to that of the Union in the Civil War. In their research on progressive taxation in World War I, Kenneth Scheve and David Stasavage show the independent effect of mass warfare in creating the conditions for the fair distribution of war's burdens, contrasting tax rates for non-participants with the far more progressive rates of the participants. Underlying these differences were changing public attitudes about taxation driven by mass mobilization, and in particular the war-driven sense of fairness—that the conscription of men should produce the conscription of wealth at the upper end of the economic ladder.[27]

As noted above, one of the virtues of the massive extraction in the world wars was that it connected the public to the conduct of the war. Even in the context of a war where the stakes were seen as existential, World War II tax proposals received considerable scrutiny. Although it seems an unlikely place to uncover evidence for the scrutiny and accountability-inducing effects of war taxes—since by all accounts it was a war with overwhelming support from the populace—archival material from the Roosevelt administration reveals folder after folder of letters to President Roosevelt about the 1943 proposal for a pay-as-you-go withholding tax. Vitriolic letters, fan mail, talking points from the Treasury Secretary to Roosevelt: to read the archival material is to read a fiscal epiphany, one infused with partisan and class politics. One of the first materials in the tax policy binder was a 1935 Confidential Report to President Roosevelt, which delves into great detail in deriding the "wealth-destroying taxation." The near-hyperbole continues throughout the report. One passage suggests that taxes are tantamount to telling people "don't produce" even though "the nation starves for credit." The report describes taxation as like a burning barn that "prevents the enjoyment of life." It then goes into great actuarial detail about the amount of credit destroyed by taxation, also referred to as "national fakery, posing as a benefaction." Only by modifying the tax structure can the US "effect the economic emancipation of the nation." That the rates would rise to 79 percent by 1937, from 63 percent in the year the report was written, suggests that the report's admonitions went unheeded.

As this correspondence suggests, even in the context of existential war the debate on war taxes produced massive outrage and claims of class warfare, despite all the efforts of the political elites who had given considerable thought both to the framing of the tax itself and to the withholding. After months of debate, the House Ways and Means Committee concluded that calling the tax a "war tax" would elicit a sense of patriotic sacrifice. "Victory tax" was an even more "euphonious name." At almost every turn, the president had to answer to his own party, the opposition, labor, churches, and corporations about the nature of the tax and decisions about war. And while the causal connection with the pace of war is difficult to pin down, it is clear that the political costs of extraction were not trivial and at least created incentives for decisive victory, as open-ended extraction would have been politically untenable.

Beyond accountability, the increase in extraction led to greater liberalization, something of a quid pro quo between the sacrifices and the societal advances, marking a rise of civic militarism in the United States. The Civil War, for example, produced an enormous expansion of veterans' benefits that ultimately spilled over into broader investment for the elderly, the working class, and families.[28] To be sure, these wars also periodically produced illiberal outcomes—for example, the suspension of habeas corpus in the Civil War and limits to free speech—but by and large liberalism increased in the wake of war: voting rights for African Americans after the Civil War and for women after World War I. As Paul Starr concludes, "liberal democracies fought and won wars, which led to further democratization, which helped to protect individual liberties once the war emergencies ended."[29]

The cycle of extraction, mass mobilization, and liberalism produced an uncomfortable tension. The liberal community had disdain for war and affection for progress. The military community's business is war, including a willingness to fight and win large-scale conflicts. How might these competing values be reconciled? Through progressive taxation, which would distribute the costs of war equitably, through decisive victory, which would end war quickly and produce public goods for the populace, and through the delivery of liberal rights, which would come in war's wake.

The cycles of ever-expanding liberalism, however, were not inevitable. More recent wars have moved away from extraction and severed the link between the public and the conduct of conflict, thereby eroding the notion of civic militarism, constraints imposed on war, and efficient paths to democratic victory in war.

Status Quo Ante: Militarism without Civic Grounding

Civic militarism has now all but disappeared in the West. Large-scale wars that required large amounts of soldiers, money, and in turn bargaining with the population for resources[30] no longer occur, whether because the advent of nuclear weapons created prohibitively high costs of war or because the "better angels of our nature" have been able to emerge.[31] The total number of war fatalities plunged in the second half of the twentieth century, a positive development, but with those declines came changes in the relationship between the state, its society, and the conduct of war.

The move away from borrowing has its contemporary foundations in the Korean War. While the United States actually financed 100 percent of the war's costs with taxes, more than any other war in its history, closer inspection reveals a different story that illustrates the state's shift from extraction.[32] As long as the country felt the Korean War was like World War II, it supported extraction. Indeed, in August 1950, a Gallup survey found that 70 percent of Americans were willing to pay more taxes to finance military operations. The polling institute reported that it had "rarely . . . in its 15 years of measuring public opinion found such heavy majorities expressing a willingness to pay more taxes for any public purpose."[33]

Relatively quickly, however, a quite different type of conflict emerged: limited war with limited stakes, no declaration of war, and no clear strategic goals, yet indefinite commitment to the use of force in Korea. President Harry Truman's efforts to engage in continued extraction through additional war taxes were quickly rebuffed once the reality of this limited war set in. Public support for either a war tax or indeed the war itself crumbled, and one member of Congress noted that "*barring a war*," any revenue proposals "will be very coldly received. . . . I am more convinced than ever that we have imposed all of the additional individual and corporate taxes our economy should bear."[34] However, Truman had studiously avoided calling the conflict a war, and therefore withdrew the proposals for war taxes from further consideration.

A similar problem occurred with regard to Vietnam, but this time President Lyndon Johnson had internalized the lessons of the recent past. Adlai Stevenson, not Harry Truman, had been the Democratic presidential nominee in 1952 because the Korean War had resulted in stalemate and taxes had tainted Truman's re-election prospects. Johnson therefore eschewed the prospect of taxes for as long as he could, aiming to avoid the trappings of war that might draw scrutiny to his Great Society programs. He engaged in gradual escalation rather than all-out mobilization. By 1966 the country had 300,000 troops in the country without technically being on a war footing, thereby avoiding the war taxes that would attract scrutiny of the conflict. Johnson admitted: "I don't know much about economics, but I do know Congress. And I can get the Great Society through right now—this is a golden time. We've got a good Congress and I'm the right President and I can do it. But if I talk about the cost of the war, the Great Society won't go through."[35]

Johnson's reluctance to impose a war tax was warranted. The public was decidedly opposed to such a tax, in large part because it did not have a sense of any existential stakes. The policy of gradual escalation and the blurred line between war and peace had muddled the terms of the debate. In May 1967 almost as many Americans (48 percent) said they did not have a "clear idea" what the war was about as those who did (49 percent). Only a minority (41 percent) thought that the war in Vietnam "may prevent World War III."[36] The public never felt about Vietnam as it had about World War II, when there were real concerns about Germany "ruling the world" and Japan "ruling Asia," as Gallup polls put it at that time. No Gallup poll over Vietnam ever probed whether the public expected the war to bring freedom to the Asian continent or result in a dramatic setback for communism.[37] In short, even if support for the conflict started at reasonably high levels, there was never any sense of the high existential stakes associated with World War II.

Thus introducing a war tax would be risky. Insofar as it would take the form of legislation, Congress would have to engage in debate, which would call into question the need for resources, which would be reported in the newspapers and alert the public, which could then push back. Johnson invoked his legislative adversary, House Chairman of the Ways and Means Committee Wilbur Mills, who favored a balanced budget to be achieved through spending cuts rather than tax increases. The president emphasized the implications for his prized social programs: "Old Wilbur Mills will sit down there and he'll thank me kindly and send me back my Great Society, and then he'll tell me that they'll be glad to spend whatever we need for the war."[38] Thus, despite the urging of Johnson's economic advisers, he resisted meaningful war taxes until the 10 percent surcharge in 1968. The case for Johnson's failure was overdetermined, but it is clear that war taxes were an important issue that coalesced and crystalized opposition to the war, alongside the questionable progress and growing casualty figures. The 1968 surcharge was the last time that an American president would institute a war tax, and for good reason politically.

Developments since the Korean War and Vietnam War confirm that, contrary to Hanson's assertion above that the connection between citizens and war in a republic is a consistent feature across time, there has been a distinct decline in civic militarism. The public has an antipathy toward total war, and its growing sensitivity to casualties and costs has meant that leaders themselves shy away from soliciting those sacrifices in blood and treasure. Inevitably this limits the type of wars that countries in the West are able to fight. They keep conflicts at the level of "police action," as in the Korean War, or engage in "gradual escalation" to avoid political debate about war. Yet as long as they cannot significantly escalate these wars—because they lack both the extractive resources of earlier periods and domestic political will—they are also unable to achieve relatively rapid and decisive victories.

Emblematic of the shift away from extraction and civic militarism—and pointing to the consequences of that shift—is the effort of legislators to impose a war tax for the Afghanistan surge in late 2009, as the war entered its ninth year and became one of the longest and costliest wars in American history. The proposed legislation would have charged a surtax on individual incomes. As its legislative sponsors, Representatives David Obey (D-WI), John Murtha (D-PA), and John Larson (D-CT) argued, "the only people who've paid any price for our military involvement in Iraq and Afghanistan are our military families . . . we believe if this war is to be fought, it's only fair that everyone share the burden. That's why we are offering legislation to impose a surtax."[39] Obey explained that "we're just trying to keep in the forefront what the financial costs are," while Representative Barney Frank (D-MA) added that "it's important for people to understand how these wars are adding to our deficits."[40]

In response to this proposal, lawmakers on both sides of the House voiced their opposition, ostensibly on the grounds that they were protecting constituents. As Representative Jerry Lewis (R-CA) suggested, Americans were "already being taxed to death."[41] Democrats other than the legislative sponsors were scarcely more supportive, hoping to avoid what they implied was a politically toxic proposal.[42] Facing such bipartisan opposition, the proposal languished despite scant direct evidence that constituents held the views that their representatives attributed to them. Moreover, debate about a war tax was so perfunctory that questions regarding that potential opposition went unexamined. What is interesting here is that, whereas previous warfare had strongly affected civilian populaces at home, governments now seek to shield civilians almost entirely from its impacts.

In both the most recent wars, Afghanistan and Iraq, the prospect of war taxes has been concentrated largely in anti-war coalitions on the left but shunned by the mainstream of both parties. The most recent proposal for a war tax came from former Democratic presidential contender Beto O'Rourke, seeking to differentiate himself in a crowded primary field. His proposal would have had households with incomes greater than $200,000 pay $1,000 a year, while those with less than $3,000 would pay $25, with the revenues going toward veterans' health care. The subtext of the proposal was distinctly antiwar: if individuals understood the cost of wars, maybe they would turn against them. Yet the very feature that would give the war tax teeth—visibility—is exactly what makes it antipathetic to political elites and therefore unlikely. However, even the occasion for discussion about wars—how we pay for them and their unending nature—appeared to be a departure from the recent past. After all, doing nothing about the policy is tantamount to doing something, by allowing the absence of opposition to enable ongoing conflict.

The lessons from recent wars are instructive. The publics of Western democracies rarely pay directly for the cost of war in the form of war taxes that in the past became lightning rods for political engagement with elected officials and their policies. Fareed Zakaria's notion of "illiberal democracy" is useful here:[43] state actors in the West (policymakers, bureaucrats, and leaders) can make use of debt financing to be free from close civilian scrutiny. Zakaria's phrase was actually targeting non-Western democracies, but some aspects of that label at least may be increasingly applicable to established Western democracies. Wars since 9/11 have expanded temporally and geographically with little accountability; they do so in part because perpetuation and expansion incur few political costs.

Yet legislators now seem even more wary than they were over seventy-five years ago to tax Americans to pay for the fight. The same policy that would create a more equitable and financially sound form of finance would also invite political scrutiny. The state is at a stage now where it is paradoxically both strong and weak: technological advances have made war financing hurdles a thing of the past; yet galvanizing the public to achieve the potential for large-scale extraction is risky and attempts are muted. If the primary goal of Congress is reelection, then demurring from periodic proposals for a war tax is no doubt wise. If the goal is good public policy, however, then the visibility of taxes, despite the unwelcome controversy it invites, will operate fruitfully in the service of democratic accountability.

Conclusion

As this historical analysis has shown, it was financing that not only set the West apart from the rest, but also resulted in large-scale, deadlier, if more efficient wars. By the time of the modern era, states in the West could raise more money and armies than states elsewhere. It is telling that the Japanese—who were humiliated by Commodore Perry's forceful dismantling of their isolationist policy of *Sakoku*—were able to defeat Russia by 1905 after adopting "Western" types of war finance. Yet we also know that it is financing that allows for states to sustain (if barely) large-scale armies. As Parker writes of the enormous wealth of Amsterdam coupled with the good credit of the United Provinces in the seventeenth century, "This combination enabled the Dutch to raise an army and go on fighting, whatever the cost, until they got their own way."[44] Financing, then, is an integral part of determining the length and magnitude of certain wars. It affects the type of wars that countries fight, the way they fight them, and the speed and decisiveness with which they are able to do so.

A second major implication of this analysis is that the turn to extraction, even if largely an aberration rather than the norm, did have the restraining effect of linking government decisions and the costs of war to society's probing. The decline of extraction has produced a decline in the public investment and scrutiny that helped create a check both on the wars the United States and others opted to wage and on the determination with which they fought. It is not surprising that the recent wars in Afghanistan and Iraq, where extraction was consciously shunned, have been the longest in American history. Without the constant reminders that come from fiscal sacrifice, the public is increasingly disconnected from wars, imposing few pressures on leaders to bring them to a rapid and decisive end.

Third, and more generally, the history of war finance offers insights about the arc of civic militarism in the West. Hanson has suggested its continuity from ancient Greece to the present, emphasizing the sense of societal cohesion and liberal notion of "free men fighting wars by consensus" as aspects of Western society. The history of extraction suggests that states in the West may look like sleeping giants: technological barriers to extraction have been largely removed; but leaders cannot whip up the sentiment for sacrifice among the public. Indeed, as Sarah Kreps argues, we may have hit an upper limit in terms of citizens' willingness to sacrifice their own incomes to pay for (war) taxes.[45]

Yet at the same time, through the mechanism of debt financing, states have been able to circumvent democratic accountability for militarized foreign policy strategies. What results is a paradox. The Western state is powerful in theory, capable of raising enormous revenues to fight and win decisively, but it is weak in practice, unable to galvanize the public to accept higher levels of extraction in return for either additional rights or the simple yet essential public good of state security. Instead, leaders have sought to reduce the visible costs of war, circumvent limits on mobilization, and loosen decision-making constraints. If this analysis is any indication, the recent past of long, open-ended, yet less lethal wars is therefore likely to be a prologue, foreshadowing the distinct likelihood of future, prolonged war.

NOTES

1. Donald J. Trump @realDonaldTrump, www.twitter.com/realDonaldTrump /status/1213593975732527112, January 4, 2020.

2. Peter Baker and Maggie Haberman, "Pentagon Rules Out Striking Iranian Cultural Sites, Contradicting Trump," *New York Times*, January 7, 2020.

3. Bruce Cumings, "Americans Once Carpet Bombed North Korea. It's Time to Remember that Past," *The Guardian*, August 13, 2017.

4. Matthew B. Ridgway, *The Korean War* (Harmondsworth, UK: Penguin Books, 1967).

5. Victor Davis Hanson, *Carnage and Culture: Landmark Battles in the Rise to Western Power* (New York: Doubleday, 2001).

6. Charles Tilly, *Coercion, Capital, and European States, AD 990–1992* (Oxford: Basil Blackwell, 1990).

7. Hanson, *Carnage and Culture,* p. 366.

8. Miguel Angel Centeno, "Blood and Debt: War and Taxation in Nineteenth-Century Latin America," *American Journal of Sociology*, vol. 102, no. 6 (May 1997), pp. 1565–1605; at p. 1566.

9. Cameron Thies and David Sobek, "War, Economic Development, and Political Development in the Contemporary International System," *International Studies Quarterly*, vol. 54, no. 1 (March 2010), pp. 267–87.

10. One exception is that of Sarah Kreps, whose *Taxing Wars* (Oxford University Press, 2018) points to the changes within the American experience over time.

11. Paul Starr, "Dodging a Bullet: Democracy's Gains in Modern War," in *In War's Wake: International Conflict and the Fate of Liberal Democracy*, edited by Ronald R. Krebs and Elizabeth Kier (Cambridge University Press, 2010).

12. Victor Davis Hanson, *The Western Way of War: Infantry Battle in Classical Greece* (University of California Press, 2000), p. 165.

13. John Brewer, *The Sinews of Power: War, Money, and the English State, 1688–1783* (London: Unwin Hyman, 1989), p. 96.

14. Gerald Leslie Harriss, *King, Parliament, and Public Finance in Medieval England to 1369* (Oxford: Clarendon Press, 1975).

15. Geoffrey Parker, *The Military Revolution: Military Innovation and the Rise of the West, 1500–1800* (Cambridge University Press, 1988), pp. 46–47.

16. Brewer, *The Sinews of Power*, p. 95.

17. Adam Smith, *An Inquiry into the Nature and Causes of the Wealth of Nations* (1776), book 5, chapter 3.

18. David Parrott, "Strategy and Tactics in the Thirty Years' War: The 'Military Revolution,'" in *The Military Revolution Debate: Readings on the Military Transformation of Early Modern Europe*, edited by Clifford J. Rogers (Boulder, CO: Westview Press, 1995), pp. 227–52, at p. 245.

19. Max Boot, *The Savage Wars of Peace: Small Wars and the Rise of the United States* (New York: Basic Books, 2014), Preface.

20. Bruce Bueno de Mesquita, James Morrow, Randolph Siverson, and Alastair Smith, "Testing Novel Implications from the Selectorate Theory of War," *World Politics*, vol. 56, no. 3 (April 2004), pp. 363–88.

21. Dan Reiter and Allan Stam, *Democracies at War* (Princeton University Press, 2002).

22. Hanson, *Carnage and Culture*, p. 366.

23. Berhard Grossfeld and James D. Bryce, "A Brief Comparative History of the Origins of the Income Tax in Great Britain, Germany, and the United States," *American Journal of Tax Policy*, no. 2 (1983), pp. 211–52.

24. Gladstone's Budget speech to Parliament, April 18, 1853, cited in Richard Aldous, *The Lion and the Unicorn: Gladstone vs Disraeli* (London: Pimlico, 2007), p. 82.

25. Karen A. Rasler and William R. Thompson, "War Making and State Making: Governmental Expenditures, Tax Revenues, and Global Wars," *American Political Science Review*, vol. 79, no. 2 (1985), pp. 491–507.

26. Tax Analysts, "Tax History Museum. 1861–1865: The Civil War," www.taxhistory.org/www/website.nsf/Web/THM1861?OpenDocument.

27. Kenneth Scheve and David Stasavage, "The Conscription of Wealth: Mass Warfare and the Demand for Progressive Taxation," *International Organization*, vol. 64, no. 4 (October 2010), pp. 529–61.

28. Theda Skocpol, *Protecting Soldiers and Mothers: The Political Origins of Social Policy in the United States* (Cambridge, MA: Belknap Press, 1993).

29. Paul Starr, "War and Liberalism," *New Republic*, no. 23 (March 5/12, 2007).

30. Ronald Krebs, "In the Shadow of War: The Effects of Conflict on Liberal Democracy," *International Organization*, vol. 63 (Winter 2009), pp. 177–210, at p. 180.

31. Steven Pinker, *The Better Angels of Our Nature* (New York: Viking, 2011).

32. Lee E. Ohanian, "The Macroeconomic Effects of War Finance in the United States: World War II and the Korean War," *American Economic Review,* vol. 87, no. 1 (March 1997), pp. 23–40.

33. George Gallup, "Strong Controls, Higher Taxes Favored by Public in Survey," *Washington Post*, August 6, 1950.

34. Robert Albright, "New Tax Hike 'Most Unlikely,' Barring War, George Holds," *Washington Post*, January 2, 1952.

35. Edward Drea, *McNamara, Clifford, and the Burdens of Vietnam* (United States Department of Defense, 2011), 28.

36. Gallup Poll, "Some people say that the war in Vietnam may prevent World War III. Others say it may start World War III. With which group are you more inclined to agree?," October 1967, 1,585 personal interviews.

37. Andrew Sidman and Helmut Norpoth, "Fighting to Win: Wartime Morale in the American Public," *Electoral Studies,* vol. 31 (2012), pp. 330–41, at p. 334.

38. David Halberstam, *The Best and the Brightest* (New York: Modern Library, 2001), p. 689.

39. "Share the Sacrifice Act Ends Borrowing to Pay for Afghan War," 19 November 2009, House of Representatives press release, www.google .com/url?sa=t&rct=j&q=&esrc=s&source=web&cd=4&ved=0CDUQFjA D&url=http%3A%2F%2Fdemocrats.appropriations.house.gov%2Fimages %2Fstories%2Fpdf%2FObey_Murtha_Larson_Call_for_War_Surtax_11.19 .pdf&ei=rYPSTobMEKXV0QHc_bkf&usg=AFQjCNFFtmUmIMal16qdKO9r v9pIiT3CHg.

40. David Rogers, "War Surtax: 'Pay as You Fight,'" *Politico*, November 23, 2009, https://www.politico.com/story/2009/11/war-surtax-pay-as-you-fight -029851, accessed May 17, 2020.

41. Janet Hook and Christi Parsons, "Afghan War Debate: How to Pay for It?," *Chicago Tribune,* November 25, 2009.

42. Mike Soraghan, "Pelosi Nixes Obey's War Tax Proposal," *The Hill*, December 3, 2009.

43. Fareed Zaakaria, "The Rise of Illiberal Democracy," *Foreign Affairs*, vol. 76, no. 6, 1997, pp. 22–43, www.jstor.org/stable/20048274, accessed August 3, 2020.

44. Geoffrey Parker, "The 'Military Revolution,' 1560–1660—a Myth?," *Journal of Modern History*, vol. 48., no. 2 (1976), pp. 196–214, at pp. 213–14.

45. Kreps, *Taxing Wars*.

TWO

Making Time an Ally

Uncovering the Perils of Tactical Military Speed

PAUL BRISTER

Military strategy scholars must be forgiven for advancing ideas of future warfare as a high-intensity, hyper-connected, and incredibly rapid activity. It has become near-impossible to discuss contemporary Western military strategy without hearing proclamations that the character of modern warfare is changing at accelerated rates; that the tempo of military operations must speed up; that forces must be deployed and employed faster to prevent an enemy *fait accompli*; that political leaders must make faster decisions to use military force; and that militaries must operate at "the speed of relevance."[1] The obsession with speed is ubiquitous, overwhelming, and dangerous. Moreover, it is revelatory of an institutional malaise caused by the failure of Western leaders to reconcile the slow pace of strategic affairs and the fast pace of tactical military operations. In important ways, therefore, the West has lost the "civic militarism" balance described in the previous chapter. This balance can be restored only if Western leaders and society identify and debate how technologies affect and shape the operational and strategic pace of their militaries.

There is little doubt that the pace of tactical military operations has accelerated. The proliferation of battlefield sensors combined with on-call standoff weapons require tactical units to constantly maneuver to ensure survival. As future weapons promise even greater speeds, the demand for lightning-fast attacks, greater battlefield dispersion, and constant repositioning of tactical assets will increase even more. Given the frightening pace of contemporary (and future) tactical operations, it is easy to see why Western defense scholars believe the effects of these tactical operations will naturally spill over into the operational and strategic levels of war, concomitantly accelerating each level. This is a problematic line of thought. History suggests that there is no such natural linkage between tactical speed and the pace required of higher operational and strategic logic.

Paradoxically, in fact, despite the accelerated speed of tactical operations, the pace and logic at higher levels of strategy may even have slowed.[2] In light of this trend, the demands on future defense scholars and strategists are immense. They must convince political leaders to rise above the tyranny of the tactical/technological and prepare themselves instead for a long strategic game. This is a difficult proposition in ideal circumstances, but is made near-impossible by the unique demands of Western politics, acquisitions processes, and unrelenting partisan media cycles. This chapter seeks to demonstrate these paradoxical disconnects between the tactical and operational levels of modern strategy, specifically highlighting the seemingly inverse relationship between tactical speed and operational and strategic pace.

Pushing back against the "need for speed," what is offered here is a more sanguine prediction with regard to the impacts of emerging technologies in future wars. The first section shows that recent calls for an increased speed of war follow a historical tradition, beginning in the Napoleonic era and running through the Iraqi "shock and awe" campaign. Although the terms of the argument have changed over time, its fundamental thrust has remained constant: that the investment in tactical military speed offers political leaders quick victories at minimal cost. Predictions of emerging technology have been used over time to bolster this argument. For over two hundred years, military strategists have pointed to the emerging technologies of their day and insisted that these systems would revolutionize war, offering a swift victory if only political leaders would allow them to strike first. For over two hundred years, these warfare prognosticators have gotten it wrong—often in bloody, tragic fashion. The second section offers an alternative perspective on the future of war, one dominated by pace-driven defensive strategies, rather than the speed-obsessed, short-duration "hyperwars" discussed within many Western military headquarters. The chapter closes with recommendations for policy-makers, defense strategists, and strategic studies scholars facing the pressure of a speed-obsessed military and the industries that fuel it.

Prediction and Paradox

Prediction is hazardous, especially about the future.
—DANISH SAYING COMMONLY ATTRIBUTED TO NIELS BOHR

Humans are notoriously bad at predicting the future. Especially (or at least equally) bad are those deemed to be "experts" in their given field.[3] The fact that many technophilic defense scholars predict the pace of future war will approach hyper-speeds should lead us to pause and question that consensus. History provides several examples of eerily similar predictions gone terribly wrong, where the employment of revolutionary technologies has indeed accelerated the speed of tactical maneuvers but done little to eliminate the fog and friction of war at operational and strategic levels—and in most cases has even served to prolong major wars. To illustrate this historical consistency, we begin with the rise of Napoleonic warfare and the evolution of modern Western strategic thought.

Napoleon's military campaigns changed forever the way Western militaries understood the utility of speed. Napoleonic maneuver turned the largely attrition-based strategy of previous eras on its head, replacing it with an annihilation-based strategy noted for rapid battlefield maneuvers, isolation of an enemy's fielded force, the decisive destruction of that force, and the ability of political leaders rapidly to translate military success into political effect.[4] These beliefs were subsequently codified by Baron de Jomini in a work that Napoleon allegedly claimed disclosed his closest military secrets.[5] A cottage industry was built upon Jomini's principles of war, giving birth to an idealized form of war.[6] The subsequent study of Napoleonic strategy drove both American Civil War and World War I military strategists to believe speed and maneuver on the battlefield offered the key to rapid political victory. They were tragically wrong. In both these wars, initial battlefield successes went to the side demonstrating boldness and swift action, but tactical speed gave way to operational pace, and both wars turned into bloody, multi-year affairs favoring the protagonist that could more effectively translate its industrial base and population into combat power. Although Jomini and Napoleon stressed speed in war, the operationalization of their theories produced military stalemate.

Before the outbreak of World War I, French politician Emile Driant concluded that new technologies and concepts would ensure that "the first great battle of the war will decide the whole war, and wars will be short."[7] Around that idea formed what would later be known as "the cult of the offensive," a consensus of military thought that coalesced around predictions of short, high-intensity wars of maneuver and the imagined power of offensive weaponry. Military commanders of the time argued that once war was imminent, it became an operational imperative to mobilize and deploy military force before their opponents, as a decisive first blow would alter the entire trajectory of the overall war. This belief led to a complete upending of civil–military relations, with the military declaring that any delay in the political decision to engage in war would spell utter doom. The manifestation of these beliefs was a rigid "war by timetable," in which military commanders pressured political leaders to make their decision to go to war early and then step aside to allow the military to translate the combat potential of their nations efficiently into tangible combat power.[8] Speed was essential, so sweeping aside prewar political dialogue saved much-needed time to launch the first strike at the enemy. Obsessed with Napoleonic maneuver and the quest for a perfect annihilation strategy, strategists at the time of World War I failed to learn from previous case studies of the American Civil War and the Boer War, both of which pointed to technology's greater impact on the defensive rather than the offensive aspects of war.[9] Instead, a fascination with emerging technology and the "need for speed" cut short necessary political dialogue, mobilized alliances, and set the world on the path to a multi-year war of attrition.

Similarly, as World War II began, both Allied and Axis military leaders believed innovative technologies afforded them advantages and—when employed correctly—the possibility of a short conflict. The rapid evolution of armor and aircraft technologies defined the era, with both holding the promise of a speedy resolution to conflict. For the Germans, armored units (augmented by tactical airpower) would be used to pierce the static defenses prevalent during World War I and drive deep into the heart of the enemy to achieve success via lightning war. While armored units and blitzkrieg tactics enjoyed initial success, the operational shift to a strategy of defense in depth slowly undercut their effectiveness. Allied strategists, by contrast, put their faith in air power and the idea that "the bomber will always get through"—an idea originating in Britain's fear of German air power but later transformed into confidence in its own abilities. Air power allowed belligerents to directly target the enemy's domestic populations in the hope of bringing the horror to their doorsteps and driving them to demand an end to the war.[10] Here again the intended effect of strategic bombing (the capitulation of a population) instead produced a "rally around the flag" effect and steeled the will of those being attacked. Yet again a fascination with emerging technology and a belief in a speedy end to war drove the world into multi-year attrition warfare, costing over 70 million lives. The subsequent involvement of the US in Vietnam would offer yet another painful lesson about technological predictions, the value of tactical speed in determining the outcome of wars, and the all-pervasive "short-war illusion."

Emerging from World War II an undisputed global superpower, the United States invested mightily in its military to maintain and expand its technological advantages. In the mid-1950s, as it stumbled into the Vietnam War, it did so in the belief that its technologically advanced military would easily defeat a backward communist opponent. Wielding a new technology that gave its infantry the ability to maneuver from the air, the United States demonstrated its awesome technological advantage via coordinated battalion-sized helicopter assaults. The ability to conduct massive bombing campaigns (demonstrated in Operations Linebacker I and II) further reinforced the idea that well-equipped soldiers would make short work of communist peasants. The Vietnam War also showcased the use of massive sensor systems, code-named Operation Igloo White, building a virtual fence between North and South Vietnam and throughout southeastern Laos. Rather than face these technologies head on, North Vietnamese forces simply shifted their operational and strategic approaches, refusing to meet the American forces in set-piece battles, engaging in a campaign of guerrilla and unconventional war, and choosing a protracted strategy designed to sap the political will of the American populace. The North Vietnamese, unable to achieve the tactical speed of US forces, instead relied upon time as their ally, knowing the support of the American people could not keep pace with their own sustained domestic support. It was a strategy that would cost lives but ultimately deliver success. Yet again, despite the incredible technological advantage the United States maintained throughout the war, these revolutionary new technologies did little to bring the war to a conclusion. US Vietnam strategists had once again mistakenly chosen tactical speed as the key to victory over the primacy of sustainable operational and strategic pace. Nearly two decades after entering Vietnam, the United States was forced into stalemate.

The promise of technology-shortening wars, in the eyes of many, bore fruit in the 1991 Gulf War. Here the United States (leading a coalition with thirty-four other countries) demonstrated immense technological prowess, combining stealth with precision-guided munitions to stun, disorient, and annihilate an Iraqi army deemed—at the time—one of the world's best. On the heels of a five-week air power campaign, ground forces expelled Iraqi forces from Kuwait in under 100 hours. The conduct of the conflict was hailed as the realization of a new, technologically enabled "strategic paralysis" theory of warfare, developed and advocated by Air Force strategists John Warden and

John Boyd.[11] At first glance, this appeared to represent the success of technology's full impact on war and a template for future wars. History would provide an opportunity to test that hypothesis as the United States led a second invasion of Iraq in 2003.

Little had changed in terms of the technological disparity between the Western coalition and Iraqi forces (although many argue Western quantitative and qualitative advantages were greater in 2003), but this time the political objective called for regime change rather than the more limited aims sought in 1991. This Rapid Dominance strategy, articulated in 1996 by Harlan Ullman and James Wade, suggested a revolutionary change was afoot, offering the potential to achieve strategic aims in minimal time. In their own words:

> Perhaps for the first time in years, the confluence of strategy, technology, and the genuine quest for innovation has the potential for revolutionary change. We envisage Rapid Dominance as the possible military expression, vanguard, and extension of this potential for revolutionary change. The strategic centers of gravity on which Rapid Dominance concentrate, modified by the uniquely American ability to integrate all of this, are these junctures of strategy, technology, and innovation which are focused on the goal of affecting and shaping the will of the adversary. The goal of Rapid Dominance will be to destroy or so confound the will to resist that an adversary will have no alternative except to accept our strategic aims and military objectives.[12]

Despite the "shock and awe" campaign in which overwhelming military power was unleashed to achieve a rapid strategic victory, the Western forces were instead confronted with another multi-year endeavor. Following an overwhelming air power display, ground forces raced toward Baghdad, destroying Iraqi units as they went. In less than three weeks Baghdad fell, and it seemed technology had—once again—won the day in relatively scant time. But the declaration of "mission success" was premature, as Iraqi resistance to Western occupation grew and insurgency blossomed. Now, nearly two decades later, Western military practitioners are still struggling to extricate forces from the Middle East, and defense scholars are still struggling to explain why this is the case. Despite an immeasurable technological advantage, the promise of a short war once again proved a fantasy.

How could defense scholars and military strategists have gotten it so wrong on so many important accounts? How have technologies destined to shorten wars lengthened them instead? In his seminal 1987 work *Strategy*, Edward Luttwak postulated that the whole realm of military strategy is "pervaded by a paradoxical logic" that "tends to reward paradoxical conduct while confounding straightforwardly logical action."[13] He also suggests that this same paradoxical logic applies to technology and its perceived utility at the start of war. Specifically, he describes "the relationship (inevitably paradoxical) between the very success of new devices and their eventual failure."[14] The driving reason behind this is the existence of a creative, thinking opponent who will direct time and resources to the development of countermeasures against the most effective weapon systems. For instance, the two technologies most likely to accelerate the end of World War I were the railroad and rifled artillery. The former promised commanders the ability to move entire units rapidly over miles of terrain to outmaneuver, outflank, and eventually annihilate an opposing military force. Yet planners discovered that sabotage often delayed movements, and to prevent this they needed to devote combat forces to the protection of these lines (thus diminishing their power projection capabilities). Similarly artillery promised to rain steel on the opponent's massed infantry units, allowing one's own force to punch through any defensive attempt and attain battlefield victory. Instead this "rain of steel" drove the infantry to dig deep defensive trenches in response, virtually turning any battlefield maneuver attempts into suicidal exercises. The armor and air power of World War II, and the heliborne forces of Vietnam, suffered similar fates.

As we enter the third decade of the twenty-first century, a familiar refrain echoes through the halls of security-minded think tanks and Western military commands. It is the same refrain that has driven militaries across time to overestimate the technologies of their respective era and rush headlong into tragedy under the false notion that a speedy first attack would deliver the decisive blow needed to bring war to an end. Believing they were operating "at the speed of relevance,"[15] technology-enamored leaders drove their countries into war at the speed of stupidity.

The Hype behind Hyperwar

> The belief in the possibility of a short decisive war appears to be one of the most ancient and dangerous of human illusions.
>
> —ROBERT WILSON LYND[16]

Today, we find ourselves in familiar intellectual territory, with a growing collection of military scholars and practitioners ushering in an era of "hyperwar." This influential group—which includes a former US deputy secretary of defense—envisions a future in which robotic swarms infused with artificial intelligence (AI) engage enemy forces at speeds exceeding human decisionmaking capacity. In the words of retired US General John Allen and technologist Amir Husain, emerging technologies will relegate humans to "providing broad, high level inputs while machines do the planning, executing, and adapting to the reality of the mission and take on the burden of thousands of individual decisions with no additional input."[17] In particular, advocates of hyperwar express concern over advances in Chinese AI as compared with the West. With powerful AI available, the hyperwar camp believes "the speed of battle at the tactical end of the warfare spectrum will accelerate enormously, collapsing the decision-action cycle to fractions of a second, giving the decisive edge to the side with the more autonomous decision-action concurrency."[18] In essence, they claim, these technologies will shrink the OODA (observe, orient, decide, act) loop into a single OODA point, and the rapid tactical successes will naturally spill over into both the operational and strategic levels of warfare, allowing military commanders to "see"—with near-perfect clarity—the strategic landscape and make war-winning decisions based upon the near-instantaneous analysis of petabytes of data.[19]

Despite my deep professional respect for the hyperwar advocates, I believe they dramatically overstate their case, ignoring past examples of "revolutionary technologies" promising—yet failing—to transform warfare into a more precise, transparent, and short-lived event. Much of the hype surrounding emerging technologies and their role on future battlefields rests in the age-old belief that emerging weapons technology favors an offensive role. With these powerful new weapons at hand, an offensive protagonist can relentlessly attack and degrade the defenses of a slow-thinking, slow-reacting opponent. Unable to orient or defend itself, the attacked country falls prey to a decisive first blow and is forced to capitulate. This argument drives belligerents to the logical conclusion that it is speed and violence of initial action that will predominate in shaping the outcome of the war to come. In the name of national defense and security, a push toward the latest offensive weaponry becomes a requirement, and rapid offensive actions are deemed an existential requirement.

This could be a misguided belief, as recent advances in technology may actually favor the defender. American military strategist T. X. Hammes suggests that these developments work to the advantage of small, smart, lethal, and multiple weapons over the few, exquisite systems upon which existing Western militaries are built.[20] Contrary to the views of the "hyperwar" camp, Hammes contends, modern technology is best utilized in denying an opponent the opportunity to seize and hold territory. Even against staggering quantitative odds, smaller countries are better positioned to employ a "porcupine strategy" that can, at best, deter a larger opponent from launching an attack altogether and, at worst, certainly delay and wear down an opposing force during an attack. Hammes argues the technological democratization of precision weaponry has "leveled the playing field between major states, smaller powers, and even non state-actors."[21] He suggests the technologies most likely to shape future battlefields are not high-tech hypersonic weaponry, fifth-generation fighter aircraft, or fully integrated AI that provides perfect clarity in the battlespace. Rather, emerging technology such as three-dimensional printing, small warheads placed on lower-tech drone systems (quadcopters), cheap space capabilities, and task-specific AI threaten to prolong wars, as aggressors become bogged down in dealing with defensive challenges that offensive technology cannot solve. Even more problematic for potential aggressors is that these defense-favoring technologies can be mobilized in hours or days, whereas weeks and months are required to mobilize an offensive thrust.[22]

Scholar and army lieutenant Brandon Euhus largely agrees with Hammes, but for different reasons. He suggests emerging technologies may actually produce paradoxical effects when employed against an enemy. Euhus deconstructs and opposes the "hyperwar" argument utilizing a Clausewitzian logic and understanding of war. He argues that although the character of war may change according to the technologics of the era, its nature remains constant: it is a contest to impose one's will on an enemy. Euhus further argues that the introduction of novel technology routinely produces the opposite of the effect intended.[23] In his masterpiece *On War*, Clausewitz himself was distinctly sceptical about the idea of a single blow determining the outcome of a war.[24] He saw war as a clash of wills, and although an initial victory might have an impact on subsequent engagements, it would be unlikely to determine the overall outcome of the contest. We would be wise to remember this theme as we enter an era where defense planners are, yet again, convinced of the possibility of rapid decisive wars and the potential for a bolt-from-the-blue *fait accompli*. This belief has—once again—convinced Western militaries to emphasize the urgency of first mover's advantage and the demand for tactical speed.

Recently, the term "*fait accompli*" has gained prominence throughout the halls of the Pentagon and, in turn, across Western defense institutions.[25] The 2014 Russian annexation of Crimea is routinely held up as the model of the *fait accompli* and the harbinger of future warfare. A second commonly cited *fait accompli* tactic in the era of near-peer conflict is China's seizure and occupation of parts of the disputed Spratly Islands (in particular Subi and Mischief Reefs) in the South China Sea, and its buildup of infrastructure there. The lessons Western militaries have gleaned from these examples is that lighting-fast offensive "bolts from the blue" are the defining features of contemporary war. Here again reality and the interpretation of that reality may be at odds. In both cases the seizure of territory did not (or more accurately should not have) come as a complete surprise to those monitoring the situation. Both land grabs were preceded by years of information warfare, legal warfare, and "salami-slicing" tactics designed to slowly wear down the will of defenders and the international community. In both cases the objectives sought (a portion of Crimea, and desolate island features in the South China Sea) simply did not infringe upon the perceived core national interests of powers capable of halting their advance. In both instances it was less a case of "we simply cannot stop them" than of "no one cares to stop them." Even now, in the context of great power competition, there remains a general lack of interest by Western powers in expelling Russian forces from Crimea. Moreover the completeness of the *fait accompli* is questionable. Even with the lackluster military support provided by Western nations, Russia finds itself frozen in conflict, taxing an already depleted domestic economy.[26] The tactical speed it exhibited in grabbing Crimean territory has now given way to the challenge of maintaining operational pace in the face of flagging domestic support.

Speed, Pace, and Maintaining Policy Primacy

As the examples in this chapter suggest, policymakers and strategic prognosticators should guard against the siren's song of tactical speed and the promise of rapid wartime success. They should instead remain grounded in the idea that tactical speed is important only as long as your wartime objectives remain limited. As they expand, the value of tactical speed gives way to the importance of operational and strategic pace. History suggests tactical speed is most useful in conflicts with minimalist aims that have little impact on the international status quo. The 1991 Gulf War, routinely hailed as the exemplar of rapid warfare, should be better remembered as a conflict defined by a status quo antebellum objective against a second-rate military force, requiring minimal mobilization of Western industrial bases or international support. Conversely, initial—often stunning—German success in the opening months of both World War I and World War II mattered little in the outcome of conflicts defined by maximalist aims. In both world wars the pace at which military potential (in terms of manpower and matériel) was transformed into military power (in terms of military units and weaponry), and the ability to sustain that transformation over time, proved the primary determinants of success. In both wars operational pace (defined as the ability to transform combat potential into combat power at or faster than the rate of battlefield attrition) was further backstopped by a sustained strategic pace, as national leaders were able to maintain international support and a coherent alliance structure. Here too Germany's World War II failures prove instructive. Despite the stunning tactical successes of its lightning-quick military operations, Germany proved operationally unable to replace wartime losses at a rate that equalled or exceeded its losses. Strategically the picture was equally dismal. As the war progressed, German alliances dissolved, with Italy becoming a military liability and Russia an enemy, while the collective ire of the international community rose against the Nazi regime. Tactical speed may have carried Germany the first few miles of the marathon, but operational and strategic limitations left it limping the last. Similarly the initial clubfooted response of Western allies morphed into a jog, then a run, and ended with a sprinting array of military forces larger than at the start of the war. The allure of tactical speed and the underappreciation of operational and strategic pace allowed Germany to combine political logic and military action and—in many cases—subjugate the former to the latter. This is a lesson democratic leaders would do well to internalize as the contemporary fascination with tactical speed approaches yet another peak.

The most commonly repeated (and routinely overlooked) aspect of military strategy is that "war is simply a continuation of political intercourse, with the addition of other means."[27] As one delves into military strategy, extreme care must be taken to ensure that the speed of future warfare does not exceed and overtake political direction. Policy primacy must remain inviolate. The Prussian master himself also declared that "war cannot be divorced from political life; and whenever this thinking occurs in our thinking about war, the many links that connect the two elements are destroyed and we are left with something pointless and devoid of sense."[28] He further emphasizes this point, stating that "policy is the guiding intelligence and war only the instrument, not vice versa."[29] The modern obsession with tactical speed among Western militaries now threatens to make military decisions the guiding intelligence, relegating policy to the position of an afterthought.

The continued push for accelerated military operations risks outrunning the nature of democracies, as chapter 10 by Nina Kollars demonstrates. Unless directly attacked, Western democracies are, by nature and design, typically slow to wage war. Politics is messy and often slow, but routinely produces policy that represents the views and support levels of the governed. This clumsy but necessary process ensures democracies can generate and sustain the operational and strategic pace demanded by the conflict faced. The rush toward automated military decisionmaking and pre-delegated authority to take military action now threatens the democratic policy process.

The idea of employing weapon systems and undertaking "hyperwar" engagements that eliminate human decisionmaking threatens to divorce military activity from political oversight. In fact such a move could upend the relationship between military activity and policy, making policy reactive and therefore subordinate to whatever effects an AI-enabled military generates. While AI may perform well at optimizing military effectiveness, there is a real chance that these optimized military decisions will subvert political reality. As warfare concepts advance, defense strategists would be wise to ensure their preferred way of war supports the nature of the political apparatus it serves.

Recommendations for Policymakers and Strategists

This chapter acknowledges and embraces the idea that emerging technologies will accelerate combat at the tactical level. The emergence of hypersonic weapons, swarming attacks enabled by advances in artificial intelligence, and man-to-machine teaming will undoubtedly provide early adopters with a distinct battlefield advantage. That said, these technologies are unlikely to change the fundamental nature of warfare, nor magically offer the solution to conducting a clean, surgical, and rapid war. In fact, while recognizing the need to invest in and integrate emerging technologies into tactical operations, the chapter suggests the speed of tactical operations will produce a paradoxical slowing at the operational and strategic levels of war. The analysis points to four distinct recommendations for national leaders to repair the institutional balance between civic and martial virtue.

First, and most importantly, policy primacy is inviolate. Political leaders will feel tremendous pressure to resort to military action, as their military commanders will demand early political decisions to avoid the strategic catastrophe associated with absorbing an opponent's initial attack. Pointing to the awesome new power of technologically advanced weapon systems, military commanders will request the delegation of authorities typically held by only the highest political leaders. Political leaders must avoid the strong temptation to act hastily and remind those clamoring to take the first punch that military action supports policy. And although policy may be the imperfect outcome of the slow, often disorganized political process, it is the foundational bedrock for establishing what operational and strategic pace the country can sustain in conflict. Both military and political leaders must be clear-eyed, neither overstating the need for early violent actions, nor falling prey to the allure of the new technology destined—at long last—to eliminate the inherent fog and friction of war and thus bring it to a speedy end.

Second, defense strategists and political leaders must invest more effort into exploring alternative second- and third-order effects of emerging technologies on the prosecution of war. Or, in simpler terms, greater emphasis must be placed on modularity, both among emerging technologies and between old and new technology. This "plug and play" aspect of technology allows battlefield military commanders opportunities to disassemble and recombine technologies in a manner demanded by the environment. The most likely uses of any technology in future war are those we cannot predict. The greatest beneficiaries of emerging technologies are therefore those most capable of rapid adaptation after the first shots are fired. Returning to the thoughts of Edward Luttwak, policymakers and military commanders should avoid technologies optimized for specific environments and instead seek "suboptimal, but inherently more resilient" technologies that lend themselves to adaptation and rapid recombination with other systems.[30] The coin of the future realm will therefore be the creation of robust technological solutions, designed to cope with errors and adjustable to environments and situations engineers did not anticipate. A rich literature exists on wartime adaptation and why militaries must prepare and deliberately plan for their reaction to the unknown. As Williamson Murray suggests, "Without intellectual preparation, the adaptation that is always necessary will come at a far higher expenditure of the lives of those on the sharp end."[31]

Third, defense scholars and academics must consistently push back against the calls for an offensively focused technological arms race, as such a competition may drive states toward war, rather than deterring one. In a superbly argued study, Joe Maiolo demonstrates how the pre–World War II faith in the power of offensive technology, the arms race to procure said technology, and an overwhelming belief that the side that "went first" would win led to a global war of attrition.[32] The promise that a massive buildup of weapons offered political leaders eventually trapped them in their own logic. The initial speed these leaders believed necessary to win the war would be replaced by the demand for a slow, long-duration, and sustained pace. By the end of the first year, all the belligerents would go about transforming both their economy and their labor force to feed the near-unquenchable demands of war. Here it is instructive to keep Hammes's thesis in mind and focus on the development of low-cost, highly effective defensive weapon systems that allow non-global superpowers to sustain the regional status quo without the assistance of other global powers. As in most periods throughout history, technological advances may benefit defenders rather than aggressors, minimizing yet again the importance of tactical offensive speed.

Finally, it is worthwhile for strategists, military practitioners, and scholars to keep in mind that war is fundamentally and eternally a clash of human wills. As such, any attempt to predict with any degree of accuracy how a war will unfold is a venture fraught with peril. As this chapter has demonstrated, previous attempts have been proven wrong time and time again, often leading to an outcome completely contrary to the original intent. As war represents the ultimate interaction between multiple thinking, reacting, adapting, and deceiving protagonists, it is an arena that defies predictions and instead demands broad study of alternative futures. We must understand that the concepts of victory and defeat are political terms, often transitory in nature, that require time and struggle to understand fully. Attempts to short-circuit this reality will end in failure.

We must be less enthralled by the concept of speed, especially at the operational and strategic levels of conflict. Instead we must explore more deeply the concept of pace in conflict and how a country can generate and sustain wartime efforts over time. The outcome of a marathon is rarely determined by the speed at which runners cover the first 100 meters. The same is true of warfare. Whether Western governments can act on this insight depends on how well they recalibrate the compromise between liberal principle and military virtue inside their institutions and thus enable a more patient and political approach to warfare.

NOTES

1. Joe Dunford, "The Character of War & Strategic Landscape Have Changed," DoDLive, April 30, 2018, www.dodlive.mil/2018/04/30/dunford-the-character -of-war-strategic-landscape-have-changed/. Dunford is citing James N. Mattis, "Remarks by Secretary Mattis on the National Defense Strategy," transcript, US Department of Defense, January 19, 2018.

2. Olivier Schmitt, "Wartime Paradigms and the Future of Western Military Power," *International Affairs*, vol. 96, no. 2 (2020), pp. 401–18. See also chapter 9 by Pascal Vennesson in this volume.

3. See Philip E. Tetlock, *Political Judgement: How Good Is It?* (Princeton University Press, 2006).

4. Antulio J. Echevarria, "Toward an American Way of War," *Strategic Studies Institute Monograph* (March 2004), www.ssi.armywarcollege.edu/pdffiles/00365 .pdf.

5. Michael Howard, "Jomini and the Classical Tradition in Military Thought," in *Studies in War and Peace* (London: Temple Smith, 1970), p. 31.

6. See Antoine-Henri Jomini, *The Art of War*, first published 1838 (Westport, CT: Greenwood Press, 1971).

7. John M. Cairns, "International Politics and the Military Mind: The Case of the French Republic, 1911–1914," *The Journal of Modern History*, vol. 25, no. 3 (September 1953), p. 282.

8. For a fuller articulation of this argument, see A. J. P. Taylor, *War by Timetable: How the First World War Began* (London: Macdonald & Co., 1969).

9. Stephen Van Evera, "The Cult of the Offensive and the Origins of the First World War," *International Security*, vol. 9, no. 1 (Summer 1984), pp. 58–107.

10. Robert Pape, *Bombing to Win: Air-Power and Coercion in War* (Cornell University Press, 1996).

11. See David S. Fadok, *John Boyd and John Warden: Air Power's Quest for Strategic Paralysis* (Maxwell AFB, Montgomery, AL: Air University Press, 1995).

12. Harlan Ullman and James Wade, *Shock and Awe: Achieving Rapid Dominance* (Washington, DC: National Defense University Institute for National Security Studies, 1996). p. 11.

13. Edward N. Luttwak, *Strategy: The Logic of War and Peace* (Harvard University Press, 1987), pp. 4–5.

14. Ibid., p. 28.

15. Mattis, "Remarks by Secretary Mattis on the National Defense Strategy."

16. Robert Wilson Lynd, *Searchlights and Nightingales* (London: J.M. Dent, 1939), p. 67.

17. John R. Allen and Amir Husain, "On Hyperwar," *Proceedings*, vol. 143, no. 7 (July 2017), pp. 30–37.

18. Ibid., p 36.

19. Ibid., p. 37.

20. T. X. Hammes, "The Melian's Revenge: How Small, Frontline, European States Can Employ Emerging Technology to Defend Against Russia," *Atlantic Council Issue Brief*, June 2019.

21. Ibid., p. 11.

22. Ibid., p. 12. See also T. X. Hammes. *Deglobalization and International Security* (Amherst, NY: Cambria Press, 2019).

23. Ibid., p. 73.

24. Carl von Clausewitz, *On War*, translated and edited by Michael Howard and Peter Paret (Princeton University Press, 1989).

25. See Elbridge A. Colby, "Testimony Before the Senate Armed Services Committee Hearing on Implementation of The National Defense Strategy," www.armed-services.senate.gov/imo/media/doc/Colby_01-29-19.pdf.

26. Andreas Umland, "Crimea Could Become an Expensive Liability for Putin," Atlantic Council, June 10, 2020, https://www.atlanticcouncil.org/blogs/ukrainealert/crimea-could-become-an-expensive-liability-for-putin/.

27. Clausewitz. *On War*, p. 605.

28. Ibid., p. 605.

29. Ibid., p. 607.

30. Luttwak, *Strategy,* p. 31.

31. Williamson Murray, *Military Adaptation in War: With Fear of Change* (Cambridge University Press, 2011), p. 9.

32. Joseph Maiolo, *Cry Havoc: How the Arms Race Drove the World to War, 1931–1941* (New York: Basic Books, 2010).

THREE

Benefit or Burden?

NATO-led Military Missions and Western Cohesion

REBECCA R. MOORE

In late March 2011, a NATO-led coalition assumed responsibility for what had been Operation Odyssey Dawn, the US mission prompted by former Libyan leader Muammar Qaddafi's threat to brutally massacre protesters in the rebel stronghold of Benghazi.[1] Operation Unified Protector (OUP) expressly aimed to protect Libyan civilians, enforce an arms embargo, and police the no-fly zone. Although only fourteen of the then twenty-eight NATO members contributed to the operation (Germany and Poland were notably among the absentees), those allies that did opt to participate were joined by five NATO partners: Sweden, Jordan, Qatar, the United Arab Emirates (UAE), and Morocco. These five not only made significant operational contributions; their active political and military support—particularly that of the Arab partners—served to enhance the legitimacy of the mission, thereby making yet another war in the Middle East more palatable for at least some allies. For a moment it thus seemed that NATO partnering in international operations had struck the right balance between aligning with like-minded liberal partners and partners that were not liberal republics but held sway on the ground. It raised the question of whether, at a time when individual Western governments were struggling at home to uphold this balance between liberal and military commitments, as evidenced in the previous two chapters, a NATO forum of international checks and balances could confer renewed strategic control of war's pace and direction.

The Libya mission raised this prospect but also highlighted distinct challenges for strategic control by international committee, especially as NATO allies wrestled with the difficulty of privileging either liberal principle or operational efficacy. NATO's Middle Eastern partners ultimately acted outside the parameters of the liberal and humanitarian-oriented UN mandate in the manner in which they aided the Libyan rebels and accelerated Qaddafi's removal from power. Although the allies had quietly acknowledged that Qaddafi needed to go, his summary execution at the hands of rebel forces, supported by NATO's Middle Eastern partners, did not just seem inconsistent with NATO's liberal values; it highlighted NATO's abdication of responsibility for Libya's longer-term future to partners whose understanding of legitimate governance diverged appreciably from that of the NATO allies.

OUP was hardly the first time that NATO has had to wrestle with the tensions that inevitably arise in waging war with partners whose behavior is not aligned with liberal values. Indeed, non-liberal as well as liberal partners have played significant and consequential roles in NATO's military missions since the mid-1990s, when thirteen of its then twenty-seven partners contributed forces to the Implementation Force (IFOR) in Bosnia.[2] Moreover, relations with partners—particularly since the September 11 terrorist attacks in the United States—have increasingly been shaped by the desire to leverage the military resources of an increasingly diverse assortment of states even in instances in which their values constituted an affront to the liberal order that NATO was purportedly seeking to promote. For example, even though NATO's mission in Afghanistan—the International Security Assistance Force (ISAF)—brought on board new Asian partners that generally subscribed to NATO values, the majority of Central Asian and Middle Eastern partners—whose cooperation had been deemed critical to the success of the mission—were headed by authoritarian, rights-abusive governments. This ultimately led to criticism that NATO was now in the business of shoring up repressive regimes.

This chapter explores the challenges the Alliance has confronted in reconciling its liberal democratic identity and values with the perceived requirements of waging war effectively. The danger for NATO is that, as it is pulled to work with disparate partners to gain effect on the ground, it is simultaneously tempted to invest in the culture of speed, highlighted in chapter 2 by Paul Brister, that threatens to corrode its commitment to liberal order in its own Euro-Atlantic neighborhood. The irony for NATO would be if its international operations corrupted its particular commitment to the "civic militarism" discussed by Sarah Kreps and Adi Rao in chapter 1, with an adverse impact on the trajectory of Western military power. Inversely, if NATO is able to forge a new balance between liberal principle and military power, it could provide an essential contribution to a continued trajectory of Western cohesion and influence. This question is investigated in the context of the ISAF mission in Afghanistan and OUP in Libya—both crisis management operations— and NATO's more recent engagement of Partnership for Peace (PfP) members Sweden and Finland in its collective defense/deterrence mission.

The Evolution of NATO Partnership

NATO's first formal partnership framework—the North Atlantic Cooperation Council (NACC)—was established in 1991 to facilitate consultation and cooperation on political and security matters and to project stability by extending eastward the liberal democratic values (democracy, individual liberty, and the rule of law) on the basis of which NATO had pacified interstate relations in Western Europe after World War II.[3] Ultimately the NACC paved the way for a web of partnership frameworks, including the PfP, the Euro-Atlantic Cooperation Council (EAPC), the Mediterranean Dialogue (MD), and the Istanbul Cooperation Initiative (ICI), among others.

In the wake of the September 11 terrorist attacks and NATO's assumption of responsibility for ISAF in 2003, however, the scope and function of NATO's partnerships began to shift as the Alliance determined that new threats required not only new *missions* and new *capabilities*, but also new *partners*.[4] This new appreciation for what partners could do for NATO ultimately prompted the Alliance to identify *cooperative security* as one of three "essential core tasks" in its 2010 Strategic Concept, while simultaneously pledging to develop "a wide network of partner relationships with countries and organizations around the globe."[5] Aiming to increase the "effectiveness and flexibility" of partners—who increasingly were expected to contribute to NATO's military missions—the Alliance also adopted a new partnership policy the following year.[6] Rather than focusing on the geographically based multilateral frameworks such as the EAPC, MD, and ICI around which NATO had historically organized its partners, the Alliance now sought to build new, more functional relationships, principally on a bilateral basis. With the adoption of a single Partnership Cooperation Menu aimed at consolidating and harmonizing various partnership activities previously available only to PfP members, NATO also made clear that its relations with partners would now be largely partner-driven.[7] Although NATO's partnership framework agreements would continue to emphasize the importance of liberal democratic values, its relations with partners—even those that shared its liberal values—were now shaped almost exclusively by a desire to leverage partner resources for NATO military operations, with little thought as to how these partners would support its commitment to the defense of liberal order.

The International Security Assistance Force (ISAF)

ISAF was a particularly notable milestone in the evolution of NATO's partnerships in so far as it served to enlarge and further diversify the Alliance's circle of partners to include states from Asia as well as official NATO partners from the Caucasus, Central Asia, and the Middle East. Unlike NATO missions in the Balkans, the ISAF mission involved actual combat. This led to significant gains in interoperability between member and partner forces, which NATO has sought to preserve with an eye to possible future crisis management operations outside Afghanistan.

Distinct from the US-led counterterrorism mission code-named Operation Enduring Freedom (OEF), ISAF was originally established by the United Nations primarily to train Afghan security forces and assist in rebuilding Afghan institutions by securing the capital city of Kabul and surrounding areas. Once NATO had assumed responsibility for the mission in 2003, it divided the country into five regional commands, establishing in each Provincial Reconstruction Teams (PRTs), which eventually covered the whole of Afghanistan.[8] Comprising teams of military and civilian personnel engaged in providing security for aid workers and helping with humanitarian assistance or reconstruction tasks, PRTs were created primarily in areas with "ongoing conflict or high levels of insecurity."[9]

NATO partners played a variety of important roles in the coalition, including sharing responsibility for leadership of the PRTs. Some contributed to the mission at a higher level than did actual NATO members, who were determined to maintain a "light footprint" in Afghanistan. Indeed, as NATO moved into the southern and eastern parts of the country, key allies (France, Germany, Spain, Italy, Greece, and Turkey), fearful of low domestic support for deployments to Afghanistan's most violent provinces, imposed significant caveats on the nature of their participation, frequently leaving the mission without adequate equipment and personnel. As Seth Jones has noted, the reluctance to deploy troops reflected not so much a debate about "whether to go into Afghanistan, but what to do there."[10] For some allies a successful counter-insurgency mission required development and reconstruction efforts, whereas they saw combat operations with their potential for civilian casualties as only likely to alienate the Afghan population. However, these uneven contributions not only undermined counterinsurgency efforts; they also generated references to a two-tier NATO—in which only some members were willing to fight. Additionally, they also raised the profile of partners, especially those that were willing to put troops on the ground in Afghanistan's more dangerous provinces.[11]

Central Asia and the Caucasus

Not all significant contributions to the ISAF mission involved the deployment of troops. Both the US-led OEF and ISAF served to enhance the geostrategic importance of NATO partners in Central Asia and the Caucasus. None of the Central Asian partners sent troops to Afghanistan, but they did make other significant contributions, including providing access to military bases, transit rights, refueling facilities, and cooperation on border security.[12] Much of this cooperation was facilitated by their participation in NATO's Partnership for Peace, which all of the Central Asian states, apart from Tajikistan, had joined in 1994. Through PfP, NATO forces had conducted training exercises in the region and become familiar with local facilities well before September 11, 2001.

Of the five Central Asian partners, it is Kazakhstan with which NATO has enjoyed the highest level of cooperation, including an Individual Partnership Action Plan (IPAP). Kazakhstan has participated in and hosted PfP training and exercises, and has also been actively working toward interoperability with Alliance forces through its membership in NATO's Interoperability Platform. Although the government briefly considered contributing a limited number to troops to ISAF in late 2010/early 2011, that deployment never materialized owing to a lack of domestic support.[13] NATO's cooperation with the remaining four Central Asian states was more limited, but all five supported ISAF through the provision of transit rights, bases, refueling facilities, and reconstruction assistance, including funding for various infrastructure projects in Afghanistan.[14]

At the same time, the absence of democratic reform in the region also meant that NATO's relations with the Central Asian states were fraught with tension. Even though liberal democratic values have been explicitly highlighted in PfP/EAPC framework documents from the start, the authoritarian nature of the Central Asian governments prompted critics—particularly during the George W. Bush administration—to accuse the US and NATO of shoring up repressive regimes with economic and military assistance in exchange for cooperation in the war on terror.[15] Russia's aggressive response to Ukraine's efforts to align itself more closely with the West in 2014 only exacerbated that tension. In the words of one NATO official, the crisis "cast a chill" over the Central Asian partnerships in causing them to "feel watched."[16] Indeed none of the Central Asian states has chosen to participate in NATO's Resolute Support Mission (RSM), the successor to ISAF.

The Caucasus states of Armenia, Azerbaijan, and Georgia, on the other hand, have all participated in both ISAF and RSM. Although the troop contributions of Armenia and Azerbaijan have been relatively small, Georgia, which desperately wishes to join the Alliance and currently participates in its RSM, was among the largest non-NATO troop contributors to the ISAF mission. At one point it provided two full infantry battalions which served alongside US forces in Helmand province—generally considered the most dangerous province in Afghanistan.[17]

Jordan and the United Arab Emirates (UAE)

The diversity of the ISAF partnership pool is also reflected in the participation of Jordan and the UAE, members of MD and ICI, respectively. Jordan, which already had strong ties to US special forces, deployed its own special operations forces in support of ISAF in both 2007 and 2009, in addition to sharing intelligence, providing demining teams, and assisting with the training of Afghan special forces on the assumption that these forces would prefer to take instruction from other Muslims.[18] Jordan's involvement was initially cloaked in secrecy, but the 2010 bombing of a Central Intelligence Agency (CIA) operations center in Khost province by a Palestinian Jordanian triple agent revealed that the Jordanians were more deeply involved than previously acknowledged.[19] Although the UAE's role was more transparent, it focused somewhat narrowly on international reconstruction efforts and assistance to schools, clinics, and libraries, and other humanitarian relief operations. UAE forces also participated in mine- and IED-clearing operations, but their number was relatively small.[20] As Daniel Brown and Ariel Ahram have observed, the interaction of Muslim troops with a Muslim population in this instance was of some benefit to NATO. Yet given a lack of domestic support for NATO in both states, "tactical gains in the campaign to win hearts and minds could not be translated to the more strategic level of public diplomacy."[21]

Global Partners

The extent to which ISAF was instrumental in generating a truly global network of NATO partners was also evident in the critical contributions made
by a number of Asian states, including Australia, New Zealand, Japan, South
Korea, and Mongolia. Dubbed "global partners," these Asian allies were not
members of any of NATO's formal partnership frameworks; yet they emerged
as important contributors at a time when even some long-standing Alliance
members were reluctant to provide the troops and other resources that NATO
commanders deemed critical to the success of the mission. Australia was in
fact the largest non-NATO contributor to ISAF, deploying troops at roughly
the same level as some NATO members. Over the course of the mission,
Australia deployed both conventional and special forces whose roles included
combat, reconnaissance and surveillance, support for reconstruction, and, finally, mentoring the Afghan National Army (ANA).[22] As Maryanne Kelton
and Aaron Jackson have observed, Australia's special forces were particularly
well suited to counterinsurgency needs in Afghanistan.[23] In fact they constituted just the sort of "niche capability" that NATO had urged all partners to
contribute. Australia's deepening ties with NATO during the course of the
ISAF mission also included an agreement in 2008 regarding the protection
of classified information, the establishment of a defense attaché in Brussels,
and the initiation of high-level reciprocal visits. Although New Zealand deployed significantly fewer troops to Afghanistan than Australia, its contributions were still at roughly the same level as those of many NATO members
and included leadership of a PRT in Bamyan province.[24] New Zealand, like
Australia, remained in the country after 2014, advising and training Afghan
security forces.

   South Korea also assumed responsibility for a PRT in Parwan province,
then under the command of Operation Enduring Freedom, but withdrew all
of its military forces in 2007, reportedly as part of deal with Taliban mili-
tants aimed at winning the release of South Korean missionaries who had
been taken hostage in the summer of that year. The withdrawal occurred just
before the transfer of the Parwan PRT to the ISAF command.[25] Although
South Korea chose not to redeploy combat forces, it did agree in late October
2009 to expand the number of civilians engaged in reconstruction and development projects in Afghanistan, in addition to sending troops and police
officers to assist in the protection of aid workers.[26]

   Among the principal non-NATO, non-partner contributors in Afghanistan, Japan played a unique role. Rather than deploying troops to the coun-

try, Japanese Maritime Self Defense Forces (JMSDF) conducted a refueling operation in the Indian Ocean in support of OEF over an eight-year period, beginning in 2001. In March 2007 Japan also finalized with NATO a framework for cooperation under which it would provide financial support for humanitarian projects in Afghanistan, with priority given to healthcare and education projects proposed by ISAF PRTs.[27] The commitment followed then Prime Minister Shinzo Abe's declaration before the North Atlantic Council (NAC) in January 2007 that Japan would "no longer shy away from carrying out overseas activities involving the SDF." Abe also pledged to strengthen cooperation between Japan and NATO with a particular focus on ISAF.[28]

Pakistan and Afghanistan

In keeping with an increasingly functional approach to partnership, NATO offered both Pakistan and Afghanistan additional access to its "toolbox" of partnership activities in 2010, including an opportunity for Pakistani officers to participate in select NATO training and education courses in the areas of peace support operations, civil–military cooperation, and defense against terrorism.[29] Over the course of the ISAF mission, however, NATO's relations with Pakistan became increasingly strained by numerous, complex disputes and events, including a friendly fire incident in November 2011 that resulted in the death of 24 Pakistani soldiers from a NATO airstrike.[30] Pakistan presented a particularly troublesome problem for NATO in that it was widely known to serve as a sanctuary for Afghan insurgents. Concern that elements of Pakistan's Inter-Services Intelligence Directorate (ISI) were supporting the Taliban and other insurgents further aggravated NATO–Pakistan relations.[31]

In 2010, NATO also established a framework for long-term cooperation with Afghanistan in the form of a Declaration on an Enduring Partnership, which included a series of agreed programs and partnership activities in such areas as capacity building and professional military education, civil emergency planning, and disaster preparedness. NATO foreign ministers then endorsed an initial list of activities in 2011, at which time they pledged that NATO and Afghanistan would continue to "pursue a partnership dialogue" aimed at determining the scope and content of their cooperation beyond 2012.[32] NATO later vowed during its 2016 summit in Warsaw to strengthen and enhance the partnership—which exists "within and alongside RSM"—through political dialogue and practical cooperation.[33]

The above descriptions of partner involvement in Afghanistan are intended not as a comprehensive account of partner contributions to ISAF, but rather as a sample of the diversity and breadth of partner roles. At its height the ISAF mission comprised 51 members, almost 30 of them NATO partners at some point (some acceded to NATO during the ISAF mission). As noted above, the ISAF mission constituted a significant step in the evolution of NATO partnerships by broadening the circle, strengthening NATO–partner relations, and resulting in significant achievements in terms of interoperability and the use of multilateral forces. In the words of one Department of Defense official, the ISAF mission "jumpstarted" the process of working with global partners.[34]

That process, however, was marked by formidable operational challenges. The complexity of the multilateral mission itself meant that any operations involving partners would also be complicated. Moreover not all partners were capable of actually deploying their capabilities. Not infrequently, NATO had to provide various types of deployment support, typically linking partners' forces to those of members in order to facilitate a useful contribution. Indeed the NATO allies routinely proved willing to pay the costs and tolerate the inconveniences associated with partner contributions. As the defense department official cited above explained, although the challenges were largely *administrative*, NATO deemed them worthy of its time and resources given the potential for partners to serve as force multipliers.[35]

The process of engaging in complex multilateral operations with partners also produced significant gains in interoperability, which NATO has sought to sustain beyond the ISAF mission. As Gale Mattox observed, "the collaboration of politically and culturally diverse nations (NATO members as well as nonmembers) that evolved during the operations—at times bumpy, at times surprisingly smooth—set a new standard for Alliance operations within a coalition from which much can learned."[36]

As the ISAF mission came to a close in 2014, NATO introduced several initiatives designed to preserve the interoperability gains achieved. The Partnership Interoperability Initiative (PII) and accompanying Interoperability Platform with variable membership, introduced at the 2014 Wales summit, aimed at deepening interoperability between NATO and its partners and supporting their joint readiness to tackle common security challenges. Twenty-five partners, most of whom had contributed to NATO's military missions, were invited to join.[37]

Post-ISAF interoperability initiatives were influenced not only by the desire to preserve gains made in Afghanistan and Libya, but also by war-weary publics and a consequent determination that the Alliance would have to do a better job of training partners and building capacity if it was to reduce its own forward deployments.[38] In this vein, NATO also introduced at the Wales summit a Defence and Related Security Capacity Building Initiative aimed at strengthening and enhancing partners' capacity to defend against external threats and build "credible, transparent, effective internal national security systems."[39] Ultimately the goal was to develop the means by which NATO could project stability without having to deploy large combat forces. Although the initiative was initially extended to just three states (Georgia, Jordan, and Moldova), the same opportunity was afforded to Iraq just ahead of the 2016 Warsaw Summit.[40]

The desire to preserve interoperability and deepen cooperation with those partners that had been deemed particularly significant contributors to ISAF and other NATO military missions also inspired the allies in 2014 to identify five states (Australia, Finland, Georgia, Jordan, and Sweden) as *Enhanced Opportunities Partners*. The idea was not to institute a new partnership framework, but rather to find a means of recognizing these states for their past contributions and enhancing opportunities for future political dialogue and cooperation.[41]

NATO's partnership management was not without controversy, however. Partly in response to Australia's expressed desire for a greater voice in NATO's decision-shaping and operational planning for the ISAF mission, the United States, together with the United Kingdom, had proposed during the 2006 Riga summit a new political framework or "stability providers forum" designed to draw Australia, Japan, South Korea, Sweden, and Finland closer to NATO.[42] A number of allies strongly resisted the proposal, fearing that the United States was unilaterally trying to restructure NATO's partnerships in favor of more functional rather than geographically oriented partnerships, and that global partners were simply the first step in the direction of a global NATO.[43]

Despite the controversy, NATO did agree at Riga "to fully develop the political and practical potential of NATO's existing cooperation programmes" and to "increase the operational relevance of relations with non-NATO countries" in two particular ways. First, NATO could "call ad-hoc meetings as events arise" with contributors or potential contributors to NATO's military missions, "utilizing flexible formats . . . based on the principles of inclusiveness, transparency and self-differentiation."[44] Second, the allies would extend partnership tools originally available only to PfP members to NATO's global partners as well as MD and ICI states, on a case-by-case basis.[45] Later initiatives aimed at sustaining political dialogue with partners included meetings of NATO core contributors to ISAF, which began during the 2012 Chicago summit.[46]

That said, the debate over the form and function of NATO partnerships that began at Riga reflects a continuing concern that, in embracing new global missions and partners, NATO has overextended itself and lost sight of its regional collective defense mission. Indeed Russia's invasion of Ukraine in 2014 only reignited a long-standing debate over NATO's identity, pitting a belief that it is time for NATO to refocus on its collective defense mission against the view that, given the increasingly global nature of contemporary threats, NATO has little choice other than to become more globally focused.

Yet despite the formidable contributions of NATO's ISAF partners and significant achievements in interoperability, there is little evidence that partners, including those that shared NATO's values, had any notable *strategic* impact on the ISAF mission. Although partners did enjoy some limited influence with respect to tactical decisions, they had very limited opportunities to influence strategic decisions at the level of the North Atlantic Council. Moreover during the course of the mission the Alliance failed to articulate clear strategic objectives, a failure for which partners bear no responsibility.[47] Indeed, further reflecting a failure to embrace the liberal dimension of its civic militarism, NATO devoted little effort to engaging partners in a manner that might serve to advance liberal order. ISAF is thus in part a story of how NATO itself, beyond considerations of NATO partners and their political character, struggled to generate strategic foresight and coherence from internal checks and balances (Kathleen McInnis examines ISAF and Protection of Civilians policy in chapter 5 of this volume). NATO did not resolve the tension between its long-term and slow-paced campaign to build stable and solid Afghan security institutions, and its short-term and fast-paced annual campaigns to wrest control of critical areas from insurgent control or influence. Despite toying with various concepts for ISAF partnering, including one that would create a global NATO partnership structure, the Alliance was unable to anchor such concepts in a balanced approach to liberal principle and military action.

Operation Unified Protector

Relative to ISAF, the NATO-led OUP mission involved a small number of partners, yet partner involvement was no less significant in terms of both operational and political contributions. Undertaken in support of two United Nations Security Council Resolutions (1970 and 1973), adopted in February and March 2011, OUP followed and assumed responsibility for what had been a US-led mission code-named Operation Odyssey Dawn. The NATO mission centered on three UN-sanctioned objectives with regard to Libya: enforcing an arms embargo, patrolling the no-fly zone, and protecting civilians. Although OUP was also shorter and more controversial within the Alliance than ISAF, the two missions were similar in some important respects.

As with ISAF, NATO found itself fighting in Libya alongside both liberal and non-liberal partners. The latter felt unconstrained by a limited UN resolution and pursued interests that did not necessarily reflect NATO's liberal values. At the same time NATO itself pursued an arguably incoherent strategy, publicly framing its objectives in terms of a limited humanitarian mission while refusing to embrace calls for either Qaddafi's removal or direct support to rebel forces, all the while working with partners whose support for these forces ultimately led to Qaddafi's demise in a manner that was inconsistent with NATO's identity and values. In declining to assume any responsibility for Libya's long-term future and neglecting the challenge of reconciling its own liberal democratic values with its political and operational reliance on non-liberal partners, NATO again failed the civic militarism test.

To some degree this failure reflected internal tensions regarding NATO's role in the region, as well as a desire on the part of many members to avoid the deployment of combat troops. Although the Alliance was joined by five partners—Sweden plus four Arab states (Jordan, Qatar, the UAE, and Morocco)—only 14 NATO members (approximately half) chose to participate. Turkey had also initially declined to support a NATO mission.[48] Indeed, as Chris Chivvis has observed, the speed at which the NAC approved the mission—roughly four weeks after it started talks—was not indicative of Alliance unity. Rather, a number of NATO allies, including Germany, "continued to object to the operation, even as they let it move ahead."[49]

The Arab Partners

At the same time NATO found itself with strong support from its four Arab partners. Owing largely to their shared distaste for the Qaddafi regime, all four proved willing to champion and ultimately assist the NATO mission.[50] Indeed the Gulf Cooperation Council, in a ministerial statement issued in early March 2011, had supported contacts with the National Transition Council (NTC)—Qatar had taken the lead in recognizing it as the sole legitimate representative of the Libyan people—and called on the UN Security Council to establish a no-fly zone. Just days later the Arab League issued an unprecedented call for military action against one of its own neighbors. That appeal advocated both a no-fly zone and the creation of safe havens for Libyan civilians, as well as cooperation with the NTC.[51] Given the general mistrust of NATO in the Arab world, the support of Arab partners played a critical role in legitimizing the mission.[52] Indeed Chris Chivvis notes that NATO made a significant, even if not fully realized, effort to put an Arab face on the operation by pushing Arab partners to take the lead in public diplomacy.[53] As he puts it: "These partnerships, which had heretofore been far from top allied priorities, suddenly took on paramount importance, because the military participation of the Arab partners would reinforce the political message that Qaddafi's actions were universally deplorable."[54]

During the course of the mission, which ran from March 23 until October 31, 2011, Jordan, Qatar, and the UAE all deployed their own special forces, provided transport flights, and facilitated the transfer of both humanitarian and military supplies to Libyan opposition forces. Qatar deployed six Mirage 2000s, which took off from Crete and flew alongside the French in joint patrols of the no-fly zones, in addition to transporting a mix of humanitarian and military supplies as well as weapons to the NTC via C-17s. These contributions were facilitated in part by embedding several Qatari officers at NATO's Joint Force Command Naples and the Allied Air Component Command Izmir to help coordinate the planning and integration of Qatar Emiri Air Force (QEAF) assets with other Allied forces.[55]

Fleshing out the Arab contribution, the UAE provided six F-16s as well as six Mirages.[56] Like Qatar, the UAE committed transports for humanitarian purposes, including carrying civilians to Jordan for medical care. Although Jordan also contributed F-16s, it assumed a much lower profile in the mission and restricted the use of its aircraft to humanitarian operations, declining to participate in air strike operations or sorties to maintain the no-fly zone.[57]

Typically these Arab partners were paired with NATO members in carrying out combat air patrols. The Emiratis, for example, worked closely with the US Air Force 363rd Intelligence, Surveillance, and Reconnaissance Wing on the logistical aspects of their F-16 deployment, with US teams providing substantial planning and support. Although UAE pilots flew their own sorties without other coalition aircraft present, US forces assisted with mission planning for both the F-16s and the Mirages. According to Bruce Nardulli, "this partnering on mission planning proved to be a key enabler for maintaining operational tempo and for tasking order commitments." That said, UAE forces did confront difficulties integrating into the NATO command network owing to their unfamiliarity with NATO processes and regulations, as well as the fact that their pilots did not have access to NATO's encrypted communications.[58] In fact NATO's restrictions on intelligence and targeting information significantly affected its ability to take full advantage of the Arab partners' contributions.

Perhaps the most important contribution made by the Arab states was the role they played in training Libyan opposition forces, which proved critical to Qaddafi's fall from power but occurred outside the NATO mandate.[59] Not only had the NATO allies expressed firm opposition to committing ground forces in Libya; they also stressed that the coalition's mandate was limited to the UN resolutions and, as noted above, did not support aid to either rebel forces or the NTC. These constraints were necessary to keep the coalition together and maintain Arab support for the operation, but they also reflected a lack of strategic clarity regarding the ultimate objective of the mission and how to achieve it. Indeed a few weeks into the mission, despite having hit most of its targets, the Alliance found itself facing a stalemate. Fabrice Pothier, an adviser to NATO's secretary general at the time, remembers this period as the "most difficult moment. . . . We had destroyed most of the military targets, but Gaddafi's troops had simply folded into the population. We were running our targets, but the problem was still there."[60] The rebels, who were poorly trained, equipped, and funded, were proving no match for Qaddafi's forces.[61] US Secretary of Defense Roberts Gates complained that the coalition faced a lack of political will and capabilities.[62] As Rob Weigill and Florence Gaub have observed, however, as the conflict dragged on, it became more apparent that the problem was not so much NATO's capacity as the limits it had set for itself. "At this point, the glaring gap between NATO's mandate—the protection of civilians—and the political objective of some NATO allies for Gaddafi to step down became fairly obvious."[63] Removing Qaddafi was outside the Alliance's mandate. Individual allies, however, were free to act outside Alliance structures.

Moreover the constraints that NATO imposed on its own mission did not apply to partners. The Arab states' participation in OUP was facilitated by membership in NATO's regional partnership frameworks (MD and ICI) as well as participation in earlier NATO missions.[64] Partners were also integrated into NATO's command and control with respect to actions undertaken in support of UN Security Council resolutions; yet much of their activity in assisting the rebels occurred within the context of their bilateral relationships with individual NATO members. As Nardulli explains it, these relationships "provided the opening for military activities not sanctioned by the UN resolutions or otherwise politically unacceptable to individual NATO members."[65]

The Qataris played a particularly important role in training and working with the opposition, even to the point of claiming that they had "acted as the link between the rebels and NATO forces."[66] Both Qatar and the UAE had special forces on the ground in Libya from the beginning, as did Britain, France, and Italy. These special forces played a role in advising, training rebel forces, and deconflicting NATO air strikes.[67]

Ironically, in order to break the stalemate NATO relied on its partners to put special forces on the ground and to arm and train the rebels, thereby leaving open the potential for activities coordinated through bilateral arrangements that were actually at odds with both the NATO mandate and the UN resolutions. Indeed a British House of Commons Defence Committee report published in January 2012 expressed concern over the manner in which the contributions of non-NATO countries were integrated into NATO command-and-control structures. The report requested that the UK government "clarify how it ensured that any bilateral alliances between non-NATO countries and the National Transitional Council were monitored to ensure that they did not impact unfavourably on the NATO mission or were contrary to the measures in the UN Resolutions."[68]

Arguably the situation also reflected a failure on the part of the Alliance to articulate clear and realizable strategic goals. NATO had adopted a mandate that was unlikely to provide a full remedy for the humanitarian crisis, which seemed inextricably linked to Qaddafi's continued hold on power. It was the Arab partners who then bridged the gap between the objective as they and some NATO members understood it—namely, the removal of Qaddafi—and NATO's limited and self-imposed mandate and means. Yet it was the limited nature of the NATO mission that served to hold the coalition together. Had NATO shown an interest in shaping Libya's long-term political future—which, ultimately, it did not—the coalition would very likely have fractured, given that the Arab partners' visions of the Arab Spring and Libya's long-term future did not necessarily match those of NATO members. In short, NATO had embraced Arab partners, believing that they provided both legitimacy and capacity that otherwise would have been lacking, but at the same time it failed to align this capacity with a long-term liberal outcome.

Sweden

Sweden served as the only non-Arab partner in the OUP coalition. Sweden was not new to NATO missions or to the Middle East region, but the speed with which it responded to NATO's request for assistance was noteworthy. Not only did the Swedish parliament quickly authorize the mission; within just two days eight JAS 39 Gripen aircraft had arrived at Sigonella Airbase in Italy. Sweden also provided a C-130 refueling aircraft and one Gulfstream IV surveillance aircraft. Notably, this was its first contribution of combat aircraft to a NATO mission, although it came with a significant caveat; namely, that the Swedish force would not be involved in strikes on ground targets.[69]

Although the deployment was not without challenges, the Swedish contribution to OUP was important and substantial. The Swedes ultimately flew at least 30 percent of the reconnaissance sorties, and both the quality of the photos and the speed and quality of their analysis were judged to be excellent.[70] The Swedish contingent was also praised for its reliability and flexibility with respect to mission tasks.[71]

The Alliance did, however, struggle briefly in ensuring Sweden's access to NATO's tactical data exchange network. Although this issue was addressed relatively quickly, Sweden, as a non-NATO member, did not initially have access to classified NATO information and communications networks, complicating the receipt of mission orders. Neither NATO nor Sweden appeared prepared for these bureaucratic obstacles, which delayed full operational capability. Adding to the challenges, Sigonella did not have fuel that was compatible with the Gripens. Although the problem was ultimately resolved satisfactorily, it "limited the extent of early missions flown."[72]

Moreover the prohibition on attacking ground targets was initially not the only caveat linked to the Swedish OUP contribution. The Swedish parliament had restricted the role of Swedish forces to just one of the three tasks outlined in the UN resolutions: implementing the no-fly zone. However, as Robert Egnell points out, maintaining the no-fly zone was an objective, not a tactic, which in some instances might require attacking ground targets. The caveat was unclear as to which tasks related to the no-fly zone the Swedish contingent was permitted to perform. In addition the restriction meant that Sweden could not gather intelligence regarding civilians in danger or breaches of the arms embargo, because these tasks were unrelated to the no-fly zone. Not until late June were the caveats lifted, with the exception of the prohibition on strikes on ground targets.[73] Despite these challenges, Sweden demonstrated relatively quickly that it possessed highly useful capabilities with the potential to be integrated quickly into NATO structures, and indeed the Swedish unit proved highly interoperable with NATO. This was a testament to the progress made since 1996, when Sweden, as a PfP member, first began working toward interoperability with NATO forces.[74]

As in Afghanistan, OUP partners served as force multipliers, providing important military capabilities at a time when many NATO allies were reluctant to get involved. Partners arguably also played a consequential role in the mission outcome, even if that outcome ultimately extended beyond OUP's mandate. As Chivvis explains it: "The participation of Jordan, Morocco, Qatar, and the United Arab Emirates and their support for Libyan opposition forces proved critical to the liberation of Tripoli, both by demonstrating Arab political support and providing additional military capabilities."[75]

Both Sweden and the Arab partners faced certain logistical challenges, requiring NATO assistance in order to deliver their full operational capabilities. Yet it was apparent during the mission that participation in NATO training and exercises, facilitated by NATO's partnership frameworks, had contributed considerably to interoperability with NATO forces and the political and military ties necessary to assist in the timely and satisfactory resolution of these challenges. As in Afghanistan, however, OUP partners had little impact on the strategic framing of the mission. According to one NATO official, this was partly due to the short timeframe. The mission was just "too short" to encompass much integration of partners into the planning process.[76] Given the nature of the governments involved and NATO's sharp distinction between partner and member, however, a larger role in shaping NATO strategy was not likely to have evolved even in the context of a lengthier mission.

Indeed OUP partners had very different rationales for their contributions. Sweden perceived the mission primarily as a humanitarian one—an opportunity to promote democracy and human rights.[77] The Arab partners, on the other hand, viewed it principally as an opportunity to remove Qaddafi from power. Although NATO ultimately proved uninterested in playing a long-term role in Libya, the allies focused primarily on partners' operational contributions, just as they had in Afghanistan, and seemingly devoted little attention to the problem of reconciling the demands of military efficiency with liberal values. Qaddafi's removal was not necessarily at odds with these values, but the means by which he was ousted clearly were inconsistent with the liberal democratic norms with which NATO has long identified. Waging an effective and legitimate fight, the allies had decided, required the embrace of at least some partners who, while militarily helpful, had long-term ambitions that deviated from NATO's. Whereas in Afghanistan NATO lost control of the pace of the war owing to its own imbalance between liberal principle and military action, in Libya it ceded this control in important ways to partners who valued military action over such principle. NATO had mobilized on an R2P (responsibility to protect) basis that promised military action anchored in and controlled by liberal and humanitarian principle; in practice, however, as NATO's inner checks and balances proved more contentious than deliberative, this liberal control ceded to fast-paced action—ultimately to the benefit of non-NATO actors.

Article 5: A Role for Partners?

Russia's 2014 invasion of Ukraine has led to a re-examination of the balance of resources devoted to NATO's regional collective defense/deterrence mission as opposed to its crisis management tasks, which had come to define the primary rationale for NATO partnerships. Fear of a resurgent Russian threat prompted the Alliance during its 2014 Wales summit to introduce a Readiness Action Plan (RAP) designed to ensure its ability "to respond swiftly and firmly" to changes in the security environment on NATO's borders and beyond.[78] Two years later in Warsaw, NATO announced that it would build on RAP by establishing an enhanced forward presence in Estonia, Latvia, Lithuania, and Poland "to unambiguously demonstrate" its commitment to deterrence and the defense of its members.[79] Not surprisingly, then, the Alliance has recently sought to increase cooperation with PfP partners Finland and Sweden "with a particular focus on ensuring security in the Baltic Sea region."[80]

Frequently referred to by the secretary general as NATO's closest partners, Sweden and Finland are among those states designated Major Non-NATO allies, a term used to identify non-member states that have close working relationships with the US military. Both have also been active in previous NATO military missions, including KFOR, ISAF, RSM, OUP, and most recently a new mission in Iraq (NATO Mission Iraq). In the wake of the Ukraine crisis, however, NATO has also come to view Sweden and Finland as critical to its deterrence/collective defense mission in Europe, in large part because of their geographical proximity to the Baltic region. Indeed Russia's efforts to build up anti-access, anti-denial capabilities near Gotland make Sweden's continued control of the island critical to the defense of the Baltic states.[81] As two of NATO's most sophisticated military partners, Finland and Sweden also offer the Alliance significant military resources. Finland has a large reserve army and could mobilize 280,000 troops quickly if necessary. Although Sweden cut the size of its armed forces following the end of the Cold War, it has been taking steps to reverse this process, including restoring a military presence on Gotland and re-introducing limited conscription.[82] In recent years both partners have been increasing investment in their armed forces and cooperation with each other and other Nordic states.

Both Sweden and Finland have also stepped up training and efforts to increase interoperability with NATO forces through their participation in exercises such as Trident Juncture and Northern Wind. Hosted by Norway, and one of NATO's largest exercises in recent years, Trident Juncture 18 involved

50,000 participants from NATO and partner states and was designed to simulate NATO's collective response to an attack.[83] Northern Wind, a Swedish high-intensity warfighting exercise, involved roughly 10,000 personnel from NATO and partner states, including Finland.[84]

In 2017 Sweden held its largest military exercise in twenty years, involving approximately 19,000 troops, roughly half of the Swedish armed forces. Aurora 17, which focused on the southeastern part of Sweden and Gotland, was clearly intended as a robust demonstration of Sweden's defense capabilities.[85] Although not technically a NATO exercise, Aurora involved a number of NATO allies, including Denmark, Estonia, France, Latvia, Lithuania, Norway, and the United States, thereby showcasing Sweden's growing interest in regional cooperation as well as its deepening interoperability with NATO forces.[86] As one NATO official observed, such exercises are not just important in helping prepare participants for possible future missions; they also serve as a deterrent by demonstrating to Russia the close cooperation between NATO and these two partners. Importantly, both Sweden and Finland have signed Host Nation Support agreements with NATO, permitting "logistical support to Allied forces located on, or in transit through, their territory, during exercises or in a crisis." The designation of Sweden and Finland as Enhanced Opportunities Partners in 2014 also paved the way for their participation in the enhanced NATO Response Force.[87]

NATO has in addition been working to enhance political dialogue with both Sweden and Finland with a focus on three priority areas: political dialogue, interoperability, and situational awareness and exchange of information. Under the 2011 Partnership Policy, both states have regular access to +2 meetings with the North Atlantic Council. Both also participate regularly in ministerial and summit meetings, and are invited to any operational meetings for missions in which they are involved. Additionally NATO now invites both partners to one policy-oriented lunch or dinner during each of its summits and ministerial meetings.[88]

Ironically, as a result of the 2014 Ukraine crisis, Sweden and Finland became important partners in NATO's collective defense/deterrence mission even though, as non-members, they are not entitled to Article 5 protections themselves. As one NATO official observed, however, both states' relations with NATO are to some degree a "two-way street" because NATO plays a significant role in their own defense strategies. In effect "Sweden and Finland, just by taking care of themselves, are taking care of NATO's northern flank."[89]

Interestingly, while Russia's intervention in Ukraine prompted NATO to highlight the distinction between member and partner in a way that was not favorable to Ukraine, the same event brought Sweden and Finland closer to NATO. Unlike Ukraine, they are not only among NATO's most militarily capable partners but also well-established liberal democracies. Indeed in this particular instance the Alliance did not have to compromise its principles in the name of military efficiency. As one NATO official noted, this also makes both states among the "easiest [partners] to work with."[90] These relationships thus constitute an opportunity for NATO to realign its partner relations to accord with the principle of civic militarism. They highlight the fact that there is no necessary trade-off between the effective use of military means and the Alliance's commitment to upholding and even extending its liberal values. However, this achievement in restoring a degree of balance within NATO as regards civic militarism has come about largely in the case of non-war, or deterrence, whereas, as noted above, NATO's earlier challenges in maintaining this balance were related to the actual use of armed force in difficult international operations—with Sweden constituting a notable exception. Thus NATO must continue to digest its operational lesson that actual war brings acute tensions between principle and action. The return to collective defense and deterrence, and to the balance it can bring, is therefore NATO's opportunity to reflect on how it can think of and if necessary engage in war as an activity where pace is not a goal but a variable in the service of durable liberal principles.

In Defense of Liberal Values

The above cases suggest that, to date, NATO's utilization of partners in its military operations is not aligned with the civic militarism that has characterized the Alliance since its inception in 1949. Although partners have come to play increasingly important roles in its military missions, serving as both "force multipliers" and "legitimacy multipliers," their integration into NATO operations has not been without significant challenges, including difficulties in communication, intelligence-sharing, and force deployment, as well as tensions over differences in core values. Given war-fatigued publics in NATO member states, however, the Alliance has generally welcomed any partner willing to contribute resources to its operations. Indeed its official policy since 2011 has been one of non-discrimination between liberal and non-liberal partners. Moreover partner contributions to its missions have generally been partner- rather than NATO-driven.

Both the ISAF and OUP missions arguably reflect significant failures on NATO's part in terms of articulating a coherent strategic vision favoring liberal outcomes and the development of effective means of achieving that vision. The above case studies also suggest, however, that the partners themselves bear little or no responsibility for this strategic incoherence. Despite their impact on NATO operations at that tactical level, they have had virtually no influence on larger strategic decisions. This is due in part to the bilateral nature of NATO's interactions with partners as well as its commitment to maintaining a clear distinction between the status of partners and members. In short, the allies bear full responsibility for the failure to develop strategies conducive to liberal outcomes. Indeed both the ISAF and OUP missions suggest that NATO has made little effort to enlist like-minded partners in actively promoting liberal outcomes. In Libya, for example, it largely abdicated responsibility for the long-term political situation to partners whose values and interests were at odds with its own. In reducing partners to little more than force multipliers or states that can offer some temporary geostrategic advantage (as was also true of the Central Asian states in Afghanistan), NATO has failed to live up to its tradition of civic militarism.

Moving forward, NATO should not abandon its non-liberal partners: effective crisis management operations will still require cooperation with a diverse assortment of partners. However, it must differentiate between partners in terms of resources and opportunities for political dialogue with the Alliance. As its increasingly close relations with Sweden and Finland have demonstrated, opportunities do exist to link the effective use of force with the pursuit of liberal outcomes. Indeed liberal partners not only share NATO's commitment to liberal order; they are also among its most militarily robust partners. Despite some limited progress in terms of engaging Sweden and Finland politically as well as militarily, NATO has done little to enlist other like-minded and militarily capable partners such as Australia, New Zealand, Japan, and South Korea in responding to the challenges to liberal order posed not only by Russia but also by the rise of China and continued threats stemming from the Middle East. If the Alliance is truly committed to the defense not only of its territory but also of the liberal values articulated in the preamble to the 1949 NATO treaty, it must make a much more deliberate effort to extend its tradition of civic militarism by engaging like-minded partners politically and militarily in pursuit of liberal outcomes, rather than treating all partners as little more than force multipliers.

Large crisis management operations have been shown to undermine NATO's civic militarism balance and have encouraged it to let tactical speed dominate its perception of time in war. To recover its balance, NATO must define a politico-strategic center of gravity with reference to collective defense and containment. It is in this domain of grand strategy and the prevention of major war that the Alliance is most able. It should thus develop its partnership framework in ways that allow like-minded partners greater influence in NATO decision-making. While this could potentially reignite the debate over a global NATO that erupted during the 2006 Riga summit, it should be noted that the states most likely to benefit from arrangements that favor liberal partners (for example Australia and Japan) are also those that currently have little interest in joining the Alliance as members. In fact in enlisting partners in response to the rise of China, a resurgent Russia, and a variety of other threats posed by state and non-state actors, the Alliance has an opportunity to move its debate on grand strategy beyond enlargement. Its most troublesome debate will, as Afghanistan and Libya also showed, take place internally, where checks and balances can produce dysfunction rather than foresight.

In a grand strategic framework, the key issue will be the potential negative impact of illiberal trends within the organization itself (such as increasingly authoritarian trends in Poland, Hungary, Turkey, and even the United States). If NATO is to succeed in reviving the institution of civic militarism, its most committed liberal members must confront these trends, just as they must labor to ensure that crisis management operations do not grow to the point where they overshadow NATO's founding commitment to military force in the service of liberal ideals. The preceding two chapters have traced how decaying political institutions and strategic culture suggest that NATO allies and partners will be hard pressed to regenerate a declining trajectory of Western power. By bringing together like-minded, liberal Western states and facilitating their strategic dialogue, NATO might still succeed in offering a multinational framework for renewal. If so, the current trajectory of decline would represent yet another crisis of the West, but notably not define its tragic destiny.

NOTES

1. David D. Kirkpatrick and Kareem Fahim, "Qaddafi Warns of Assault on Benghazi as U.N. Vote Nears," *New York Times*, March 17, 2011, www.nytimes.com/2011/03/18/world/africa/18libya.html.

2. Sean Kay, "Partnerships and Power in American Grand Strategy," in *NATO: The Power of Partnerships*, edited by Håkan Edström, Janne Haaland Matlary, and Magnus Petersson (Palgrave Macmillan, 2011), p. 26.

3. NATO, "Declaration on a Transformed North Atlantic Alliance" (The

London Declaration), July 6, 2001, www.nato.int/docu/comm/49-95/c900706a
.htm. See also Rebecca R. Moore, *NATO's New Mission: Projecting Stability in a
Post-Cold War World* (Westport, CT: Praeger Security International, 2007), pp.
9–32.

4. Marc Grossman, "21st Century NATO: New Capabilities, New Members,
New Relationships," US Department of State, *U.S. Foreign Policy Agenda*, vol. 7,
no. 1 (March 2002).

5. NATO, "Active Engagement, Modern Defence, Strategic Concept for the
Defence and Security of the Members of the North Atlantic Treaty Organisation,"
Lisbon, November 10, 2010, www.not.into/lisbon2010/strategic-concept-2010
-eng.pdf.

6. NATO, "Active Engagement in Cooperative Security: A More Efficient and
Flexible Partnership Policy," April 15, 2011, www.nato.into/nato_static/assets/pdf
/pdf_2011_04/20110415-Parnership-Policy.pdf.

7. Ibid. Author telephone interviews with US Department of State official, February and August 2011.

8. Michael E. O'Hanlon and Hassina Sherjan, *Toughing It Out in Afghanistan*
(Brookings, 2010), p. 24.

9. William Maley, "Provincial Reconstruction Teams in Afghanistan: How
They Arrived and Where They Are Going," *NATO Review*, August 2007, www
.nato.int/docu/review/2007/issue3/english/art2.html.

10. Seth G. Jones, *In the Graveyard of Empires: America's War in Afghanistan*
(New York: W. W. Norton, 2010), pp. 248–50.

11. Patricia A. Weitsman, *Waging War: Alliances, Coalitions, and Institutions of
Interstate Violence* (Stanford University Press, 2014), p. 105.

12. A. Elizabeth Jones, Assistant Secretary of States for European and Eurasian
Affairs, Testimony before the Subcommittee on the Middle East and Central
Asia, House International Relations Committee, Washington, DC, October 29,
2003, www.state.gov/p/eur/rls/rm/2003/25798.htm. See also US Department of
State Fact Sheet, "Frequently Asked Questions about U.S. Policy in Central Asia,"
Bureau of European and Eurasian Affairs, Washington, DC November 27, 2002,
www.state.gov/p/eur/rls/fs/15562.htm.

13. RFE/RL, "Afghan War Veterans Oppose Kazakh Participation in ISAF,"
May 25, 2011, www.rferl.org/a/afghan-war-veterans-oppose-kazakh-participation
-isaf/24204941.html.

14. "Partners in Central Asia," NATO Backgrounder, November 2007, www
.nato.int/nato_static_fl2014/assets/pdf/stock_publications/20140505_140505
-Backgrounder_CentralAsia_EN_lowres.pdf.

15. Author e-mail interviews with members of NATO's international staff, June
and August 2009. See also "Security Forum Discusses Key Challenges in Central
Asia," June 24–25, 2009, www.nato.int/cps/en/natolive/news-55920.htm.

16. Rebecca R. Moore, "The Purpose of NATO Partnerships," in *NATO's
Return to Europe: Engaging Ukraine, Russia, and Beyond* (Georgetown University
Press), p. 178.

17. Ernesto Londono, "Georgia's Role as U.S. Coalition Partner has Honed Its Army, Bolstered NATO Hopes," *Washington Post*, August 13, 2014, www .washingtonpost.com/world/national-security/georgias-mettle-as-us-coaltion -partner-has-honed-its-army-bolstered-nato-hopes/2014/08/13/431f192a-1bea -11e4-ab7b-696c295ddfd1_story.html.

18. Daniel P. Brown and Ariel I. Ahram, "Jordan and the United Arab Emirates: Partners in Afghanistan," in *Coalition Challenges in Afghanistan: The Politics of Alliance*, edited by Gale A. Mattox and Stephen M. Grenier (Stanford University Press, 2015), p. 207.

19. Ibid., p. 208. See also Ian Black, "Jordan Embarrassed as Bombing Reveals CIA Link," *The Guardian*, January 6, 2010, www.the guardian.com/world/2010/ jan/06/Jordan-embarrased-cia-link.

20. Brown and Ahram,"Jordan and the United Arab Emirates," p. 209.

21. Ibid., p. 210.

22. Maryanne Kelton and Aaron P. Jackson, "Australia: Terrorism, Regional Security, and the U.S. Alliance," in *Coalition Challenges in Afghanistan*, edited by Mattox and Grenier, p. 231.

23. Ibid., p. 234.

24. Esther Pan, "NATO Takes on Afghan Security," July 27, 2006, *Council on Foreign Relations*, https://www.cfr.org/backgrounder/nato-takes-afghan-security.

25. "South Korean Hostages Head Back Home from Afghanistan," *New York Times*, August 31, 2007.

26. Choe Sang-Hun, "South Korea Says It Plans Afghanistan Deployment," *New York Times*, November 1, 2009.

27. NATO, "NATO Cooperation with Japan," updated March 9, 2009, NATO Topics, www.nato.int/issues/nato_japan/index.html.

28. Shinzo Abe, "Japan and NATO: Toward Further Collaboration," January, 12, 2007, www.nato.int/docu/speech/2007/s070112b.html.

29. NATO, "First Visit by Top Pakistani Officer to NATO," NATO Update, November 17, 2006, www.nato.int/docu/update/2006/11-november/e1117a.htm. Author telephone interviews with NATO International Staff members, August 2009.

30. Pakistan responded to the friendly fire incident by shutting down NATO's supply routes to Afghanistan and removing the US from an air base used to facilitate drone attacks. Anne Gearan, "Pakistan, U.S. Assume Less Cooperation in Future," Associated Press, http://hosted2.ap.org/APDEFAULT/3d281c11a 96b4ad082fe88aa0db04305/Article_2012-01-02-US-Pakistan-US/id-3734a5 528d454a6db26974bc2093d4ae.

31. See, for example, O'Hanlon and Sherjan, *Toughing It Out in Afghanistan*, p. 15.

32. NATO, "Afghanistan and NATO's Enduring Partnership," January 2012, www.nato.int/nato_static/assets/pdf/pdf_2011_04/20110414_110414-Afghan Partnership.pdf.

33. NATO, "NATO and Afghanistan," March 5, 2019, www.nato.int/cps/en/ natohq/topics_8189.htm.

34. Author telephone interview with Department of Defense official, June 2019.

35. Ibid.

36. Gale Mattox, "Going Forward: Lessons Learned," in *Coalition Challenges in Afghanistan,* edited by Mattox and Grenier, p. 288.

37. NATO, "Wales Summit Declaration," press release (2014) 120, September 5, 2014, www.nato.int/cps/en/natohq/official_texts_112964.htm.

38. Author telephone interview with NATO official, August 5, 2019.

39. Defence and Related Security Capacity Building Initiative, July 12, 2018, www.nato.int/cps/en/natohq/topics_132756.htm.

40. Author e-mail interview with NATO official, February 2016. Although defense capacity building and improved interoperability with partners preceded the 2014 Ukraine crisis, in its aftermath the Alliance was quick to extend both defense capacity building and PII to partners to its east (including Ukraine) as well as to the Middle East, where its focus shifted in light of developments in Iraq as well as Syria, including the rise of the Islamic State in Iraq and Syria (ISIS).

41. Author interviews with Department of State official, January 2015. See also "Warsaw Summit Communiqué" press release (2016) 100, July 9, 2016, www.nato .int/cps/en/natohq/official_texts_133169.htm.

42. R. Nicholas Burns, "Briefing on NATO Issues Prior to Riga Summit," Washington, DC, November 21, 2006.

43. Author interview with Department of State official, January 2007. Karl -Heinz Kamp, "'Global Partnership': A New Conflict Within NATO?," *Analysen und Argumente* aus der Konrad-Adenauer-Stiftung, 29 (2006), p. 3, https:// www.kas.de/c/document_library/get_file?uuid=42579544-972c-db55-91a0 -341ec273a6dc&groupId=252038. The US ambassador to NATO, Ivo Daalder, had explicitly called for NATO's door to be opened to any liberal democratic state willing to contribute to NATO's responsibilities. See Ivo H. Daalder and James M. Lindsay, "An Alliance of Democracies," *Washington Post*, May 23, 2004, B7; and Ivo Daalder and James Lindsay, "Democracies of the World Unite," *The American Interest* Online (Winter 2006–07), www.the-american-interest.com/aiz/aricle .cfm?ID+219&MId=6.

44. NATO, "Riga Summit Declaration," press release (2006) 150, November 29, 2006, www.nato.int/docu/pr/2006/p06-150e.htm.

45. Ibid., and author telephone interview with US Department of State official, January 2007.

46. NATO, "Chicago Summit Declaration," press release (2012) 062, May 20, 2012, www.nato.int/cps/en/natolive/official_texts_87593.htm.

47. Mattox, "Going Forward: Lessons Learned," p. 294.

48. Chris Chivvis, *Toppling Qaddafi: Libya and the Limits of Liberal Intervention* (Cambridge University Press, 2014), p. 77.

49. Ibid., p. 97.

50. Ibid., p. 99.

51. Bruce R. Nardulli, "The Arab States' Experiences," in *Precision and Purpose:*

Airpower in the Libyan Civil War, edited by Karl P. Mueller (Santa Monica, CA: RAND Corporation), p. 343.

52. See, for example, Ivo H. Daalder and James G. Stavridis, "NATO's Victory in Libya: The Right Way to Run an Intervention," *Foreign Affairs*, vol. 91, no. 2 (March/April 2012), pp. 2–7.

53. Chivvis, *Toppling Qaddafi*, p. 99.

54. Ibid., p. 71.

55. Nardulli, "The Arab States' Experiences," pp. 353 and 362.

56. Chivvis, *Toppling Qaddafi*, pp. 99–100.

57. Nardulli, "The Arab States' Experiences," p. 346.

58. Ibid., pp. 356–57.

59. Ibid., pp. 340–41.

60. Quoted in Rob Weigill and Florence Gaub, *The Cauldron: NATO's Campaign in Libya* (Oxford University Press, 2018), p. 160.

61. Chivvis, *Toppling Qaddafi*, pp. 106–07.

62. Remarks by Secretary Gates at the Security and Defense Agenda, Brussels, Belgium, June 10, 2011, https://archive.defense.gov/Transcripts/Transcript.aspx?TranscriptID=4839.

63. Weigill and Gaub, *The Cauldron*, pp. 160–61.

64. Jordan, the UAE, and Morocco had all participated in the Kosovo and ISAF missions.

65. Nardulli, "The Arab States' Experiences," p. 364.

66. Ibid., p. 366. See also Chivvis, *Toppling Qaddafi*, pp. 154–59.

67. Chivvis, *Toppling Qaddafi*, p. 155.

68. UK Parliament, Defence Committee, Ninth Report: Operations in Libya, https://publications.parliament.uk/pa/cm201012/cmselect/cmdfence/950/95002.htm.

69. Ryan C. Hendrickson, "Sweden: A Special NATO Partner?," *NATO Review*, 2013, www.nato.int/docu/review/2013/Partnerships-NATO-2013/Sweden-partnerships/EN/index.htm.

70. Robert Egnell, "The Swedish Experience: Overcoming the Non-NATO-Member Conundrum," in *Precision and Purpose*, edited by Mueller, pp. 322–23; Hendrickson, "Sweden: A Special NATO Partner?"

71. Egnell, "The Swedish Experience," p. 323.

72. Ibid., pp. 322–23 and 330.

73. Ibid., pp. 332–33.

74. Ibid., p. 325.

75. Chivvis, *Toppling Qaddafi*.

76. Author telephone interview with NATO official, August 5, 2019.

77. Egnell, "The Swedish Experience,", p. 313.

78. NATO, "Wales Summit Declaration."

79. NATO, "Warsaw Summit Communiqué."

80. NATO, "Relations with Sweden," October 4, 2018, www.nato.int/cps/en/natohq/topics_52535.htm.

81. Kenneth Dickerman and Loulou d'Aki, "Inside the Swedish Military Presence on Gotland, the Most Strategic Island for Defense Against Russian Aggression," *Washington Post*, August 30, 2018, www.washingtonpost.com/news /in-sight/wp/2018/08/30/inside-the-swedish-military-presence-on-gotland-the -most-strategic-island-for-defense-against-russian-aggression.

82. Author interview with NATO official, August 8, 2019.

83. NATO, "The Swedish Armed Forces Participate in Trident Juncture," November 7, 2018, www.shape.nato.int/news-archive/2018/the-swedish-armed -forces-participate-in-trident-juncture-.

84. NATO, "NATO Allies Participate in Swedish Exercise Northern Wind," www.shape.nato.int/news-archive/2019/nato-allies-participate-in-swedish -exercise-northern-wind.

85. See for example, Government of Sweden, "Swedish Armed Forces Exercise Aurora 17 will increase military capability," September 13, 2017, www.government .se/articles/2017/09/swedish-armed-forces-exercise-aurora-17-will-increase -military-capability.

86. Finland also participated in Aurora 17.

87. NATO, "Relations with Sweden," October 4, 2018, www.nato.int/cps/en/ natohq/topics_52535.htm.

88. Author telephone interview with NATO official, August 8, 2019.

89. Ibid.

90. Ibid.

FOUR

The Future of the West

What If the United States Pulls Out of NATO?

TOBIAS BUNDE

Can the West exist without the United States? Can NATO remain the main platform for Western collective action in the military sphere in the face of increasingly diverging understandings of what the West is all about? Will there be such a thing as a "collective intentionality"[1] called "the West?" Or are we entering an era of "Westlessness?"[2] This chapter probes these questions by envisioning a medium-term scenario in which Donald Trump wins reelection in 2020 and "the United States pulls out of NATO, leaving its legacy infrastructure to be rescued by European cooperation."[3] Instead of spelling out multiple alternative worlds, it describes the implications of a specific scenario that may at first appear extreme and certainly contradicts the hitherto prevailing narrative of Western progress on the way to the "end of history." To be sure, NATO has survived all its manifold crises and proved wrong all the doomsayers who predicted its immediate demise.[4] Unlike in previous predicaments, however, the forty-fifth president of the United States has been one of the most vocal critics of the Alliance. As a result, more and more scholars, journalists, and politicians are considering a withdrawal of the US from NATO or the overall dissolution of the Alliance to be occurrences that must not be discounted.[5]

The following scenario is the result of a combination of plausible events and key driving forces identified in the academic literature, including different geopolitical outlooks in North America and Europe, a regionalization of threat perceptions, different approaches concerning the appropriate strategy for an era of renewed great power competition, the rise of illiberal political forces in NATO member states, generational and demographic changes, intensified debates about transatlantic burden-sharing, and diverging attitudes regarding the use of force that could erode "civic militarism" as the basis for NATO's mutual defense commitment. The scenario serves to illuminate the serious implications for European security of a US withdrawal from NATO, highlighting some of the manifold security challenges that European member states would have to face. None of these are preordained. But they need to be described and understood lest they become ugly reality one day. As Herman Kahn noted in 1962, "the serious, even if temporary, consideration of extreme examples jerks us out of our peaceful world and stimulates our imaginations."[6]

Brussels, September 2024

After two rocky years in office, Karel Svoboda was exhausted but quite proud of himself. He was the first NATO secretary general hailing from a former member state of the Warsaw Pact. And for a while he feared he would actually be NATO's last secretary general. Last year, when it was clear that most member states would not reach the benchmark of spending 2 percent of their GDP on defense by 2024, President Donald Trump, narrowly reelected in November 2020, announced the US withdrawal from NATO. Of course, Svoboda first heard about it on Twitter.

For many observers at the time, this meant the end of NATO. But Svoboda—strongly supported by the "Bucharest Nine," an informal but increasingly influential forum of member states on the eastern flank—had swiftly orchestrated an emergency meeting in Brussels that made clear that the remaining NATO members were determined to keep the Alliance alive.[7] Although some leading politicians in Paris and elsewhere briefly speculated about upgrading the European Union, most saw the unique value of the NATO framework. Not only did it include the British, the Canadians, and the Norwegians, it had also developed a well-oiled bureaucratic machinery and standard military procedures over the past decades. The EU could not offer something comparable in the short run, despite the significant progress made in recent years.[8]

It was no minor success for Svoboda that the structure of NATO was preserved. But what about the substance? He was sitting in the huge new, shiny headquarters at Boulevard Léopold. For some cynics, the airy building with lots of glass was a symbol of the new NATO, basically an overblown but

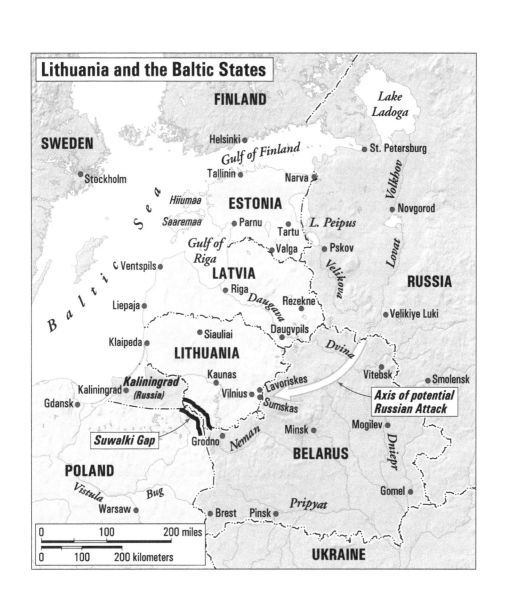

Lithuania and the Baltic States

FINLAND

Lake
Ladoga

SWEDEN

Helsinki •

Gulf of Finland

• St. Petersburg

Volkhov

• Stockholm

Tallinin •

Narva •

• Novgorod

Hiiumaa

ESTONIA

Saaremaa

• Parnu

B a l t i c   S e a

Tartu

L. Peipus

Gulf of
Riga

Valga

• Pskov

Velikova

Lovat

⊂ Ventspils •

LATVIA

RUSSIA

• Riga

Daugava

Rezekne •

• Velikiye Luki

Liepaja •

Daugvpils •

Dvina

• Siauliai

LITHUANIA

• Vitebsk

• Smolensk

Klaipeda •

Kaunas
•

Lavoriskes

**Axis of potential
Russian Attack**

**Kaliningrad
(Russia)**

Vilnius • • Sumskas

Kaliningrad •

Mogilev •

Gdansk •

Suwalki Gap

Grodno • *Neman*

Minsk • •

Dniepr

BELARUS

POLAND

Vistula

Bug

Pripyat

Gomel •

Warsaw •

• Brest   Pinsk

| 0 | 100 | 200 miles |
| 0 | 100 | 200 kilometers |

UKRAINE

hollow structure, filled with hot air and very fragile. Could this Alliance work without the United States?

The easiest task was to fill the political and military leadership positions hitherto occupied by US officials. After all, each NATO member was interested in having new senior posts in Brussels. But would they also be able to fill the political and military gap? At the very least, the Trump administration had agreed to slow down the withdrawal of troops in order to make possible a reasonably controlled "Europeanization" of the Alliance.[9] Had the president prevailed, US troops would have already left entirely. But concerted efforts by military leaders and the remaining transatlanticists in Congress had been able to limit the immediate damage. Yet even if the military was slow-walking the president's decisions, the withdrawal of the majority of the US troops was a done deal. Most importantly, the rotational troops forward deployed to central and eastern Europe as part of the European Reassurance Initiative after the Russian annexation of Crimea in 2014 had been the first to leave.

Svoboda's predecessors had repeatedly underlined the need for European NATO members to make every effort to move toward the 2 percent goal by 2024. But European leaders had become so used to US complaints about unfair burden-sharing that they refused to believe that Trump would eventually follow through. A strategic error of extraordinary proportions, Svoboda thought. Now European members would have to spend much more than 2 percent of their GDP on defense if they wanted to have a decent level of security, let alone completely fill the gaps the US withdrawal had left. At the moment the Europeans were far from meeting the requirements of what was known in NATO parlance as a Major Joint Operation Plus (MJO+), which meant defending the Alliance against a near-peer competitor. The Alliance was running short of practically everything, but the NATO planners had come up with a priority list for the coming years that included crucial combat-enabling capabilities such as air-to-air refueling, large-scale command-and-control capabilities, long-range precision-strike capabilities, satellite communications, and uninhabited aerial systems. The cost of the equipment required to match the main capability shortfalls for an Article 5 scenario was at least a quarter of a trillion euros.[10]

But Svoboda did not only worry about material challenges. Most of the time he thought about whether there was enough "civic militarism" left in Europe. For years public opinion polls had shown a discrepancy between the limited willingness of the Europeans to defend their allies in the event of a conflict with Russia, and the widely shared belief that the United States would use force in such a case.[11] Now that the US was leaving, would the Europeans get their act together? Svoboda's job would not become easier.

Berlin, November 2024

Thomas Müller stood on the balcony of the German Chancellery, watching a few people pass by the Reichstag building in front of him. From old photos, the Chancellor knew quite well what this special place had looked like in the past and what political turmoil it had experienced. On a rainy day like today, it was easier to see the fragility of it all. Would this Germany, "the best we've ever known," as then-President Joachim Gauck had described it at the Munich Security Conference a decade ago, a stable liberal democracy, a vibrant social-market economy, at peace with its European neighbors—would this Germany last?

Next week US citizens would vote for a new president. But whatever the outcome, it was clear that a new era for Germany, Europe, and the world had begun. For many countries the rapidly changing role of the United States during the Trump era had presented serious challenges. For Germany it had required a complete overhaul of its worldview. No other country, he thought, had adapted as perfectly to the "pax Americana." This country was so dependent on the US-led liberal international order—economically, military, but also intellectually—that it had been close to impossible to imagine something else. And even those who had sensed that a new approach was needed were either not willing or not able to act accordingly. His predecessor, Angela Merkel, had missed the opportunity to convince her compatriots of the need for a stronger German role in defense when she was still immensely popular and the federal budget provided some room for maneuver.[12] While she carefully steered the country toward gradual military adaptation after the annexation of Crimea, Merkel never took a major public risk in foreign and defense policy. Again and again people quoted her Trudering beer tent speech of 2017, in which she told the audience that "the times in which we could rely fully on others—they are somewhat over" and that the Europeans had to "really take our fate into our own hands."[13] But—like most in her generation—she was reluctant to act on it. In hindsight it was a dramatic failure of collective leadership.

Now much—perhaps too much—depended on Germany, and on the Chancellor. Abroad, most people overestimated German power and influence, as all the lazy talk of Merkel as the "leader of the free world"[14] demonstrated.

At home, in contrast, most people underestimated their country's role. Müller had to convince them that Germany could make a difference—and that it had to move quickly, adapt to the new circumstances and assume a comprehensive leadership role if the European way of live was to be preserved. In this new context Berlin was no longer able to "outsource" the military dimension.

Of course there were those who made the case for a "neutral" Germany that focused on its own business. If the extreme-right Alternative für Deutschland, the leading opposition party, had its way, Berlin would adopt a narrow-minded view of its national interests and not think too much about the rest of Europe. He was convinced that this would end badly—both for Germany and for Europe as a whole. Europe could deal with nationalist parties in Poland or Italy, at least for a while. But it would not survive a nationalist Germany.[15] One of NATO's major accomplishments had been to "denationalize" security policy to a large degree. The Chancellor feared the continued disintegration of Europe and thus had one essential goal: keeping Europe together. This had not been an easy task even when Europe still had the luxury of being under the US security umbrella while grappling with the financial and economic crises, migration, and Brexit. Today it was a tall order.

Obviously, keeping Europe together would be expensive. Today the 2 percent controversy that had plagued Germany's foreign policy debate just a few years ago seemed surreal. But even now fiscal conservatives were reluctant to massively increase spending on defense. Some witty students had planted a banner in front of the Bundestag: "The world is crumbling but hey, we still have a balanced budget!" The Chancellor was confident, though, that the Bundestag would agree on a major budget increase and that the country would soon reach the 2 percent benchmark. Yet as his advisers argued, Germany would need to spend much more than that. He, however, thought that change could only be gradual. He had to convince the members of parliament and keep a coalition together.

Most importantly, it would take time to ramp up German and European defenses—time he possibly did not have.[16] For now, he had to convince the incoming US president that a managed withdrawal over a longer period was the best option for the United States too. Müller had no illusions that the next president would reverse Trump's decision. But from a strictly national point of view he was bent on making sure that a considerable number of US forces would remain on German soil. After all, Germany and the facilities in Ramstein or Landstuhl, he thought, were still of use to the US. Maybe the new president could be convinced at least to make a statement to the effect that Europe would still be covered by US extended nuclear deterrence? Next month the Chancellor wanted to introduce legislation that would make it even more attractive for Washington to have a strong base in Germany. He knew that the Polish government had upped its proposals to build new infrastructure and even pay for a residual US presence. Even if his coalition partner did not like it, Müller had to be a bit more forthcoming as well.

At present managing an emboldened Russia was the major challenge. At least since Trump's reelection, the team in the Kremlin was on a roll, and Vladimir Putin could not believe his luck. Just a few months ago Putin had ensured his election as the president of the new Union of the Russian Federation and Belarus.[17] While Russia's economy was a mess and the young generation was increasingly frustrated with the regime, his foreign policy was still popular. This made it even more dangerous.

In his new position, Putin continued to offer the well-known mix of seemingly gracious offers for cooperation and thinly veiled threats. In a recent speech he alluded to Russia's European vocation, easily walking back his previous rhetoric highlighting the country's specific "Eurasian" identity, and called on the Europeans eventually to fulfill the dream of an all-inclusive European security architecture. Russia, he noted, was ready to "play a constructive role commensurate with its status and taking into account the new circumstances." Six times in his speech, he referred to Russia's nuclear arsenal.

Müller understood the message. And he knew that Germany's NATO allies on the eastern flank had become increasingly nervous since Russian troops had moved into Belarus. But he was also under pressure domestically. This morning, the weekly *Die Zeit* had published an open letter by fifty German intellectuals, artists, actors, and former politicians who called for a new approach in Germany's Russia policy. Of course the "new" approach was anything but new, but essentially meant German acquiescence in a Russian sphere of influence in eastern Europe. He knew that next week's edition would very likely feature a response by some of Germany's leading foreign policy and Russia experts—notably absent from the first group—highlighting the myopia behind this strategic thinking.[18] But he also understood that the authors of the open letter expressed sentiments widely shared among parts of the population—and that it would only add to the concerns of Germany's eastern neighbors that it was merely a matter of time until the Germans and the Russians began to negotiate the contours of a new "Rapallo" over their heads.

To a certain degree he could comprehend these fears. But he and many of his compatriots were also tired of the never-ending suspicions. His colleague in France got away with making the case for a rapprochement with Russia every time there was a minor positive movement in the Kremlin, while the

Germans were watched suspiciously. After all, it was Berlin that had made sure the post-2014 sanctions were not reversed. Now the Bundeswehr was slowly becoming the backbone of Europe's territorial defense efforts.[19] The Germans provided the bulk of the troops that stepped in as substitutes for the US soldiers in NATO's Enhanced Forward Presence on the eastern flank. Still, he would be the first to blame. When Germany did not do enough Berlin was criticized for its lack of resolve or commitment. When it went ahead it was often accused of wanting to dominate Europe—lately even in the military sphere.[20] Now Müller could much better understand the frustration voiced by previous US presidents who were criticized by their allies for whatever they did. Behind closed doors, he often wondered aloud whether Germany was able to play the leadership role now required. Could Berlin successfully balance the diverging interests in NATO?

Last week a political cartoon, drawing on the well-known image of Bismarck as an exceptional juggler who could keep five balls in the air at the same time, had shown Müller buried under about twenty smaller and larger balls, with his allies and neighbors pulling him in different directions. The headline read: "Europe's central power." He could relate to it.

Washington, DC, April 2025

President Jorge Miller was going through some foreign policy memos. He had tasked his national security apparatus with proposing a number of options for updating the US approach to working with allies. The first memo began with a quote from a 2010 Council on Foreign Relations report: "If the North Atlantic Treaty Organization (NATO) did not exist today, the United States would not seek to create it."[21] As the author of the report, James Goldgeier, noted back then, if the US had to build a new alliance from scratch, it would debate whether to form some kind of great power concert or a value-based global alliance of democracies. The president agreed. While some of his advisers from the "old guard" of the Democratic Party had urged him to rejoin NATO, he sided with those who thought that there was no turning back the clock. America could not just put together broken instruments of the mid-twentieth century to respond to the challenges of the mid-twenty-first century. He needed something new. At the same time he was not willing to abandon the role of the United States as a force for good in the world. He had always liked the idea of a global value-based alliance.[22] Maybe this was the new grand bargain he could offer the Europeans. After all, he could do with a little help from Europe on the global level—if only for political support and legitimacy.

Miller's campaign platform had emphasized the need to repair the US image in the world. But his first two trips to Europe and Asia had driven home the message that this was even more challenging than he had imagined. Wherever he went he was met with relief but not with enthusiasm. Clearly this was not comparable to the Obama effect fifteen years ago. One evening in Berlin, a former German foreign minister had bluntly told him: "Mr. President, this all sounds wonderful—and we're happy to hear you believe in multilateral cooperation and in strengthening international organizations. But why should we believe that anything we'll do together now will survive the next administration?" He did not really know how to respond. The political polarization in the US had indeed become a major problem for its foreign policy.[23] He did not say it aloud but he was not sure himself whether the Republican Party could recover from the Trump era at all. Looking at his own party and its voters, he saw an ironic twist: those increasingly influential societal groups that would shape the future of the Democratic Party were both more and less European at the same time. Their worldview was closer to the Europeans, but they did not have the same emotional attachment to Europe, nor were they willing to continue an imbalanced partnership in which the Americans had to do the hard work.[24] In this century the West had to be defined in global, not Euro-Atlantic terms.

While Miller was keen on rebuilding relations with like-minded democracies, he was thus determined not to return to the status quo ante. Although he wanted to give the Europeans a hand and was willing to provide cover for a transition period, he had stated in no uncertain terms that he would not support any military measures that would let the Europeans believe the Americans might come back. From his point of view it was hardly comprehensible that the rich democracies of Europe were not able to defend themselves collectively against Russia, a second-rate economic power with a GDP the size of Spain's. The United States' attention had moved to the Indo-Pacific—for everybody to see in plain sight. The ups and downs of NATO–Russia relations since the 1990s notwithstanding, several administrations had consistently shifted the US strategic posture to this region for the past two decades.[25] In 2019, when some in central and eastern Europe still pointed to the increased investment of the Trump administration in the European Deterrence Initiative as a symbol of the long-term US commitment to Europe, then-Acting Secretary of Defense Patrick M. Shanahan had told the audience at the annual Shangri-La Dialogue that the "US Indo-Pacific Command has four times the assigned forces as any other geographic combatant command."[26] If there still was one topic that Democrats and Republicans in Washington could agree upon, it was the need to check the rise of China. Europe was and would remain a secondary concern. The United States had abandoned the two-major-wars doctrine for good. The one high-intensity war that the US military was prepared to fight would not take place in Europe.[27] It was wrong to pretend otherwise.

Warsaw, June 2025

In Warsaw, the chairman of Prawo i Sprawiedliwość (PiS, Law and Justice), Jarosław Kaczyński, was in a bad mood. In a closed meeting with his advisers, he had again complained about the Polish fate: "It seems we are destined to be betrayed by our allies." He and many others had wanted to believe that the US was different, and Polish politicians had put their eggs in just one basket. In contrast to most other Europeans, they had welcomed Donald Trump. When he came to power, the government felt encouraged as a favorite ally. Trump came to Warsaw early on in his presidency and promoted a view of NATO and the West that Kaczyński shared, emphasizing culture, history, and religion instead of liberal democracy and human rights.[28] Although Warsaw was irritated by his strange affection for Vladimir Putin, the government courted President Trump for years. Sensing that European efforts to strengthen their common defense were going nowhere anyway, Poland doubled down on its transatlantic orientation. It was one of the first European allies to reach the 2 percent goal and demonstrated its support for US foreign policy even if this sometimes meant breaking the European consensus. But proposals for a "Fort Trump," a major permanent US military base in Poland, never bore fruit.[29]

After Trump's decision to withdraw from NATO, alarmism reigned in Poland. Polish politicians had called on their interlocutors in the US to not abandon their country. The optimists pointed to the strong bilateral partnership, but no one was quite sure whether Trump's lukewarm statement of support would mean anything. There was no alternative: Kaczyński had to rely on his fellow Europeans. He was glad that the European NATO members had agreed to make up for the United States' forward presence. But was the refurbished NATO Enhanced Forward Presence a meaningful tripwire? After all, activating a tripwire only made sense if it also triggered something behind it. Just last week, a political confidant who had always criticized the PiS team for not trying to build a better relationship with Berlin and Paris told him that this was a mess of Kaczyński's own making. Kaczyński thought that the French and the Germans were to blame for the poor relationship, but he had to admit that this was now an unfortunate basis for asking for help. He could only hope that Berlin and Paris would understand that it was in their interest to strengthen what was essentially their very own defense along the eastern flank.

Poland, for its part, would spend almost 5 percent of its GDP on defense by next year. But this would not change Poland's position on the map, sandwiched between the Western European powers and Russia. Since their accession to NATO (and, in particular, since the Russo-Georgian war in August 2008), the "new member states" had argued that there must not be different levels of security within the Alliance. Today this concern was even more acute. Would Article 5 now be a "layered commitment?"[30]

London, July 2025

She had been dealt a very weak hand. Prime Minister Patricia Jones had entered No. 10 Downing Street in the midst of a deep recession, heading a country still deeply divided. "Global Britain" and all the other promises the Brexiteers had made had turned out to be a chimera.[31] The UK was still waiting for a trade deal with the US, and without the EU, the "special relationship" was nothing special anymore. As some had warned years ago, Britain was in danger of turning into "an Atlantic version of Australia."[32]

Theoretically, Jones thought, the best course for the UK was to reapply for membership of the EU. The countries on the Continent were still by far the most important trading partners of the UK, and in this new era of great power competition, being part of a bigger club was certainly advisable. The first five years of "Global Britain" had driven this message home. Yet rejoining the EU was not an option, for political reasons. She would only reopen wounds that had hardly healed since the tumultuous years after the fateful 2016 referendum. The British people had had enough of bold decisions, they wanted to see pragmatic solutions that improved the economic situation and avoided a further polarization of their society. She had thus campaigned on a pragmatic platform—and her foreign policy would follow this path.

Immediately after Brexit, the UK had strengthened its role in NATO because it offered "an elegant solution to combine British independence from the EU with the necessity of close collaboration in the face of security challenges."[33] Although she thought the US withdrawal from NATO was a dangerous move, she was determined to see it as an opportunity for the UK. After all, Britain's military assets, though significantly depleted, were now even more valuable than before.[34] Even though the French had initially thought of abandoning NATO completely, endowing the EU with the defending the continent, she and many leaders had been able to preserve the Alliance. In the end Paris also knew that the Europeans just could not do without the UK after the US had announced it would leave NATO. For Jones, this might provide a good starting point for a better, and more beneficial, relationship with the EU. Maybe there was a win-win situation here: military strength in exchange for economic strength. The absolute non-necessity of all of this never ceased to amaze her. Yet if it hadn't been for the Brexit chaos, she, a Liberal woman, would very likely not be where she was now.

Paris, August 2025

Emmanuel Macron also had *"une certaine idée de la France."* In times like these, France had to step up. The Germans would have to carry the bulk of the conventional burden but they did not have nuclear weapons. When Trump announced the withdrawal of the remaining non-strategic nuclear weapons from European soil last year, Macron knew he had to make a move. Thus he publicly announced, specifying language he had used previously,[35] that the *force de frappe* was French-owned and French-operated but essentially a *European* deterrent, based on the understanding that the notion of "all the means in their power" expressed in Article 42.7 of the Lisbon Treaty, the EU's mutual security guarantee, unquestionably included nuclear weapons. Since Macron's announcement, Rafale jet fighters, albeit without nuclear weapons, were regularly being sent to airfields on the Eastern flank for assurance pur-poses. But this was just a short-term remedy that needed to be underwritten by more practical and visible implementation. The president had to decide. If he did not move quickly, Poland—and maybe others—would sooner or later try to acquire nuclear weapons themselves. Europe, he was sure, would quickly disintegrate if its members did not feel secure. His military planners and political advisers were now working on various options for the future of French extended deterrence for Europe.[36] One was to base French weapons in other NATO/EU member states. Macron was ready to deploy a part of the French airborne nuclear arsenal, maybe about a dozen French nuclear-tipped missiles, to Germany in order to underline the French commitment. Warsaw would certainly welcome French nuclear weapons on Polish soil as well. An-other option was to replicate NATO's nuclear sharing arrangement, at least to a certain degree. Some allies would take part in SNOWCAT (Support of Nuclear Operations With Conventional Air Tactics) deterrence, while other allies could provide dual-capable aircraft, ideally French-made. French indus-try lobbyists had strongly suggested France go in this direction, sensing huge contracts for the French defense industry. New thinking in the nuclear realm was certainly needed.

Yet Macron was also skeptical for several reasons. He knew that this new nuclear role would require major investment in the *force de frappe*. And, as he was reminded every day, there were other urgent demands both at home and on NATO's southern flank, where France bore the lion's share of the burden. He agreed with his colleagues in NATO member states bordering the Mediterranean that the Alliance had to stick to a 360-degree outlook and must not be fully absorbed by a confrontation in the east. Indeed he believed the most important threat was to be found in the south. Obviously, an enhanced deterrent posture would provoke anger in Russia. Above all, Macron did not want to end up in a new Cold War–like confrontation either in Europe or on a global scale. He and his advisers were therefore also wary of President Miller's plans for a global alliance of the world's leading democracies, tantamount to a "global NATO." From their point of view, this would only lead to China and Russia closing ranks, as an alliance of democracies would inevitably bring about an alliance of non-democracies. While Paris would side with the rest of the West if push came to shove and would, for instance, support Washington in its efforts to preserve freedom of navigation, President Macron was bent on ensuring that France (and Europe, for that matter) was not seen as a junior partner of the US. And just like his predecessors, he wanted to preserve some French room for maneuver.[37] In the new circumstances he believed that Europe had to go to greater lengths to avoid Russia's complete absorption into the Chinese orbit. He knew that such a policy was not popular in central and eastern Europe. But he was even more convinced of its necessity than when he had made the case for a cautious rapprochement with Russia during his first term.[38] After all, what was the alternative to some kind of settlement with Russia? After the US withdrawal from NATO, accepting Georgia or Ukraine as members was out of the question anyway. What difference would it make if NATO publicly admitted this? In the end, as so many German politicians had stressed over and over again, sustainable peace in Europe was only possible with Russia, not against Russia. In this new situation there was nothing to be gained from an overly confrontational posture. Probably, in this regard, the Germans were right after all; it made sense to continue a dual-track policy: as much cooperation and détente as possible, as much deterrence as necessary.[39]

If Macron did not credibly offer détente but focused on strengthening deterrence alone by, for instance, deploying French nuclear weapons to Poland, many citizens in western Europe would call him a warmonger. He could already almost hear those French and German politicians and pundits complaining that the presence of French nuclear weapons in central and eastern Europe would break the promises NATO had made in the NATO–Russia Founding Act—an argument that nobody in central and eastern Europe could understand. After all, Russia had long violated all basic principles of the Founding Act, and the security environment had clearly changed.[40] In addition he knew, just like his German partner, how hard it was to convince their compatriots to ramp up military support on NATO's eastern flank. It would be even harder if some of their allies continued to follow in the footsteps of Viktor Orbán, the Hungarian prime minister who had effectively put to rest liberal democracy in his home country. It was increasingly difficult to argue that NATO was protecting liberal democracy if political leaders in Poland and other countries followed Orbán's illiberal playbook. Why, critics asked, should we defend those who themselves already undermine the values we are supposed to uphold?[41] After all, NATO was supposed to be an alliance of liberal democracies. Macron was not willing to use European funds to enrich kleptocracies, nor did he want to give them cover if they undermined core European values.[42] Somehow he had to square the circle. How much deterrence was necessary to convince the Russians that an attack on their neighbors would come at an unacceptable price without completely undermining his initiative for a European détente? How much assurance was needed to prevent Poland and others from pursuing their own nuclear program without giving them a blank cheque on everything? How could he use his leverage to maximize French influence? In his mind he foresaw the big speech in which he could put it all together.

Suddenly his national security adviser burst into the room. She had not even knocked. With a frightened look on her face she said: "Mr President, Chancellor Müller and the NATO Secretary General are on the line. There is something happening on the eastern flank."

NATO and the West beyond 2025: Demise or Renewal?

For the past decades, the prevailing narrative of the West's past, present, and future used to be one of progress—following a "Whig interpretation of history," one of teleological development and drawing a straight line "from Plato to NATO" and toward the "end of history."[43] In recent years, analysts have discussed the implications of a "post-Western world" or whether the West "has lost it."[44] But just as the narrative of unidirectional progress is misleading, the demise of the West is far from inevitable.

Even if the West as a whole may be in relative economic decline, there is no material reason to believe that the Western world will be unable to defend itself and to preserve its particular way of life against external threats. After all, the combined power of Europe's and North America's liberal democracies will remain second to none for a while.[45] But to bring it to bear, they need to continue to understand "themselves and their actions in terms of a shared identity"[46] or a shared destiny, a *Schicksalsgemeinschaft*, rather than a transactional partnership with sometimes converging and sometimes conflicting interests. German Federal President Frank-Walter Steinmeier put it well in a speech about the enduring importance of the transatlantic partnership: "I firmly believe that we need each other if democracy and freedom are to have a future in this world of rivalry and conflicts and if the West is to remain more than merely a point on the compass. We need the transatlantic partnership for this."[47]

Whether the West remains a "collective intentionality"—and whether NATO remains its "executive arm"—will depend on the ability of Western societies to preserve a common understanding of the core features of the Western project. To be sure, the West has never been a monolithic concept, constantly merging and obscuring various intellectual, cultural, and religious traditions as well as being used for various political purposes.[48] But while there have always been different interpretations of what the West was about, some of today's disagreements go to the heart of the collective identity of the transatlantic security community as an alliance of liberal democracies. Yet it is precisely this collective identity that, time and again, has been a crucial factor in NATO's persistence and its ability to overcome internal crises.[49] While there is of course potential for renewal and convergence, it can be argued that illiberal forces across the West are attempting to dismantle precisely those institutions that have allowed the "strong self-healing tendencies"[50] of an alliance of liberal democracies to work. The current risk is that the West as defined by this book, as an institutional practice of directing military power by liberal government, will decline and morph into an illiberal West—a Euro-Atlantic, white, Judeo-Christian, thus a geographically, racially, and religiously bound entity that will seek to defend itself against other cultures or religions.[51]

The scenario above highlights some of the existing centrifugal forces that point toward an ongoing erosion of the West's collective identity and, in consequence, of NATO cohesion. In 2003, Mikkel Vedby Rasmussen asked: "Was the West a collective intentionality relevant for 'post-history'?"[52] Today the question is whether it will be relevant for the return of history.

NOTES

I would like to thank the editors, the anonymous reviewer, and the participants in the authors' workshop at Chatham House for helpful feedback on earlier drafts of the chapter.

1. See Mikkel Vedby Rasmussen, *The West, Civil Society and the Construction of Peace* (Basingstoke, UK: Palgrave Macmillan, 2003), pp. 145–46: "In the twentieth century the West constituted a collective identity because states that defined themselves as Western acted on the basis of a shared ontology and epistemology. They understood themselves and their actions in terms of a shared identity. I term this 'collective intentionality.'"

2. See Tobias Bunde and others, "Munich Security Report 2020: Westlessness" (Munich: Munich Security Conference, 2020).

3. This was the task given to me by the editors. Just like the scenarios analyzed at the New Era Foreign Policy Conference, this contribution envisions an alternative world that could come into being "in the medium (five to seven year) term and [is] designed to tease out issues scholars and policymakers may encounter in the relatively near future so that they can begin thinking critically about them now. This timeframe offers a period distant enough from the present as to avoid falling into current events analysis, but not so far into the future as to seem like science fiction." Naazneen Barma and others, "'Imagine a World in Which': Using Scenarios in Political Science," *International Studies Perspectives,* vol. 17 (2016), pp. 117–35, at p. 122. For a variety of scenarios for the transatlantic relationship in 2025, see Sonja Kaufmann and Mathis Lohaus, "Ever Closer or Lost at Sea? Scenarios for the Future of Transatlantic Relations," *Futures,* vol. 97 (March 2018), pp. 18–25.

4. See in detail Wallace J. Thies, *Why NATO Endures* (New York: Cambridge University Press, 2009).

5. See, for example, "Europe Alone: July 2024. What if America Leaves NATO?," *The Economist,* July 6, 2019. See also the "ugly scenario" in Sten Rynning, "NATO's Futures: The Atlantic Alliance Between Power and Purpose," NDC Research Paper 2 (Rome: NATO Defense College, March 2019), pp. 28–31; Douglas Barrie and others, "Defending Europe: Scenario-based Capability Requirements for NATO's European Members," Research Paper (London: International Institute for Strategic Studies, April 2019); Liana Fix and Bastian Giegerich, "European Security in Crisis: What to Expect If the United States Withdraws from NATO," War on the Rocks, November 30, 2019.

6. Herman Kahn, *Thinking About the Unthinkable* (New York: Horizon Press, 1962), p. 185.

7. On the "Bucharest Nine," see Sergiy Gerasymchuk, "Bucharest Nine: Looking for Cooperation on NATO's Eastern Flank?," *Ukrainian Prism* (Kyiv: Friedrich Ebert Foundation, July 2019).

8. In this sense, using Glaser's phrase, NATO would still be better than any of the competing options. See Charles L. Glaser, "Why NATO Is Still Best: Future

Security Arrangements for Europe," *International Security*, vol. 18 (Summer 1993), pp. 5–50.

9. Some authors have called for a planned Europeanization of NATO over the next 10–15 years, supported by the US, in order to avoid such an abrupt breaking point. See Jolyon Howorth, "EU–NATO Cooperation: The Key to Europe's Security Future," *European Security*, vol. 26 (2017), pp. 454–59, at p. 458.

10. According to an IISS report, the estimated cost "to match capability shortfalls in an Article V scenario ranges between US$288bn and US$357bn, in current (2019) terms." Barrie and others, "Defending Europe," p. 38.

11. See Moria Fagan and Jacob Poushter, "NATO Seen Favorably across Member States," Pew Research Center, February 9, 2020, www.pewresearch.org/global /2020/02/09/nato-seen-favorably-across-member-states/. According to the data, "there is widespread reluctance to fulfill the collective defense commitment outlined in Article 5 of NATO's founding treaty," while publics "are more convinced that the U.S. would use military force to defend a NATO ally from Russia."

12. It is telling that Merkel did not echo the speeches given by Federal President Joachim Gauck, Foreign Minister Frank-Walter Steinmeier, and Defense Minister Ursula von der Leyen at the Munich Security Conference in 2014, which had all called for assuming "more responsibility" in foreign and security policy, in a major foreign policy speech of her own. On the so-called Munich consensus, see Bastian Giegerich and Maximilian Terhalle, "The Munich Consensus and the Purpose of German Power," *Survival*, vol. 58 (April–May 2016), pp. 155–66.

13. Quoted in Alison Smale and Steven Erlanger, "Merkel, After Discordant G-7 Meeting, Is Looking Past Trump," *New York Times*, May 28, 2017, https:// nyti.ms/2rclSO1. For a critique of the stark contrast between Merkel's analyses and her actions, see René Pfister, "Merkel's Dark View of the World We Live In," *Der Spiegel*, June 5, 2018, https://spon.de/affdT.

14. See Rick Noack, "Germany Won't Become the 'Leader of the Free World' After All, and the Germans Don't Mind," *Washington Post*, February 21, 2018.

15. A nationalistic Germany would not necessarily mean a more militaristic Germany. More likely, it would be an isolationist Germany, less willing to support European institutions. See also Philip Stephens, "Europe Should Beware a Nationalist Germany," *Financial Times*, June 21, 2018.

16. See Barrie and others, "Defending Europe," p. 3: "If the funding to meet shortfalls were available, the IISS assesses that the recapitalisation across the military domains would take up to 20 years, with some significant progress around the ten- and 15-year marks."

17. On this speculation, see Andrew Higgins, "As Putin Pushes a Merger, Belarus Resists with Language, Culture and History," *New York Times*, June 29, 2019, https://nyti.ms/2KOg2gm.

18. Similar open letters were published in the past. See, for example, Mario Adorf and others, "Wieder Krieg in Europa? Nicht in unserem Namen!" [War in Europe Again? Not in Our Name!], *Die Zeit*, December 5, 2014, www.zeit.de/ politik/2014-12/aufruf-russland-dialog. See also the response by more than 100

experts on Russia and Eastern Europe: Sabine Adler and others, "Friedenssicherung statt Expansionsbelohnung" [Securing Peace Instead of Rewarding Expansion], *Die Zeit*, December 11, 2014, www.zeit.de/politik/2014-12/aufruf-friedenssicherung -statt-expansionsbelohnung.

19. On the military reorganization and capability planning of the Bundeswehr and its role in NATO, see Claudia Major, "NATO's Strategic Adaptation. Germany Is the Backbone for the Alliance's Military Reorganisation," SWP Comment 16 (Berlin: Stiftung Wissenschaft und Politik, March 2015); Rainer Glatz and Martin Zapfe, "Ambitious Framework Nation: Germany in NATO. Bundeswehr Capability Planning and the 'Framework Nations Concept,'" SWP Comment 35 (Berlin: Stiftung Wissenschaft und Politik, September 2017).

20. A US withdrawal from NATO would be likely to bring up a modern iteration of the "German question" that NATO had arguably solved. See Sten Rynning, "Germany Is More Than Europe Can Handle: Or, Why NATO Remains a Pacifier," NDC Research Paper 96 (Rome: NATO Defense College, September 2013).

21. James M. Goldgeier, "The Future of NATO," Council Special Report 51 (New York: Council on Foreign Relations, 2010), p. 3.

22. This idea has a long tradition in US foreign policy and has been discussed in various forms by both Democrats and Republicans. See Tobias Bunde and Timo Noetzel, "Unavoidable Tensions: The Liberal Path to Global NATO," *Contemporary Security Policy*, vol. 31 (August 2010), pp. 295–318.

23. See Kenneth A. Schultz, "Perils of Polarization for U.S. Foreign Policy," *Washington Quarterly*, vol. 40 (Winter 2018), pp. 7–28.

24. For some public opinion data on the "Millennials," see Trevor Thrall and others, "The Clash of Generations? Intergenerational Change and American Foreign Policy Views," Chicago Council on Global Affairs, June 25, 2018, https: //shar.es/aXlqz5.

25. This reorientation did not begin with the Obama administration's "rebalancing" efforts but in the mid-2000s. See Nina Silove, "The Pivot Before the Pivot: U.S. Strategy to Preserve the Power Balance in Asia," *International Security*, vol. 40 (Spring 2016), pp. 45–88.

26. Patrick M. Shanahan, "Remarks at the IISS Shangri-La Dialogue 2019," Singapore, June 1, 2019, www.defense.gov/Newsroom/Transcripts/Transcript /Article/1871584/acting-secretary-shanahans-remarks-at-the-iiss-shangri-la -dialogue-2019/.

27. For decades the US strategy was based on the conviction that its military had to be ready to fight in two major regional contingencies simultaneously. In contrast, the 2018 National Defense Strategy announced that the US military would now prepare for defeating aggression by a top-tier competitor, while only deterring in a second theater. See Jim Mitre, "A Eulogy for the Two-War Construct," *Washington Quarterly*, vol. 41 (Winter 2019), pp. 7–30. This has major implications for Europe. See Hal Brands, "What If the U.S. Could Fight Only One War at a Time?," Bloomberg Opinion, June 11, 2019, www.bloomberg.com/opinion/articles/2019 -06-11/two-war-strategy-overhaul-creates-many-risks.

28. Trump emphasized, for example, "the bonds of culture, faith and tradition that make us who we are." See Donald J. Trump, "Remarks by President Trump to the People of Poland," Warsaw, July 6, 2017, www.whitehouse.gov/briefings -statements/remarks-president-trump-people-poland/.

29. Lara Seligman and Robbie Gramer, "'Fort Trump' for Poland? Not Quite," *Foreign Policy*, June 12, 2019, https://foreignpolicy.com/2019/06/12/fort-trump -for-poland-not-quite/.

30. Rynning, "NATO's Futures," pp. 30–31.

31. For evaluations of the idea of "Global Britain" as a potential role for the UK post-Brexit, see Benjamin Martill and Monika Sus, "Post-Brexit EU/UK Security Cooperation: NATO, CSDP+, or 'French Connection?,'" *British Journal of Politics and International Relations,* vol. 20, no. 4 (2018), pp. 846–63, at p. 849; Christopher Hill, "Turning Back the Clock: The Illusion of a Global Political Role for Britain," in *Brexit and Beyond: Rethinking the Futures of Europe*, edited by Benjamin Martill and Uta Staiger (London: UCL Press, 2018), pp. 183–92.

32. François Heisbourg, "Europe's Defence: Revisiting the Impact of Brexit," *Survival*, vol. 60 (December 2018), pp. 17–26, at p. 21.

33. Martill and Sus, "Post-Brexit EU/UK Security Cooperation," p. 857.

34. For an evaluation of the potential impact of Brexit on the UK's ability to achieve its level of ambition and capability, see James Black and others, "Defence and Security After Brexit. Understanding the Possible Implications of the UK's Decision to Leave the EU," Compendium Report (Santa Monica, CA and Cambridge, UK: RAND Corporation, 2017).

35. In his 2020 speech at the École de Guerre, Macron said French nuclear weapons had "a truly European dimension" and that "France's vital interests now have a European dimension." See Emmanuel Macron, "Speech of the President of the Republic on the Defense and Deterrence Strategy," Paris, February 7, 2020, www.elysee.fr/emmanuel-macron/2020/02/07/speech-of-the-president-of-the -republic-on-the-defense-and-deterrence-strategy.en.

36. The options discussed in this paragraph are based on Bruno Tertrais, "Will Europe Get Its Own Bomb?," *Washington Quarterly*, vol. 42 (Summer 2019), pp. 47–66, at pp. 58–59.

37. Badie referred to this mindset, to which all French presidents of the Fifth Republic returned, as "Gaullism without de Gaulle." See Bertrand Badie, *New Perspectives on the International Order: No Longer Alone in This World* (Cham, Switzerland: Springer International Publishing, 2019), pp. 109–11. On the competing traditions in French strategic thinking, of which "Gaullism" is just one, see Alice Pannier and Olivier Schmitt, "To Fight Another Day: France Between the Fight Against Terrorism and Future Warfare," *International Affairs*, vol. 95, no. 4 (July 2019), pp. 897–916, at pp. 898–99.

38. See Emmanuel Macron, "Ambassadors' Conference – Speech by M. Emmanuel Macron, President of the Republic," Paris, August 27, 2019, https: //lv.ambafrance.org/Ambassadors-conference-Speech-by-M-Emmanuel-Macron -President-of-the-Republic: "I also think that pushing Russia away from Europe

is a major strategic error, because we are pushing it either toward isolation, which heightens tensions, or toward alliances with other great powers such as China, which would not at all be in our interest." See also Rynning, "NATO's Futures," pp. 33–38.

39. Tobias Bunde, "NATO Back on Dual-Track?," East West Institute, May 19, 2016, https://shar.es/aXlrIR.

40. This has become a never-ending debate with a continued repetition of the same arguments. For two examples of the respective positions, see Nadja Douglas, "Is the NATO-Russia Founding Act Still Relevant?," ZOiS Spotlight 11, May 24, 2017, https://en.zois-berlin.de/publications/zois-spotlight-2017/is-the-nato-russia-founding-act-still-relevant; and John R. Deni, "The NATO-Russia Founding Act: A Dead Letter," Carnegie Europe, June 29, 2017, https://carnegieeurope.eu/strategiceurope/71385.

41. This argument has already been made by libertarians in the US. See, for instance, Ted Galen Carpenter, "NATO's Worrisome Authoritarian Storm Clouds," *Mediterranean Quarterly*, vol. 26 (December 2015), pp. 37–48, at p. 48: "Incurring risks, including a possible confrontation with a nuclear-armed Russia, to protect such free-riding 'allies' is bad enough, even if they are bona fide democracies. But it would be far worse to incur such risks on behalf of autocratic allies masquerading as democracies." On the rise of illiberalism as a major challenge for NATO cohesion, see Tobias Bunde, "Die Entwertung der NATO. Warum die 'illiberale Internationale' das Nordatlantische Bündnis gefährdet," *Sicherheit und Frieden*, vol. 37, no. 1 (2019), pp. 19–23.

42. See Agata Kondzińska, Bartosz T. Wieliński, and Tomasz Bielecki, "French Foreign Minister: We No Longer Want to Pay for Poland and Hungary," *Euractiv*, September 5, 2018, www.euractiv.com/section/future-eu/news/french-foreign-minister-we-no-longer-want-to-pay-for-poland-and-hungary/; Steven Erlanger, "As Poland and Hungary Flout Democratic Values, Europe Eyes the Aid Spigot," *New York Times*, May 1, 2018, https://nyti.ms/2FxHyrf.

43. Herbert Butterfield, *The Whig Interpretation of History* (London: Bell, 1931); David Gress, *From Plato to NATO: The Idea of the West and Its Opponents* (New York: Free Press, 1998); Francis Fukuyama, *The End of History and the Last Man* (New York: Free Press, 1992).

44. Oliver Stuenkel, *Post-Western World: How Emerging Powers Are Remaking Global Order* (Cambridge: Polity Press, 2016); Kishore Mahbubani, *Has the West Lost It? A Provocation* (London: Allen Lane, 2018).

45. According to Michael Beckley, the US has unique advantages over rivals that can preserve its status as the preeminent power for decades to come. See Michael Beckley, *For the Unrivaled: Why America Will Remain the World's Sole Superpower* (Cornell University Press, 2018). This argument can be extended to the West as a whole.

46. Rasmussen, *The West, Civil Society and the Construction of Peace*, pp. 145–46.

47. Frank-Walter Steinmeier, "Reopening of Goethe Institute Boston," October

31, 2019, www.bundespraesident.de/SharedDocs/Reden/EN/Frank-Walter -Steinmeier/Reden/2019/10/191031-Boston-Goethe-Institut.html.

48. See the contributions in Gunther Hellmann and Benjamin Herborth, eds., *Uses of "the West": Security and the Politics of Order* (Cambridge University Press, 2016).

49. Thies, *Why NATO Endures*; Tobias Bunde, "NATO's Identity Crisis: The Transatlantic Identity Terrain and the Patterns of Conflict and Cooperation Within the Alliance," PhD Dissertation (Berlin: Freie Universität Berlin, 2016).

50. Thies, *Why NATO Endures*, p. 19.

51. See, for example, President Trump's speech in Warsaw: "We must work together to confront forces, whether they come from inside or out, from the South or the East, that threaten over time to undermine these values and to erase the bonds of culture, faith and tradition that make us who we are. . . . If left unchecked, these forces will undermine our courage, sap our spirit, and weaken our will to defend ourselves and our societies." Donald J. Trump, "Remarks by President Trump to the People of Poland," Warsaw, July 6, 2017.

52. Rasmussen, *The West, Civil Society and the Construction of Peace*, p. 146.

PART II

Western Perceptions of Time and the International Normative Order

A Normative Order under Pressure

AMELIE THEUSSEN

Norms—defined as "beliefs shared by a community about who they are, what the world is like, and given these two things, what they can and should do in given circumstances"[1]—provide the framework within which Western governments interpret war. Norms are the rules of the game and thereby serve to regulate behavior. They are used to justify one's own actions, such as the resort to armed force, and judge the action of others as legitimate or illegitimate. The current international normative order relating to war and warfare was largely built after World War II, even though the origin of many norms can be traced back even beyond World War I. Under Western leadership, in the war's aftermath, many of the legal norms relating to the use of force in international relations were codified in the United Nations Charter, and the rules regarding the means, methods, and conduct of warfare are set out in the Geneva Conventions.[2] Other legal norms are enshrined in the numerous other conventions that have been agreed upon since, with varying numbers of signatories, as well as in customary law. Aside from the legal norms, other ethical or moral norms also guide the use of force by the West. This normative order represents a specific Western perception of time in politics and war, based on a clear distinction between peace and war, and weighing humanitarian concerns against military necessity. Together with military organizations created after World War II, it allowed the West to build strong collective security arrangements, which are the cornerstone of Western military power, and Western democracies and post–World War II institutions have regarded themselves as guardians of this favorable international normative order.

For many decades this normative context has been relatively stable, albeit frozen in great power competition. Since the end of the Cold War and the US unipolar moment,[3] however, this order has been increasingly challenged from multiple directions. First, President Donald Trump's policy of "America first" and the resulting US withdrawal from the international stage threatens the survival of the international liberal order,[4] of which the international normative order is part, by withdrawing its strongest guardian. This was symbolically highlighted in June 2018, when President Trump rejected a G7 communiqué reaffirming the importance of a "rule-based international order."[5]

Second, other state actors, such as Russia, China, and India, have emerged as international competitors and put forward their own interpretations of existing norms. Russia has on multiple occasions accused the West of a "creative application" of international legal norms such as the non-use of force.[6]

Emerging forms of conflict such as hybrid and cyber warfare pose a third challenge for the existing normative order. Fundamental disagreements about the applicability of established norms to cyberspace and hybrid forms of conflict—also within the West—have ignited calls for revisions or the creation of new norms,[7] emphasizing differing interpretations of norms and diverging fundamental perceptions of time, politics, and war.

Fourth, many opponents—especially the numerous non-state actors that have emerged as main adversaries in contemporary wars—neglect the norms of armed conflict, which might in turn lead Western states to abandon these norms in their fight against such adversaries, as they perceive the rules as hindering the defeat of an opponent fighting thus "unfairly."[8] Going even further, Tanisha Fazal argues that "the standards for compliance [with international norms] have risen so high that . . . full compliance is impossible even for the best-resourced militaries,"[9] while for others the complexity and restrictive nature of international law have made it irrelevant.[10] Is it that the existing norms are too constraining for the West to fight and win contemporary wars?

All of these factors point toward the emergence of new interpretations and new norms, not necessarily aligned with the Western perception of time, but instead challenging it as the underlying factor of a universal normative order. There is no doubt that a normative order is the expression of certain actors' preference and a certain set of circumstances; in the case of the norms regarding war and warfare, these actors are "the West," and the set of circumstances is the West's experience with two world wars and its later military engagements. While normative orders can be relatively stable, as the current international normative order has been since the end of the World War II, norms do not exist independently of time; indeed they develop, change, rise, and fall in the context of changing circumstances. A normative order is not static, but constantly in flux—either norms are being reaffirmed or they are being contested, expanded, changed, or dismissed. Finnemore and Sikkink's norm "life cycle" is one conceptualization of the changing of norms that clearly shows the connection to time.[11] Yet the mutability of norms, including legal norms, goes beyond their emergence, acceptance, and internalization. In fact every reference to or usage of a norm has the potential to alter this norm. This means that norms go through a continuous cycle of change: the existing normative structure provides the frame within which actors choose and justify their course of action, and within which their behavior is evaluated by others. However, this existing normative structure cannot account for all possible courses of action and circumstances, and norms within the structure may be in conflict with one another. This leads to debates about a norm's applicability and content—and these debates always change the norm in question, by modifying its strength, its breadth, or its context.[12]

In light of the fundamental challenges raised against the existing normative order, the temporal context of a norm and its susceptibility to change over time call for an investigation into how the existing normative order represents a specific Western perception of time in politics and war—and what this says about the future of Western power. It seems the universality of the existing order is increasingly being questioned, with peer competitors and other actors producing their own interpretations of existing norms and even new norms, none of which are necessarily aligned with the Western temporality enshrined in existing norms. This section considers how these current norms are built on certain Western conceptions of time, which are themselves increasingly contested. It analyzes both the existing normative framework and the changes it is undergoing, as well as how these normative changes will affect Western power.

In chapter 5, Kathleen J. McInnis explores the role of norms of civilian protection in the case of Afghanistan, and gives some answers to the question posed above about the constraints imposed by norms. She analyzes how a clash of temporalities at the tactical and strategic level and among different allies and missions exacerbated campaign mismanagement, resulting in a prolonged campaign and increased civilian casualty numbers. This undermined Western efforts in Afghanistan.

Chapters 6 are 7 broaden the inquiry, investigating whether clashes of different temporalities are systemic to the existing normative structure relating to war and warfare, inhibiting the West's ability to use military force. In chapter 6, Natasha Kuhrt looks at conflicting norms of intervention. She argues that it is not so much the case that either Russia or China has a fundamentally different understanding of international norms, but that Russia in particular has been able to exploit the indeterminacy and lack of consensus on norms of intervention within the West itself. Internal Western disagreements based on different temporalities between the need for speedy intervention and the need to avoid prolonged conflicts create ambiguity about the applicability and extent of the norms, allowing Russia to act "below the radar." By fleshing out these differing interpretations, this chapter shows how this indeterminacy in the West hinders its ability to use its force and leads to a regionalization of norms of intervention.

In chapter 7 Amelie Theussen and Peter Viggo Jakobsen argue that Russia and China are able to exploit the clear distinction between wartime and peacetime enshrined in the normative system and Western thinking about war. Great power competition in the form of gray zone conflict is a clash of temporalities: the West's strict separation between peacetime and wartime contrasts with a more comprehensive, long-term war-focused approach by Russia and China. As traditional distinctions between war and peace are being broken down, this poses a major challenge for the West: the creation of a constant state of low-level conflict hinders decisive responses on its part. Nevertheless, Theussen and Jakobsen suggest, focusing on existing peacetime mechanisms while being prepared for war might just be the solution the West is seeking.

Finally, the scenario by Ernst Dijxhoorn in chapter 8 envisions China taking control of parts of Djibouti and asks the reader to consider how the West could respond in light of these fundamental challenges to the normative order. The chapter asks whether the West would be able to respond to the increasingly divergent normative framework and defend its interests (including the continuation of the existing normative order), and if so, under which conditions and how. This raises fundamental questions about whether the West can continue its privileged position as the originator of the normative context within which war will be interpreted, or whether it must adapt to new frameworks and interpretations.

NOTES

1. Theo Farrell, *The Norms of War: Cultural Beliefs and Modern Conflict* (Boulder, CO: Lynne Rienner, 2005).

2. One should not forget the continued importance of the Hague Conventions of 1899 and 1907.

3. Charles Krauthammer, "The Unipolar Moment," *Foreign Affairs*, vol. 70, no. 1 (1990/1991), pp. 23–33.

4. Joseph Samuel Nye, Jr., "The Rise and Fall of American Hegemony from Wilson to Trump," *International Affairs*, vol. 95, no. 1 (2018), pp. 63–80.

5. Julian Borger and Anne Perkins, "G7 in Disarray after Trump Rejects Communiqué and Attacks 'Weak' Trudeau," *The Guardian*, June 10, 2018, www.theguardian.com/world/2018/jun/10/g7-in-disarray-after-trump-rejects-communique-and-attacks-weak-trudeau.

6. Russian Ministry of Foreign Affairs, "Foreign Policy Concept of the Russian Federation (Approved by President of the Russian Federation Vladimir Putin on November 30, 2016)," December 1, 2016, ww.mid.ru/foreign_policy/official_documents/-/asset_publisher/CptICkB6BZ29/content/id/2542248.

7. Sascha-Dominik Bachmann and Hakan Gunneriusson, "Hybrid Wars: The 21st-Century's New Threats to Global Peace and Security," *Scientia Militaria: South African Journal of Military Studies,* vol. 43, no. 1 (2015), pp. 77–98; George R. Lucas, "Emerging Norms for Cyberwarfare," in *Binary Bullets: The Ethics of Cyberwarfare*, edited by Fritz Allhoff, Adam Henschke, and Bradley Jay Strawser (Oxford University Press, 2016); Brian M. Mazanec, *The Evolution of Cyber War: International Norms for Emerging-Technology Weapons* (Lincoln, NE: Potomac Books, 2015).

8. Marco Sassoli, "The Implementation of International Humanitarian Law: Current and Inherent Challenges," *Yearbook of International Humanitarian Law,* vol. 10 (2007), p. 57.

9. Tanisha M. Fazal, *Wars of Law: Unintended Consequences in the Regulation of Armed Conflict* (Cornell University Press, 2018), p. 5.

10. Stephen Hopgood, *The Endtimes of Human Rights* (Cornell University Press, 2013); Martti Koskenniemi, *From Apology to Utopia: The Structure of International Legal Argument*, reissue with a new Epilogue (Cambridge University Press, 2005); Eric Posner, *The Twilight of Human Rights Law*, Inalienable Rights Series (Oxford University Press, 2014).

11. Martha Finnemore and Kathryn Sikkink, "International Norm Dynamics and Political Change," *International Organization*, vol. 52, no. 4 (1998), pp. 887–917.

12. Wayne Sandholtz, "Dynamics of International Norm Change: Rules against Wartime Plunder," *European Journal of International Relations*, vol. 14, no. 1 (2008), pp. 101–31.

FIVE

Civilian Casualties and Contemporary Coalition Operations

The Case of Afghanistan

KATHLEEN J. MCINNIS

This chapter argues that different perceptions of temporality—between coalition partners, and between the tactical and strategic levels—help explain why the Afghanistan campaign may have been mismanaged, extending its duration and increasing the number of civilian casualties, despite clear dedication to norms of civilian protection.[1] The chapter offers a reflection upon the Afghanistan experience in the hope that meaningful contemplation of US and allied shortcomings might encourage current and future military campaign practitioners to avoid repeating avoidable mistakes.

While the operations in Afghanistan are arguably outliers, there are two main reasons why the campaign there has been selected as the subject of inquiry here. In the first instance, considerable material, including primary source material, is publicly available on the campaign and its evolution since its inception in 2001. This makes Afghanistan considerably easier to examine than other recent campaigns, for which many of the details remain classified. The second reason is that the case of Afghanistan poignantly illustrates many of the features of other contemporary military campaigns; it can therefore usefully provide lessons that may help current and future participants in, and managers of, military campaigns.

Preventing Civilian Casualties as a Strategic Imperative

It was mid-2008 when I found myself in the garden of the International Security Assistance Force (ISAF) headquarters compound, having coffee with the NATO Senior Civilian Representative for Afghanistan. He was a portrait of fatigue and frustration. Then-President Karzai had just given General David McKiernan, the commander of ISAF at the time, a very shrill earful regarding an operation that had resulted in civilian casualties in southern Afghanistan. As a result, in Karzai's estimation, the coalition was rapidly becoming worse than the Soviet forces in the 1980s—a dire comparison indeed. The point Karzai was making was clear: if ISAF and the Government of Afghanistan were waging a campaign for legitimacy and the support of the Afghan people, bombing civilians and noncombatants actually undermined the coalition's ability to win that campaign. Civilian casualties also eroded support for ISAF within coalition capitals. Consequently, if the ISAF mission was to spread security and stability for the benefit of the Afghan people, were NATO forces doing more harm than good in the country?

The stakes regarding the issue of civilian casualties were being raised higher and higher with each loss of civilian life, and the conversation with President Karzai was a wakeup call. Shortly thereafter a tactical directive on minimizing civilian casualties was issued for ISAF.[2] General Stanley McChrystal, upon assumption of ISAF command after McKiernan's dismissal, issued his own tactical directive, which aimed to reduce civilian casualties and required ISAF forces to partner with their Afghan counterparts in conducting operations.[3] These steps were not without controversy; at the time some observers contended that such limitations on ISAF's ability to act were contrary to key principles of warfare, namely the necessity to use overwhelming violence to compel an adversary to accept a given political outcome. Preventing civilian casualties was a lesser priority. According to this view, failure to apply force in such an overwhelming manner simply prolonged the campaign.[4]

US and NATO policymakers and military commanders alike tended to disagree with this dissenting view. ISAF was not a "conventional" military campaign, and perceptions that ISAF was not taking sufficient steps to prevent civilian casualties were quickly becoming the fastest route to a speedy ejection of coalition forces from Afghanistan. Still, concerns emerged that the emphasis placed on civilian casualty prevention was hampering ISAF's ability to prosecute operations effectively. By the time that General David Petraeus took command of ISAF, the key question was how to strike the right balance between preventing civilian casualties and giving coalition forces adequate authorities and resources for force protection—not whether overwhelming force should be applied to win the campaign.[5]

Within the Iraq (2003–10) campaign, concern about the corrosive effects of civilian casualties on strategic-level matters was also becoming apparent. Speaking on behalf of the National Security Council at a pre-deployment conference for Iraq and Afghanistan-bound US Army Advise and Assist Brigades, a senior White House official argued that tactical-level accidents, and in particular civilian casualties, distracted senior-level attention from—and often undermined progress during—critical negotiations such as those taking place over the US–Iraq Status of Forces Agreement.[6] The character of the Iraq and Afghan campaigns led defense institutions, including the US Department of Defense, to the overall conclusion that "the sympathy and support of the civilian population are frequently important objectives in non-international armed conflict. In order to ensure such support, commanders and their forces may operate under rules of engagement that are more restrictive than what the law of war requires."[7]

Yet despite the general consensus that harming civilians undermines campaign progress by undermining public support for coalition forces and the governments they support,[8] civilian casualties—even seemingly easily avoidable ones—do occur.[9] In 2019 more than forty pine nut farmers in Afghanistan were reportedly mistaken for Islamic State terrorists while sitting around a campfire at the end of their workday; they were killed in a drone strike.[10] If such tactical, and often preventable, errors can have such enormous strategic impact, why do these incidents keep happening?

The easy answer, of course, is that civilian casualties are part and parcel of warfare itself; as states wage war to advance their interests, some degree of harm to civilians is inevitable.[11] Yet what if one were to set that maxim aside and instead ask whether there are other structural factors within these recent military campaigns that may have contributed to instances of civilian casualties, despite extensive efforts to prevent them? Are there deeper issues with the prosecution of contemporary military campaigns that are exacerbating the risks that civilians will be caught in the crossfire? Chris Kolenda, a prominent US national security practitioner and scholar, has hinted that the way the Afghan campaign was designed may indeed have exacerbated civilian harm:

> Even better civilian protection, however, will not overcome an absent or bankrupt strategy. Why did the U.S. take so long to recognize that protection of Afghan civilians mattered? *Failure to understand the nature of the conflict*

*and to devise a credible strategy to succeed prolonged the conflict and the human
suffering.*[12]

In other words, policies and procedures to prevent and mitigate civilian
harm amount to nothing if there is no credible, coherent campaign and strategy. Unfortunately, during significant periods of NATO's operations in Afghanistan, campaign coherence, coherent strategy, and a coherent theory of
victory were all missing. It is, upon reflection, a staggering case of mismanagement that very likely contributed to prolonged hostilities. If civilian casualties
are an inevitable aspect of war, what moral responsibility do we bear for prolonging the campaign—creating time and space for more civilian casualties to
occur—through our own strategic and operational incompetence?

After a brief exploration of norms, norms of civilian protection, and their
application in contemporary warfare, this chapter asks whether a clash of temporalities among allies and between strategic and tactical levels caused the
failure to design a coherent military campaign, the failure to formulate and
advance a coherent strategy, and the failure to produce a coherent theory of
victory, all of which prolonged the war and ultimately exacerbated the potential for civilian casualties. Certainly the United States and other NATO
militaries have gone to considerable lengths to avoid civilian harm in a narrow
sense by adopting and promulgating policies to prevent and mitigate civilian
casualties—efforts that are both laudable and sensible. But in a broader sense
US and NATO capitals must now reckon with the fact that their own strategic and operational decisionmaking had a large bearing on the campaign's
duration and the attendant loss of civilian life.

Norms and Civilian Harm

Although considerable scholarship is devoted to the understanding of norms
and how they affect international relations and state behavior,[13] this chapter
uses Farrell's definition of norms, which are "beliefs shared by a community
about who they are, what the world is like, and given these two things, what
they can and should do in given circumstances. . . . Norms function to regulate behavior by defining the rules of the game."[14] While they can be difficult
to pinpoint, norms can have significant impact upon the policy preferences of
states, including choices surrounding the conduct of war.

Several areas of scholarship explore those norms and their application to
the conduct of war, and issues surrounding civilian casualties in particular.
The war convention scholarship explores when it is legitimate to use force,

who are appropriate belligerents, and against whom legitimate force might be applied.[15] International humanitarian law articulates a set of norms to which states ought to adhere during the conduct of war, including humane treatment of prisoners, protection of neutral medical workers, and minimization of harm to non-belligerents.[16] With the increasing use of advanced technologies to prosecute contemporary wars, such as precision-strike capabilities and enhanced air power, other scholars have explored risk transference from US and NATO/allied forces to combatants and noncombatants alike.[17] Finally, with the advent of armed drone technology and its use on the battlefield, recent scholarship has explored the moral and ethical costs of using such unmanned aerial vehicle platforms on the battlefield.[18]

These debates are not confined to academia or legal scholarship; they are also reflected in public critiques and scrutiny of US and allied conduct during conflict. Most prominent in public discussions are those instances in which beliefs about what constitutes "good" conduct during war are thought to be violated.[19] The accidental bombing of the pine nut farm referred to above provoked a huge international outcry.[20] Even more recently, the Trump administration's pardoning of Navy SEAL team member Eddie Gallagher, a man accused of murdering civilians in Iraq, provoked a public outcry including (but not limited to) deep expressions of concern about what this might mean for military order and discipline, and adversaries' adherence to the laws of war; it even resulted in the resignation of the Secretary of the Navy.[21] The public—and private—horror expressed by defense policy practitioners and military personnel alike when it is perceived that the norms governing the proper conduct of war have *not* been followed suggests that such norms are intact, at least for the time being. Further, the fact that US and allied governments need to justify their actions when accused of causing civilian casualties is evidence that such norms exist; as Finnemore and Sikkink note, without such norms governments would not feel compelled to mention the issue at all.[22]

Public commentary is one thing, however; adoption of norms by governments is quite another. Are US and allied governments really taking norms of civilian protection seriously? A cursory overview of relevant policy literature suggests that while more work can always be done to prevent civilian harm, the United States, and NATO states more broadly, appear to have accepted the norm that Western militaries must take considerable precautions to minimize civilian casualties. In addition to the issuances of the tactical directives mentioned at the beginning of this chapter, measures to prevent civilian casualties, as Colin Kahl argues, are not only embedded in policy direction, they are often integrated into pre-deployment training as well as operational planning and execution.[23]

More recently prevention of civilian casualties has also been the subject of standalone doctrine published by the United States Army. ATP 3-07.6 *Protection of Civilians*, published on October 2015, notes that Army units

> comply with the law of war and other relevant bodies of law to minimize civilian harm. Additionally, Army units avoid actions that undermine the efforts of other actors to improve human security. . . . Army units perform offensive, defensive, and stability tasks that mitigate harm to civilians and create an environment conducive to the protection of civilians.[24]

Subsequently, on July 1, 2016, the White House issued Executive Order 13732, *United States Policy on Pre- and Post-Strike Measures to Address Civilian Casualties in U.S. Operations Involving the Use of Force*.[25] This was followed by a number of other measures, including those mandated by legislation. For example, Congress mandated the issuance of an annual Department of Defense report on civilian casualties in theaters of "active hostilities" (P.L. 115–91); the issuance of a DoD report on civilian casualty policy (P.L. 115–232, section 936) that required DoD policy to address eight key aspects of civilian casualty policy;[26] and the appointment of a senior DoD civilian responsible for civilian casualty policy.[27]

Prevention of civilian casualties was also integrated into the US military's capstone doctrinal document, *Joint Publication 3.0 Operations*, which argues that prevention of civilian casualties is not only a strategic and tactical necessity but also consistent with values and behaviors of contemporary military service professionals:

> Civilian casualty mitigation directly affects the success of the overall mission. Even tactical actions can have strategic and second-order effects. Minimizing and addressing civilian casualty incidents supports strategic imperatives *and are also at the heart of the profession of arms*. Failure to minimize civilian casualties can undermine national policy objectives and the mission of joint forces, while assisting the enemy. Additionally, civilian casualties can incite increased opposition to joint forces. Focused attention on civilian casualty mitigation can be an important investment to maintain legitimacy and accomplish the mission.[28]

The most recent *Annual Report on Civilian Casualties in Connection with United States Military Operations*, issued in May 2019, notes the following:

the protection of civilians is fundamentally consistent with the effective, efficient, and decisive use of force in pursuit of U.S. national interests. Minimizing civilian casualties can further mission objectives; help maintain the support of partner governments and vulnerable populations, especially during counterterrorism and counterinsurgency operations; and enhance the legitimacy and sustainability of U.S. operations critical to U.S. national security. As a matter of policy, U.S. forces therefore routinely conduct operations under policy standards that are more protective of civilians than is required by the law of war.

U.S. forces also protect civilians because it is the moral and ethical thing to do. Although civilian casualties are a tragic and unavoidable part of war, no force in history has been more committed to limiting harm to civilians than the U.S. military. This commitment is reflected in DoD's consistent efforts to maintain and promote best practices that reduce the likelihood of civilian casualties, take appropriate steps when such casualties occur, and draw lessons from DoD operations to further enhance the protection of civilians.[29]

As counter–Islamic State operations were being conducted, then-Secretary of Defense James Mattis was so sensitive to the issue of civilian casualties that he personally convened a group of watchdog organizations to help devise better ways to account for and mitigate harm to non-belligerents.[30]

On the other side of the Atlantic, NATO has also taken steps to prevent and mitigate civilian harm during operations. During the ISAF campaign NATO's headquarters in Brussels created a civilian harm protection cell within its operations division.[31] At its Warsaw summit in July 2016, it also adopted a "NATO Policy for the Protection of Civilians" and has begun developing concepts for its implementation.[32]

So it seems that prevention of civilian casualties is a norm that was instigated by strategic efficacy—that is, the recognition that civilian harm undermines strategic-level campaign progress—and is being further strengthened and codified in official documentation on both sides of the Atlantic. All this stands in stark contrast to many other actors' wartime behavior. Watching the behavior of Russia in Georgia and Chechnya, or even the Taliban's indiscriminate violence in Afghanistan, it appears that the prevention of civilian casualties and adherence to the laws of armed conflict factor less prominently in the calculations of other belligerents.[33]

While it is arguably a positive development that the United States and its allies are taking the prevention of civilian casualties seriously, all these efforts raise the underlying question of whether they have focused a little too much on pruning the trees rather than putting out the forest fire itself. In 2007, Rus-

sian President Vladimir Putin stood up at the Munich Security Conference
and asked whether the United States was a sufficiently responsible actor to be
trusted with global security. Pointing to the invasion of Iraq and its disastrous
fallout, Putin noted:

> Unilateral and frequently illegitimate actions have not resolved any problems.
> Moreover, they have caused new human tragedies and created new centres of
> tension. Judge for yourselves: wars as well as local and regional conflicts have
> not diminished. Mr Teltschik mentioned this very gently. *And no less people*
> *perish in these conflicts—even more are dying than before. Significantly more,*
> *significantly more!* Today we are witnessing an almost uncontained hyper use
> of force—military force—in international relations, force that is plunging the
> world into an abyss of permanent conflicts.[34]

As abhorrent as the speech seemed to us at the time—we were in Afghanistan helping Afghans, after all—policymakers would do well to reflect
on Putin's 2007 critique. Ultimately, while the United States and its partners
have attempted to make war as clean an endeavor as possible at a tactical level,
at the operational and strategic levels significant campaign management missteps have arguably created the conditions in which the risks of civilian casualties were exacerbated. Indeed, this is a central theme embedded within the
Afghanistan Papers, a trove of documents released by the *Washington Post* that
depict mismanagement and inertia at the heart of the Afghan campaign.[35]
The forces opposing the Government of the Islamic Republic of Afghanistan certainly share the blame for the campaign's endurance. They were able
to gain and sustain indigenous public support as well as external sanctuary
which kept them on the battlefield, and their infamously brutal behavior and
unwillingness to negotiate with the legitimate government in Kabul to end
the war lessened our own imperative to find a solution that would do so. But
to place all the blame squarely on the shoulders of our adversaries is to side-
step important scrutiny of the moral culpability of the US and NATO in the
conduct of the war. As lofty as the goals and intentions for the campaign may
have been, hindsight review of the evidence suggests that we could have done
things a lot better. Indeed the issue of civilian casualties and their prevention
forces us to grapple with our own missteps and mistakes that may have led to
the continued duration of the campaign.

Did the US and its allies prolong the campaign through mismanagement?
If so, might different perceptions of temporality—between coalition participants, and between the tactical and strategic levels—help explain why this
mismanagement might have occurred? Could a clash of temporalities have

had an impact on the conduct and planning of the Afghanistan campaign? The remainder of this chapter applies the analytic lens of temporality to exploring different aspects of the Afghanistan campaign and asks how its architecture and overall design, by prolonging the campaign, may have contributed to civilian harm.

Context: Establishing NATO's International Security Assistance Force (ISAF)

ISAF was established in 2001 at the Bonn Conference. Under a United Nations mandate, its mission, initially limited in geographic scope to Kabul and its environs, was to assist the nascent Afghan Transitional Authority as it reconstructed Afghanistan. Different nations, starting with the United Kingdom, took command of ISAF every six months. In 2003 NATO assumed responsibility for ISAF.[36] Its mandate was revised to cover all of Afghanistan, paving the way for ISAF's eventual growth.

The first expansion out of Kabul was to northern Afghanistan, completed by mid-2004. Germany provided the bulk of forces and accordingly assumed command of the newly established Regional Command (RC)-North. By mid-2006, ISAF assumed responsibility for operations in western Afghanistan, with Italy in command of RC-West. Nearly simultaneously, ISAF expanded its area of responsibility to include eastern and southern Afghanistan, a transition completed by late 2006. The United States contributed its forces and resources along the eastern border with Pakistan and therefore led RC-East. Regional Command-South was led on a trilateral rotational basis, alternating every six months between the UK, Canada, and the Netherlands.

In order to better command and control the temporary "surge" of US Marines flowing into southern Afghanistan, in 2010 ISAF created RC-Southwest. By the end of 2010, the United States was leading three of the six regional commands. Over time, the number of coalition partners contributing to ISAF steadily increased until eventually it comprised approximately 133,000 troops from 50 nations.[37] Gradually the "RC" system of command and control in Afghanistan led to the formation of coalitions-within-coalitions; as a result, at its height, ISAF itself consisted of seven distinct coalitions (Capital, North, West, Southwest, South, East, and Afghanistan-wide).

Missing: Campaign Coherence?

These mini-coalitions were forged through interactions between nations at operational—and in some cases strategic—levels. At the operational level the dynamics between the different regional commands varied considerably. For example, the level and type of threats faced by the nations in RC-North were markedly different from those in RC-South. This led in turn to differing interpretations of how best to implement ISAF's mandate between the various regional commands.

One notable example was the debate over "counterinsurgency" (COIN) versus the "comprehensive approach." As the insurgency began heating up between 2006 and the end of 2008, nations operating in southern Afghanistan began arguing for the delivery of a greater degree of aggressive tactical-level patrolling and blended civilian-military assistance at local levels—in other words, an operational approach informed by counterinsurgency principles. The assessment of those operating in northern Afghanistan, by contrast, was still that aggressive patrolling of this kind was not necessary because the operating environment in that part of the country was deemed relatively permissive. This style of campaign management was called the "comprehensive approach." While the main difference between the two terms was rooted in the relative roles and missions of civilian versus military actors on the ground, these notions of which kind of actor was most suitable to lead a country's operations on the ground were arguably influenced by different conceptions of the timescales in which progress would be made during the campaign. A civilian-led "comprehensive approach" was more akin to traditional peacekeeping, whereby coalition and Afghan forces could take a more indirect, passive, and longer-term approach to campaign management. Counterinsurgency, by contrast, was more militarily aggressive; while its proponents recognized that political and civilian leadership was critical to campaign success, the military was the primary instrument for eradicating challenges to the Kabul-based Afghan government.[38]

The practical upshot was that nations within a particular regional command were often (although not always) more likely to agree on a given operational approach than those in different ones. This, of course, had implications for campaign design and rules of engagement, with states operating in southern Afghanistan—where the "closer" fight was located—generally arguing for more permissive rules of engagement for the overall campaign than their counterparts in the north. It also led to problems in bringing the whole campaign together at the country-wide level; the differences in approach led to "seams" in the coalition that ISAF's adversaries were able to exploit. For example, in 2011, forces opposed to the Government of Afghanistan infiltrated the north, and in particular Kunduz.[39] This eventually led to the "Kunduz" incident in 2015, in which more than 142 people, many not believed to be combatants, were killed during a major battle between the Taliban and Government of Afghanistan forces.[40]

Complicating matters quite significantly, the coalitions comprising ISAF were not the only ones operating in Afghanistan at that time. Although many of its details remain classified, Operation Enduring Freedom existed alongside ISAF, initially performing two primary missions: Afghan National Defense and Security Forces (ANDSF) training, and "black" counterterrorism operations. And it was the latter that led to stark instances of civilian casualties that were aggravating strategic-level relations between the Government of Afghanistan and NATO/ISAF. This contributed to a growing concern among senior policymakers that campaign incoherence and the lack of unity of command were undermining the coalition's ability to achieve its objectives.

Serious efforts were undertaken in 2009 to bring coherence to the ISAF and OEF missions, leading to the transfer of the security force training mission to ISAF, and the "dual-hatting" of the US four-star general then in theater, General McChrystal. Full integration of the two operations at the time was deemed impossible owing to allied objections to conflating ISAF's stability operations mission with OEF's counterterrorism operations.[41] It was therefore believed that dual-hatting COMISAF as COMOEF would bring more operational coherence to the ongoing efforts in Afghanistan, primarily by improving command and control over special operations forces in theater.[42]

Yet, surprisingly, all these efforts to improve campaign coherence still fell short. In the first instance the US Marines deployed to Helmand province in 2009/10 designed their operational command-and-control arrangements to exist almost wholly outside ISAF. They reported instead to the Marine component command of United States Central Command, which in turn reported to COMCENTCOM and the commandant of the Marine Corps.[43] The Marines themselves were a part of the "surge" of 33,000 troops that began flowing into Afghanistan in late 2009 and were withdrawn in late 2012.[44] And while those Marines helped create a degree of stability in Helmand province within a very short time, the gains proved to be temporary. According to the Special Inspector General for Afghan Reconstruction, in 2018 and 2019 Helmand province was the location of the most enemy-initiated attacks in Afghanistan and also had some of the highest numbers of civilian casualties.[45]

Yet this move, while frustrating to senior leaders in both Kabul and Washington, ultimately pales in comparison with the failure to provide effective command and control to Afghan forces partnered with, and trained by, the Central Intelligence Agency. While details of their operations and composition are sensitive, as the *New York Times* reported in 2018:

> The [CIA-trained] units have also operated unconstrained by battlefield rules designed to protect civilians, conducting night raids, torture and killings with near impunity, in a covert campaign that some Afghan and American officials say is undermining the wider American effort to strengthen Afghan institutions.[46]

In other words, since 2001 Afghanistan has been the terrain for no fewer than nine distinct military campaigns, some of which appear to have been responsible for civilian casualties so significant that they threatened the overall success of international and coalition efforts in the country. And these examples focus only on the military; institutional silos between the military, diplomats, aid workers, and so on added still greater complexity and made coherence extraordinarily difficult. In any case the sheer number of distinct military operations—each with its own rules of engagement, risk tolerance, and different sense of temporality—presented an enormous command-and-control challenge and, as already noted, created seams across the campaign that adversaries were able to exploit.

The absence of campaign coherence raises a number of questions about the duration of the Afghanistan war. If there had been a shared sense of temporality and timeframes among the actors in these coalitions, might a more common operational approach have been adopted and implemented? Might these vulnerable seams across the different mini-coalitions have been prevented from emerging? Above all, if there had been a greater degree of coherence—and command and control—might the campaign have been brought to a swifter conclusion, thereby saving civilian lives?

Missing: Campaign Continuity?

Shortly after I became a policy officer for the ISAF campaign in the US Department of Defense, I was introduced to an Afghan saying about the war: "The coalition has the watches, but we have the time." The admonition was clear: US and coalition forces were in a hurry to make progress (whatever that meant) but the Afghans—and adversaries—on the ground could easily just wait us out. It was a powerful reminder of the clash of temporalities between the coalition and the Afghans themselves.

Yet getting into the nuts and bolts of the operation, it soon became clear that there was another implication to the saying: this desire to make progress and declare victory quickly was reinforced at a tactical level. As one observer of the Afghan campaign noted, "The modern COIN forces are like aliens parachuting in and staying only for short rotations with no sense of the landscape."[47] Within the US system, commanders and their military units would deploy to Afghanistan and within a month of their arrival would usually assess that the conditions in their area of responsibility were dire. The stoplight chart—a map depicting whether conditions were good (green), bad (red), or somewhere in between (yellow)—was invariably covered in red. By the end of their tours, however, that stoplight chart was largely green. A new commander would take over and the cycle would continue.[48] This is why many observers remarked at the time that ISAF at the time had waged ten one-year campaigns rather than one ten-year campaign.[49]

Many other coalition partners—Canada, for example—had shorter, six-month tours in Afghanistan, which further compounded the temporality problem. The main US solution at the time was to extend tour lengths from nine to twelve months.[50] Yet this did not necessarily address the stoplight chart problem. The view at the time was that, because commanders are generally evaluated according to whether they are able to make progress in their respective missions, campaign continuity was in tension with inherent human bias, whereby commanders were generally predisposed to see the accomplishments of their predecessors negatively and evaluate their own accomplishments favorably. Given how difficult it was to measure progress in the Afghan campaign in a meaningful way, it was also difficult to assess whether those commanders were right or wrong, but it certainly created significant opportunities for disjuncture between deployments.[51]

To be fair, efforts were made to address this issue of context and continuity. The United States initiated "Af-Pak Hands"—a program of intensive training on Afghanistan and Pakistan followed by several deployments to the region—in order to improve the quality of advice given to commanders in theater.[52] While the program was initially hailed as a success,[53] it became a "retention nightmare," which is a fundamental challenge for a program that has long-term personnel commitments as its core requirement.[54] After significant criticism, the program is being discontinued in 2020.[55]

The absence of campaign continuity meant it was very difficult to bring together these efforts over time. This was inherently problematic as, according to the US government's own counterinsurgency manual, such operations are of long duration.[56] Once again the issue of multiple temporalities—tactical short term versus strategic long term—comes into play and raises the question as to whether the campaign was unnecessarily prolonged, and the risk of civilian harm inherently exacerbated as a result.

Missing: Coherent Strategy?

The lack of campaign coherence necessarily affected strategy too. If we define strategy as the alignment of ends (goals), ways (methods), and means (resources), then applied to Afghanistan one cannot help but wonder whether well-documented mismatches and shortcomings between these three dimensions of strategy have also been a contributing factor to civilian casualties.[57] How can a campaign's goals be successfully accomplished if the ends, ways, and means to do so frequently shift to the point of incoherence?

Ends

George Harrison, borrowing from Lewis Carroll, once quipped: "If you don't know where you're going, any road will take you there." This is how it has apparently gone with the campaign in Afghanistan. Although NATO and its member states have, on various occasions, attempted to bring strategic coherence to the international assistance effort, at a fundamental level the different stakeholders have had different views on their exact purpose for being there, and the timeframes in which strategic aims could be accomplished. And some statements on behalf of the coalition arguably have contradicted, or at least confused, other statements made by ISAF participant states and by NATO ISAF member states themselves. For example, in 2008 the latter argued at Bucharest:

> Our vision of success is clear: extremism and terrorism will no longer pose a threat to stability; Afghan National Security Forces will be in the lead and self-sufficient; and the Afghan Government will be able to extend the reach of good governance, reconstruction, and development throughout the country to the benefit of all its citizens.[58]

Yet in 2009 President Barack Obama argued that it was the United States' core goal to "disrupt, dismantle and defeat al Qaeda in Pakistan and Afghanistan, and to prevent their return to either country in the future."[59]

Despite diplomatic attempts to underscore that there was no daylight between the US and NATO positions, the fact of the matter is that the leader of the NATO ISAF coalition was bringing a fundamentally different emphasis to its activities in Afghanistan, bringing in the former Joint Special Operations Commander (JSOC), General McChrystal, in order to implement President Obama's vision, and, as noted above, authorizing the temporary "surge" of forces into Afghanistan. In still another contrast, some NATO member states, Germany for example, emphasized the humanitarian aspects of the mission for much of the campaign; its narratives underscored that German forces were deployed to Afghanistan to create a shield under which reconstruction activities could take place.[60]

Was the mission reconstruction a long-term endeavor? Was it empowerment of the Government of Afghanistan? Was it counterterrorism—a more tactical, short-term activity? Was it all three? As Doug Lute, a former White House official responsible for the wars in Iraq and Afghanistan, observed: "We were devoid of a fundamental understanding of Afghanistan—we didn't know what we were doing. . . . What are we trying to do here? We didn't have the foggiest notion of what we were undertaking."[61] The answer to this question continues to vary, and as a result developing and implementing a theory of victory for Afghanistan remains elusive.[62] Indeed the only common ground between the Taliban and the United States is that neither side wants American troops in Afghanistan any longer. This leads to an obvious point: without an understanding of how to terminate the war (in fact the Taliban offered to surrender in 2001 and 2003), or what success looks like in that country, the war has continued well beyond anybody's expectations at the outset of the campaign. And so too have civilian casualties.

Ways

Given the variety of different concepts of the goals for the campaign in Afghanistan, it is hardly surprising that the ways in which states have sought to accomplish their goals have also varied. Yet with the transition from ISAF to the current campaign, Resolute Support and its US-led counterpart, Operation Freedom's Sentinel, the main efforts now appear to be fairly straightforward: training and advising the Afghan National Defense and Security Forces through Resolute Support, and counterterrorism operations through Sentinel.

Achieving the tactical-level objectives of both these operations requires speed. With respect to the ANDSF training mission, the stated goal has been to field a sufficiently large, sufficiently competent security force capable of protecting territory controlled by the Government of Afghanistan. Yet attrition has been a persistent problem with both the Afghan National Army and the Afghan National Police. This means that the de facto goal for Resolute

Support has been to train and field ANDSF rapidly enough to take account of that attrition. Accordingly the prevention of civilian casualties and the importance of civilian protection has constantly been given short shrift by NATO ISAF trainers. One can hardly blame the trainers; in 2010 at least, Afghans were given only six weeks of training before being sent to the front lines.[63] Prioritizing the rapid fielding of ANDSF has been inherently in tension with the goal of building a sustainable, capable security force that can prevent civilian harm. This ended up having massive impacts on the overall campaign; ANDSF were widely reported to be corrupt and predatory, which alienated local Afghans from the government in Kabul.[64]

With respect to Resolute Support, its operational approach to counterterrorism appears to emphasize the elimination of actors that could pose a threat to the United States and its allies—including the Government of Afghanistan—before they can actually realize those threats. Time is of the essence. Yet by making speed the primary way of accomplishing counterterrorism objectives, this aspect of the campaign appears to be more like "whacking a mole" or "mowing the grass" than anything more durable. And the necessity for speed can lead to significant civilian casualties, as the most recent incident with the pine nut farmers tragically demonstrated. Here once again the priority that the coalition has placed upon speed is inherently in tension with the goal of preventing civilian casualties. Minimizing civilian harm takes time, careful planning, rigorous training, and careful management—all factors that have at times been absent during tactical counterterrorism operations, when speed is essential.

Means

The primacy of the military in the Afghan campaign has naturally led to the problems in Afghanistan being framed in a manner that requires a military solution. Yet in the best of circumstances, military forces can only do so much in the absence of political objectives that they can pursue. In any case, experiences in countering violent extremism (CVE) in other theaters have suggested to some observers that they may not always be the appropriate instrument to take the lead in addressing the problem of terrorist groups and insurgencies in a meaningful way.[65] This is because the underlying factors that might cause individuals to join terrorist groups are rooted in complex local societal and governance dynamics.

Yet despite our admonitions that these problems do not lend themselves to military solutions, nonmilitary CVE efforts are dwarfed by those conducted by the military, in terms of both resources and personnel.[66] With respect to the Afghanistan campaign, coordination between civilian actors and the military was notoriously fraught and not synchronized, adding another dimension to the coherence challenge.[67] It is therefore hardly surprising that civilian casualties persist; when the military remains the primary instrument to accomplish an objective, civilian casualties often follow. All this means recent US decisions to curtail aid expenditures to Afghanistan significantly are particularly tragic.[68]

Conclusions

The above discussion suggests that despite efforts to strengthen and promulgate the norms of civilian protection during military campaigns, the strategic and operational sloppiness with which the Afghan campaign has been conducted may have actually prolonged that war, leading to the loss of more noncombatant lives. Moreover clashes of temporalities—between short, speedy tactical operations and longer-term strategic imperatives, and among the coalition allies—appear to be related to these issues of mismanagement. Yes, the adversaries of the Afghan government have had a vote, and yes, they are responsible for unspeakable violence. Yet the behavior of these belligerents does not exonerate the United States and its partners from their own real normative shortcoming: the failure to treat the Afghan campaign with the strategic-level seriousness it requires. The price of this carelessness has been the loss of innocent lives.

It is with this in mind that efforts to prevent civilian casualties, however admirably intentioned, can take a darker turn. By making ourselves feel better that we are prosecuting wars as cleanly as possible, are we making it easier to fail in demanding answers to the more fundamental issues of campaign strategy and management: why are we there in the first place, in what timeframes should we reasonably expect progress, and how we can achieve our goals? And so, almost twenty years after the United States initiated hostilities in Afghanistan, Afghan civilian lives are still in the balance. Reflection upon our own damaging behavior and the role of clashing temporalities is required if we are to avoid making the same preventable mistakes in the future.

NOTES

1. Kathleen J. McInnis served in the Pentagon from 2006 to 2009 and currently serves as Specialist, International Security at the Congressional Research Service. All views are solely those of the author and do not necessarily reflect the views of either the Congressional Research Service or the United States Government.

2. Center for Civilians in Conflict, "The Sum of All Parts: Reducing Civilian Harm in Multinational Coalition Operations," January 23, 2019, p. 8.

3. International Security Assistance Force Headquarters, "Tactical Directive," July 6, 2009; Theo Farrell and Rudy Chaudhuri, "Campaign Disconnect: Operational Progress and Strategic Obstacles in Afghanistan, 2009–2011," *International Affairs*, vol. 87, no. 2 (March 2011), pp. 271–96. at p. 273.

4. Harry D. Tunnell IV, "Open Door Policy—Report from a Tactical Commander," Memorandum for the Honorable John McHugh, Secretary of the Army, August 20, 2010.

5. Radio Free Europe, "Petraeus Clarifies Rules to Avoid Civilian Casualties," August 4, 2010.

6. White House Official, "Remarks before the Advise and Assist Brigade Conference," Pinehurst, NC, July 2009.

7. General Counsel of the Department of Defense, "Department of Defense Law of War Manual," December 2016, p. 1047.

8. Christopher D. Kolenda, Rachel Reid, Chris Rogers, and Marte Retzius, "The Strategic Costs of Civilian Harm: Applying Lessons from Afghanistan to Current and Future Conflicts," Open Society Institute, June 2016, www .opensocietyfoundations.org/uploads/1168173f-13f9-4abf-9808-8a5ec0a9e4e2/ strategic-costs-civilian-harm-20160622.pdf.

9. It should be noted that civilian casualties are difficult to capture accurately and to account for, as they are often plagued with methodology and attribution problems. Further, while the United States goes to considerable lengths to verify civilian casualties, many other battlefield belligerents do not. Most figures should therefore be viewed with caution.

10. Ahmad Sultan and Abudl Qadir Sediqi, "U.S. Drone Strike Kills 30 Pine Nut Farm Workers in Afghanistan," Reuters, September 19, 2019, www.reuters .com/article/us-afghanistan-attack-drones/u-s-drone-strike-kills-30-pine-nut -farm-workers-in-afghanistan-idUSKBN1W40NW.

11. Department of Defense, *Annual Report on Civilian Casualties in Connection with United States Military Operations in 2017*, p. 3.

12. Emphasis added. Christopher D. Kolenda as quoted in Kolenda and others, "The Strategic Costs of Civilian Harm," p. 3.

13. See, for example, Gregory A. Raymond, "Problems and Prospects in the Study of International Norms," *Mershon International Studies Review*, vol. 41, no. 2 (November 1997), pp. 205–45; Martha Finnemore and Kathryn Sikkink, "International Norm Dynamics and Political Change," *International Organization*, vol. 52, no. 4 (1998), pp. 887–917; Thomas Risse and Kathryn Sikkink, "The

Socialization of International Human Rights Norms into Domestic Practices: Introduction," in *The Power of Human Rights: International Norms and Domestic Change*, edited by Thomas Risse, Stephen C. Ropp, and Kathryn Sikkink, Cambridge Studies in International Relations 66 (Cambridge University Press, 1999), pp. 1–38; Nina Tannenwald, *The Nuclear Taboo: The United States and the Non-use of Nuclear Weapons Since 1945*, Cambridge Studies in International Relations 87 (Cambridge University Press, 2007).

14. Theo Farrell, *The Norms of War: Cultural Beliefs and Modern Conflict* (Boulder, CO: Lynne Rienner Publishers, 2005).

15. See, for example, Neta C. Crawford "Just War Theory and the US Counterterror War," *Perspectives on Politics*, vol. 1, no. 1 (2003): pp. 5–25; Mark Evans, ed., *Just War Theory: A Reappraisal* (London: Palgrave Macmillan, 2005); Michael Walzer, *Just and Unjust Wars* (New York: Basic Books 1991), p. 158.

16. For example, the 1864 Geneva Convention, the 1949 Geneva Conventions, and the 1977 Additional Protocol II.

17. Christopher Coker. *Globalisation and Insecurity in the Twenty-first Century: NATO and the Management of Risk* (Routledge, 2014); Christopher Coker, *Humane Warfare* (Routledge, 2003); Mary Kaldor, *New and Old Wars: Organised Violence in a Global Era* (John Wiley & Sons, 2013).

18. Loren de Jonge Schulman, "Weird Birds: Working Paper on Policymaker Perspectives on Unmanned Aerial Vehicles and their Impact on National Security Decision-Making," Center for a New American Security, April 2018; Michael J. Boyle, "The Costs and Consequences of Drone Warfare," *International Affairs*, vol. 89, no. 1 (2013), pp. 1–29; Medea Benjamin, *Drone Warfare: Killing by Remote Control* (London: Verso Books, 2013); Ryan J. Vogel, "Drone Warfare and the Law of Armed Conflict," *Denv. J. Int'l L. & Pol'y*, vol. 39 (2010), p. 101.

19. Rahim Faiez and Kathy Gannon, "UN Says US Strikes Cause Civilian Casualties in Afghanistan," Associated Press, October 9, 2019.

20. See, for example, Kathy Gannon, "Anger Grows at Civilian Deaths by U.S., Afghan Forces," Associated Press, October 6, 2019, www.militarytimes.com/flashpoints/2019/10/06/anger-grows-at-civilian-deaths-by-us-afghan-forces/; Charles P. Pierce, "How Many Future Terrorists Did We Create Yesterday?," *Esquire* (online), September 19, 2019.

21. Editorial Board, "The Moral Injury of Pardoning War Crimes," *New York Times*, November 22, 2019; David Barno, as quoted in Anna Mulrine Grobe, "Does Trump's Navy SEAL Pardon Undermine Military Justice?," *Christian Science Monitor*, November 27, 2019; Finnemore and Sikkink, "International Norm Dynamics and Political Change."

22. Faiez and Gannon, "UN Says US Strikes Cause Civilian Casualties in Afghanistan": "A U.N. report released on Wednesday criticized American airstrikes earlier this year against alleged drug facilities in Afghanistan, saying they were unlawful and caused significant civilian casualties. . . . In a two-page rebuttal to the U.N. report, the U.S. military said the May strikes followed a year-long intelligence operation to locate and monitor the drug labs. The strikes took place in

daytime, to allow for effective identification of those entering and leaving the area, it said." See also Finnemore and Sikkink, "International Norm Dynamics and Political Change."

23. Colin H. Kahl, "In the Crossfire or the Crosshairs? Norms, Civilian Casualties, and US Conduct in Iraq," *International Security,* vol. 32, no. 1 (2007), pp. 7–46.

24. Headquarters, Department of the Army, "ATP 3-07.6 Protection of Civilians," October 2015.

25. The White House, "Executive Order 13732 United States Policy on Pre- and Post-Strike Measures to Address Civilian Casualties in U.S. Operations Involving the Use of Force," July 1, 2016.

26. The eight areas listed in legislation are: (1) uniform processes and standards across the combatant commands for accurately recording kinetic strikes by the United States military; (2) the development and dissemination of best practices for reducing the likelihood of civilian casualties from United States military operations; (3) the development of publicly available means, including an Internet-based mechanism, for the submittal to the United States Government of allegations of civilian casualties resulting from United States military operations; (4) uniform processes and standards across the combatant commands for reviewing and investigating allegations of civilian casualties resulting from United States military operations, including the consideration of relevant information from all available sources; (5) uniform processes and standards across the combatant commands for—(A) acknowledging the responsibility of the United States military for civilian casualties resulting from United States military operations; and (B) offering ex gratia payments to civilians who have been injured, or to the families of civilians killed, as a result of United States military operations, as determined to be necessary by the designated senior civilian official; (6) regular engagement with relevant intergovernmental and nongovernmental organizations; (7) public affairs guidance with respect to matters relating to civilian casualties alleged or confirmed to have resulted from United States military operations; and (8) such other matters with respect to civilian casualties resulting from United States military operations as the designated senior civilian official considers appropriate.

27. U.S. Public Law 115-232, Section 936.

28. The Joint Staff, "Joint Publication 3-0 Joint Operations," January 17, 2017, Incorporating Change October 22, 2018, p. III-46. Emphasis added.

29. United States Department of Defense, *Annual Report on Civilian Casualties in Connection with United States Military Operations in 2018?,*" April 29, 2019.

30. Missy Ryan, "After Bloody Insurgent Wars Pentagon Launches Effort to Prevent Civilian Deaths," *Washington Post,* February 4, 2019.

31. Marla Keenan and Victoria Holt, "Preparing to Protect: Advice on Implementing NATO's Protection of Civilians Policy," *NATO Allied Command Transformation OPEN Publications,* July 2018.

32. NATO, "NATO Policy for the Protection of Civilians, July 9, 2016."

33. Hew Strachan, "Clouds of War and Strategic Delusions: Britain's Strategic

Outlook Requires Realism about the Kind of Conflicts We Are Prepared and Willing to Fight," *Standpoint*, February 26, 2020.

34. Vladimir Putin, "Remarks at the 43rd Munich Conference on Security Policy," *Washington Post* (courtesy of the Munich Conference on Security Policy), February 12, 2007, www.washingtonpost.com/wp-dyn/content/article/2007/02/12/AR2007021200555.html. Emphasis added.

35. Craig Whitlock, "The Afghanistan Papers: A Secret History of the War," *Washington Post*, December 9, 2019.

36. North Atlantic Treaty Organization, "Nato Isaf History" (www.isaf.nato.int/history.html), accessed October 16, 2016.

37. North Atlantic Treaty Organization, "Isaf Placemat Archives" (www.web.archive.org/web/20170622145156/http://www.nato.int/cps/en/natolive/107995.htm).

38. For further discussion of the differences between the two approaches, see Michael J. Williams, *The Good War: Nato and the Liberal Conscience in Afghanistan* (Palgrave Macmillan, 2011), pp. 106–09.

39. Mohammad Hamed, "Suicide Bomber Kills 30 as Afghan Violence Spreads," Reuters, February 21, 2011.

40. Zach Beauchamp, "Kunduz: The Taliban's Biggest Victory in Years, Explained," Vox, September 29, 2015.

41. Robert Gates, *Duty: Memoirs of a Secretary at War* (Random House, 2014).

42. Robin Schroeder, "Not Too Little, but Too Late: ISAF's Strategic Restart of 2010 in Light of the Coalition's Previous Mistakes," in Joachim Krause and Charles King Mallory IV, *Afghanistan, Pakistan, and Strategic Change: Adjusting Western Regional Policy* (Routledge, 2014).

43. Gates, *Duty*.

44. Rajiv Chandrasekaran, "The Afghan Surge Is Over: So Did It Work?," *Foreign Policy*, September 25, 2012.

45. Special Inspector General for Afghan Reconstruction, *SIGAR Quarterly Report*, January 30, 2020, pp. 69 and 71.

46. Mujab Mashal, "CIA's Afghan Forces Leave a Trail of Abuse and Anger," *New York Times*, December 31, 2018.

47. Isaiah Wilson, as quoted by Jeff Eggers, "Lessons Learned Record of Interview, Special Inspector General Lessons Learned 01-00125," published by Craig Whitlock, "The Afghanistan Papers," *Washington Post*, December 9, 2019.

48. As one observer notes, "Commanders were regularly throwing out their predecessor's plans and priorities, even when both embraced COIN, which many [Commanders] didn't." Interview with Bob Crowley, Special Inspector General for Afghan Reconstruction Lessons Learned Interview, 8/3/2016, as found in Craig Whitlock, "The Afghanistan Papers," *Washington Post*, December 9, 2019.

49. Heather Reed, "Wartime Sourcing: Building Capability and Predictability through Continuity," *Military Review*, May–June 2011, p. 62.

50. For example, a press release describing the extension of OEF units' rotations in Afghanistan stated: " 'These adjustments to our force flow strategy are an

important element in supporting the commander of ISAF's efforts to *develop greater campaign continuity* in regard to maximizing experience and stability in Operation Enduring Freedom,' said Lt. Gen. J. D. Thurman, the U.S. Army's deputy chief of staff for operations." Emphasis added. US Department of Defense, "Army Announces New Afghanistan Troop Rotation," press release no. 679-00, September 3, 2009, https://archive.defense.gov/releases/release.aspx?releaseid=12949.

51. Anthony Cordesman, *Measures of "Progress" in Afghanistan in the Spring of 2012: The Need for Strategic Focus, Transparency and Accountability* (Washington, DC: Center for Strategic and International Studies), May 9, 2012, http://csis.org/files/publication/120510_Afghan_Military_Progress.pdf.

52. Chairman of the Joint Chiefs of Staff, Afghanistan/Pakistan Hands (APH) Program, Chairman of the Joint Chiefs of Staff Instruction 1630.01B. While the version that is publicly available reflects revisions from July 2016, the program was initiated in late 2009, www.jcs.mil/Library/CJCS-Instructions/udt_46626 _param_orderby/Info/udt_46626_param_direction/descending/.

53. T. X. Hammes, "Raising and Mentoring Security Forces in Afghanistan and Iraq," in *Lessons Encountered: Lessons from the Long War*, edited by Joseph Collins and Richard Hooker (Washington, DC: National Defense University Press, 2015), p. 320, http://ndupress.ndu.edu/Publications/Books/Lessons-Encountered /Article/915950/chapter-4-raising-and-mentoring-security-forces-in-afghanistan -and-iraq/; Steven Heffington, "AFPAK to APAC Hands: Lessons Learned," War on the Rocks, January 7, 2014.

54. Major General Samuel C. Mahaney, Commentary: "The AFPAK Hands Program was a Retention Nightmare; It's Been Transformed," *Air Force Times*, August 20, 2018.

55. J. P. Lawrence, "A Decade Long Program to 'Turn the Tide' in Afghanistan Is Ending, Long after Military Shifted Its Focus," *Stars & Stripes*, August 17, 2019.

56. US State Department, *U.S. Government Counterinsurgency Guide*, January 2009, p. 12.

57. Doug Lute, "Lessons Learned Record of Interview, Special Inspector General for Afghan Reconstruction," as found in Craig Whitlock, "The Afghanistan Papers," *Washington Post*, December 9, 2019.

58. NATO, "ISAF's Strategic Vision," April 3, 2008.

59. The White House, "A New Strategy for Afghanistan and Pakistan," March 27, 2009.

60. Timo Noetzel, "The German Politics of War: Kunduz and the War in Afghanistan," *International Affairs*, vol. 87, no. 2 (2011), pp. 397–417.

61. Lute, "Lessons Learned Record of Interview."

62. Christopher Kolenda, "Slow Failure: Understanding America's Quagmire in Afghanistan," *Journal of Strategic Studies,* vol. 42, no. 7 (2019), pp. 992–1014.

63. The author raised this with senior leaders of the NATO Training Mission-Afghanistan in 2011. They shrugged, noting that although their leadership maintained that ANDSF training had to emphasize both quantity and quality, the reality was that quality came at the expense of quantity.

64. Andrew Legon, "Ineffective, Unprofessional and Corrupt: The Afghan National Police Challenge," Foreign Policy Research Institute E-Notes, June 3, 2009.

65. In an off-the-record interview with a US Agency for International Development official, the interlocutor noted that experience performing CVE/counter-Boko Haram missions in Africa suggests that appropriately targeted quick impact programs—such as putting in solar-powered lights in key community areas or providing sewing machines to local women—that empower local communities can turn noncombatants from tacit supporters to adversaries of extremist groups. "Off the record interview with US Agency for International Development Official," August 16, 2019. See also The White House, Office of the Press Secretary, "Fact Sheet: The White House Summit on Countering Violent Extremism," February 18, 2015; Michael Igoe, "20 Years After a Shocking Attack, US Aid Groups Grapple with Countering Violent Extremism," Devex, August 7, 2018.

66. For example, as of 2019 the US State Department had a total of 93 personnel assigned to the mission of Countering Terrorist Extremists/Countering Violent Extremism, and plans to allocate approximately $386 million towards such efforts in fiscal year 2020. By contrast, the Department of Defense has significant components of US Special Operations Command, a 4-star Combatant Command, focused on comparable missions. USSOCOM's FY2020 budget request was for $13.8 billion, and USSOCOM requested a force structure of 66,553 military and 6,651 civilian personnel. While State Department initiatives often do not require significant resourcing or personnel, the balance of civilian and military activities and resources appears skewed. United States Department of State, *FY 2020 Budget Justification*, p. 10; Andrew Feickert, "U.S. Special Operations Forces (SOF): Background and Issues for Congress," Congressional Research Service, March 28, 2019.

67. Olga Oliker, Richard Kauzlarich, James Dobbins, and others, *Aid During Conflict: Interaction Between Military and Civilian Assistance Providers in Afghanistan, September 2001–June 2002* (Santa Monica, CA: RAND Corporation, 2004).

68. Lara Jakes, "U.S. Cuts $100 Million in Aid to Afghanistan, Citing Government Corruption," *New York Times*, September 19, 2019. By contrast, the United States appropriated $4.9 billion in FY19 to support the Afghan Security Forces, many of which are viewed by observers as having significant problems with corruption themselves (on ANDSF corruption, see, for example, Special Inspector General for Afghan Reconstruction, *Reconstructing the Afghan National Defense and Security Forces: Lessons from the U.S. Experience in Afghanistan*, September 2017, pp. xiv, 131–41). Department of Defense, *Fiscal Year 2020 Overseas Contingency Operations Request: Afghan Security Forces Fund*, Office of the Under Secretary of Defense (Comptroller)/CFO.

SIX

Conflicting Norms of Intervention

When and How to Use Military Force?

NATASHA KUHRT

This chapter looks at the ongoing changes in and reinterpretations of the norms of intervention. It considers, first, the prohibition on the use of force, and its exceptions, and then issues related to self-defense and UN Security Council (UNSC) authorization, as well as the Responsibility to Protect (R2P). It seeks to answer two main questions: how does the West's understanding of these norms limit it in its use of force, and does it prevent the West from adapting to the changing pace of modern conflicts, while other interpretations by Russia or China and others enable them to adjust better?

Existing Norms on the Use of Force

The norm of non-intervention and the prohibition on the use of force at the heart of the UN Charter, while ostensibly intact, have been eroded to some extent by the fact that since the early 2000s international law has appeared to bifurcate into two spheres: UN Charter law and customary international law (based on state practice and *opinio juris*). This bifurcation has caused significant ambiguity and disagreements regarding the norms of intervention within the West, which is torn between two temporalities: a need for swift intervention to protect civilians, and a wish to avoid protracted armed conflict. The resulting indeterminacy of the norms relating to the use of force allows competitor states such as Russia to use legal arguments that mirror the West's in their interventions.

Discussions in the UNSC regarding whether to intervene in Iraq, when it was argued that there was law *outside* the Charter, have potentially undermined the norm. Moreover, the repeated use of force against Iraq by the ad hoc coalition in the run-up to the 2003 conflict had met with no real opposition or objection from other P5 members. However, it appears that forming a consensus on intervention among Western powers has become even more difficult since the operation in Libya, despite the fact that for many that intervention was viewed as R2P *par excellence*. The reasons for this difficulty are multiple, but one factor is that the apparent agreement on R2P achieved in 2005 was based on support for a diluted version that merely papered over divisions, not simply between West and non-West but also within the West itself. It is the indeterminacy surrounding the "settledness" of the norm of R2P that Russia and, to a much lesser extent, China have sought to exploit—in Russia's case by a form of mimicking or mirroring of Western justifications and argumentations. Arguably this may confer an advantage on Russia in terms of a readiness to intervene, while discussions in the West regarding the legitimacy of any intervention may slow down decision-making.

In addition the West's unwillingness to commit militarily in the wake of the campaigns in Iraq and Afghanistan, and then Libya, has further emboldened Russia in particular (in Crimea, eastern Ukraine, and Syria). Debate tends to focus simply on rejection or acceptance of R2P, but scrolling back to 2005 it is clear that the version of R2P accepted there was itself flawed, perhaps even "hollow," to use Aidan Hehir's term,[1] leading to uncertainty as to whether R2P could even be called a norm. In terms of international law, in fact, the absence of *opinio juris* and state practice would tend to rule out seeing R2P as a norm in the legal sense.

According to the UN Charter, force cannot be used except if "an armed attack occurs" and when Article 51, the right to self-defense, is activated as a result. However, debate on how to measure the gravity of an attack, and the rise of non-state actors, have called into question the scope of Article 51. The attacks of 9/11 already gave rise to a debate as to whether an armed attack could even emanate from a non-state actor (in this case al Qaeda), but these concerns were largely swept aside as the "Global War on Terror" gathered pace. They have, however, partly resurfaced as a result of the situation in Syria, although the norm on the prohibition of the use of force has to a large extent remained intact and been upheld in various cases brought before the International Court of Justice (ICJ). Moreover the US drone strike in early 2020 that killed Iranian general Qasem Soleimani, the commander of the Quds forces of Iran's Islamic Revolutionary Guard Corps and the second most powerful person in Iran, has raised fresh doubts and concerns regarding US unilateral use of force, particularly questions regarding both necessity and attribution of responsibility.

Further, force can be authorized, if the UNSC exercises its primary responsibility, deems that a threat to international peace and security exists (or that there is a breach of the peace or act of aggression), and authorizes enforcement action under Chapter VII of the Charter, under the auspices of collective security (there are numerous examples, including Iraq 1990; Somalia 1993; Haiti 1994). At the same time, there has been an increasing resort to peacekeeping operations (PKOs) where UN forces aim to ensure adherence to existing peace agreements but require the use of force that goes beyond mere self-defense, entailing the defense of the mandate by "all necessary means." These operations still take place theoretically with the consent of the host state. In these cases force is used tactically, and sometimes even strategically. Moreover, the move to stabilization missions—the Democratic Republic of Congo (DRC); Central African Republic (CAR); Mali—which seek to restore or support the "legitimate authority" in a given country and frequently involve counterinsurgency operations in parallel, has given rise to concerns regarding the corrosion of one of the three key principles of peacekeeping: impartiality.

The development of the R2P doctrine and the related emerging norm of civilian protection adds further complexity to debates on the use of force. In peacekeeping, the need to protect civilians has increasingly come into conflict with the need to ensure security and defend the mandate.

After the end of the Cold War and, with it, bloc voting in the UNSC, Russia, preoccupied with internal problems, appeared to go along with enforcement resolutions sponsored by the West, even those containing language that now spoke of *internal issues* as threats to international peace and security. Examples include the intervention in Somalia in response to a grave humanitarian crisis; the intervention in Yugoslavia in response to a civil war and grave violations of international humanitarian law; the need to restore the democratically elected government in Haiti, and to respond to genocide in Rwanda; and a whole host of "threats" which were all largely internal. Thus the notion of the threat to international peace and security had expanded dramatically. The environment in which many of the interventions took place required action under Chapter VII, by "all necessary means," and often without the consent of the host government.

China tended to abstain on these interventions, while Russia displayed increasing discomfort with the expansion of Chapter VII actions. China and Russia both resisted attempts to include human rights provisions in mandates; for example, both spoke out regarding the mission in Haiti to "restore the legitimately elected President and authorities of the government of Haiti."[2] In the end China did vote for the resolution, although Russia abstained, explicitly stating that human rights violations should not be viewed as threats to international peace and security.[3] However, this may miss the point that the UNSC has at times intervened in situations where the threat has begun as a "soft" one, for example in Somalia or Bosnia, but where humanitarian assistance could eventually only be delivered with the help of military force. It was this development that appeared to demonstrate for some an emerging norm of humanitarian intervention.

The next section focuses in more detail on this development, and the contested doctrine of Responsibility to Protect, but also discusses the growing trend for R2P to be mainstreamed into peace support operations in the guise of "protection of civilians."

Humanitarian Intervention and the Responsibility to Protect

Humanitarian intervention is not yet recognized as a norm, but is rather an exception to the use of force that remains very controversial. Even the intervention in Kosovo was deemed unlawful, although it was justified ex post facto as legitimate on ethical and moral grounds.

What is humanitarian intervention? Broadly speaking it is the use of military force to intervene in a state without the host state's consent, in order to avert or halt mass egregious human rights abuses. This has been described as a "right to intervene," in the words of Bernard Kouchner, the co-founder of Médicins Sans Frontières.[4] For those who take a strict interpretation of international law, intervention is prohibited, irrespective of the grounds, unless sanctioned by the UNSC. Few if any interventions under UNSC auspices can be termed humanitarian interventions in the strict sense of the word.

This brings us back to the problem of the UN Charter itself and the ambiguity of its wording. The Charter appears to commit to the protection of human rights in its preamble, and yet the Charter also strongly protects state sovereignty in Purposes and Principles, Article 2(4), whereby "members shall refrain from the threat or use of force against the territorial integrity or political independence of any state."[5]

The Development of R2P and the West (Kosovo to Iraq)

The Responsibility to Protect, which evolved as a result of the 1999 intervention in Kosovo, was initially viewed as a means to bridge the gap between non-intervention and sovereignty by reconceptualizing sovereignty as responsibility. In the 2001 Report on Intervention and State Sovereignty, clear criteria were set out for any intervention.

However, disagreement over Kosovo was already evident between West and non-West. But even within the West, making any generalization about "Western norms" of intervention is difficult, to say the least. Germany's foreign minister at the time very clearly stated that NATO's decision must not set a precedent; France took a similar line. The UK was rather less circumspect and under Prime Minister Tony Blair showed enthusiasm for drawing up criteria for intervention in situations of egregious human rights abuses, but there was lack of agreement on it within the UNSC. Yet there was resistance from other west European states, notably Germany, to the idea of setting out such criteria. And the United States was clear that it preferred not to set out any intervention criteria but rather to treat each case individually on its merits.[6]

In Kosovo a similar problem was encountered to the US airstrikes on Syria in 2017: aerial strikes were criticized for bombing targets from great heights and failing sufficiently to distinguish between combatants and non-combatants, resulting in an acceleration of ethnic cleansing of Kosovar Albanians. Moreover the campaign, widely expected by NATO to last only a few days, took far longer: 78 days, to be exact. As Adam Roberts points out, the issue of what sorts of military force or means were used to carry out the intervention in Kosovo was "bound to affect judgements about the legality of the operation."[7] In essence the effectiveness of an operation will influence perceptions of legality and legitimacy. The recently developed Western aversion to sustaining casualties, encapsulated in the use of bombing from great heights, led to widespread criticism of the campaign despite the initial support for it among the general public in the West.

The operation in Iraq is of course not usually seen as a humanitarian intervention, but it was also at times justified as such, whether (as argued by the US and UK) as either implied authorization via SCR 1441 or as "revived authorization" via Iraq's apparent breach of ceasefire resolution SCR 687, or by others as self-defense based on evidence of weapons of mass destruction. However, the overwhelming use of force and the lack of planning for the aftermath were generally held to be inconsistent with humanitarian intervention. Thus Tony Blair used R2P-type language in an attempt to legitimize the

Iraq intervention ex post facto: "we have a responsibility to act when a nation's people are subjected to a regime such as Saddam's."[8] The overall aim of the operation was to get in and out quickly, and the campaign was expected to be swift—General Tommy Franks optimistically foresaw a drawdown of US forces from 140,000 to only 30,000 by September 2003.[9] The US envisaged a warm welcome from the Iraqis, who would be grateful for their liberation from Saddam's tyranny, and then a swift handover to an Iraqi transitional government. This soon became a patently unrealizable objective.

Such attempts as Blair's to justify the intervention in humanitarian terms may already have helped to discredit the idea of R2P, even if Iraq was not explicitly described as an R2P operation. Moreover if we look beyond the binary of West versus non-West, a third category, of former colonial states, was particularly concerned by Western (Iraq, Afghanistan) as well as Russian (Georgia/ South Ossetia 2008, see below) invocations of R2P or humanitarian intervention as pretexts for military operations. While the objective was for R2P to be detached from the idea of humanitarian intervention, for R2P to "drive a stake through the heart of the term 'humanitarian intervention,' "[10] the results have been mixed. Many states in the "Global South" view R2P and humanitarian intervention as interchangeable, although the African Union has now incorporated R2P into its constitution. Russia also persists in conflating the two.

In the run-up to the 2005 World Summit at which all countries signed up to the R2P, a preparatory document that fed into the summit, the UN High-level Panel Report on Threats, Challenges and Change,[11] set out the need for the recognition of such a doctrine according to the 2001 International Commission on Intervention and State Security (ICISS) report. The high-level panel had set out criteria for intervention that were similar to the precautionary principles of the 2001 report (and remarkably similar to Just War theory). However, by the time of the 2005 summit these criteria were noticeable by their absence. The United States was particularly concerned to ensure that no legal criteria for intervention were spelled out.[12] As Michael Byers suggests, the Outcome Document did not create "any new rights, obligations or limitations for the Security Council, since the council already had the discretionary power to authorise force for the full range of human rights and humanitarian concerns." What it may have done was to create a new form of political leverage, as those who favored intervention could now "point to this collective statement of intent."[13]

Even before the 2005 summit, Iraq had again exposed cleavages, not just between West and non-West, but also regarding the use of force between, on the one hand, the United States, the United Kingdom, and Australia, and on the other Russia, China, France, and Germany. It was not clear, however, whether the norm of non-intervention had been eroded by the Iraq operation: some argued that the strong resistance to US and UK argumentation, and the fact that the operation had not been explicitly authorized by Resolution 1441 or a second resolution, left the authority of the UNSC largely intact rather than damaged.

R2P after the 2005 World Summit

By the time of the 2005 World Summit, then, when all member states affirmed the "existence" of a responsibility to protect, the doctrine had been so watered down that to call it a norm was almost devoid of meaning.

Further, even when there is agreement that the threshold for intervention has been reached, it does not follow that such an intervention will take place where political will is lacking: no one disputes the fact that there is a responsibility; the dilemma is rather how this should be implemented. This is in large part due to the fact that even where intervention under pillar three of R2P[14] could be justified, the focus is mainly on prevention in terms of nonmilitary means of discouraging and halting atrocities, with military force very much the last resort.[15] Because there are no enforceable obligations on states, even with the advent of R2P, the fact remains that, as before 2005, in the absence of political will nothing will be done. As discussed above, the 2005 World Summit Outcome Document[16] did not change the essence of the problem, as states merely reaffirmed their obligations under the UN Charter. While the 2009 debates in the UN General Assembly on implementing R2P have at times been held up as a key moment in the development of the norm, ultimately consensus was achieved only on the less contentious elements: as Aidan Hehir termed it, on the "lowest common denominator of R2P."[17]

The case of Darfur, from 2004 onward, illustrates the problem well. Although this was not a case of R2P in the sense of being an intervention mainly predicated on its invocation, there were elements of an R2P case to be made. Only a peacekeeping force was authorized (in 2006), however, rather than a strategic military force to avert ongoing atrocities, as in Kosovo. R2P was invoked only loosely, with UNSCR 1706 in 2006 referring back to the previous year's Resolution 1674 and the World Summit Outcome Document. As Michael Byers notes, however, "most governments, instead of rushing to participate in this new and legally robust mission, either ignored the authorisation or cited commitments elsewhere."[18] It should be noted further that a timely intervention had already been called into question in 2005, when the UNSC authorized a commission to investigate ongoing atrocities in Darfur, in order to determine whether these constituted genocide, or rather crimes against humanity, thus delaying deployment of a peacekeeping force. At the time, the UN Commission of Inquiry on Darfur[19] did emphasize that crimes against humanity were "no less heinous," yet this did not increase pressure for a timely intervention. The US insisted it was genocide, although as President George W. Bush stated at the time, this did not mean it would necessarily take action.

Libya and After

The Libyan case in 2011 revealed disunity on intervention. Deep disagreements within the EU meant it was unable to act. Germany in particular was reluctant to intervene militarily and ultimately abstained on the vote in the UNSC on Resolution 1973 ("all necessary means"), despite puzzlingly having originally set out plans for a no-fly zone. Germany saw big risks, anticipating large-scale loss of life, the possibility of protracted military conflict, and the impossibility of a quick, clean, military intervention.[20]

In a sense Germany was merely measuring a proposed intervention against the criteria that had originally been set out in the original version of R2P as proposed by ICISS; this differed from the "R2P-lite version" of 2005 in assessing whether there was a high chance of success. These precautionary principles had also been suggested ahead of the 2005 World Summit in the UN Secretary General's High-Level Panel Report,[21] but did not feature in the final version of the R2P doctrine at the summit itself.

One norm that is increasingly problematic and may potentially affect the West's ability to respond in a decisive manner in conflict situations is the emerging norm of "protection of civilians" (discussed in more detail in chapter 5 by Kathleen McInnis). This norm, often viewed as a "close cousin" of R2P,[22] appears to have strengthened, within the UN system at least, as the fortunes of R2P have waned. As Christine Gray notes, "reference to the protection of civilians has become routine after the experience of Rwanda."[23] The two norms have become more intertwined, and developed in parallel, but are very often conflated. As Mats Berdal suggests, the two debates overlap, but at the same time they are distinct.[24] This conflation is dangerous because it may allow countries that are less mindful of human rights concerns, such as Russia, to exploit the gray zone or ambiguity of these norms—what John Karlsrud terms "cognitive slippage."[25] It is important to recall that originally a "line in the sand" had been drawn between the R2P third pillar and peacekeeping operations. Countries contributing troops wanted a clear distinction made between consent-based peacekeeping operations and interventions under the responsibility to protect. Thus peace support operations would fall under the second pillar, the "prevention" pillar,[26] rather than the interventionist third.[27] It seems that at least some countries of the West wish to avoid becoming involved in another potentially protracted war, favoring taking a more long-term approach under pillar two instead of buying into the need for speedy (and, it was expected, brief) intervention under pillar three. This demonstrates a clash of temporalities for intervention within the West itself.

As with Iraq, the legality of the US strikes on Syria was also somewhat dubious, resting on the doctrine of "pre-emption," where force can be used to address an "imminent" threat. However, on the whole the international community has been less sanguine about accepting arguments based around a "preventive" use of force—that is, where imminence is reconceptualized as a threat that may not yet have crystalized. As Christine Gray notes, the US has developed a "very wide interpretation of imminence" that "does not require any imminence in time"[28] (another example of a similar interpretation might be the strike on Soleimani, mentioned above). This interpretation has generally been supported by the UK even though its parliament rejected a motion to intervene in Syria, once again signaling a reluctance to accept casualties after the Libya operations.

Russian Attitudes

Although Russia had been part of the original committee (ICISS),[29] tasked with elaborating this new concept, within a few years disillusion had set in. At the UN World Summit in 2005, along with China and other non-Western powers, Russia signed up to the idea of R2P, and in 2009 it supported an enhanced role for Protection of Civilians in UN peacekeeping. However, these minor normative shifts were not matched by Russian positions on a range of key votes in the Security Council over Zimbabwe (2007) and Myanmar (2008), or in the UN Human Rights Council over Sri Lanka (2009), as well as Syria later. In each case Russia cited its concerns over sovereignty to block international action in response to severe human rights abuses and conflict. These positions were largely an extension of earlier Russian opposition to overt military intervention by Western states in Kosovo and Iraq; Russia again cited those aspects of international law that prioritize state sovereignty as constraining any such actions.

The Libyan case appeared to highlight that Russia's approach to intervention differed from that of the West. However, it also showed that there was not a homogeneous view within the Russian elite. There was both opposition and support for intervention. Russia had initially agreed on the need to protect civilians: UN envoy Vitalii Churkin stressed the need to uphold general humanitarian values as a reason for abstaining from rather than vetoing the draft resolution.[30] Yet there was Russian disquiet regarding the imposition of a no-fly zone (which may have brought back memories of Iraq in the run-up to 2003, in particular regarding the vagueness and ambiguity of the scope of the use of force).

In the former Soviet republics, however, Russia's adoption of a different set of norms and practices with regard to sovereignty and intervention suggests only a partial adherence to the concept of universal international law. In response to what it viewed as security threats to its interests and to populations for which it felt a state-level responsibility, Russia intervened militarily in the South Ossetian region of Georgia in 2008, and subsequently engineered the secession of both South Ossetia and Abkhazia from Georgia, although their declarations of independence were recognized only by three other states. It became embroiled in conflicts in Crimea and eastern Ukraine in 2014–2015, supporting the secession and eventual annexation of Crimea in March 2014, and providing covert military support to armed separatists in eastern Ukraine. These actions appeared to be in clear contradiction to Russia's global position on international norms and legal frameworks of sovereignty.[31]

Here we might remind ourselves of the difference between Russian and Western interventions. If we assume that Russian interests in its neighborhood—in South Ossetia/Abkhazia and Ukraine (though not Syria)—are strongly linked to domestic concerns, this is different from Western intervention in Kosovo which, it has been suggested, was for the US and some Western states merely an "*ad hoc* operation to weaken Serbia and 'stabilise' the Balkans;"[32] that is, there was no real national value attached to it, although many strove to describe the Balkans as firmly located in Europe. These examples then served as valuable lessons for Russia's aggression in Georgia and Ukraine after 2008. It is argued that Russia, which has succeeded in exerting power through the exploitation and weaponization of the principle of self-determination by minority groups in the context of "passportization," has redrawn the distinction between legitimate intervention and foreign illegal involvement in another state's affairs.[33] Whether or not one agrees with this assessment, it is certainly the case that strong national interests may make an intervention more effective—an argument also made by Michael Walzer.[34]

Yet the most striking aspect of Russian behavior in South Ossetia in August 2008 and Crimea in 2014 is the way in which it has sought to hold up a mirror to the West by using similar legal arguments as justification for these interventions. On South Ossetia, Russia used the language of the responsibility to protect, arguing that it had a duty to protect Russian citizens from imminent genocide, and using passportization policies to effect this. Russia subsequently recognized South Ossetia and Abkhazia, apparently in response to the widespread recognition of Kosovo's unilateral declaration of independence in February 2008; indeed it had immediately warned that any rush to recognize Kosovo's move would mean Russia "invoking universal principles" with regard to South Ossetia and Abkhazia. In the case of Crimea, while ultimately incorporating the entity into Russia proper, rather than leaving it as a de facto entity like South Ossetia and Abkhazia, Russia—at least initially—specifically invoked the case of Kosovo. The 2010 ICJ advisory opinion on the legality of Kosovo's declaration of independence stated that it could not be deemed "either lawful or unlawful." Putin explicitly referred to both this and the 1998 Quebec ruling by the Canadian Supreme Court: the latter famously noted that "international law contains neither a right of unilateral secession nor the explicit denial of such a right,"[35] adding that the issue was ultimately a matter of politics rather than law.

Russia has thus confused observers by both criticizing Western actions that appeared to fall short of strict international legal justification (Kosovo; Iraq) and then carrying out its interventions with similarly flawed or dubious justifications (Georgia, Syria, Crimea). For Michael Ignatieff, "Putin is serving up a series of international law justifications that are parodic versions of some of the ones that he didn't like in the 1990s."[36] Does this "parody" serve a purpose? Perhaps. As Keir Giles notes: "the existence of mutually contradictory Russian narratives is not an inherent disadvantage as described in some Western analysis." Why? "As the main objective of these measures is to dazzle and disorient [the] Western public, running several parallel narratives is not a deficiency, but an asset and important feature of Russian strategic deception."[37]

Russia is continuing to see and use what is sometimes called "lawfare" (see also chapter 7 by Amelie Theussen and Peter Viggo Jakobsen), as a nonmilitary method, as part of a confluence of political, military, and legal options, as explicitly highlighted in the 2014 "Military Doctrine of the Russian Federation" and falling under the wider scope of the 2015 "Russian Federation's National Security Strategy."[38]

Russia participates only minimally in peacekeeping missions, but through its support for the regionalization of peacekeeping via the African Union and its insistence on involving regional organizations such as the AU in certain stabilization missions, it seeks to push back against Western involvement:

this has been particularly in evidence in Francophone Africa, where it has attempted to discredit France and its standing via propaganda campaigns and lobbying at the UNSC. Since Libya, Russia tends to see the West as conflating the two norms, using protection of civilians as an excuse for intervention. A Russian academic view of peacekeeping highlights the difference in approach:

> For the United States and many European countries, the goal of peacekeeping and conflict resolution is to protect individual rights and freedoms and to accomplish a "democratic transition" by replacing authoritarian regimes with liberal-democratic alternatives. For Russia as well as many other emerging powers, the goal of conflict resolution and peacekeeping is to preserve and strengthen the local state structures so that they can support law and order on their territory and stabilize the situation in the country and the region.[39]

Russia specifically criticized the UN stabilization mission in the CAR for its emphasis on human rights. At the time of discussions on renewing the mandate for the CAR, on which Russia abstained, it circulated an official note:

> in which we explained we could not support the linking of human rights issues to the protection of civilians, since the latter involves the use of force based on Chapter VII of the UN Charter . . . there can be no question of monitoring human rights with the use of force.[40]

In general, on the use of force Russia has both criticized the way in which international law has been stretched since 9/11 and simultaneously sought to exploit this "stretching." The fact that law is both a "legitimation of the powerful and a tool for resistance of the weak"[41] makes it particularly useful for states such as Russia that hope to challenge the dominant Western discourse.

In large part this mirrors the uncertainty since at least the mid-1990s regarding both the locus of authority for enforcement action and the justification for such action (in Just War theory: right authority, just cause), as well as the growing gap between legality and legitimacy that was crystalized by Kosovo but had been emerging since the intervention in Yugoslavia earlier that decade. It may be no coincidence that Russia's intervention in Syria was at the invitation of the Syrian government, which apparently conferred on it both greater legality and legitimacy. Although there is some controversy over whether a government may invite an outside power in to assist it in defeating non-state actors in what amounts to a civil war, no Western countries have seriously challenged Russia's right to help the Syrian government, given Assad's "invitation." This gives Moscow a certain strategic advantage in Syria.

China's Approach

China's commitment to sovereignty and its strong stance against secession-ism has been a central element of its domestic and foreign policies since 1949.[42] This has been strengthened by the continued movements for greater autonomy or outright secession in the borderlands of Xinjiang and Tibet. Non-interference remains a central tenet in Chinese foreign policy, but in the twenty-first century China's position has been challenged by two simultane-ous processes that have made its commitment to these norms more difficult to maintain.

On the one hand, the international community's increasing commitment to emerging norms such as R2P is challenging China's position on sovereignty and non-interference in the name of humanitarian ideals. While in many ways resisting such norm promotion, China has itself become more involved in the politics of third states, largely as a result of the "pull" factor of its own extensive overseas investments. The huge increase in the number of Chinese nationals working and living in different countries has also forced it to take a more active role in protecting its nationals overseas (see Ernst Dijxhoorn's scenario, chapter 8 in this section).

China appears to be increasingly enthusiastic regarding participation in UN peacekeeping missions as an opportunity to gain military experience in a global strategic environment, and given its investments in African countries, in particular, this is helping to contribute to regional stability.

China opposes robust mandates that risk compromising impartiality. As Peter Ferdinand notes: "For good or ill, [China] argues that if the SC be-comes bogged down in unsuccessful and never-ending peace-keeping opera-tions, where it is perceived to have intervened on one side rather than another, this diminishes the readiness of other governments to turn to it as the main and most authoritative place to resolve future international disputes. In this respect it represents a different perspective on the role of the UN in upholding global governance, because it does not seek so much to lead as to mediate."[43]

However, while this may have been true in 2013, China has since stepped up its peacekeeping activities, taking part in stabilization missions by, for ex-ample, sending combat troops to take part in the UN peacekeeping operation in Mali. The increasing Chinese deployment to PKOs means that the Chi-nese military (PLA) "can further develop its limited strategic power projection capabilities."[44]

In relation to R2P, views differ on the extent to which China has acqui-esced in the development of the R2P norm. Rhetorically China has largely been resistant to this emerging norm, with a UN ambassador warning that "while discussing the issue of protection of civilians in armed conflict, the concept of 'responsibility to protect' should continue to be approached with caution by the Security Council."[45] Moreover R2P as restated in the 2005 World Summit Outcome Document was specifically described by China as "a very cautious representation of the responsibility to protect . . . it is not appropriate to expand, willfully to interpret, or even abuse this concept."[46] Sarah Teitt argues that nevertheless we can see a shift in China's reaction to R2P. She notes, for example, that in situations where China has opposed Security Council resolutions on Sudan, it nevertheless played a key role in brokering the 2006 Addis Ababa Annan Plan to deploy peacekeeping forces in Sudan, and appointed a Special Envoy to Sudan. Similarly, although it vetoed a UNSC resolution on Myanmar, it played a key role in persuading the Myanmar government to provide a visa to UN Special Envoy Ibrahim Gambari.[47]

On the other hand—and this is the second ongoing process affecting China's approach—this increasing range of challenges to its own non-intervention norm should not be viewed as the "socialization" of China into liberal versions of sovereignty norms. Rather, as with some other international norms, it appears to be promoting its own, localized version of R2P, taking the central role of the state in R2P and prioritizing that element in its own reworking. In its 2011 position paper for the UN General Assembly, China did not address the R2P issue, but did address the notion of "protection of civilians," the phrase that came to the fore in the Libya crisis. In the paper it argued that "responsibility to protect civilians rests first with the government of the country involved. When providing assistance, the international community and external organizations should adhere to the principles of 'impartiality, neutrality and objectiveness,' obtain the consent of the host country, fully respect its sovereignty and territorial integrity, and refrain from interfering in local political disputes or impeding the peace process."[48] Chin and Thakur argue that its interpretation of R2P "is one way that China is shaping global norms and rules, interpreting Western Enlightenment principles through a Confucian lens of governance that stresses an essential unity between citizens and state, rather than giving primacy to human rights as claims against the state."[49] Thus although China's new global role may reformulate its commitment to "non-interference" in practice, it will continue to resist a cosmopolitan view of sovereignty derived from notions such as human security.

Moreover, although it has expressed concern over Russia's actions in the near abroad, China's opposition to Russian interventions in Georgia and Ukraine has been rather muted relative to its critique of Western-led inter-

ventions. This may reflect the fact that China also has developed more assertive policies in its own local neighborhood than its principled stance on
non-interference in the rest of the world might suggest. In no case has China
entertained the kind of military intervention seen in Russian policies, yet the
restraint of its critiques of Russia indicates a certain ambivalence in its response. While China's assertiveness in relation to its neighbors may not be as
new a phenomenon as media reports suggest,[50] its broader regional policies
suggest a new phase of foreign policy that seeks to build alternative institutions based on alternative norm sets in its immediate region.

India's Position

India has also played an important role in shaping sovereignty norms and
resisting many aspects of a more interventionist norm set developed since the
1990s. As a major player in UN peacekeeping, India has been persuaded to
support—sometimes reluctantly—a range of peacekeeping missions that reflect an increasingly interventionist mode of robust PKOs. For the most part,
however, at a global level India has strongly opposed the increasingly interventionist approach of the international community, through concepts such as
humanitarian interventionism, in the context of Kosovo in 1999, and later in
agreeing to the more formalized concept of R2P at the UN World Summit in
2005. But it has been reluctant to see the norm translated into practice, particularly where it involves military action without a UN mandate.[51] A strong
commitment to sovereignty remains central to Indian policy at a global level.

At the same time, although India shares with Russia such principles as respect for sovereignty, non-intervention, and non-interference (both actual and
verbal) in other states' domestic affairs, including opposition to democracy
promotion,[52] it has no desire to challenge the Western normative hegemony
head on. Indian policymakers do not want these norms and principles to
affect its cooperation agenda with the US. India has always been ambivalent
about non-intervention as its position has often been driven by the realist logic
of national interest rather than by inviolable foreign policy principles. For
example, its abstention from UNSC Resolution 1973 on Libya in 2011 demonstrated not so much an anti-Western stance but rather a desire, among other
things, to avoid angering its substantial Muslim population by appearing to
support Western interventionism.[53] New Delhi is most likely skeptical about
the premise of Western covert involvement in, and engineering of, events like
the Arab Spring or the "color revolutions" in the former Soviet states. If anything, India, as a peace-loving and hegemony-averse nation, might be un-

comfortable with Russia's advocacy of spheres of influence and its practical application of this advocacy through its interference in the Ukraine crisis and seizure of Crimea.[54]

India's policy toward Syria reflects its stance against any kind of military intervention.[55] It had earlier opposed the Iraq intervention, and also criticized NATO airstrikes on Serbia during the Kosovo crisis, saying they were a violation of the UN Charter. Already in October 2011 India had abstained from a draft UNSC resolution condemning Assad's crackdown on pro-democracy protests. The following August it abstained from a UN General Assembly resolution that expressed "grave concern" about the escalation of violence. The reason India gave for this decision was that the resolution referred to Arab League calls for Assad to step down and for UN member states to sever ties with Syria. India did vote in favor of a February 2012 UNSC draft resolution that would implement a peace plan proposed by the Arab League, but only after a call for Assad to step down was dropped.

The Perspective of the RIC States

Russia, India, and China meet annually as an "RIC" grouping, and are agreed on the need for a more "just and democratic multipolar international system" as well as rejecting "forced regime change from the outside in any country," while emphasizing the core principles of respect for state sovereignty and non-interference in the internal affairs of other states.[56]

While the RIC states appear to be converging in their views, in the area of peacekeeping the three main penholders, the US, the UK, and France, which craft the mandates for peacekeeping missions, are less and less in agreement over approaches. For example, regarding the Central African Republic, there has been disagreement between France and the US over the mission.[57] The former US national security adviser John Bolton warned that the US would no longer support peacekeeping missions in Africa that failed to make any progress. Concern has been expressed that China and Russia will seek to take advantage of US withdrawal to advance their own interests, for example to ensure access to mineral resources; notably, Russia deployed a private military firm to the CAR and has been providing military training to the government. It was, in addition, successful in persuading the UNSC to lift an arms embargo so that it could supply arms to the government forces in the CAR, while there have been accusations that Russia is also making contact with opposition leaders. This is similar to its strategy in Syria, where it seeks to present itself as a "revitalized great power, international mediator, humanitarian actor and effective counter-terrorism partner."[58] As Michael Kofman points out, in Syria, Russia was signing deals or ceasefires with some leaders, while others became more radicalized. Kofman cites Senator John McCain's assertion that "Russia presses its advantage militarily, creates new facts on the ground, uses the denial and delivery of humanitarian aid as a bargaining chip, negotiates an agreement to lock in the spoils of war, and then chooses when to resume fighting. This is diplomacy in the service of military aggression. And it is working because we are letting it."[59]

What is the overall effect of such practices? Peacekeeping operations can create, modify, and dilute established international norms. They define what appropriate practice can be, and in international law, chipping away at the margins threatens to embolden other states such as Russia and China. Sean Murphy has written about the fundamental interpretive differences between lawyers who see the *jus ad bellum* as protean, evolving, and enabling the emergence of new exceptions to the prohibition on the use of force, and those who see it as fixed, static, and restrictive of the use of force (as in Russia).[60] These views reflect fundamental disagreements between states, as shown by the considerable difficulties encountered by the NATO states in identifying a legal theory to justify their actions to protect civilians in Kosovo.

The withdrawal of the US from peacekeeping in Africa is matched by its reluctance to intervene elsewhere. This is an important point as the ineffectiveness of the airstrikes on Syria carried out by the Trump administration in 2017, for example, highlighted the problem of a reluctance to intervene and accept casualties (see also chapter 5 by Kathleen McInnis).[61] Thus in Syria, rather than the United States seizing on Russia's desire to get out, it was Moscow that took advantage of the US wish to see an end to the humanitarian catastrophe without having to intervene.[62] This demonstrates the stark contrast between the West's desire to avoid casualties and Russia's clear readiness to accept them to achieve strategic goals.

Conclusion

R2P will not guarantee that states will intervene to prevent another Rwanda, "not simply because R2P imposes no such hard obligation, but . . . because the requisite degree of global solidarity for sustaining an effective operation still does not exist."[63] The as yet underdeveloped regionalization of R2P, while promising in terms of the potential for more timely deployment, may not be the panacea that Western states are hoping for.

In 2009 UN Secretary General Ban Ki-moon admitted that the concept of R2P remained underdeveloped. He emphasized that "the responsibility to protect does not alter, indeed it reinforces the legal obligations of Member States to refrain from the use of force except in conformity with the Charter," and that "if principles relating to the responsibility to protect are to take full effect and be sustainable, they must be integrated into each culture and society without hesitation or condition, as a reflection of not only global but also local values and standards."[64] This is part of the problem: the call to "regionalize" R2P is more likely to result in an inconsistent application of the concept, and detracts from any idea of universality. It may not be possible to have it both ways. As the secretary general himself then cautioned in 2012, the national and international responsibilities that had been agreed to at the 2005 World Summit "must not be diluted or diminished through reinterpretation at the regional, sub-regional or national levels."[65]

The West itself is torn between a perceived need for speed, in that action for the protection of civilians needs to be committed to and conducted with urgency, and a desire to avoid war and additional interventions by focusing on the long-run perspective enshrined in pillar two of R2P. We need to acknowledge that the West's unwillingness to intervene has been exploited by actors like Russia who seek to challenge the Western liberal world order. Russia uses the West's own legal argumentation to highlight what it views as a dangerous stretching of the law. UNSC Resolution 1973 on Libya perfectly highlighted the ambiguity of much of what passes for international law. As Michael Byers observes, "the authorisations in Res 1973 gave space for different public positions concerning the permissible extent of force." This was very similar to UNSC Resolution 1441 on Iraq, which also reflected the difficulty in crafting UN resolutions to reflect the views of all UNSC members. For Byers, the "result is an intermediate one on the legal-illegal spectrum of military action: between the legal and the illegal, there is now the deliberately arguable." Ultimately this "gray zone" creates "a form of temporary conditional permission that can harden into legality or illegality depending on how contested facts are subsequently clarified."[66]

Finally, then, it is not so much that Russia and China have a different understanding of norms or international law, but that they (particularly Russia) have been able to exploit the indeterminacy and disagreement over many of these norms amongst Western powers in order to act "below the radar"—for example, in both Crimea and eastern Ukraine, Russia has used various forms of warfare to do so. China has not yet challenged the West in the same way, but its cautious proposals on the R2P, "responsible protection," indicate that if it takes a more active role in international affairs in the future, it may be more entrepreneurial regarding norms than one might have expected. Russia so far merely resists or "mocks" the norms.

Further, the West's unwillingness to accept the risk of civilian casualties—due in large part to the greater public scrutiny of Western states (see chapter 5 by Kathleen McInnis), as shown, for example, in the UK parliament's unwillingness to countenance intervention in Syria—means that states like Russia and China with lower levels of public accountability may be more likely to take risks. The "prevention" pillar of R2P is rightly emphasized, but this can also mean a failure to intervene in a timely fashion in situations where a delay may exacerbate a humanitarian crisis. As Thomas Weiss notes: "By the time that all the alternatives to military force have been explored, many of the people for whom humanitarian intervention is intended to save could be dead or have fled."[67]

Finally, the conflation of R2P and the norm of civilian protection in both peace support missions and enforcement missions has increased suspicion in countries like Russia or China regarding regime change. This, along with the general Western aversion to accepting risk in terms of civilian casualties, may put R2P in jeopardy in the longer term and allow Russia and China to take the initiative, where their national interests are clearer. The line in the sand that was drawn between peacekeeping and the third pillar of R2P needs to be reaffirmed and more clearly delineated. The 2005 "consensus" on intervention was nothing of the sort: it merely reflected an affirmation of pre-existing obligations, thus leaving room for the overstretching of the R2P that was seen in Libya. Work must be done to attempt to refashion a consensus, perhaps to elaborate the now abandoned criteria for intervention as envisaged by the 2001 Commission.

NOTES

1. Aidan Hehir, "The Responsibility to Protect: Sound and Fury Signifying Nothing?," *International Relations*, vol. 24, no. 2, (2010), pp. 218–39.

2. UNSCR, Resolution 940, http://unscr.com/en/resolutions/940.

3. Xinhuanet, "UN Mission in Haiti Should Not Be Excessively Involved in Human Rights Matters: Chinese Envoy," April 13, 2019, www.xinhuanet.com/english/2019-04/13/c_137972706.htm.

4. Gareth Evans, "The Evolution of the Responsibility to Protect: From Concept and Principle to Actionable Norm," in *Theorising the Responsibility to Protect*, edited by Ramesh Thakur and Michael Maley (Cambridge University Press, 2015), pp. 16–38, at p. 18.

5. *Charter of the United Nations and Statute of the International Court of Justice* (New York: United Nations, Dept of Public Information), p. 6.

6. Michael Byers and Simon Chesterman, "Changing the Rules about Rules?," in *Humanitarian Intervention: Ethical, Legal and Political Dilemmas*, edited by J. L. Holzgrefe and Robert O. Keohane (Cambridge University Press, 2003), pp. 177–204, at p. 195.

7. Adam Roberts, "NATO's 'Humanitarian War' over Kosovo," *Survival,* vol. 41, no. 3 (Autumn 1999), pp. 102–23, at p. 108.

8. Cited in Thomas Weiss, *Humanitarian Intervention: Ideas in Action* (Cambridge: Polity Press, 2007), p. 124.

9. Jeremy Greenstock, *Iraq: The Cost of War* (London: William Heinemann/ Penguin, 2016), p. 242.

10. Jacinta O'Hagan, "The Responsibility to Protect: A Western Idea?," in Thakur and Maley, eds., *Theorising the Responsibility to Protect*, pp. 285–305, at p. 300.

11. Report of the United Nations Secretary-General's High-level Panel on Threats, Challenges and Change, *A More Secure World: Our Shared Responsibility*, December 2004, A/59/565, http://www.un.org/en/ga/search/view_doc.asp.

12. Hehir, "The Responsibility to Protect: Sound and Fury Signifying Nothing?," p. 231.

13. Michael Byers, "International Law and the Responsibility to Protect," in Thakur and Maley, eds., *Theorising the Responsibility to Protect,* pp. 101–24, at p. 110.

14. Pillar Three states that: "If a state is manifestly failing to protect its populations, the international community must be prepared to take appropriate collective action, in a timely and decisive manner and in accordance with the UN Charter." See https://www.globalr2p.org/what-is-r2p/.

15. David Carment and Martin Fischer, "R2P and the Role of Regional Organisations in Ethnic Conflict Management, Prevention and Resolution: The Unfinished Agenda," *Global Responsibility to Protect*, vol. 1, no. 3 (2009), p. 267.

16. 2005 UN World Summit Outcome Document, https://www.unsceb.org/ content/2005-world-summit-outcome-responsibility-protect, accessed August 19, 2020.

17. Aidan Hehir, *The Responsibility to Protect: Rhetoric, Reality and the Future of Humanitarian Intervention* (Basingstoke, UK: Palgrave Macmillan, 2012), p. 120.

18. Byers, "International Law and the Responsibility to Protect," p. 112.

19. 2005 UN Commission of Inquiry on Darfur, https://www.un.org/ ruleoflaw/blog/document/report-of-the-international-commission-of-inquiry-on -darfur-to-the-united-nations-secretary-general/, accessed August 19, 2020.

20. David Curran, "The European Union and the Third Pillar," in *The Responsibility to Protect and the Third Pillar: Legitimacy and Operationalization*, edited by Daniel Fiott and Joachim Koops (Basingstoke, UK: Palgrave Macmillan, 2014), pp. 146–71, at p. 154.

21. Report of High-level Panel on Threats, Challenges and Change, *A More Secure World*.

22. Emily Paddon Rhoads and Jennifer Welsh, "Close Cousins in Protection:

The Evolution of Two Norms," *International Affairs*, vol. 95, no. 4 (July 2019), pp. 597–617.

23. Christine Gray, *International Law and the Use of Force*, 4th ed. (Oxford University Press, 2018), p. 324.

24. Mats Berdal, "United Nations Peacekeeping and the Responsibility to Protect," in Thakur and Maley, eds., *Theorising the Responsibility to Protect*, pp. 223–49, at p. 235.

25. John Karlsrud, "United Nations Stabilisation Operations: Chapter 7 and a Half," *Ethnopolitics*, vol. 18, no. 5 (2019), pp. 494–508.

26. Pillar Two states that: "The wider international community has the responsibility to encourage and assist individual states" in meeting the responsibilities of Pillar One.

27. Curran, "The European Union and the Third Pillar," p. 148.

28. Gray, *International Law and the Use of Force*, p. 236.

29. International Committee on Intervention and State Sovereignty, 2001.

30. Ministerstvo innostrannykh del Rossiiskoi Federatsii, Zayavleniye ofitsial'nogo prestavitela MID Rossii A.K. Kukhashevicha o situatsii vokrug Livii, [Ministry of Foreign Affairs of the Russian Federation, "Russia's Position on the Situation in Libya"], March 19, 2011.

31. Lauri Mälksoo, *Russian Approaches to International Law* (Oxford University Press, 2017).

32. Hakan Gunnerieusson and Sacha Dov Bachmann, "Western Denial and Russian Control: How Russia's National Security Strategy Threatens a Western-based Approach to Global Security, the Rule of Law and Globalization," *Polish Political Science Yearbook*, vol. 46, no. 1 (2017), pp. 9–29, at p. 18.

33. Ibid., p. 19.

34. Michael Walzer, *Just and Unjust Wars: A Moral Argument with Historical Illustrations* (New York: Basic Books/Harmondsworth: Penguin, 1992).

35. Supreme Court of Canada, Reference re Secession of Quebec, Case Number 25506 (August 20, 1998), https://scc-csc.lexum.com/scc-csc/scc-csc/en/item/1643/index.do, accessed August 20, 2020.

36. Michael Ignatieff, "Is the Age of Intervention Over?," Talk at Chatham House, March 19, 2014.

37. Keir Giles, *Handbook of Russian Information Warfare* (Rome: NATO Defense College, 2016), p. 58; emphasis added.

38. Gunnerieusson and Bachmann, "Western Denial," p. 15.

39. M. Bratersky, "Russia and Peacekeeping Operations: Conceptual and Practical Components of Russia's Policy," *International Organisations Research Journal*, vol. 13, no. 1, pp. 157–70, at p. 157.

40. S/PV8521-E-S/PV.8521, 8521st meeting of the UN General Assembly, Tuesday, May 7, 2019.

41. Christine Chinkin and Mary Kaldor, *International Law and New Wars* (Cambridge University Press, 2017), p. 565.

42. Allen Carson, "Helping to Keep the Peace (Albeit Reluctantly): China's

Recent Stance on Sovereignty and Multilateral Intervention," *Pacific Affairs*, 2004, pp. 9–27; Zhongying Pang, "China's Non-Intervention Question," *Global Responsibility to Protect,* vol. 1, no. 2 (2009), pp. 237–52; Sarah Teitt, "The Responsibility to Protect and China's Peacekeeping Policy," *International Peacekeeping*, vol. 18, no. 3 (2011), pp. 298–312, at p. 214.

43. Peter Ferdinand, *The Positions of Russia and China at the UN Security Council in the Light of Recent Crises* (European Parliament: Directorate General for External Policies, Policy Department, 2013), p. 14.

44. Pieran Wang, "China and the Third Pillar," in Fiott and Koops, eds., *The Responsibility to Protect,* pp. 78–97, at p. 82.

45. Cited in Natasha Kuhrt, "Russia, the Responsibility to Protect and Intervention," in Fiott and Koops, eds., *The Responsibility to Protect and the Third Pillar*, pp. 97–115.

46. Ramesh Thakur, "R2P after Libya and Syria: Engaging Emerging Powers," *Washington Quarterly,* vol. 36, no. 2, pp. 61–76.

47. Teitt, "The Responsibility to Protect and China's Peacekeeping Policy," p. 214.

48. People's Republic of China, "Position Paper of the People's Republic of China at the 66th Session of the United Nations General Assembly," September 9, 2011.

49. Gregory Chin and Ramesh Thakur, "Will China Change the Rules of Global Order?," *Washington Quarterly*, vol. 33, no. 4 (October 2010), pp. 119–38.

50. Alastair Iain Johnston, "How New and Assertive Is China's New Assertiveness?," *International Security*, vol. 37, no. 4 (2013), pp. 7–48.

51. Madhan Mohan Jaganathan and Gerrit Kurtz, "Singing the Tune of Sovereignty? India and the Responsibility to Protect," *Conflict, Security & Development*, vol. 14, no. 4 (2014), pp. 461–87.

52. Bernd von Muenchow-Pohl, "India and Europe in a Multipolar World," Carnegie Endowment for International Peace, May 10, 2012.

53. C. Raja Mohan, "India, Libya and the Principle of Non-Intervention," *ISAS Insights*, National University of Singapore, no. 122, 2011.

54. Mikhail Troitskiy, "Unable to Lead, Reluctant to Follow: Russian, Chinese, and Indian Approaches to Balancing and Bandwagoning with the West," *PONARS Eurasia* no. 334, 2014.

55. Indian Ministry of External Affairs Annual Report, 2017–18 on Syria, www.mea.gov.in/Images/amb1/MEA-AR-2017-18-03-02-2018.pdf.

56. Alexander Lukin, *Pivot to Asia: Russia's Foreign Policy Enters the 21st Century* (New Delhi: ViJ Books India, 2017).

57. Richard Gowan, "What the U.N. Peacekeeping Mission in CAR Reveals About Security Council Gridlock," *World Politics Review*, November 19, 2018, www.worldpoliticsreview.com/articles/26785/what-the-u-n-peacekeeping-mission -in-car-reveals-about-security-council-gridlock.

58. Natalia Bugayova and Darina Regio, "The Kremlin's Campaign in Africa: Assessment Update," Institute for the Study of War, August 2019.

59. Michael Kofman, "The Russian Quagmire in Syria and other Washington Fairy Tales," *War on the Rocks*, February 16, 2016.

60. Sean Murphy, "Protean Jus ad Bellum," *Berkeley Journal of International Law*, vol. 27, no. 1 (2009), pp. 22–52.

61. David Smith and others, "As Warplanes Return to Scene of Sarin Attack, Trump Defends Missile Launch," www.theguardian.com/world/2017/apr/08/syria -khan-sheikun-sarin-attack-strike-trump-views-unclear, *Observer*, April 9, 2017.

62. Kofman, "The Russian Quagmire."

63. Jonathan Graubart, "War is Not the Answer: The Responsibility to Protect and Military Intervention," in Thakur and Maley, eds., *Theorising the Responsibility to Protect*, pp. 200–21, at p. 209.

64. United Nations General Assembly, *Implementing the Responsibility to Protect*, 12 January 2009, www.un.org/ruleoflaw/files/SG_reportA_63_677_en .pdf, accessed January 11, 2019.

65. Hugh Glanville, "Intervention in Libya: from Sovereign Consent to Regional Consent," *International Studies Perspectives* (2012), pp. 1–18.

66. Byers, "International Law and the Responsibility to Protect," p. 114.

67. Weiss, *Humanitarian Intervention*, p. 104.

SEVEN

In the Shadows

The Challenge of Russian and Chinese
Gray Zone Conflict for the West

AMELIE THEUSSEN

PETER VIGGO JAKOBSEN

Over the course of the last decade, Russia and China have emerged as the foremost competitors to US American supremacy. In their attacks on Western primacy, these competitor states target the very foundations of the Western order and its underlying understanding and practice of war. Their actions aim to exploit the Western distinction between peacetime and wartime embodied in the existing normative framework for war by remaining below the threshold of war. This gray area between war and peace as distinct conditions is what gives this form of conflict its name: "gray zone conflict." Gray zone conflict creates a fundamental problem for the West because it limits the Western ability to use its superior military force against adversaries not playing by Western rules. This chapter analyzes these challenges, investigating why the West has difficulties responding to conflicts in the gray zone between peace and war, and what the West can do to address these challenges. It shows gray zone conflict as a clash of different temporalities: the strict Western distinction between wartime and peacetime, and the more comprehensive approaches by Russia and China that deliberately exploit this distinction.

The perceptions of what war is and how it is being fought are undergoing major changes, which affect the international normative framework regarding war and warfare. Nowadays, wars between major powers are not fought with conventional military means on an open and geographically limited battlefield. Instead, these wars are primarily fought in the shadows, with the involvement of non-state actors, on boundless battlefields encompassing all domains and potentially endless in time. This is not to say that other forms of war and conflict do not exist, where the violence crosses the threshold of armed conflict and inter- or intrastate wars ensue; these are addressed in other chapters in this book. Yet, for reasons explained below, much contemporary great power competition takes place in the gray zone. For the West the principal challenge of these conflicts is that they remain below NATO's Article 5 threshold—they do not easily trigger the collective self-defense clause at the heart of the Alliance, but they undermine the foundations of Western power: its liberal institutions, the existing normative order, and its supreme military might.

Clearly, the West also engages in this gray zone, as shown, for example, in the US use of drones outside active battlefields, the reliance on black operations by special operations forces, and the US/Israeli Stuxnet attack on Iranian nuclear centrifuges. Other actors, smaller states, and non-state actors make use of gray zone warfare too, but given the main theme of this book— the Western perception of time and its impact on continued Western military power—this chapter focuses on Russia and China as the foremost competitors to the US-led West. It argues that both states are able to expand their power by exploiting the strict Western distinction between peacetime and wartime enshrined in the normative order, which limits the West's ability to respond to such challenges by using its superior military strength. Moreover, the distinction itself prevents the Western mindset from taking an integrated approach. For the West to be able to address these conflicts, the effects of the strict wartime/peacetime dichotomy need to be clearly understood, and a revised understanding of what war looks like nowadays may be necessary.

The first part of the chapter looks at the reasons for the emergence of such gray zone conflicts and defines their common characteristics. It then analyzes the Western understanding of the distinction between wartime and peacetime. Wartime is the exceptional state in the existing normative order; and conflict has to reach a certain level of violence to trigger a shift from the peacetime paradigm to wartime. The perception and practice of great power competition and contemporary war are quite different in Russia and China, however: as the subsequent sections show, these states take advantage of this strict Western distinction to undermine Western power by exploiting the speed of attacks in the gray zone and slowing down a response by the West. The chapter ends with suggestions for how the West can ensure its ability to respond in a timely and adequate way to such challenges posed by gray zone conflicts, by recognizing the strengths of the distinction between wartime and peacetime and returning to the array of peacetime mechanisms that are already available.

Emerging Challenges to the Western Understanding and Practice of War

The dominant Western understanding of war has been heavily influenced by Clausewitz's thinking (see also chapter 2 in this volume, by Paul Brister). The dominant reading of Clausewitz interprets war as the threat and use of organized military force in pursuit of political objectives involving two or more actors. In this understanding, war is interactive and competitive; it is not one-sided slaughter of undefended victims. Just as it takes two to tango, it takes a minimum of two to fight a war. War is conceptualized as a collective activity undertaken on behalf of groups (tribes, ethnic groups, states), and it is usually defined as violent and highly intensive.[1] This interpretation was reinforced by the Western experience with "total" or industrial war—the Napoleonic wars, the two world wars, the Cold War confrontation with the Soviet Union.[2] The result is a preoccupation with major conventional war. Western militaries are primarily trained for and geared to deterring and fighting major conventional wars, as is evident in their education, doctrines, organization, and equipment.[3]

The organized, interactive of use of armed force in pursuit of collective political objectives is regarded as the essence or nature of war in this tradition. By contrast, the character of war is regarded as highly variable because it is a function of the contextual factors and the actors involved. Clausewitz characterized war as "a true chameleon" because of its constant adaption to the prevailing cultural, economic, political, social, and technological conditions.[4]

The West's contemporary understanding of war is, as noted, a product of its experience with major conventional wars from the Napoleonic wars until the first Gulf War in 1990–91, which was interpreted by many to validate this focus. Many of these wars were symmetrical confrontations between opponents fielding conventional (and after 1945, in some cases nuclear) forces against each other. The Western states thought and fought in similar ways and adhered to the same rules and norms related to the resort to armed force and conduct of war (*jus ad bellum* and *jus in bello*). But with the collapse of the Soviet Union, the symmetry characterizing these wars and confrontations disappeared. This created a fundamentally different context, in which the United States initially enjoyed unparalleled economic, technological, and military superiority that became clear for all to see in the one-sided victory by the American-led coalition in the first Gulf War. As Mattis and Hoffman have noted, the new situation created "a compelling logic for states and non-state actors to move out of the traditional mode of war and seek some niche capability or some unexpected combination of technologies and tactics to gain an advantage."[5]

The futility of confronting and fighting the United States on its own terms using the same understanding of war, its norms, rules, tactics, and weapons, has been the single most important factor characterizing war in the post–Cold War era. But it has interacted with the rise of new powers, notably China and India, the process of globalization, and the rapid development and diffusion of new technologies such as communications and missile technology, the cyber domain, and drones, that have given even small states and non-state actors greater destructive powers and global reach.[6] This interaction has given rise to profound changes in the character of war that scholars and practitioners are struggling to understand. The state of intellectual confusion is evident in the proliferation of new terms proposed to make sense of the process. They include terms such as asymmetric war,[7] cyber war,[8] fourth generation warfare,[9] gray zone conflict,[10] hybrid war,[11] irregular war,[12] new wars,[13] postmodern war,[14] unrestricted war,[15] war of the third kind,[16] and war amongst the people.[17]

Regardless of the term preferred, most post–Cold War attempts to understand the changing character of war highlight three features that challenge the predominant Western understanding of war. First, the strategic purpose of war is to achieve political objectives without triggering a superior (Western) conventional military response. While most thinkers believe that the threat and use of military force have continued to play an important role, they emphasize that war is increasingly about avoiding the use of force altogether, thus neutralizing the military instrument. Most hostile activities are conducted in the gray zone between war and peace, and below the threshold that would legitimate a military response in accordance with international law (see below).

This leads to a second point: the declining importance of military force. Direct, overt use of military force is no longer seen as decisive. Instead, the new concepts prioritize the use of nonmilitary domains and means. The key to winning is no longer the ability to use force successfully to defeat opponents on the battlefield, but the ability to coordinate and synchronize an ever-increasing number of nonmilitary instruments and actors in order to undermine the target's capacity and willingness to resist the demands of the attacker. Use of force remains the *ultima ratio*, but the focus in literature has shifted to gray zone short of war and to use of force that does not trigger a conventional military (Article 5) response from the West.

Finally, most scholars agree that the increased emphasis on nonmilitary means has blurred the distinction between war and peace on which the Western understanding of war is based. This also undermines the effectiveness of the existing legal frameworks and norms regulating war understood as involving the use of force. The growing use of "lawfare," defined as the "the strategy of using—or misusing—law as a substitute for traditional military means to achieve an operational objective,"[18] is highlighted as indicative of this trend.[19]

The next three sections examine how these three changes in the character of war outlined here are affecting the Western, Russian, and Chinese understanding and practices of war. As will become clear, it is the West that has the greatest difficulty in addressing the challenges produced by these changes—a situation that allows Russia and China to exploit Western weaknesses.

The Western Perception of Contemporary War

The distinction between war and peace as separate and distinguishable situations has a long Western tradition. More than two thousand years ago, the Roman statesman and philosopher Cicero highlighted the connection between time, war, and legal norms. His famous saying *"inter arma silent leges"* [In time of war, laws are silent] points to the exceptional status of wartime that allows the suspension of civil laws in cases of military emergencies. In a similar vein, one of the founding fathers of international law, Hugo Grotius, wrote in 1625 that *"inter bellum et pacem nihil est medium"* [Between war and peace, there is no intermediate state],[20] pointing to a fundamental difference between wartime and peacetime, with nothing in between the two conditions. It is clear that war is seen as something limited in time, a temporary state.[21] When war is over, peace follows.

This perception of a dichotomy between war- and peacetime is also visible in the international (legal) norms regulating behavior in and around war. This is not surprising; the traditional norms regulating armed conflict are based on the Western experiences of major interstate war, most notably the two world wars, and an understanding of war as political activity. A strict distinction exists between wartime and peacetime, each having its own legal rule set. In regard to *jus ad bellum*, the UN Charter prohibits states from resorting to the use of armed force in their relations, with two exceptions: UN Security Council authorization and self-defense against an armed attack.[22] Peace is the "normal" state of affairs and war the exception. Also NATO's Article 5 refers to an "armed attack" as trigger for its collective defense agreement. The law that governs the way in which warfare is conducted (*jus in bello*) distinguishes between two different types of armed conflict.[23] International armed conflicts are exchanges of armed force between two or more states, while non-international armed conflicts take place between a state's armed forces and armed non-state actors, or between two or more of such violent non-state groups.[24]

According to the International Criminal Tribunal for the former Yugoslavia (ICTY) in the highly influential *Tadić* case, the threshold for an international armed conflict—war between states—is crossed "whenever there is a resort to armed force between States."[25] For proponents of this "first-shot" theory, there is no requirement for a certain level of intensity of violence for a situation to be a war between states. Nevertheless, in state practice and expert opinion, another view, allowing for "border 'incident[s]', falling short of an armed conflict," has been prevalent.[26] For non-international armed conflicts, a certain threshold regarding the intensity of the violence and organization of the parties to the conflict is necessary for the situation to amount to a war; this is assessed for each situation.[27]

Interestingly, in the social sciences it is the norm to use a minimum threshold of one thousand combat-related deaths for categorizing an armed conflict as war;[28] this seems to follow the logic that a certain level of violence and deaths is required for the situation to amount to a war.[29] Only when this threshold is crossed does a situation amount to wartime, bringing with it the rights and obligations specified in international humanitarian law (among others, the right to employ armed force for combatants and the right to target military objectives).

This analysis of the existing thresholds for war highlights three key notions that are crucial for the distinction between wartime and peacetime in the existing normative framework: the use of *armed* force, a certain *intensity* of this armed force, and a degree of *organization* of the parties. But as this chapter shows, the current character of war in the gray zone challenges all three of these factors in different ways, creating fundamental problems for the Western perception of the wartime/peacetime distinction and undermining the international normative order.[30]

The first issue is that some of the actions falling under the description of the contemporary character of war given above are not violent per se. In particular, aspects of information and cyber warfare do not have a direct kinetic impact but only amount to indirect kinetic effects and sometimes do not have these effects at all. Nobody has been killed by a cyber attack—at least not yet, and not directly.[31] Nevertheless, the US/Israeli Stuxnet attack, for example, succeeded in disrupting and delaying Iranian efforts to develop nuclear weapons by causing the destruction of centrifuges, displaying the potential for powerful *indirect* kinetic effects of such cyber attacks. There remains a debate over how far these actions can be understood to amount to an armed attack as required by NATO's Article 5 (or Article 51 of the UN Charter), but NATO Secretary-General Jens Stoltenberg confirms that "for NATO, a serious cyberattack could trigger Article 5 of our founding treaty."[32] The US has also made it very clear that cyber attacks and similar actions could cross the threshold between peace and war and trigger wartime.[33] Nevertheless, the challenge of the conflicts in the gray zone addressed in this chapter lies precisely in the fact that these actions are designed to stay "below the threshold" of armed conflict, and both NATO and the US seem to refer to the extreme cases as crossing the threshold—constituting cases of "wartime." This speaks to the intensity of force that would be required; beyond these extreme cases, Western countries and institutions such as NATO and the EU struggle to address threats that are clearly perceived to exist in the gray space between war- and peacetime.[34]

How should the West understand and address these attacks from actors (countries and non-state actors alike) it is not "at war with"? It is important to acknowledge that this understanding of time is merely a part of the culture of a specific age—and as Clausewitz argues about the character of war as mentioned above—that is susceptible to change. Mary Dudziak argues that "we imagine wars to be bound in time, but the American experience is to the contrary. Since 9/11, war has been framed in a boundless way, extending anywhere in the world that the specter of terrorism resides."[35] The US "War on Terror" after 9/11 has led many to criticize the perceived lack of achievable goals to reach a conclusion of the war and subsequently peacetime, and the expansion of war into a condition defined as perpetual, endless, or forever wars, boundless in geography and time.[36] This is precisely why the term "War on Terror" was criticized so heavily—because this fight against terrorism was not war in the traditional understanding of the West.

Today, activities below the threshold of armed attack are no longer seen as episodic forms of crime, espionage, subversion, or similar, but instead as part of the new great power competition between the US, its allies, and other actors such as Russia and China. It is thus important to recognize that this contemporary character of war in the gray zone allows for activities that can achieve strategic outcomes while remaining under the defined thresholds of armed conflict. With its strict peacetime/wartime dichotomy, the West is struggling to address gray zone activities by its peer competitors, as these activities seem to be part of a larger, comprehensive approach by organized actors to undermine Western power that is more akin to a prolonged military campaign than to ad hoc diplomatic skirmishes. The following two sections analyze the Russian and Chinese approaches to gray zone conflict and highlight their comprehensive characteristics.

The Russian Perception of Contemporary War

Russia does not share the West's strict distinction between war- and peacetime, and exploits the existing distinction in international law to avoid eliciting a strong Western response. In fact, at least since the 1990s, Russian military thinkers have thought of the future of war as a blurred condition, situating conflict between war and peace. In line with the three challenges of the contemporary character of war outlined above, already in 1995, Makhmut Gareev pointed to disinformation campaigns as the opening stages of a war, a more important role for subversion, and an increasing reliance on indirect means to reach limited political objectives.[37] Chekinov and Bogdanov's analysis of Russian military experts writing on the character of future war offers "enough evidence that the early 21st century is really the beginning of a new 'military age' for humanity—an age of high-tech wars" characterized by information and psychological warfare and the importance of asymmetric actions that combine indirect "political, economic, information, technological, and ecological . . . actions and nonmilitary measures" to balance the opponent's conventional military superiority.[38]

What has gotten most attention in recent years is without a doubt the Russian understanding of the character of war in the twenty-first century formulated by the Chief of the General Staff of the Armed Forces of Russia, Valery Gerasimov:

> The very "rules of war" have changed. The role of nonmilitary means of achieving political and strategic goals has grown, and, in many cases, they have exceeded the power of force of weapons in their effectiveness. The focus of applied methods of conflict has altered in the direction of the broad use of political, economic, informational, humanitarian, and other nonmilitary measures—applied in coordination with the protest potential of the population. All this is supplemented by military means of a concealed character, including carrying out actions of informational conflict and the actions of special-operations forces. The open use of forces—often under the guise of

peacekeeping and crisis regulation—is resorted to only at a certain stage, primarily for the achievement of final success in the conflict.[39]

It is important to note that, contrary to popular understanding, what Gerasimov writes should not be seen as a Russian blueprint for war against the West; rather, it depicts Russia's understanding of what conflicts in the twenty-first century look like based on its perception of how the West is fighting.[40] In this context, the development of Russia's gray zone strategies has to be seen as a reaction to what it sees as Western gray zone activities and threats. Finally, for presidential adviser Vladislav Surkov, writing under his often-used pseudonym Nathan Dubovitsky, future warfare will involve everyone and everything, all possible aspects of life. War would be total, but nevertheless remain discreet and elusive.[41]

In short, the Russian perception of the contemporary conflict spectrum focuses on nonmilitary means that can be used in conjunction with military means, either simultaneously or, increasingly, consecutively. The open use of military force is the last stage of the war, not the first as in the Western perception of wartime analyzed above. The Russian approach follows no clear distinction between peace, conflict, and war.[42] As Oscar Jonsson points out, the Russian understanding of war "has always been closer to the view of permanent struggle and insatiable insecurity."[43] Some even go so far as to argue that the Russian understanding of war has fundamentally shifted toward information warfare and political subversion as the most important contemporary forms of war; and that Russian leaders have in fact perceived themselves to be at war with the West (the US and its allies) for the last decade—a war that is being fought through non-violent means.[44] Importantly, Russian decision-makers regard as acts of war certain actions intended by the West as limited, non-escalatory responses to Russian aggression—for example, the Western sanctions on Russia after the invasion of Ukraine—because they perceive them to be engineered to achieve regime change in Russia.[45]

It is important not to overstate the newness of the underlying ideas: Keir Giles, for example, argues that while Russian information warfare capabilities have been developing rapidly in recent years, the underlying principles can be traced back to the Cold War.[46] Nevertheless, the point here is not that all of these ideas are fundamentally new, but that Russia has in fact managed to integrate "military tools with other tools of pressure in innovative ways, and made use of a seamless transition from peace to conflict."[47]

The conflict in Ukraine, but also the Russian interference in the US elections in 2016, serve as good examples for how Russia is playing with the threshold of war defined in Western understanding. In Ukraine, Russia has used incremental violence over time to reach its political objectives with the least possible disturbance to the international community. This does not mean that it did not employ conventional force on a major scale in Ukraine—it did—but the accompanying intelligence and (mis-)information campaigns were crucial for the success of this military operation.[48] This approach not only allows for a certain amount of plausible deniability but also reduces the costs of the Russian engagement in Ukraine.[49] Additionally, in the information domain Russia conducts subversive actions through espionage and manipulation. These relatively low-cost means of political warfare allow it to affect public opinion and political will, and manage crises indirectly.[50] The US presidential election of 2016 is the perfect example of the usefulness of the cyber domain as an instrument for manipulation through information control and propaganda conducted as a subversive campaign falling well below the threshold of war. In fact it is estimated that this propaganda was able to reach up to 126 million users on Facebook alone.[51]

This is underlined by Russia's strategy of using legal arguments to justify its actions, displaying an ability to exploit Western disagreements about the normative order, as Natasha Kuhrt analyzes in chapter 6. This lawfare used by Russia "aims to blur the legal and illegal, to create justificatory smokescreens, in part by exploiting some areas of uncertainty in international law, while making unfounded assertion of 'facts.'"[52] An example of this strategy occurred in 2014, when the deputy secretary of the Russian National Security Council called for a global conference with the aim of revising existing international law, because "there are no agreed rules and the world may become an increasingly unruly place."[53] Looking at Russia's behavior and arguments as a permanent member of the United Nations Security Council on a wide array of issues (including on Iran, North Korea, and Syria), it is clear that it persistently challenges the West's role "as the privileged custodians and interpreters of core principles of international order."[54] Yet, in this context it is important to acknowledge that the West, and above all the US, is also trying to reinterpret and redefine the existing normative order, as for example in the US attempt to broaden the definition of preemption after 9/11.

The Chinese Perception of Contemporary War

Even though it may be the most blatant, Russia is not the only non-Western actor exploiting the Western perception of a clear distinction between wartime and peacetime, enshrined also in the existing legal norms regulating the resort to and use of armed force. Western states and other Asian states also accuse China of activities in the gray zone staying just below the threshold of war, despite publicly being more supportive than Russia of the existing international normative order.

It is noteworthy in this context that the Chinese perception of time is fundamentally different from the linear Western perception: based on Confucianism and Taoism, Chinese culture focuses on the collective rather than the individual, and time is perceived to be polychronic, non-linear, and repetitive, allowing a very different time horizon for actions.[55] Moreover the political set-up matters; it allows China to have a longer timeframe than Western liberal democracies, with their frequent elections and party competition (see also chapter 1 by Sarah Kreps and Adi Rao). This perception is represented in the 1999 book *Unrestricted Warfare* by two colonels of the Chinese People's Liberation Army (PLA). In addressing the future of warfare in an age of globalization and looking at how China can defend itself against the militarily and technologically superior US undergoing a revolution in military affairs, Qiao Liang and Wang Xiangsui argue that "the new principles of war are no longer 'using armed force to compel the enemy to submit to one's will [Clausewitz's dictum],' but rather are 'using all means, including armed force or non-armed force, military and nonmilitary, and lethal and non-lethal means to compel the enemy to accept one's interests.'"[56] Battle would be everywhere and infinitely, breaking down the distinctions between combatants and civilians, between what is a battlefield and what is not. Warfare would be omnipresent in a society: environmental warfare, financial warfare, trade warfare, cultural warfare, legal warfare, and many others.[57] This clearly goes against the American-led thinking of the revolution in military affairs, whose advocates argued that advances in technology and network-centric weaponry would allow for speedy, short, and precise wars, allowing a swift victory over the opponent (as discussed in part III of this volume). It also shows that China's perception of contemporary war and how to fight it, like Russia's, emerges from its understanding of the West, especially the US, as a threat, and the best possible way to respond to that.

This is further reflected in a revision to the Political Work Guidelines of the PLA in 2003, where China introduced what became known as the "three warfares": public opinion warfare, psychological warfare, and legal warfare. They are tools of political warfare, with the aim of creating political power. Public opinion warfare aims to shape domestic and international public opinion; psychological warfare targets foreign decisionmakers and aims to influence how they view China; and legal warfare shapes the legal context in building the legal justifications for Chinese actions. The importance of political warfare stems from a perceived lack of capabilities to fight the world's most advanced militaries,[58] but it has to be seen not just as representing the PLA's perception and practice of contemporary war, but as "expressions of the CCP's [Chinese Communist Party] intentions and day-to-day operations" that sees "influence operations and active measures as a normal way of doing business."[59]

Not unlike Russia, China seems to attempt to alter the status quo through small and gradual changes, which "even if ambiguous in nature, are more likely to be accepted by an opponent in ultimately altering its perception over time."[60] This allows the changes to remain under the threshold of eliciting a strong opposing response, little by little creating status quo changes as *faits accomplis*. This is especially visible in the South China Sea, a region which China has consistently treated as falling within its sphere of influence. In particular, the construction and militarization of islands in the South China Sea have been seen as China's attempts to undermine international law and seek geopolitical advantage for itself. The slow and continuous build-up of military capabilities here has shifted the balance of power in the region to such an extent that Admiral Philip S. Davidson, the head of the United States Indo-Pacific Command, emphasized in congressional testimony that "China is now capable of controlling the South China Sea in all scenarios short of war with the United States."[61] Interestingly, especially in the maritime domain, China is blurring the distinction between military and civilian, through using civilian and proxy forces such as the Coast Guard and People's Armed Forces Maritime Militia to bolster the PLA Navy.

Aside from the territorial claims in the South China Sea, China is also engaging in "information operations and disinformation, political and economic coercion, cyber and space operations, and provocation by state-controlled forces" as part of its gray zone approaches.[62] Cyber operations are seen as enablers for other gray zone activities. For example, in 2018 the assessment of the then US director of national intelligence, Dan Coats, was that "Russia, and other foreign countries, including China and Iran, conducted influence activities and messaging campaigns targeted at the United States to promote their strategic interests" in the weeks leading up to that year's congressional elections.[63] In 2015, a large-scale hack of the US Office of Personnel Management (OPM) was discovered, presumably conducted by possibly state-sponsored Chinese hackers; data on background checks, security clearance, 4.2 million personnel files, and 5.6 million digital images of government employee fingerprints were stolen before the security breach could be resolved.[64] China's

Belt and Road Initiative (BRI) and Digital Silk Road are other examples of the country's gray zone activities, allowing for potential debt-trap coercive diplomacy whereby China could deploy military forces into an acquired infrastructure project, or use digital networks provided by companies such as Huawei as tools for intelligence gathering and political coercion.[65] Just as in the South China Sea, these policies illustrate China's long operational time horizon. The scenario in the next chapter addresses such a threat, envisaging China using infrastructure in Djibouti built as part of the BRI to occupy parts of the country in the Horn of Africa.

According to observers, China is seen to have "the greatest capacity and long-term capability to exploit gray zone tactics to undermine liberal democratic systems" in the West, as its power is rising. Russia, on the other hand, does not have the same promising future as a global superpower.[66] Of course, activities in the gray zone below the threshold of armed conflict are being conducted by a multitude of other actors as well, but those two make up the largest competitors to Western political and military power.

How Gray Zone Conflicts Challenge the West

As the analysis above shows, gray zone activities are used precisely because they limit the West's reaction possibilities and negate its superior conventional military power. It is thus worth investigating exactly how the strict division between war- and peacetime in the existing normative system impedes a strong Western response to these activities. Conflicts in the gray zone have specific characteristics with temporal implications—in fact, gray zone activities can simultaneously speed up and slow down a conflict, making a timely response virtually impossible.

Attacks in the gray zone can be conducted much faster than conventional military attacks. In particular, operations in the cyber domain allow for instant and simultaneous attacks worldwide (even though preparing such an attack, like the 2015 hack of the OPM, may have taken many months). Additionally, disinformation campaigns allow for constant "attacks" that can create an ongoing state of low-level conflict, which does not fit with the peacetime/wartime dichotomy in the existing normative order.

The speediness and pervasive nature of such attacks makes the establishment of a normal, attack-free baseline difficult. One challenge these gray zone conflicts pose is that they paralyze the ability to see what is normal, especially in the cyber and information domain. In order to be able to identify an attack in the gray zone, one needs to know what a state of no attack looks like. If the establishment of such a baseline is not possible, detecting attacks becomes almost impossible and a timely response is negated. Threats in the gray zone may share the overall characteristics identified in the first part of this chapter, but the instruments used vary depending on the goals of the attack and the weakness targeted. Additionally, the diversity of nonmilitary instruments and domains that can be used in such attacks makes monitoring them increasingly difficult. All of this makes early warning challenging and attacks difficult to predict, leading to a situation where "we are much less likely to correctly understand, or even see, the mysteries and puzzles of hybrid threats until the effects are already underway."[67] This connects back to the requirements noted above of *armed* force and a certain *intensity* for the threshold between peace and war to be crossed; even with constant attacks, the kinetic effect is most likely still missing, and without an established baseline it is very difficult to assess the intensity of the attacks.

A second challenge for the defending/responding side, contributing to a slowing down of conflict, is the uncertainty about responsibility for the attacks. Attacks in the gray zone are intentionally designed in ways that sow doubts about their attribution and the identity of the attackers: "the use of proxies, plausible deniability, and the strategic exploitation of ambiguity and uncertainty of who or what the adversary is . . . create problems for analysts using a traditional and even current warning intelligence paradigm that is premised on knowledge of an easily identified adversary."[68] This impedes rapid and coherent responses, as intelligence services and decisionmakers scramble to understand where an attack has come from and who is responsible for it. It also leads back to the requirement to be able to assess the degree of organization of the parties that is necessary for a situation to amount to an armed conflict, especially if links between state and non-state actors are unclear. Attribution here has to be seen as a continuum of varying degrees of certainty and not as a yes/no answer. In addition it is dependent on the level of resources a government is willing to expend on attributing a certain action with reasonable certainty. For this, of course, it also matters how important the consequences of the action are to the government in question. If no vital interests are at stake, it may be easier to look the other way. Consequently a gray zone attack does not have to be unattributable, but only shrouded enough to cause doubt about the attribution and thus delay a response or limit the considered options.[69] Prime examples are Russia's initial denial of its involvement in Ukraine, despite multiple reports of "little green men,"[70] and its continued denial of involvement in the downing of Malaysian Airlines Flight 17 in 2014; other examples abound, such as hacker groups acting on behalf of the Russian or Chinese government, and the activities of the Chinese naval militia mentioned above.

Finally, this ambiguity of gray zone attacks and the connected challenges highlighted here are bound to create discussions among allies about the applicable norms and how to react appropriately. It forces liberal democracies to question and justify "the legitimacy of their responses with much greater scrutiny than non-democratic actors," greatly restraining their courses of action.[71] This not only further slows down the decisionmaking process and response, but could in a serious case "impede a rapid and coherent response under [NATO's] Article 5,"[72] resulting "in a strategic imbalance that threatens and undermines the strategic advantage NATO provides."[73] Posing all these challenges at once means not only that gray zone warfare willfully exploits the existing normative system based on a strict distinction between war- and peacetime, but also that the West's response mechanisms are slowed, leaving it unable to bring conventional military power to bear in time.

Countering Chinese and Russian Gray Zone Warfare

Gray zone conflict below the threshold of armed conflict thus presents a host of significant challenges to the international normative order and Western military power, giving rise to the question of how they can be mitigated. Of course the fundamental problem in addressing gray zone challenges lies in their being deliberately designed to avoid crossing the threshold from peacetime into wartime. More specifically with regard to NATO, the purpose of hybrid warfare is precisely "to lower the risk of triggering the use of NATO's capabilities, which are more appropriate for conventional or even nuclear war."[74] How can one address a threat that was specifically intended to inhibit a strong, coherent, and unified response?

Instead of trying to replicate the Russian and Chinese perceptions of the gray zone as comprehensive, long-term war, the solution this chapter proposes for the West lies in maintaining the dichotomy between wartime and peacetime that exists in the normative order and constitutes the backbone of Western liberal and democratic values. By accepting that the threshold of armed conflict (or war) has not been crossed, attention can be focused on peacetime mechanisms and solutions, within NATO, the EU, and their individual member states.

The core of NATO is the allied states' Article 5 collective defense commitment, but owing to the character of gray zone conflict this would only find application in the most extreme cases. Nevertheless, NATO has experience of engagements below the threshold of armed conflict through its other two pillars, crisis management and collective security—for example in the form of training missions and global partnerships (see also chapter 3 by Rebecca R. Moore). The consulting procedure under Article 4 is also a possibility and was used by Poland and Lithuania in April 2014. Since 2015 NATO's strategy for countering hybrid warfare has rested on three pillars: preparation, deterrence, and defense. Preparation includes the constant gathering, sharing, and assessing of information, notably through the Joint Intelligence and Security Division at NATO Headquarters; support for member states' efforts to identify national vulnerabilities and mitigate them; serving as a hub for expertise, for example through counter-hybrid support teams; and training of joint military and nonmilitary responses and decision-making processes. Deterrence is improved through increasing the preparedness of forces, including a strengthening of the decisionmaking process and command structure. Finally, defense rests on a continued commitment to the core purpose of the Alliance, underscored by the forces' ability to react quickly.[75]

While NATO is the only international organization in the West that has the military resources for credible deterrence, it is clear that a military solution alone does not sufficiently address the challenges posed by hybrid warfare in the gray zone. Cooperation with other actors is crucial. Cooperation with the European Union especially has been strengthened (for example through the establishment in 2017 of the European Centre of Excellence for Countering Hybrid Threats), but more is still needed, particularly joint exercises. The EU has a broader spectrum of relevant capabilities and instruments at its disposal than NATO as a purely military alliance, precisely because gray zone conflicts are fought in other domains than the military, and in peacetime. It can therefore be expected to take on a larger role and more tasks in countering hybrid warfare. However, there are important limits to EU–NATO cooperation owing to differences in membership, goals, and working methods.[76]

Individual states too (possibly with help from NATO or the EU) can work to better address threats below the threshold of armed conflict by enhancing resilience, for example through strong civil societies and robust law enforcement.[77] Resilience refers to the ability to manage the consequences of dangers, and it matters little whether the failure of an electrical grid or communications network was caused by a storm, a bomb, or a cyber attack. Focusing on being prepared for the aftermath, whatever its cause, requires a better pooling of resources and expertise in preparing for and dealing with such potential consequences of gray zone conflict.[78]

Regarding the international normative order, it is not enough simply to reiterate that international law and norms apply to these conflicts in the gray zone. This chapter has shown that there are fundamental problems with determining how and when the existing norms actually apply in these situations, making the vague claim of their application useless. Specific answers need to be given about how and when the norms apply, and what constitutes acceptable and unacceptable behavior in the twenty-first century, as norms are often created through state behavior (state practice is an integral part of identifying customary law, for example).

In the absence of limits and rules, it is likely that a crisis will occur, even if triggered by a misunderstanding and without intention. Thus, even if they may be disregarded on occasion, an agreement on the rules and norms applicable in these cases of contemporary conflict is crucial to prevent just such misunderstandings from arising and escalating.[79] However, this is hindered by the fact that greater openness about behavior and norms increases the risk that the enemy is able to address and correct weaknesses, making espionage and attacks more difficult in the future; it may also direct attention to one's own vulnerabilities and strategies. Nevertheless, many weaknesses and tools are already well known, and some—especially in the cyber realm—cannot be improved, avoided, or fixed as the case may be. Hence the requirement for increased openness about the need for norms does not pose an insurmountable obstacle to the creation of new norms—and should not be viewed as such.[80] Especially among allies it is crucial to reach a shared understanding of how to approach gray zone conflict, and particularly how to determine when the threshold to war is crossed. A simple prohibition of the use and possession of "weapons" in the gray zone will certainly not be possible, because of the dual-use nature of many gray zone methods: often they are civilian instruments that can be weaponized.

While democracies are widely regarded as a highly resilient form of government, their liberal values and democratic accountability prevent Western states from employing similar levels of ambiguity in their actions. Of course they are able to employ some gray zone instruments such as cyberattacks, but it is important not to engage in actions that fundamentally undermine the principles and norms that undergird Western power.[81] It is vital for the West to understand the more comprehensive Russian and Chinese approaches to gray zone conflict and how they exploit the Western peacetime/wartime distinction. But the West should support the existing normative order, which serves as a foundation of its power, instead of undermining it by weakening its stance. Instead of accepting, with Mary Dudziak, that "wartime has become the only kind of time we have,"[82] the West should beware of calling every action "warfare" and accepting the gray zone as a space where no norms apply; this only increases the dangers of escalation. Remembering the values and norms of peacetime might help to make space for competition and dialogue between states, provide better solutions (some of which have been outlined above) to address the challenges of conflicts below the threshold, and eventually perhaps find a path to developing common norms.

NOTES

1. Hew Strachan, *The Changing Character of War—A Europaeum Lecture Delivered at the Graduate Institute of International Relations, Geneva on 9th November 2006* (Oxford: Europaeum, 2007), www.europaeum.org/wp-content /uploads/2017/09/The-Changing-Character-of-War-Hew-Strachan-Europaeum -Lecture-2006.pdf.

2. Kalevi J. Holsti, *The State, War, and the State of War* (Cambridge University Press, 1996); Rupert Smith, *The Utility of Force: The Art of War in the Modern World* (London: Allen Lane, 2005).

3. Cornelius Friesendorf, *How Western Soldiers Fight: Organizational Routines in Multinational Missions* (Cambridge University Press, 2018).

4. Carl von Clausewitz, *On War* (1834), translated and edited by Michael Howard and Peter Paret (Princeton University Press, 1984), p. 89.

5. James N. Mattis and Frank Hoffman, "Future Warfare: The Rise of Hybrid Wars," *U.S. Naval Institute Proceedings*, vol. 131, no. 11 (November 2005), p. 18.

6. Thomas X. Hammes, "3-D Printing Will Disrupt the World in Ways We Can Barely Imagine," War on the Rocks, December 28, 2015; Jean-Loup Samaan, "Missile Warfare and Violent Non-state Actors: The Case of Hezbollah,"*Defence Studies*, vol. 17, no. 2 (2017), pp. 156–70.

7. Ivan Arreguin-Toft, "How the Weak Win Wars: A Theory of Asymmetric Conflict," *International Security*, vol. 26, no. 1 (Summer 2001), pp. 93–128.

8. John Arquilla and David Ronfeldt, *Cyberwar is Coming!* (Santa Monica, CA: RAND Corporation, 1993); Thomas Rid, *Cyber War Will Not Take Place* (Oxford University Press, 2013).

9. Thomas X. Hammes, *The Sling and The Stone: On War in the 21st Century* (St. Paul, MN: Zenith Press, 2004).

10. John Chambers, *Countering Gray-Zone Hybrid Threats: An Analysis of Russia's "New Generation Warfare" and Implications for the US Army* (West Point, NY: Modern War Institute, 2016); Michael Mazarr, *Mastering the Gray Zone* (Carlisle, PA: Strategic Studies Institute, 2015).

11. Frank Hoffman, *Conflict in the 21st Century: The Rise of Hybrid Wars* (Arlington, VA: Potomac Institute for Policy Studies, 2007).

12. United States Department of Defense, "Irregular Warfare," Joint Operating Concept, 11 September 2007.

13. Mary Kaldor, *New and Old Wars: Organized Violence in a Global Era* (Stanford University Press, 1999).

14. Hans-Georg Ehrhart, "Postmodern Warfare and the Blurred Boundaries between War and Peace," *Defense & Security Analysis*, vol. 33, no. 3 (2017), pp. 263–75; Chris Hables Gray, *Postmodern War: The New Politics of Conflict* (New York: Guildford Press, 1997).

15. Qiao Liang and Wang Xiangsui, *Unrestricted Warfare* (Beijing: PLA Literature and Arts Publishing House, 1999).

16. Holsti, *The State, War, and the State of War*.

17. Smith, *The Utility of Force*.

18. Charles J. Dunlap Jr., "Lawfare Today: A Perspective," *Yale Journal of International Affairs* (Winter 2008), pp. 146–54.

19. Aurel Sari, "Legal Resilience in an Era of Gray Zone Conflicts and Hybrid Threats," Exeter Centre for International Law Working Paper (2019/1), pp. 16–19.

20. Cicero, *Philippica VII*; Hugo Grotius, *Ius Bellum et Pacis*, Book III, Chapter XXI.

21. Mary L. Dudziak, *War Time: An Idea, Its History, Its Consequences* (Oxford University Press, 2012).

22. Relevant articles: Prohibition of the Use of Force, Art. 2(4); Security Council Authorization, Art. 39 together with Art. 42; Self-defense, Art. 51.

23. When drafting the Geneva Conventions, it was decided to use the notion of "armed conflict" instead of "war" because it "deprives belligerents, in advance, of the pretexts they might in theory put forward for evading their obligations. There is no need for a formal declaration of war, or for the recognition of the existence of a state of war, as preliminaries to the application of the Convention. The occurrence of de facto hostilities is sufficient." Jean Simon Pictet and others, *Commentary on Geneva Convention III Relative to the Treatment of Prisoners of War* (Geneva: International Committee of the Red Cross, 1960), pp. 22–23; International Committee of the Red Cross, *Commentary on the First Geneva Convention: Convention (I) for the Amelioration of the Condition of the Wounded and Sick in Armed Forces in the Field*, edited by Knut Dörmann and others, 2nd ed. (Cambridge University Press, 2016), para. 202.

24. Common Article 2 and 3 of the Geneva Conventions, respectively.

25. International Criminal Tribunal for the former Yugoslavia (ICTY), *Prosecutor v. Duško Tadić a/k/a "Dule." Decision on the Defense Motion for Interlocutory Appeal on Jurisdiction* (1995), para. 70.

26. Gary Dean Solis, *The Law of Armed Conflict: International Humanitarian Law in War*, 2nd ed. (Cambridge University Press, 2016), p. 162. See also International Law Association: Committee on the Use of Force, *Final Report on the Meaning of Armed Conflict in International Law* (London, 2010), pp. 14, 17–18, 24, 26–27 for state practice (yet it is important to note that there are instances of contrary state practice as well: for example, the US operation in Grenada in 1983 and the UK's invocation of the Geneva Conventions when British sailors were detained by Iran in 2007); Yoram Dinstein, *War, Aggression and Self-Defence*, 5th ed. (Cambridge University Press, 2011), p. 11, for a view emphasizing the perception of the situation by the antagonists.

27. The famous formulation by the ICTY in the Tadić case states that "an

armed conflict exists whenever there is a resort to armed force between States or protracted armed violence between governmental authorities and organized armed groups or between such groups within a State." ICTY, *Prosecutor v. Dusko Tadić a/k/a "Dule,"* para. 70.

28. Therése Pettersson and Peter Wallensteen, "Armed conflicts, 1946–2014," *Journal of Peace Research,* vol. 52, no. 4 (2015), pp. 536–50; Melvin Small and J. David Singer, *Resort to Arms: International and Civil War, 1816–1980* (Beverly Hills, CA: Sage, 1982), pp. 205–06.

29. It might be worth briefly considering the difference between the notions of "war" and "armed conflict." As mentioned above (note 23) during the drafting of the Geneva Conventions it was decided to use "armed conflict" instead of "war." There is a difference between war as it is used colloquially in the media, politics, and the wider field of political and social sciences, and war as legal term, which can be exemplified through Hedley Bull's distinction "between war in the loose sense of organized violence which may be carried out by any political unit . . . and war in the strict sense of international or interstate war." Hedley Bull, *The Anarchical Society: A Study of Order in World Politics,* 3rd ed. (Basingstoke, UK/New York: Palgrave, 2002), p. 178.

30. Herfried Münkler, "Hybride Kriege: Die Auflösung der binären Ordnung von Krieg und Frieden und dessen Folgen" [Hybrid Wars: The Dissolution of the Binary Order of War and Peace, and Its Consequences], *Ethik und Militär: Kontroversen der Militärethik und Sicherheitskultur* (2015/2).

31. Rid, *Cyber War Will Not Take Place* (see particularly chapter 2: Violence); Robert E. Schmidle, Michael Sulmeyer, and Ben Buchanan, "Non-Lethal Weapons and Cyber Capabilities," in *Understanding Cyber Conflict: 14 Analogies,* edited by George Perkovich and Ariel E. Levite (Georgetown University Press, 2017), p. 31.

32. Jens Stoltenberg, "Nato Will Defend Itself," *Prospect,* October 2019, p. 4.

33. The White House, "International Strategy for Cyberspace: Prosperity, Security, and Openness in a Networked World," May 17, 2011, https://info.publicintelligence.net/WH-InternationalCyberspace.pdf.

34. European External Action Service, "Countering Hybrid Threats," Food-for-thought paper (May 2015); European Commission and the High Representative of the Union for Foreign Affairs and Security Policy, "Joint Communication to the European Parliament and the Council: Joint Framework on Countering Hybrid Threats. A European Union Response" (April 2016); NATO, "NATO's Response to Hybrid Threats," 2019, www.nato.int/cps/en/natohq/topics_156338.htm; Henry Kissinger, *World Order* (New York: Penguin Books, 2014) p. 344.

35. Dudziak, *War Time,* p. 5.

36. Aside from the War on Terror, the notion of perpetual, endless, or forever war has also been employed to describe the Vietnam War, US operations in Latin America, the war against drugs and others.

37. Makhmut A. Gareev, *If War Comes Tomorrow?: The Contours of Future Armed Conflict,* translated by Yakov Vladimirovich Fomenko, 1st ed. 1995 in Russian (Abingdon, UK: Routledge, 1998).

38. Sergei Chekinov and Sergei Bogdanov, "The Nature and Content of New-generation War," *Military Thought*, vol. 22, no. 4 (2013), pp. 14 and 16, respectively.

39. Valeriy Gerasimov, "Tsennost' nauki v predvidenii," *Voyenno Promyshlennyy Kuryer*, February 26, 2013, http://vpk-news.ru/articles/14632. Translation of parts in Mark Galeotti, "The 'Gerasimov Doctrine' and Russian Non-Linear War," *Moscow's Shadows*, July 6, 2014, https://inmoscowsshadows.wordpress.com/2014/07/06/the-gerasimov-doctrine-and-russian-non-linearwar/.

40. Mark Galeotti, "I'm Sorry for Creating the 'Gerasimov Doctrine,'" *Foreign Policy*, March 5, 2018.

41. N. Dubovitsky, "Bez neba," *Russkiy Pioner*, March 12, 2014, http://ruspioner.ru/honest/m/single/4131; quoted in András Rácz, "Russia's Hybrid War in Ukraine: Breaking the Enemy's Ability to Resist," Finnish Institute of International Affairs Report no. 43 (Helsinki: 2015), p. 37.

42. Dave Johnson, "Russia's Approach to Conflict: Implications for NATO's Deterrence and Defence," in *NATO's Response to Hybrid Threats*, edited by Guillaume Lasconjaririas and Jeffrey A. Larsen (Rome: NATO Defense College, 2015), pp. 137–60.

43. Oscar Jonsson, *The Russian Understanding of War: Blurring the Lines between War and Peace* (Georgetown University Press, 2019), p. 157.

44. Ibid.

45. Ibid., pp. 5–6, 157.

46. Keir Giles, "Russia's 'New' Tools for Confronting the West: Continuity and Innovation in Moscow's Exercise of Power," Research Paper, Russia and Eurasia Programme (London: Chatham House, 2016), www.chathamhouse.org/sites/default/files/publications/2016-03-russia-new-tools-giles.pdf.

47. Kristin Ven Bruusgaard, "Crimea and Russia's Strategic Overhaul," *Parameters*, vol. 44, no. 3, Autumn 2014, p. 81.

48. Mark Galeotti, "'Hybrid War' and 'Little Green Men': How It Works, and How It Doesn't," in *Ukraine and Russia: People, Politics, Propaganda and Perspectives*, edited by Agnieszka Pikulicka-Wilczewska and Richard Sakwa (Bristol: E-International Relations Publishing, 2015), pp. 149–56, www.e-ir.info/wp-content/uploads/2016/06/Ukraine-and-Russia-E-IR-2016.pdf.

49. Even though the costs have risen through the prolonged Russian campaign in eastern Ukraine. Alexander Lanoszka, "Russian Hybrid Warfare and Extended Deterrence in Eastern Europe," *International Affairs,* vol. 92, no. 1 (2016), pp. 175–95; Amos Fox, "Understanding Modern Russian War," *Fires* (September–October 2017), pp. 20–25. For an analysis of why the operation in Crimea was successful but the Donbas is more difficult for Russia, see Galeotti, "'Hybrid War' and 'Little Green Men.'"

50. Benjamin Jensen, Brandon Valeriano, and Ryan Maness, "Fancy Bears and Digital Trolls: Cyber Strategy with a Russian Twist," *Journal of Strategic Studies*, vol. 42, no. 2 (2019), p. 219.

51. Of course this does not say anything about whether Russia actually man-

aged to influence the voting behavior of these people. Mike Isaac and Daisuke Wakabayashi, "Russian Influence Reached 126 Million through Facebook Alone," *New York Times*, October 30, 2017.

52. Roy Allison, "Russian 'Deniable' Intervention in Ukraine: How and Why Russia Broke the Rules," *International Affairs*, vol. 90, no. 6 (November 2014), p. 1259.

53. Eugenie Lukyanov, in statement to RIA Novosti, July 2, 2014, cited in Allison, "Russian 'Deniable' Intervention," p. 1267.

54. Allison, "Russian 'Deniable' Intervention," p. 1268.

55. Gordon S. Redding, "Cognitions as an Aspect of Culture and Its Relation to Management Processes: An Exploratory View of the Chinese Case," *Journal of Management Studies*, vol. 17 (1980), pp. 127–48; quoted in Paul S. Kirkbride, Sara F. Y. Tang, and Robert I. Westwood, "Chinese Conflict Preference and Negotiating Behaviour: Cultural and Psychological Influences," *Organization Studies*, vol. 12, no. 3 (1991), pp. 365–86.

56. Qiao Liang and Wang Xiangsui, *Unrestricted Warfare* (Beijing: PLA Literature and Arts Publishing House, 1999), translated by the Foreign Broadcast and Information Service (1999), p. 7, https://archive.org/details/Unrestricted _Warfare_Qiao_Liang_and_Wang_Xiangsui/mode/2up. Original quotes kept.

57. Liang and Xiangsui, *Unrestricted Warfare*. See also David Barno and Nora Bensahel, "A New Generation of Unrestricted Warfare," War on the Rocks, April 19, 2016.

58. Dennis J. Blasko, "The New PLA Joint Headquarters and Internal Assessments of PLA Capabilities," *China Brief*, vol. 16, no. 10.

59. Peter Mattis, "China's 'Three Warfares' in Perspective," War on the Rocks, January 30, 2018.

60. Peter Callamari and Derek Reveron, "China's Use of Perception Management," *International Journal of Intelligence and CounterIntelligence*, vol. 16 (2003), p. 3.

61. Quoted in Hannah Beech, "China's Sea Control Is a Done Deal, 'Short of War with the U.S.,'" *New York Times*, September 20, 2018.

62. Kathleen H. Hicks, Joseph Federici, and Connor Akiyama, "China in the Grey Zone," *Strategic Analysis* no. 4 (2019) (Helsinki: Hybrid Center of Excellence, April 2019), p. 3.

63. Jonathan Landay and Mark Hosenball, "Russia, China, Iran Sought to Influence U.S. 2018 Elections: U.S. Spy Chief," Reuters, December 21, 2018.

64. Brendan I. Koerner, "Inside the Cyberattack That Shocked the US Government," *Wired* (October 23, 2016).

65. Hicks, Federici, and Akiyama, "China in the Grey Zone."

66. Ibid.

67. Patrick Cullen, "Hybrid Threats as New 'Wicked Problems' for Early Warning," *Strategic Analysis* (Helsinki: Hybrid Center of Excellence, May 2018).

68. Ibid., p. 5.

69. Oliver Fitton, "Cyber Operations and Gray Zones: Challenges for NATO," *Connections QJ*, vol. 15, no. 2 (2016), pp. 109–19.

70. Allison, "Russian 'Deniable' Intervention," pp. 1257–58.

71. Fitton, "Cyber Operations and Gray Zones," p. 113.

72. Peter Braun, "Fighting 'Men in Jeans' in the Grey Zone between Peace and War," Policy Brief no. 18 (August 2019) (Rome: NATO Defense College), p. 5. See also Johnson, "Russia's Approach to Conflict."

73. Fitton, "Cyber Operations and Gray Zones," p. 113.

74. Lanoszka, "Russian Hybrid Warfare," p. 190.

75. NATO, "NATO's Response to Hybrid Threats."

76. Danish Institute for International Studies, *Europæisk Forsvarssamarbejde og det Danske Forsvarsforbehold*, Copenhagen, December 2019. [Available in English as *European Defence Cooperation and Denmark: The Danish Opt-Out on Defence* (April 2020).]

77. Lanoszka, "Russian Hybrid Warfare."

78. Roger Clarke and Owen Jackson, "Building Resilience: Hybrid's Weakness?," Working Paper (Helsinki: Hybrid Center of Excellence, April 2019).

79. Kissinger, *World Order*, pp. 346–47.

80. Jeppe Teglskov Jacobsen, "Fælles internationale normer i cyberspace kræver mere åbenhed" [Common International Norms in Cyberspace Require More Openness], Danish Institute for International Studies Policy Brief, Copenhagen, August 2019.

81. Fitton, "Cyber Operations and Gray Zones;" Hicks, Federici, and Akiyama, "China in the Grey Zone."

82. Dudziak, *War Time*, p. 8.

EIGHT

Competing Norms

*What If China Takes Control of
Djibouti to Protect Its People?*

ERNST DIJXHOORN

This chapter describes a scenario, set in the near future, in which China uses armed force to occupy key infrastructure in the northwestern part of the city of Djibouti, including the Doraleh Container Terminal, Djibouti Dry Port, and Doraleh Multi-Purpose Port. In the scenario, China presents "the West" with a *fait accompli* and justifies the use of force with a competing interpretation of norms of international law regarding the doctrine of Protection of Nationals Abroad (PNA). Other hypothetical events with implications for China–Western relations might be more likely—for instance actions in the South China Sea or a conflict emerging as a result of enforcement of the Hong Kong national security law that came into effect on June 30, 2020[1]—but looking at a more extreme event rather than gradual change forces us to think about the implications of a shifting balance of power, competing interpretations of norms of international law, and the impact of a rising China on "the West" and its ability to deploy armed force to protect its values and shared interests.

Even though the scenario described here is hypothetical, the idea is rooted in real-life developments. For a long time, China's foreign policy was guided by what Deng Xiaoping described as "hide your strength and bide your time," but China became too powerful to hide its strength, and under President Xi Jinping is taking on a more assertive role.[2] This includes a proactive approach to foreign trade and international economic affairs, and more forceful behavior in security matters.[3] Beijing displays a combination of soft power and financial might through the Belt and Road Initiative (BRI), which, while driven by China's need to look abroad for economic expansion and surplus industrial capacity, also buys political influence abroad.[4] Djibouti's main importance to China lies in its location on the Bab-el-Mandeb Strait, which connects the Indian Ocean and the Mediterranean. Because of this strategic location on the maritime sea routes between Asia and Europe, China invested heavily in Djibouti's infrastructure as an essential part of the BRI.[5] It also financed large infrastructure projects such as the Addis Ababa–Djibouti Railway, which strengthened Djibouti's position as a gateway to landlocked Ethiopia and provided loans to the country.[6]

In 2017, on the seventieth birthday of the People's Liberation Army (PLA), China opened its first overseas naval base in Djibouti, close to the commercial Container Terminal at Doraleh, which was also built by the state-owned China Merchants Holdings.[7] China describes the base as a logistics facility to support anti-piracy operations and UN peacekeeping deployments.[8] But the base also gives the PLA the opportunity to react quickly to other emergencies in the region. China held military exercises in Djibouti in 2017 that included tanks and other heavy weaponry to make sure Chinese troops are able "to protect themselves and resist attacks from terrorists, pirates, local armed forces, or even foreign troops."[9] These were widely reported in Chinese state-owned media to show the audiences at home and abroad that China is a rejuvenated nation and that its navy will prevent another century of humiliation. This makes the Chinese presence in Djibouti also a matter of prestige.[10] In short, Djibouti is on the fault line where the strategic rivalry between China and "the West" might play out.

Traditionally, China adhered to a strict interpretation of the principle of non-interference in the domestic affairs of other states, and it still does so in theory. However, over the last decade the Chinese government has been willing to use armed force to protect citizens and their interests abroad, even if that is at odds with the principle of non-interference (as analyzed in chapter 6 by Natasha Kuhrt).[11] In the hypothetical scenario described here, China uses the PNA doctrine to justify its actions. This chapter assesses the discrepancy in interpretation of the norm between and among Western powers and Russia and China. The West's response to the scenario described would be informed not only by its interests in Djibouti but also by the perceived need to protect

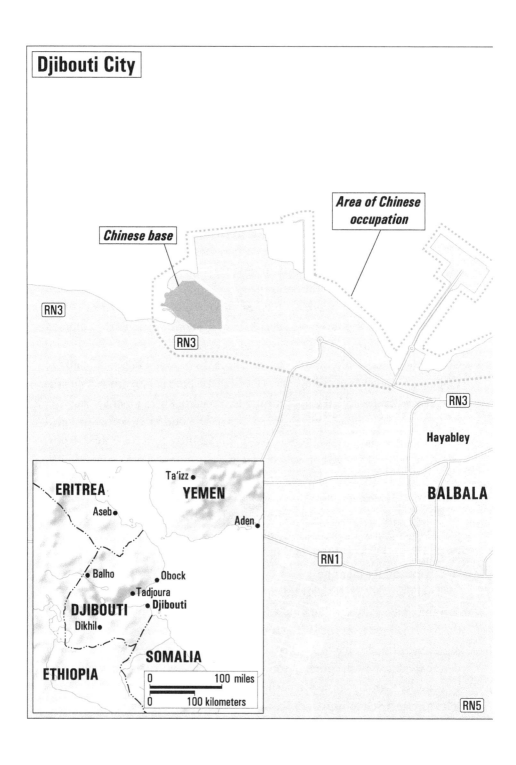

Djibouti City

Area of Chinese occupation

Chinese base

RN3

RN3

RN3

Hayabley

BALBALA

RN1

ERITREA

YEMEN

Ta'izz

Aseb

Aden

Balho

Obock

Tadjoura

DJIBOUTI

Djibouti

Dikhil

SOMALIA

ETHIOPIA

| 0 | 100 miles |
| 0 | 100 kilometers |

RN5

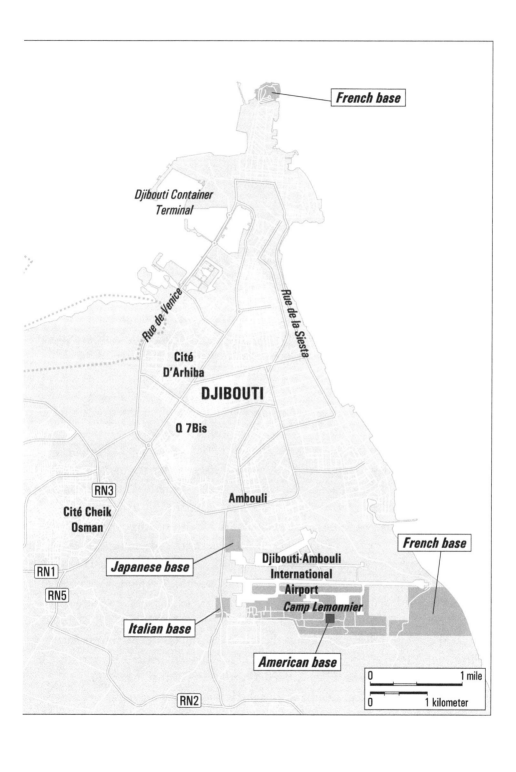

French base

Djibouti Container
Terminal

Rue de Venice

Rue de la Siesta

Cité
D'Arhiba

DJIBOUTI

Q 7Bis

RN3

Cité Cheik
Osman

Ambouli

RN1

RN5

Japanese base

Djibouti-Ambouli
International
Airport

French base

Camp Lemonnier

Italian base

American base

RN2

| 0 | 1 mile |
| 0 | 1 kilometer |

the international rule of law. In order to gauge how Western states might react, the chapter also assesses their response to the annexation of Crimea by Russia based on a similar argument of protecting nationals abroad.

Finally, the chapter examines the ability of Western states to act decisively when presented with a *fait accompli* by China, and considers their motivations and the coercive instruments at their disposal in such a situation. In particular, it asks to what extent diplomatic and political measures, economic sanctions, and military force might be employed in response to a Chinese takeover of parts of Djibouti, and considers the limits of Western power to compel China to return to a status quo.

As explained in the introduction to this book, time is of the essence in war. This is especially true when choosing to confront an opponent with a *fait accompli*. To use a strategy that requires taking the initiative suddenly to change the status quo requires expert timing at both the political and the tactical level. A *fait accompli* strategy requires the objective to be reached quickly so as to give a potential defending power little or no time to react adequately.[12] Usually this strategy involves some level of surprise—surprise that, as described in the introduction to this book, may be the result of the parties' different temporal horizons.

In a hypothetical scenario as described in this chapter, whether potential Western defenders of Djibouti sovereignty would accept the new status quo would depend on a number of variables. One of them would be the interpretation by various Western states of the doctrine of the "Protection of Nationals Abroad," and the willingness of "the West" to stand up for the international normative order that it has shaped for a long time. Western states have long regarded themselves as guardians of the international normative order, but norms of war and warfare change: as Natasha Kuhrt explains in chapter 6, the erosion of the norm of non-intervention has led to uncertainty and disagreement among Western states. This allows for competing interpretations of norms by Russia and China to justify their actions. Combined with the aversion to risk and casualties in the West described in chapter 5 by Kathleen McInnis, this limits the ability of the West to decide the pace of war. Moreover the political discussion about the legality of military deployments that in some Western countries will precede any action will hamper a Western response to any *fait accompli*. This chapter further argues that, when confronting the US and its Western allies with a *fait accompli* in Djibouti, China does not have to be able to beat the West in a direct military confrontation. It just has to correctly calculate the willingness of the West to respond, and must be able to make leaders in Washington and European capitals believe that restoring the former status quo in Djibouti is so costly that they are deterred from launching a military response.

Scenario

On January 9, 2021, Axmed Liibaan Dhuule, the *New York Times* correspondent for East Africa, had only just come home from a night out in Nairobi, when at 4:00 a.m. he was woken up by a phone call. Still only half-awake, Axmed did not immediately recognize the person talking to him in rapid Somali. But when his fixer in Djibouti told him that sightings of Chinese special forces had been reported across Djibouti City, he immediately realized this would change the balance of power in the region. By the time the US woke up on Saturday morning to yet another presidential Twitter storm, much remained unclear about what exactly had happened in Djibouti the previous night, but Axmed could report the following:

NAIROBI, January 9, 2021. In the early hours of Saturday morning, Chinese special forces took control of parts of the capital city of the East African country of Djibouti in what appeared to be a well-planned and swiftly executed military operation.

On Friday evening a flotilla of the Chinese Navy (PLAN) including a Type 054A guided-missile frigate, a Type 903A supply ship, and a Type 052D destroyer docked at the naval facility in Djibouti opened in 2017 to support Chinese anti-piracy operations in the Gulf of Aden. Shortly after 3:00 a.m. local time, the first reports came in that Chinese special forces had taken control of the Doraleh Container Terminal, Djibouti Dry Port, the Doraleh Multi-Purpose Port, and other key infrastructure on the northwestern side of the city of Djibouti. Although the actions of the Chinese military came after weeks of rising tensions in the small East African country, the use of military force by China took the Djibouti government, international observers, and Western powers by surprise.

Street protests in Djibouti started in late November when President Ismaïl Omar Guelleh announced he would seek a fifth successive term in office and ordered the pre-emptive arrest of several opposition leaders. On December 19, tensions escalated after police used live ammunition against protesters burning tires and installing roadblocks on the main route from the ports of Djibouti to Ethiopia. After these clashes protesters started to co-ordinate their actions against government buildings with the radical faction of the Front for the Restoration of Unity and Democracy (FRUD-Armé), the remnant of an armed opposition group that opposed the ruling party in the late 1990s.

In recent weeks the anger of protesters also turned toward the large Chinese presence in Djibouti, and on Monday demonstrators burned Chinese flags in front of the Chinese Embassy on Rue Addis Ababa. The anger toward China is the result of a highly contested debt-for-equity swap earlier this year in which President Guelleh signed over ownership of Djibouti's port facilities on a 99-year lease to China Merchants Holdings after Djibouti had been unable to meet the interest payments on Chinese loans. In an interview in July 2019 Djibouti's finance minister, Ilyas Moussa Dawaleh, still defended the Chinese loans as "crucial for preventing an eruption of protest among Djibouti's poor and unemployed." However, the poor and unemployed of Djibouti did not benefit from Chinese investments in the country and, over the course of the last weeks, arson attacks and vandalism against companies affiliated with China have taken place across the country. Additionally, officials in Ethiopia expressed fears that the Chinese-owned Addis Ababa–Djibouti Railway on which the Ethiopian economy heavily depends would be sabotaged.

Reports in the Chinese daily newspaper the *Global Times* on January 3 that two Chinese engineers had been found dead in Djibouti caused a storm on the Chinese social media platform Weibo, with nationalist commentators calling for the government to do more to protect Chinese citizens abroad. Their demands have continued even after the Chinese Ministry of Foreign Affairs released a statement that the two men had died in a tragic accident while unloading a container and the incident was not connected to the ongoing protests in Djibouti.

In Washington officials said they were monitoring the situation in Djibouti closely. Only eight miles from the port facilities now occupied by Chinese special forces, the US Navy operates Camp Lemonnier—with almost 4,000 troops the largest US military base in Africa and home to its regional drone operations. In an emergency meeting on Friday night at Trump International Golf Club in West Palm Beach, President Trump's security advisers and Members of Congress discussed whether to impose new sanctions on Chinese officials. However, President Trump has so far held back from taking measures. On Friday night Mr Trump took to Twitter to attack former attorney general William Barr, who claims in his upcoming book that the president interfered with the Justice Department, but Mr Trump kept silent on the events in Djibouti.

Former US security adviser John Bolton tweeted: "I warned @realDonaldTrump this would happen! The US has to take decisive action now to protect our national security and restore our credibility." A spokesperson for House Speaker Nancy Pelosi told journalists that she "condemns the use of military force by China and urges President Trump to take immediate action to ensure the sovereignty and territorial integrity of Djibouti and protect US interests in the region." French President Emmanuel Macron called for a European task force to be sent to Djibouti. In an official statement, Chinese officials declared that "China has an obligation to protect its nationals and their economic interests abroad, and the right to do so in the light of recent attacks in Djibouti." According to the statement, "Chinese security forces will maintain their presence in Djibouti until peace and security have been restored."

China's Motivations for Intervening in Djibouti

The large investments of Chinese state-owned enterprises (SOEs) in African infrastructure, mining, and energy sectors, combined with a high appetite for risk among privately owned Chinese companies, has led to a large number of Chinese nationals living in relatively unstable countries, and to Chinese citizens abroad being attacked, taken hostage, and killed.[13] Nationalist opinions are less censored online, and whenever Chinese are attacked and kidnapped, or their economic interests are threatened, there are growing demands domestically for Beijing to be more proactive in protecting Chinese overseas citizens and economic interests.[14] Since the mid-2000s the Chinese military have become increasingly involved when Chinese citizens abroad are at risk.[15] China has conducted 17 non-combatant evacuations over the last decade; for instance, at the beginning of the civil war in Libya in 2011, the PLA evacuated more than 35,000 Chinese nationals, and in 2015 a Chinese frigate moved 629 Chinese workers and 279 nationals of other countries from war-torn Yemen to Djibouti.[16] Moreover the deployment of the Chinese Navy (PLAN) since 2008 to protect Chinese ships against pirates off the Somali coast provided operational experience and showed China's ability to engage in combat operations outside its claimed territorial waters.[17] As Natasha Kuhrt also shows in chapter 6, since 2014 China has been contributing combat troops to UN peacekeeping operations (PKOs). By doing so, it conveys the image of a "responsible stakeholder" in the international order, and PKO missions contribute to stability in countries with heavy Chinese investments.[18] These missions are also a way to obtain operational experience for the PLA and demonstrate its ability to operate far beyond China's borders.[19]

Despite the increased need to protect citizens abroad, in theory China remains largely wedded to the principle of non-interference.[20] However, there has been a shift in the interpretation of these norms in China. This means that the interests concerned in Djibouti are so important to China that the use of force cannot be excluded as an option. So far, China has always had other options than substantial sustained military action abroad—in Libya and Yemen for instance, evacuation of nationals was possible without occupying territory. Yet there is no reason to believe China would not be willing to take control over parts of Djibouti territory if it deemed this necessary to protect its nationals and their (economic) interests.

A Response from "the West"

China is not the only state that has considerable economic and strategic interests in Djibouti. In addition to military bases operated by France, Italy, and Japan, 4,000 US and allied troops are stationed at Camp Lemonnier, the largest US military base in Africa and main US drone base in the region.[21] As this camp is located only eight miles southeast of the new Chinese naval facility, the US military has been viewing the growing Chinese presence in Djibouti with unease.[22] According to AFRICOM's commanding General Thomas Waldhauser, access to Djibouti's container port is central to US missions in Somalia and East Africa.[23] The Trump administration even expressed concern that Djibouti might hand over control of the Doraleh port to Chinese state-owned enterprises.[24] As China reportedly holds around 80 percent of Djibouti's national debt, it might be able to leverage this to exert control over Djibouti's ports.[25] In September 2019 then National Security Adviser John Bolton stated that if this happened "the balance of power in the Horn of Africa—astride major arteries of maritime trade between Europe, the Middle East, and South Asia—would shift in favor of China."[26]

The West might be motivated to respond to the use of force by China to sustain its sphere of influence, or it might be motivated by normative concerns. Either way, Western states would employ the language of international law to justify their response, whether or not this response was in accordance with international law. Therefore, the justification of the response of Western states would depend on an assessment of the legality of Chinese actions in Djibouti under existing norms of international law. While norm setting in international law has been largely dominated by the West, this position is under increasing pressure as China and especially Russia have criticized the West's selective application of norms of international law, above all the prohibition on the use of force.[27] In parallel, non-Western powers have put forward their own interpretations of norms of international law (see chapter 6 by Natasha Kuhrt and chapter 7 by Amelie Theussen and Peter Viggo Jakobsen).[28] The annexation of Crimea by Russia showed how the West reacted to that example of "competing interpretations of norms" of non-interference. In this scenario, China seeks to legitimize its action under the doctrine of the "Protection of Nationals Abroad," a concept that refers to the "conducting of a military intervention in the territory of a third state aimed at the protection and/or rescuing of threatened nationals of the intervening state."[29] PNA has been the focus of renewed interest since the Russian Federation used it as a justification for the use of force in Georgia in 2008 and in Crimea and eastern Ukraine in 2014.[30] However, the legality under international law of PNA without the consent of the territorial state is debated and remains controversial.[31]

Before the entry into force of the UN Charter in 1945, it was generally accepted that PNA could be justified if: (i) there was an imminent threat of injury to nationals; and (ii) there was a failure or inability on the part of the territorial sovereign to protect them; and (iii) the action of the intervening state was strictly confined to the object of protecting its nationals against injury.[32] As also highlighted in the previous chapters, current international law prohibits the "threat or use of force against the territorial integrity or political independence of any state" in Article 2(4) of the UN Charter and provides only two exceptions to that rule: use of force authorized by the UN Security Council under Chapter VII, and self-defense under Article 51 of the Charter.[33] Some scholars argue that PNA operations are an exercise of the right of self-defense under Article 51 as "an attack against nationals abroad can be equated to an attack against the state itself."[34] Other proponents argue that PNA constitutes an exception of customary law to Article 2(4), separate from Article 51.[35] Those claiming that PNA is contrary to Article 2(4) altogether base their argument on the *travaux préparatoires* of the Charter (and the absence of the concept in it).[36]

Besides a lack of scholarly consensus on PNA, there is little consistency in the practice of states.[37] Some Western states used PNA as an extension of self-defense as justification for intervening in other states.[38] The UK invoked PNA during the 1956 Suez crisis; the US did so in the Dominican Republic (1965), Grenada (1983), and Panama (1989); and Israel used it to justify the Entebbe raid of 1976.[39] When PNA is limited to a rescue operation, lasting no longer than the evacuation itself, and does not include a long deployment or occupation, states can usually count on little condemnation, or can even gain support from the international community.[40]

However, PNA can also be abused for political purposes by states to aid and assist "their" businesses, or to justify occupation or annexation.[41] The alternative interpretations of the norms of intervention based on PNA put forward by Russia stretched the norm further than most states were willing to accept. In the case of South Ossetia and Abkhazia their citizens were essentially Georgians that by "passportization" were made Russian nationals, thereby creating a "legitimation" of intervention in these two regions.[42] In 2014, in relation to the revolution in Ukraine, the Russian Federation further extended the argument that it had the right to protect all Russian-language speakers.[43] The reaction of the West to the annexation of Crimea can shine some light on its potential response when confronted with the use of military force by a member of the P5, under the pretext of PNA.

The US vehemently condemned the Russian involvement in Ukraine in February and March 2014 and quickly installed sanctions against "Persons Contributing to the Situation in Ukraine."[44] Since March 2014, the EU has progressively imposed restrictive measures against Russia in response to what it called the "illegal annexation of Crimea" and "deliberate destabilization of Ukraine."[45] UNGA Resolution 68/262 affirming the General Assembly's commitment to the territorial integrity of Ukraine and underscoring the invalidity of the 2014 Crimean referendum was supported by 100 member states; eleven members voted against the resolution, while 58 states abstained, including China.[46] Moreover Russia was suspended from the G8. However, while this *fait accompli* on the ground in Crimea was widely condemned by Western states and resulted in diplomatic measures and economic sanctions, the scope of the West to react militarily was severely limited (as analyzed by Amelie Theussen and Peter Viggo Jakobsen in chapter 7).

Dealing with a Fait Accompli

In this scenario China confronts Djibouti, regional allies, and Western states with a *fait accompli,* transforming the existing situation in a quick, decisive manner before the other side can react.[47] Opponents in such a situation have to choose between "accepting the new status quo, or going to war (or at least threatening war or some other punishment) to try to undo the transformation."[48] In this strategy it is crucial to correctly gauge the level of loss the defender will accept: "take too much and the defender will prefer war to tolerating the loss."[49] The strategy of creating a *fait accompli* shifts roles and puts the burden of the initiative for coercion or violence and the risks of a further escalation onto those who want to reverse the new situation.[50] However, doing so successfully requires expert timing and gauging the interests of the opponent. The remainder of this chapter will assess whether China calculated the interests of, and agreement among, Western states correctly in this scenario, and what their scope for response would be.

In the introduction to this book it is argued that the West is a set of particular institutional practices rather than a permanent unitary actor. In *Defending the West,* James Gow argues that "defining the West is largely a question of who shares values and interests that need defending."[51] The question is whether "the West" as a "political-security phenomenon based on shared values and interests" can come to an agreement about a timely response to defend these values, and its shared interests, when confronted with a show of Chinese force in Africa.[52] Some Western states have historically been more willing than others to take action to defend the rule-based international order.[53] The motivation to react to a Chinese military intervention in Djibouti would also differ across the spectrum of Western states as their economic and strategic interests in the region differ, as do their relationships with China. The BRI is in principle a soft power instrument, but it is not always clear where diplomacy ends and financial dependence begins. China invested in key infrastructure of some NATO (and EU) member states, for instance Greece's Piraeus port.[54] Within NATO, diverging interests make it difficult to reach political unity to devise a strategy to deal with a large power like China that "is neither an open rival nor a partner."[55] Thus economic and financial dependency might constrain the possibilities of some "Western" states to react to a Chinese intervention in Djibouti.

As NATO is a consensus-based alliance, internal tensions as well as China's influence on some of its members make it more likely that the West would operate in a coalition, rather than an alliance, in response to the scenario described. If not for military reasons then at least for "the umbrella of legitimacy provided by international support."[56] However, coalitions "demand international recognition of the threat or problem to be resolved, and agreement to the necessity for action, so as to underpin the legitimacy of the work in hand."[57] On the one hand, a strong leading state that can provide unity of command is necessary. On the other hand, gathering as much international support as possible, both political and in terms of states willing to commit forces and resources, is a requirement for a coalition to be effective.[58] While the US has traditionally been the leading state in Western coalitions, the Trump administration has been signaling a retreat from its traditional role on the international stage. Agreement among Western states about the need to take action against China, or even a shared political objective, does not mean they can come to an agreement on a single campaign plan (as shown in Kathleen McInnis's analysis of Afghanistan in chapter 5) and on what coercive measures to use to make China restore the former status quo.

In terms of possible diplomatic responses, isolating China from the West is both impossible and undesirable. China has the ability to maintain relations with other states if relations with Western states sour, and a pariah status would only strengthen nationalist sentiments. As in 2014 in relation to Crimea, draft UN Security Council resolutions "condemning flagrant violation of international law" would be vetoed. China cannot be suspended from the G8 as it is not a member. Expressing anger by summoning the ambassador is both "a piece of diplomatic theatre" and a symbol of serious political will.[59] However, if it is not backed up by the threat of other measures, it is unlikely to impress China.

States can also impose a range of economic sanctions in reaction to a perceived violation of international norms.[60] In theory, reduced prosperity as a result of sanctions will lead to the target reconsidering its behavior, to changes in its leadership, or a reduced military ability. However, the effectiveness of sanctions is much debated; states often have alternatives to bypass sanctions, and they unite populations against a common enemy.[61] They might be understood as further escalation or even an act of war, as Amelie Theussen and Peter Viggo Jakobsen show in their analysis of Russia's understanding of contemporary gray zone conflict in chapter 7. China would veto UN Security Council sanctions but other (multilateral) sanction regimes would also be hard to implement, not least because China has the world's second-largest economy. Sanctions are a double-edged sword, and in most Western societies economic downturn as a result of Chinese counter-sanctions would be hard to sell to the electorate. [62]

In the scenario described, the most important issue is whether the political will highlighted by Clausewitz would exist in the West to use decisive military force to compel China to restore the territorial integrity of Djibouti.[63] In recent decades the West has shown it does not shy away from using force, but it has also demonstrated that it avoided risk, or transferred risk to civilians in the war zone, and that it lacked the political will to use military power in a decisive manner if that would incur the risk of large numbers of casualties, as Kathleen McInnis illustrates in chapter 5.[64] In a (hypothetical) case like this—where a nuclear power is directly involved and would have to be confronted—the question is to which side the balance would tip, with the military force required to end a Chinese takeover of (parts of) Djibouti on one side and the interests at stake for the West on the other.

An adequate military response against a great power without risking an escalation of violence when confronted with a *fait accompli* is difficult, as was shown when Russia annexed Crimea. Nuclear powers directly engaging each other militarily over Djibouti might be hard to imagine. However, as Lawrence Freedman pointed out, previous predictions of the obsolescence of major war turned out to be "quite correct on the irrationality of warfare but wrong on their assumptions that rationality would prevail, or at least in terms of appreciating the short-term conditions that might lead countries to act so decisively against their long-term interests."[65]

In this scenario, a Chinese *fait accompli* strategy may fail if it provokes a stronger response than had been calculated and the West chooses to escalate rather than relent. Colin Gray argued in 2005 that "'decisive war' between major states currently is enjoying an off-season for one main reason: so extreme is the imbalance of military power in favour of the United States that potential rivals rule out policies that might lead to hostilities with the superpower."[66] China is attempting to end that superiority by enormous investments in its armed forces and especially by developing a blue-water navy that is increasingly able to project power across the world to protect the country's expanding economic interests.[67] By early 2020 it had two aircraft carriers, of which one is fully operational.[68] According to US officials, the PLAN is already able to inflict "heavy damage to or losses of American warships or major bases."[69] In a congressional testimony, US Admiral Philip S. Davidson warned that "China is now capable of controlling the South China Sea in all scenarios short of war with the United States."[70] This explains why no US aircraft carrier has passed through the Taiwan Strait since 2007.[71] The West has been unable to react to China's behavior and maritime claims in the South China Sea, or to Beijing's refusal to accept the arbitration rulings issued under the United Nations Convention on the Law of the Sea. This shows that in order to reach its political objectives in the South China Sea, China does not need a navy that can defeat the US Navy; it needs a navy that can make intervention in the region too costly for the US, and many analysts believe it already possesses this.[72]

While the Chinese Navy is undeniably gaining strength fast, China operates only one overseas base, while the US military operates 34 sites across Africa alone.[73] The US has 11 aircraft carriers against China's single operational carrier, and SIPRI estimates China's defense spending in 2019 at US$261 billion, against US$732 billion spent by the US in the same year.[74] The West still has an advantage in military technology and battle experience. However, as in the South China Sea gray zone warfare situation (as analyzed in chapter 7 by Amelie Theussen and Peter Viggo Jakobsen), when confronting the US and its Western allies with a *fait accompli* in Djibouti, China does not have to be able to beat the West in a direct military confrontation. It just has to have enough military force to deter leaders in Washington and European capitals from launching a military response to undo the new status quo.

Conclusion

The hypothetical scenario described in this chapter depicts events that are not outside the realm of possibility, given the right circumstances: economic recession, a US president distracted by domestic scandals, and a trade war between China and the US, combined with a situation in which political violence in Djibouti threatens Chinese citizens and commercial interests there, and growing domestic demands for the Chinese government to protect its citizens abroad.

The possible reaction of Western powers to such a scenario would be influenced by the legal justification that China would use to legitimize the use of force, and the extent to which this argument differed from the interpretation and application of the norm by Western powers. The argument used in this scenario, the doctrine of the "Protection of Nationals Abroad," lacks a clear basis under the UN Charter, and there is insufficient consistent conduct and *opinio juris* for a customary norm of PNA as the basis of an exception to the prohibition on the use of force to have been formed. Nevertheless, a number of Western states have, like China in this case, engaged in PNA over the years, and when states react to an imminent threat of injury to nationals, when the territorial state fails to protect them, and when their action remains confined to protecting their nationals against injury, condemnation from the international community is usually limited.[75] However, if, as described in this scenario, PNA were used by China as a pretext to take control over infrastructure in Djibouti, and it went further than absolutely necessary to protect its nationals, this would be such a flagrant violation of existing norms of international law that the West would be forced to react.

The use of the diplomatic instrument in this scenario would be limited, as China would be able to veto UN Security Council resolutions, and the political isolation of China is both implausible and undesirable. Experience teaches us that China would not be impressed by political condemnation of its actions. Against smaller states, economic sanctions can be installed and maintained, despite the debate on their effectiveness. But China has the second largest economy of the world; it has other options, and economic sanctions would adversely affect the economies of Western countries.

Comparing such a scenario with the Russian intervention in and subsequent annexation of Crimea shows that the West's response options are limited when a permanent member of the Security Council confronts it with a *fait accompli*. In this particular case, this is primarily because it is not clear in how far "the West" could come to an agreement about using coercive measures against China to defend shared interests and values. A *fait accompli* reverses existing relationships in that those who want to restore the status quo have to take the initiative to use armed force, and they now bear the risks of a further escalation. Even if there were an agreement among Western states that the use of force by China was a flagrant violation of norms of international law that merited a response, that is no guarantee that they could agree on what such a response should entail. A *fait accompli* strategy means that the existing relationship is changed almost instantly. "The West," accustomed to setting the pace of warfare, in this scenario would be denied any possibility to do so, apart from the pace of its response. A miscalculated or ill-timed *fait accompli* strategy could be very costly, but it is not unthinkable that a Chinese calculation that a lack of coherence would prevent the West from acting in unison in response to such a situation is correct.

The requirement for consensus in decision-making within NATO and diverging interests among members may make it difficult for the Alliance to respond. While the scenario described would not lead to an Article 5 situation, members openly questioning the principle of collective defense of Article 5 could also hamper the Alliance's ability to take other collective security measures. It is telling that President Macron called NATO "brain dead," albeit in a warning that Europe needs to start acting as a strategic power.[76] Yet it is highly doubtful whether the EU could act as a strategic power in the scenario presented here. Given the limited scope of action by alliances because of the need for consensus, Western countries need coalitions of the willing when confronting China, both for military reasons and legitimacy. The withdrawal of the US from Syria signals that it is less willing to play its traditional role in leading a coalition, even when faced with strategic opponents such as Russia taking over that role in a region. The fact that the Netherlands will contribute to a French-led naval mission in the Strait of Hormuz but ruled out joining a US-led coalition to protect the shipping lanes from Iranian interference shows a division in opinions on how to deal with adversaries and a diverging willingness to risk escalation.

Finally, coming to a shared understanding of the political objective of a military reaction to China might prove difficult for the West. Not only do different Western states have different ideas about the use of force—the divergence is especially marked between the US and Europe—but as became clear in the previous chapters in this section, they also have a different relationship with China. Moreover, as this scenario shows, their interests in Djibouti differ, and this will influence their response.

Although China's military and especially its naval capacities are increasing fast, it is not ready to take on the West in a direct confrontation outside what it claims as its own territorial waters. Nevertheless, in presenting the West with a *fait accompli*, it would not need to be able to confront it directly, but only to convince Western states that the costs of escalating a conflict over control of parts of Djibouti will be too high. In a scenario in which the West is taken by surprise and confronted with a *fait accompli* by China, it will be difficult to agree on an adequate response.

NOTES

1. "Hong Kong National Security Law Full Text | South China Morning Post," https://www.scmp.com/news/hong-kong/politics/article/3091595/hong-kong -national-security-law-read-full-text, accessed July 27, 2020.

2. Charles Clover, "Xi Jinping Signals Departure from Low-Profile Policy," *Financial Times*, October 20, 2017, https://www.ft.com/content/05cd86a6-b552 -11e7-a398-73d59db9e399.

3. Jacques deLisle and Avery Goldstein, eds., *China's Global Engagement: Cooperation, Competition, and Influence in the Twenty-First Century* (Brookings Institution Press, 2017).

4. Ministry of Foreign Affairs of the People's Republic of China, "President Xi Jinping Delivers Important Speech and Proposes to Build a Silk Road Economic Belt with Central Asian Countries," September 9, 2013, www.fmprc.gov.cn/mfa _eng/topics_665678/xjpfwzysiesgjtfhshzzfh_665686/t1076334.shtml.

5. "How Tiny Djibouti Became the Linchpin in China's Belt and Road Plan," *South China Morning Post*, April 28, 2019, www.scmp.com/news/china/diplomacy /article/3007924/how-tiny-african-nation-djibouti-became-linchpin-chinas-belt.

6. Geoffrey York, "Djibouti's Debt-Defying Stunt: Taking China's Money without Accepting China's Control," July 16, 2019, *Globe and Mail*, www .theglobeandmail.com/world/article-djiboutis-debt-defying-stunt-taking-chinas -money-without-accepting/.

7. "China Formally Opens First Overseas Military Base in Djibouti," Reuters, August 1, 2017, www.reuters.com/article/us-china-djibouti-idUSKBN1AH3E3.

8. Office of the Secretary of Defense, "Military and Security Developments Involving the People's Republic of China 2019," Annual Report to Congress, Washington, May 2, 2019, p. 16.

9. "Live-Fire Exercises Conducted by PLA Base in Djibouti—China—China daily.Com.Cn," www.chinadaily.com.cn/china/2017-11/25/content_34966883 .htm.

10. David Lague and Benjamin Kang Lim, "Special Report: China's Vast Fleet Is Tipping the Balance in the Pacific," Reuters, April 30, 2019, www.reuters.com/ article/us-china-army-navy-specialreport-idUSKCN1S612W.

11. Mathieu Duchâtel, Oliver Bräuner, and Hang Zhou, *Protecting China's Overseas Interests: The Slow Shift Away from Non-Interference*, SIPRI Policy Paper 41, June 2014.

12. Alexander L. George and Richard Smoke, *Deterrence in American Foreign Policy: Theory and Practice* (Columbia University Press, 1974), p. 537.

13. Jonas Parello-Plesner and Mathieu Duchâtel, *China's Strong Arm: Protecting Citizens and Assets Abroad*, Adelphi Papers, 451 (London: Routledge, 2015), p. 20; Mathieu Duchâtel, Oliver Bräuner, and Zhou Hang, *Protecting China's Overseas Interests: The Slow Shift Away from Non-interference,* SIPRI Policy Paper 41, June 2014.

14. Chen Zheng, "China Debates the Non-Interference Principle," *Chinese Journal of International Politics*, vol, 9, no. 3 (September 2016), p. 350, https://doi.org/10.1093/cjip/pow010.

15. Parello-Plesner and Duchâtel, *China's Strong Arm*, p. 10.

16. Ibid., pp. 12–13; "China Evacuates Foreign Nationals from Yemen in Unprecedented Move," Reuters, April 3, 2015, https://www.reuters.com/article/us-yemen-security-china-idUSKBN0MU09M20150403.

17. Andrew S. Erickson and Austin M. Strange, *No Substitute for Experience: Chinese Antipiracy Operations in the Gulf of Aden*, CMSI Red Books, Study No. 10 (Newport, RI: U.S. Naval War College, 2013), p. 2; Alison A. Kaufman, "China's Participation in Anti-Piracy Operations off the Horn of Africa: Drivers and Implications" (Alexandria, VA: CNA Analysis and Solutions, 2009), p. 1, https://apps.dtic.mil/dtic/tr/fulltext/u2/a503697.pdf.

18. Parello-Plesner and Duchâtel, *China's Strong Arm*, p. 14.

19. Office of the Secretary of Defense, "Military and Security Developments Involving the People's Republic of China 2019."

20. Erickson and Strange, *No Substitute for Experience*, p. 14; Zheng; "China Debates the Non-Interference Principle," p. 350.

21. CNIC, "Camp Lemonnier, Djibouti," www.cnic.navy.mil/regions/cnreuraf cent/installations/camp_lemonnier_djibouti.html.

22. Arwa Damon and Brent Swails, "China and the United States Face off in Djibouti," CNN, www.cnn.com/2019/05/26/africa/china-belt-road-initiative -djibouti-intl/index.html.

23. Ibid.

24. "Remarks by National Security Advisor Ambassador John R. Bolton on the Trump Administration's New Africa Strategy," The White House, www.whitehouse .gov/briefings-statements/remarks-national-security-advisor-ambassador-john-r -bolton-trump-administrations-new-africa-strategy/.

25. Damon and Swails, "China and the United States Face off in Djibouti."

26. "Remarks by National Security Advisor Ambassador John R. Bolton on the Trump Administration's New Africa Strategy."

27. Clover, "Xi Jinping Signals Departure from Low-Profile Policy."

28. "Address by President of the Russian Federation," http://en.kremlin.ru/ events/president/news/20603.

29. T. Ruys, "The 'Protection of Nationals' Doctrine Revisited," *Journal of Conflict and Security Law,* vol. 13, no. 2 (13 August 2008), pp. 233–71, https://doi .org/10.1093/jcsl/krn025.

30. Onur Güven and Olivier Ribbelink, "The Protection of Nationals Abroad: A Return to Old Practice?," in *Fundamental Rights in International and European Law*, edited by Christophe Paulussen and others (The Hague: T.M.C. Asser Press, 2016), pp. 45–72, https://doi.org/10.1007/978-94-6265-088-6_3. While Russia's legal justification for intervention at some point shifted toward "intervention by invitation," originally in Crimea it was that of the "Protection of Nationals Abroad."

31. Francis Grimal and Graham Melling, "The Protection of Nationals Abroad: Lawfulness or Toleration? A Commentary," *Journal of Conflict and Security Law*, vol. 16, no. 3 (January 2, 2012), pp. 541–54, at p. 541, https://doi.org/10.1093/jcsl/krr021.

32. Ruys, "The 'Protection of Nationals' Doctrine Revisited,", p. 541; C. Humphrey M. Waldock, "The Position Under Customary Law," *The Regulation of the Use of Force by Individual States in International Law*, Collected Courses of the Hague Academy of International Law: 081 (Leiden/Boston: Brill | Nijhoff, 1951), p. 467, https://doi.org/10.1163/1875-8096_pplrdc_ej.9789028611825.451_517.2.

33. United Nations, "Charter of the United Nations," 1 UNTS XVI § (1945), www.unwebsite.com/charter.

34. Ruys, "The 'Protection of Nationals' Doctrine Revisited," p. 235. Ruys lists as examples D. W. Bowett, L. Doswald-Beck, C. Greenwood, G. Fitzmaurice, A. Gerard, O. Schachter, and R. B. Lillich.

35. Ibid., p. 236.

36. Güven and Ribbelink, "The Protection of Nationals Abroad," p. 52. Another argument is that PNA is a form of Humanitarian Intervention. However, the two concepts differ in that one involves the protection of the state's own nationals abroad and the other of foreign nationals against their own government.

37. Ruys, "The 'Protection of Nationals' Doctrine Revisited," p. 233.

38. Ibid., p. 233.

39. Ibid., pp. 238–51.

40. Güven and Ribbelink, "The Protection of Nationals Abroad," p. 49.

41. Ibid., p. 49.

42. Ibid.

43. Ibid.

44. "Executive Order—Blocking Property of Certain Persons Contributing to the Situation in Ukraine," whitehouse.gov, March 6, 2014, https://obamawhitehouse.archives.gov/the-press-office/2014/03/06/executive-order-blocking-property-certain-persons-contributing-situation.

45. "EU Restrictive Measures in Response to the Crisis in Ukraine—Consilium," www.consilium.europa.eu/en/policies/sanctions/ukraine-crisis/.

46. UN General Assembly, "Resolution 68/262 on the Territorial Integrity of Ukraine," A/RES/68/262 § (2014).

47. Dan Altman, "By Fait Accompli, Not Coercion: How States Wrest Territory from Their Adversaries," *International Studies Quarterly,* vol. 61, no. 4 (December 29, 2017), pp. 881–91, https://doi.org/10.1093/isq/sqx049.

48. Ahmer Tarar, "A Strategic Logic of the Military Fait Accompli," *International Studies Quarterly,* vol. 60, no. 4 (June 13, 2016), p. 743, https://doi.org/10.1093/isq/sqw018.

49. Altman, "By Fait Accompli, Not Coercion," p. 886.

50. Glenn Herald Snyder and Paul Diesing, *Conflict among Nations: Bargaining, Decision Making, and System Structure in International Crises*, Princeton Legacy Library (Princeton University Press, 2016), p. 227.

51. James Gow, *Defending the West* (Cambridge: Polity Press, 2005), p. 16.

52. Ibid., p. 17.

53. Robert Kagan, *Of Paradise and Power: America and Europe in the New World Order* (New York: Vintage Books, 2004).

54. International Institute for Strategic Studies, "How Should NATO Respond to China's Growing Power?," www.iiss.org/blogs/analysis/2019/09/nato-respond-china-power.

55. Ibid.

56. Andrew Graham, *Military Coalitions in War* (Oxford University Press, 2012), p. 321, https://doi.org/10.1093/oxfordhb/9780199562930.013.0022.

57. Ibid., pp. 324–25.

58. Ibid., pp. 324–25.

59. Roland Hughes, "What Happens When an Ambassador Is Summoned?," BBC News, September 10, 2019, sec. World, www.bbc.com/news/world-48949534; Rob de Wijk, *The Art of Military Coercion: Why the West's Military Superiority Scarcely Matters* (Amsterdam University Press, 2014), p. 110, https://doi.org/10.1515/9789048519415.

60. Council on Foreign Relations, "What Are Economic Sanctions?," www.cfr.org/backgrounder/what-are-economic-sanctions.

61. de Wijk, *The Art of Military Coercion*, p. 112.

62. World Economic Forum, "How Effective Are Economic Sanctions?," www.weforum.org/agenda/2015/02/how-effective-are-economic-sanctions/.

63. Carl von Clausewitz, *On War*, edited and translated by Michael Howard and Peter Paret (New York: Knopf, 2007), p. 83.

64. Martin Shaw, "Risk-Transfer Militarism, Small Massacres and the Historic Legitimacy of War," *International Relations,* vol. 16, no. 3 (December 2002), pp. 343–59, https://doi.org/10.1177/0047117802016003003.

65. Lawrence Freedman, "Introduction," *Adelphi Papers,* vol. 45, no. 379 (January 2006), p. 6, https://doi.org/10.1080/05679320600661624.

66. Colin S. Gray, "Combatting Terrorism," *Parameters, US Army War College Quarterly,* vol. 35, no. 1 (2005), p. 22.

67. Office of the Secretary of Defense, "Military and Security Developments Involving the People's Republic of China 2019."

68. Office of the Secretary of Defense, "Military and Security Developments Involving the People's Republic of China 2020."

69. Lague and Lim, "Special Report."

70. Steven Lee Myers, "With Ships and Missiles, China Is Ready to Challenge

U.S. Navy in Pacific," *New York Times*, August 29, 2018, sec. World, www.nytimes .com/2018/08/29/world/asia/china-navy-aircraft-carrier-pacific.html.

71. Lague and Lim, "Special Report."

72. Myers, "With Ships and Missiles, China Is Ready to Challenge U.S. Navy in Pacific."

73. Nick Turse, "U.S. Military Says It Has a 'Light Footprint' in Africa. These Documents Show a Vast Network of Bases," *The Intercept* (blog), December 1, 2018, https://theintercept.com/2018/12/01/u-s-military-says-it-has-a-light -footprint-in-africa-these-documents-show-a-vast-network-of-bases/.

74. SIPRI Military Expenditure Database, https://www.sipri.org/databases/ milex, accessed July 27, 2020.

75. Ruys, "The 'Protection of Nationals' Doctrine Revisited," p. 541; Waldock, "The Position Under Customary Law."

76. "Emmanuel Macron Warns Europe: NATO Is Becoming Brain-Dead," *The Economist*, November 7, 2019, https://www.economist.com/europe/2019/11/07/ emmanuel-macron-warns-europe-nato-is-becoming-brain-dead.

PART III

Military Operations and Temporality

Speed, Time, and Western Military Power

OLIVIER SCHMITT

The final part of this book is concerned with warfare, or the conduct of military operations. Part I discussed civil militarism as a foundation for strategy, and explored whether recent Western military setbacks were reflective of a disconnect between political institutions and military practices. In turn, Part II discussed normative orders as anchors of temporality: norms reflect specific perceptions *of* time, but also evolve *over* time, thus constantly reshaping the context of war-making. Adopting a more granular perspective, Part III looks in more detail at war-making. Here again we observe that perceptions of time shape the Western ability to generate military power, particularly because of a confusion between time and speed.[1]

Perceptions of time in warfare have three main dimensions.[2] First, time is conceived of as "timing," especially in the tactically oriented literature: tactical commanders are supposed to "seize the opportunity" in order to achieve battlefield dominance, and the military professional literature is replete with advice on how to combine maneuver and fire in order to make the most of specific situations.

Second, time can be conceived as a resource to be managed, or as a currency. This type of thinking is particularly evident in sentences such as "in counter-insurgency, times favors the insurgent." In fact time is neutral and does not, by itself, favor anyone: such a saying is a category error since it is about motivations, not time. It is actually a shorthand for "the insurgents' will to fight is higher than the counterinsurgents," which will lead to the latter's defeat if the fight drags on without the insurgent being clearly defeated."[3] The confusion of time with commitment is revelatory of a perception of time as a resource which has to be managed, and not as a context for strategic action.

The third way to perceive time in warfare is by conflating it with speed, which is what this section focuses on. Speed in the conduct of military operations has long been thought to be a critical factor in achieving battlefield successes. As Basil Liddell Hart wrote: "Of all qualities of war, it is speed which is dominant, speed of both mind and movement."[4] More recently, the intellectual cornerstone for the emphasis on speed in Western armed forces conceptually began with John Boyd and his OODA loop, which was a way to conceptualize the role of tempo (or pace) and speed in warfare and contributed to the adoption of maneuver warfare in the US Marine Corps.[5] The emphasis on speed was confirmed by the adoption of the "AirLand Battle" doctrine in 1982 with the new iteration of the *Field Manual 100-5: Operations.* FM-100-5 emphasized *agility*, defined as the ability to "act faster than the enemy," which would be enable US forces to generate sufficient mass through better synchronization. The emphasis on speed intensified after the end of the Cold War and with the intellectual domination of the "Revolution in Military Affairs" and "Transformation" paradigms.[6] In a context of "peace dividends" and decreasing budgets, the services tried to maximize their fighting power by capitalizing on what were already US military advantages: doubling down on the flexibility and modularity of the forces. For example, in 1997 Major General Robert Scales produced a report entitled *Knowledge and Speed*, which was supposed to provide a blueprint for future force requirements in the US army. Of course, the path toward full modularity and information dominance was far from direct, not least because of the stabilization operations that were initiated in Afghanistan and Iraq, but the wartime paradigm guiding operational concepts was still about increasing the speed and tempo of operations.[7]

The importance of speed became deeply ingrained in US operational thinking, General James Mattis (who commanded the 1st Marine Division in the 2003 Iraq war) even declaring "we knew that the centre of gravity was speed . . . *speed equals success.*"[8] Current technological developments, such as the rise of mature precision-strike regimes and the convergence between cyber and electronic warfare, seem to be accelerating the pace of warfare at the tactical level. In order to cope with such changes, it is probably tempting for Western armed forces to do "more of the same." For example, General David Allvin, the US Joint Staff's director of strategy, plans, and policy, declared that speed has to be a characteristic of the US forces: "We have to up our game in speed of recognition, speed of decision and speed of action, because it is coming at us that fast."[9] Emerging technologies in sensors and data-fusion capabilities already generate discourses that are eerily similar to the "Network-Centric Warfare" visions of the 1990s: a blog post author for the US Army Training and Doctrine Command (TRADOC) recently wrote that "one of the greatest leaps that has yet to come and is coming is the ability to significantly increase the speed of the decision-making process of the individual at the small unit level. To maximize individual and small unit initiative to think and act flexibly, soldiers must receive as much relevant information as possible, as quickly as possible."[10] Such claims need to be qualified and put in their proper strategic and political contexts, which is the purpose of the chapters in this section. The core argument is that Western military organizations desperately try to optimize for speed, but their efforts are frustrated by battlefield conditions; they could have negative civil-military consequences and may be based on problematic perceptions of the strategic value of speed.

The recent history of the tension between a Western desire to achieve speed on the battlefield and the operational challenges encountered by Western forces is explored by Pascal Vennesson in chapter 9. Vennesson shows how doctrinal preferences for achieving speed were usually frustrated in recent military interventions, leading to "uneasy attempts to fight both fast and slow," and thus questioning the assumptions on which most Western military transformation efforts are based.

Chapter 10 by Nina Kollars shows that this preference for speed is still very much ingrained in Western militaries. Looking at the example of the Multi-Domain Battle doctrine in the US armed forces, Kollars argues that the belief in *information superiority* as a way to achieve battlefield dominance through faster decisionmaking is dangerous for the political control of military efforts and may even be counterproductive.

While Kollars dispels the myth of information as the key to victory, in chapter 11 Heather Williams looks at some preconceived ideas about the effect of speed on strategic stability. Although recent discussions of hypersonic glide vehicles and artificial intelligence have adopted alarmist tones and warned against potential major risks to strategic stability, Williams shows that the jury is still out and that speed, by itself, is not necessarily a destabilizing factor: as always, political conditions, not technology, will determine the degree of risk to international stability.

Finally, the scenario by Stéphane Taillat and Joseph Henrotin in chapter 12 explores whether Western armed forces would still be able to fight if they were denied one of the key enablers of their speed of operations: digital communications. By questioning this perception of time favoring speed on the battlefield, this section therefore raises uncomfortable questions about the sustainability of Western military power and the effectiveness of Western approaches to warfare.

NOTES

1. Andrew R. Hom, *International Relations and the Problem of Time* (Oxford University Press, 2020).

2. Elie Baranets, "Who Benefits from Time? A Critical Analysis of the Use of Time in War Studies," *Temporalités: Revue de Sciences Sociales et Humaines*, no. 21 (2015), online.

3. Ivan Arreguin-Toft, *How the Weak Win Wars: A Theory of Asymmetric Conflict* (Cambridge University Press, 2005).

4. Basil H. Liddell Hart, "The Development of the 'New Model' Army: Suggestions on a Progressive, but Gradual Mechanicalization," *Army Quarterly*, no. 9 (1924), p. 48.

5. Ian T. Brown, *A New Conception of War: John Boyd, the U.S. Marines, and Maneuver Warfare* (Quantico, VA: Marine Corps University Press, 2018).

6. Jeffrey Collins and Andrew Futter, eds., *Reassessing the Revolution in Military Affairs: Transformation, Evolution and Lessons Learnt* (Basingstoke, UK: Palgrave, 2015).

7. Olivier Schmitt, "Wartime Paradigms and the Future of Western Military Power," *International Affairs*, vol. 96, no. 2 (2020), pp. 401–18.

8. Quoted in Anthony King, *Command: The Twenty-First Century General* (Cambridge University Press, 2019), p. 259. Emphasis added.

9. Jim Garamone, "Military Global Integration Is About Change, Joint Staff Official Says," U.S Department of Defense, May 15, 2019.

10. Richard Nabors, "Warfare at the Speed of Sound," *Mad Scientist* (blog), April 26, 2018, https://madsciblog.tradoc.army.mil/48-warfare-at-the-speed-of-thought/.

NINE

Fighting, Fast and Slow?

Speed and Western Ways of War

PASCAL VENNESSON

This chapter addresses the challenge of speed in military operations.[1] When they confront this issue, Western war planners face a trade-off. They tend to seek maximum operable speed—that is, the fastest pace or tempo of operations that will enable them to exploit mobility and surprise. Speed helps to ensure their freedom of action by retaining the initiative.[2] A faster pace provides a reserve of time and, simultaneously, rushes their adversaries and reduces their range of options.

However, a higher operational tempo implies a number of shortcomings. First, speed entails higher risks because the shorter timescale does not allow for more comprehensive planning, nor for reassessment following errors.[3] Indeed a vast body of evidence accumulated in the psychology of judgment and decisionmaking shows that fast thinking frequently leads to severe and systematic errors.[4] Second, a faster tempo at the tactical and operational levels may run counter the political need to slow down the war. For example, compellence as well as thinking on limited nuclear war often rely on "set-piece warfare," which includes advance warnings, a slower time schedule, and the postponement of decisions.[5] With a slower pace of war, political leaders gain time to reflect and may be better positioned to control and patiently affect the course of events. Third, an exclusive focus on speed risks missing the need for well-calibrated strategic moves: it may become too predictable and ultimately unable to destabilize the adversary, or inadequate when the intensity level of conventional fighting is low and there is no benefit from faster movements. Finally, the quest for speed and short war runs into trouble when it confronts a rival political-military sense of time explicitly designed to frustrate that very preference. Mao Zedong famously emphasized both during the Second Sino-Japanese War (1937–45) and at the beginning of the Chinese Civil War (1945–49) that his priority was to keep the war going as long as possible and that he intended to shape time in order to force the enemy's will to yield.[6] In the first decades of the twenty-first century, sowing confusion through cyber propaganda, increasing deniability, preventing access through anti-access/area denial (A2/AD) capabilities and mature reconnaissance-strike complexes exemplify the continuing efforts to frustrate Western war planners' preference for speed.

How do military planners seek to "win time" and carry out operations as fast as possible while adjusting speed to prevailing conditions, such as the most suitable rhythm for their own force and the actions of the enemy? Can they fight *both* fast *and* slow? This chapter explores how Western military planners face this dilemma of operational speed, with a focus on the United States, the United Kingdom, and France, the three main warfighting nations in the West.[7] It is important to acknowledge that there is no such thing as one Western military culture, however, and some of the differences in these three states' conceptions of operational speed are highlighted below.[8] The focus here is on the operational level of war, which prescribes how military forces, such as army divisions or corps, naval task forces, or aircraft wings, are to achieve theater strategic ends by interconnecting a series of battles or engagements in the course of a campaign.[9]

Western ways of war are best characterized by uneasy attempts to fight both fast and slow. To be sure, Western militaries—and this is not unique to "the West"[10]—may have a preference for fighting quickly to achieve decisive results in a short campaign or war.[11] However, as they engage in a competitive strategic interaction with their adversaries, they simply cannot decide on their own to fight at the pace of their choosing. In fact the adaptive and paradoxical logic of strategy is likely to lead to situations in which the more they seek to fight fast, the more their adversaries have incentives to force them to fight slow.[12] The rhythm of operations and the ways in which the war is kept as short as possible or extended for as long as possible are part of the political and military stakes. Western warfighting has been characterized by a variety of uneven and challenging efforts to adapt to a slower pace of operations and wars of much longer duration than were initially expected and wished for.

In short, Western war planners may prefer to fight fast and win short wars but they end up having to fight fast and slow, which proves harder and more unsettling than expected.

The first part of this chapter explores how Western defense intellectuals and war planners approach speed conceptually, in their doctrinal understandings, and operationally, in their actual modes of engagement.[13] The second part then turns to the three Western states' efforts to adjust to the war tempo of specific adversaries in Iraq, Afghanistan, and Mali.

Fighting Fast: Strategic Imperative and Organizational Culture Preferences

Time, closely associated with space, is a central component of strategy, especially at the operational level of war. The attempt to fight speedily in order to keep the war short, while not universally sought after, is an important component of one pattern of strategy—violent conflict aiming at military victory.[14] Attempted several times by Frederick II of Prussia, for instance during the Silesian campaign, this pattern originated in the era of the wars of the French Revolution; Napoleon, particularly attuned to the value of time, constantly pressed his subordinates to accelerate execution.[15] This operational priority was dominant, though not always successfully implemented, in Europe from the nineteenth to the first half of the twentieth century. As Basil Liddell Hart noted: "Every gain in speed increases not only the attacker's security but the defender's insecurity. For the higher the speed the greater the chance of, and scope for, surprise. Speed and surprise are not merely related; they are twins."[16] Although their views are not identical, war planners in the US, the UK, and France all take speed seriously in their doctrines and operations.

Speed and the American Way of War

In the mid- and late 1990s, many analysts, including Michael Ignatieff, David Deptula, and Eliot Cohen, agreed that a "new" American way of war was emerging. One of its core components was the idea of defeating an opponent swiftly, within a few weeks, and decisively.[17] In 1998 the Department of Defense *Vision 2010* officially endorsed that conception of speed in warfare. This was not merely a matter of altering doctrinal documents, significant though they are in helping the military define a common view of the conduct of war and improve training. A key assumption underlying the Stryker Brigade Combat Team put into place by the US Army in 1999–2002, for example, was that protracted warfare was either unlikely or could be precluded by combat information superiority and the quick use of precision fire.[18] The institutional memories of the 1990–91 Gulf War focused largely on the swift, 100-hour ground campaign and less on the one-month air campaign, let alone the earlier six-month deployment phase.[19]

At each level of war—political-strategic, operational, and tactical— defense intellectuals and planners in the US often approach time in absolute terms and tend to emphasize speed as their core priority. The preponderance of speed was striking in the quick battle victories at the outset of the wars in Afghanistan and Iraq (2001–03). As he led the 2003 invasion of Iraq, General Tommy Franks thought he was implementing this way to use operational speed, noting that the way to win the war was "by getting inside the enemy's decision cycle. Remember: Speed kills . . . the enemy."[20] At the head of the 1st Marine Division during the early stages of the war, General James Mattis also prioritized speed and claimed that, in fact, "the centre of gravity [of the Iraqi campaign] was speed."[21] Speed was therefore confirmed as the best yardstick to measure future wars and presented as an important factor of success at the tactical and operational level. These swift initial victories led many to conclude that "today, and in the future, armed conflict is expected to be short, decisive and accompanied with a minimum of casualties."[22] Defense intellectuals considered that speed was the predominant trait required to ensure victory on the battleground, and proponents of this "New American way of war" posited that "rapid blows on carefully selected centers of gravity" would bring about "a quick and bloodless victory."[23] Speed was the best way to rob the enemy of the time required to respond. These brisk attacks were assumed to "create cascading effects" that would lead to the enemy's "psychological paralysis and loss of control."[24] If victory was understood as the defeat of adversary's armed forces on the battlefield, the American military appears to have found a swift way to achieve it. In sum, a strong preference for speed is embedded in US military organizational culture. As encapsulated in the July 2019 Army Doctrine Publication no. 5-0 (ADP 5-0) devoted to the conduct of operations: "A goal of the operations process is to make timely and effective decisions and to act faster than the enemy. A tempo advantageous to friendly forces can place the enemy under the pressures of uncertainty and time. Throughout the operations process, making and communicating decisions faster than the enemy can react produces a tempo with which the enemy cannot compete. . . . The speed and accuracy of a commander's actions to address a changing situation is a key contributor to agility."[25]

Maneuver and Speed in the British Military

The question of speed and mobility is also an important component of the evolution of operational art in the UK.[26] By the 1990s, attrition and maneuver began to be seen not as alternatives but as complementary.[27] The Gulf War showed the importance of a capacity for mass fire effects. In effects-based warfare, armies could maneuver to bring fire to bear, while also using fire power to be able to maneuver. Despite the complementary nature of attrition and maneuver, the first edition of the joint defense doctrine published in 1997 favored the latter. It defined maneuver theory as a "warfighting philosophy that seeks to defeat the enemy by shattering his moral and physical cohesion—his ability to fight as an effective, coordinated whole—rather than by destroying him physically through incremental attrition."[28]

The central idea of maneuver in British operational thinking is more than just mobility; it involves setting the tempo of operations and uses pre-emption and surprise to dislocate an enemy. The British military doctrine—notably *Army Doctrine Publication (ADP) Land Operations* (published in 2010 and updated in 2017), the capstone doctrine for British Land Forces—considers time as an important factor at both tactical and operational levels. Significant features of the "Manoeuvrist Approach" that it sets forth are "momentum, tempo and agility, which in combination lead to shock and surprise."[29] Momentum, defined as a "product of velocity and mass," is designed to keep an enemy off-balance to retain the initiative.[30] The aim of the "Manoeuvrist Approach" is to operate at a higher tempo than adversaries and have a psychological impact by stunning them and rendering them "incapable of rational decision making."[31]

The British doctrine understands time as a relative factor, through the concept of tempo. Tempo is defined as "rate of operations relative to an enemy's," and war planners advocate acting faster than the enemy to gain an advantage. Speed of decisionmaking is necessary to hold an initiative but must be followed by speedy action. Time of execution is often more important than how "perfect" a plan is for success.[32] In the face of new and changing situations, the land forces must be able to sustain a high tempo by adapting more rapidly than adversaries. Flexibility is considered a principle of war and defined as "the ability to change rapidly, appropriately and effectively to new circumstances."[33] Flexibility includes how responsive and adaptable the force is, which are time-dependent traits. Responsiveness measures "speed of action, reaction and how quickly the initiative can be seized or regained," while adaptability emphasizes the necessity to 'learn quickly, to adjust to changes in a dynamic situation, and amend plans" in a rapid and effective manner.[34] In Afghanistan and Iraq, the British Army proved eager in looking for action and ready to seek battle. This brought at times quick but only temporary successes as there were not enough troops to hold what was seized.[35]

While British land doctrine seeks to maximize the speed of decisionmaking and action, it also recognizes the need to keep a variable pace. For example, as Christopher Elliott notes, instead of rapidly assaulting Basra in the early phase of the Iraq campaign, Major General Robin Brims decided to halt his 1st Armoured Division for a week outside the city.[36] Instead of rushing into a long and hard slog in urban terrain, which would have destroyed the civil infrastructure and alienated the population, he waited for the Baathists to melt away, thereby facilitating the early occupation of the city. Some operations also require a steady and persistent pace. War planners highlight persistence as one of the four attributes that inform doctrine and the design of land forces. Persistence refers to "the capacity of land forces to extend their presence in an area for long periods of time" so as to develop "engagement, control, and influence" in the local context.[37] For stability operations, the focus is not speed at all costs but preparing for the long term under legitimate authority in the host nation.

Speed and the French Military

French military doctrine considers time to be an important factor at all levels of warfare.[38] At the strategic level, "responsiveness is reinforced by the dynamic management of the build-up of forces, under the direction of its Joint Operations Centre (CPCO). The graduated readiness of the forces results in different postures and warning orders (characterized by more or less short time-frames, from a couple of hours to several days or weeks), and in the operational readiness level that has been reached. . . . At the operational level, the operational modules on alert (managed by *EMIA-FE54* and formed from the operational pool) provide the strategic level with the guarantee of an initial response capability, especially as part of initial entry."[39] Military readiness is considered as "crucial to the success of engagement" in both training and operations. The proper succession of preparation phases contributes to efficient operational readiness and allows the force to respond speedily, while optimizing the utilization of resources.[40]

Tactically, high responsiveness is achieved by increased flexibility and agility "in terms of organization, command and action" to deal with modern military challenges.[41] War planners recognize uncertainties as an "essential part of strategy, manoeuvre and combat." Uncertainties are often time-sensitive; for example, in sudden crises that may develop rapidly and have "immediate or long-term consequences." Another time-related uncertainty is the duration of military engagements: "The longer a conflict lasts, the more it develops its own dynamic, which might differ from the initial expectations. A long-term confrontation also raises the issue of the constancy and determination of the coalition and public opinion."[42] Moreover constant and timely adaptation help the French armed forces "to maintain a capability for long-distance action." Without adaptability, they would not be able to "rapidly apprehend the characteristic specific to each theatre, or changes in an environment within the same campaign."[43] War planners also emphasize the importance of agility in planning, and throughout the course of a military engagement, in order for forces to adapt to highly volatile situations and to be able to "combine joint actions, from the lowest tactical levels, without being confined to preconceived patterns."[44]

French war planners do not focus exclusively on winning time and rapid action, however. They generally acknowledge that lengthy operational preparation matters and that great battles are often won long before the day of combat.[45] General Bernard Barrera, commander of the 2013 Serval operation in Mali, points out that the motivation of troops is a long-term enterprise.[46] While responsiveness and readiness are important, war planners also recognize the need to sustain operations over time: "The duration of a military operation corresponds less and less to the political tempo, which is cadenced by the level of acceptance of the intervention by public opinion and risks of the situation becoming bogged down."[47] Action must be kept consistent with the accomplishment of the "desired end state" and it is through endurance and continuous supply that the force may fulfill its mission.[48] Moreover military planners recognize that time is relative to one's adversaries. They advocate "achieving and maintaining decisional superiority" over them, with a "faster decision and order dissemination process." They seek to gain an advantage from the "decreased ability of the adversary to make timely and well-grounded decisions," which "greatly reduces or paralyses its capacity for action."[49] For example, at the start of the Serval operation the force deployed had to cover 1,000 km to reach Timbuktu but its intelligence and logistics were limited, it lacked command and recovery vehicles, and its radio communications were inadequate. Yet General Barrera framed the situation as a "speed race": he considered it out of the question to wait for six months before starting the progression and got ready to launch it in 36 hours.[50] His objective was to capture Timbuktu and the Gao bridge as quickly as possible.

This focus on operational speed is related to the necessity of high-speed information flows for faster and more effective decisionmaking in military action. The doctrine states that a faster information flow of "Open Source Intelligence (OSINT) and Military-Related Intelligence (MRI) feeds into situational awareness, which in turns leads to better understanding." Furthermore "the OSINT available in real time leads to significantly accelerat[ing] the cycle of production and dissemination of MRI, to which it contributes." At the same time, military planners recognize that pure speed of information flows does not translate into information superiority and knowledge of the battle space. "The efficient management of ever-growing flows of information is imperative" so as not to "overload or inhibit the decision-making capacity of the military chief and his Force Headquarters (FHQ)."[51]

Military planners also note the importance of synchronizing the use of armed forces to maintain time efficiency, specifically through the Combined Joint Expeditionary Force (CJEF), a "rapidly deployable force that is formed based on specific needs. . . . It can gather up to two land battlegroups, one mixed air wing, and one maritime component based on a capital ship (aircraft carrier or amphibious ship)" and "can act within a bilateral framework or in support to NATO-led, UN-led or EU-led operations."[52] Because of its speedy deployability, the CJEF is an "early entry force" and does not have the capabilities to ensure long-term military action such as peacekeeping. The Army favors light armor as it modernizes and remains roughly in the Stryker weight class. This is because "developers have focused on maintaining their predecessors' mobility while enhancing their capabilities, primarily by means of technology-enabling networked warfare."[53] The high mobility of armored vehicles gives the Army some flexibility "with regard to how it gets armoured vehicles to the theatre of operations and moves them around once there, and to what extent it draws on vehicle fleets already in the region as opposed to dispatching them from France."[54]

What comes before speed of military action is speed of decisionmaking and organization. Hence time matters not just tactically but operationally as well. French expeditionary forces had various mechanisms to give their commanders a "significant level of flexibility and organizational adroitness" to respond rapidly to new threats. The various units were well versed in reorganizing into more efficient formations to deal with changing situations. Indeed during the Serval operation, "as French forces poured into Mali and mission objectives shifted from day to day, week to week, the GTIAs and SGTIAs formed and re-formed quickly and operated as effective and coherent units."[55]

The Army's investment in network and information management systems also increased the speed of information flows "down to individual vehicles and dismounted soldiers," as well as enhancing situational awareness.[56] Project Scorpion, the overall system of networking systems, "is intended to make French units more effective despite being more dispersed and often smaller" and is "a key to fighting the kind of fast-paced and relatively low-budget manoeuvre warfare that the French would like to fight." Networking technology has also enabled the digitization of logistics operations, which has allowed units not only to work faster but to remain efficient for longer.[57] Finally, the Army optimizes readiness through a system of "centralizing vehicle maintenance and fleet management and, in effect, rationing out vehicles to units as needed in a roughly just-in-time approach rather than having units maintain their own vehicle fleets."[58] This increases the speed of the troops by "ensuring that units have access to ready vehicles when they need them, rather than having them deal with pools of vehicles that are only partially operable, if working at all."[59]

Recognizing the Limits of Fast Fighting

In sum, although they address the issue of speed in different ways, war planners in the US, the UK, and France all recognize its significance in multiple dimensions: doctrine, technology, networking, and actual engagements. They all display a preference for speed as a way to increase their own freedom of action and simultaneously to deprive their adversaries of theirs. It is important to avoid caricatures, however. Planners and commanders do consider the risks and rewards associated with increasing or reducing the tempo of an operation. They seek to adjust their speed by taking into consideration a variety of factors such as their enemy's disposition, the attrition of key enemy and friendly capabilities, the availability of logistics to continue their movement at the same speed, or the capacity of friendly units to keep pace (or not). They also recognize that there will be discrete moments in an operation where they may decide to slow the tempo in order to set particular conditions, for example taking account of the availability of intelligence or specific capabilities prior to an attack. In short, while some war planners may at times confuse speed with haste, they generally distinguish one from the other. The core issue remains, however: Western militaries may have a preference for operational speed and for short wars, but the actual wars in which they have been and remain involved, notably in Iraq, Afghanistan, and Mali, are long-drawn-out struggles. In short, Western war planners may prefer to fight fast, but what happens when their adversaries force them to fight slow?[60]

Fighting Slow: Adjusting the War Tempo?

Aware of the preference of Western countries for operational speed and wars of the shortest possible duration, their adversaries naturally tend to design their own strategy to frustrate this attempt to keep the fighting swift and the war short.[61] As a consequence, the experience of Western countries has been not only to plan for their preferred quick operations but also to adapt to actual wars in which their adversaries refuse the high-intensity conventional fight and opt for a protracted war relying on guerrilla, terrorist tactics and propaganda. Counterinsurgency campaigns often require years, if not decades, and rarely lend themselves to swift victories. They also demand a carefully attuned adjustment of the tempo of operations, with periodic shifts from fast to slow. Moreover the trade-offs associated with operational speed are not limited to irregular warfare. The constant quest for speed in warfare raises a number of challenges that have been clearly identified with regard to the planning of nuclear operations, such as the risks of loss of control and the weakening of command, control, and intelligence mechanisms.[62] Similar issues are likely to come into play when robots and artificial intelligence will have an increased impact on the conduct of operations. In short, the question of slower operational tempos cannot simply be wished away. The protracted wars in Iraq, Afghanistan, and the Sahel region elicited an acknowledgment, at least among some defense intellectuals and military planners, of the need to reexamine the role of speed in war as well as to unpack what "victory" in such wars should really mean.

Uneven Adaptation: The United States

The initial phases of the wars in Afghanistan and Iraq were based on creating "'effects' in the most immediate military terms."[63] As historian Brian Linn notes, there was an absence of systematic thinking about "the intermediate and long-term impacts of 'loss of control' in states that were coercive theocracies, dictatorships, or fragile tribal alliances."[64] The American military's focus on speed led to a creation of "U.S. armed forces that were organized, equipped and trained only for rapid, decisive operations," unprepared and unable to handle long-haul conflicts. At the outset of these wars, the dominance of speed in ensuring battlefield successes blindsided planners and led to their inability to achieve national objectives and end the wars conclusively. The subsequent insurgencies that sprang out of the initial successes indicated that the American strategies were disconnected from the pace of the war. The different services "selected and promoted officers who were skilled at managing the complicated control systems of EBO/NCW" but were "intellectually unprepared to deal with the unforeseen consequences of battlefield victory."[65]

However, between 2004 and 2011 a genuine doctrinal and operational effort was made to alter this accepted way of war, including its time dimension. For a while the military was forced to accept that it was not permitted to fight under its favorite conception of time, for which it was best suited. The publication of the "U.S. Army Field Manual No. 3-24" on "Counterinsurgency" in December 2006 marked a departure from the previous decade's emphasis on speed and technology, and promoted a more flexible approach to warfare.[66] War planners acknowledged that insurgencies are "protracted by nature" and that the counterinsurgents should prepare for a "long-term commitment."[67] In such a context, they also advocated that at times "doing nothing is the best reaction."[68] This relative de-emphasis of speed, along with an understanding that military forces have to "deal with a spectrum of challenges simultaneously, ranging from conventional war to humanitarian aid," reflected a doctrine that was less focused on speed as an unmitigated operational good and more concerned about the pace of developments on the ground.[69]

The introduction of the US Army's 2008 capstone combat doctrine "FM-3: Operations" also seemed to promise a different understanding of pace and speed: "The Army's experience makes it clear that no one can accurately predict the nature, location, or duration of the next conflict. . . . This doctrine addresses the needs of an Army responsible for deploying forces promptly at any time, in any environment, against any adversary. This is its expeditionary capability. Once deployed, the Army operates for extended periods across the spectrum of conflict, from stable peace through general war. This is its campaign capability."[70] Differing markedly from the battlefield focus of its 1993 predecessor, "FM 100-5: Operations" acknowledged the changed character of war. War was no longer perceived deterministically as short and decisive, but as eluding prediction of its "nature, location or duration."[71] Moreover by presenting the Army's "campaign capability" as spanning the range from "stable peace through general war," the doctrine attempted reconciliation with the previously overlooked strategic pace of war. By stating that "winning battles and engagement is important but alone is not sufficient" and that "shaping the civil situation is just as important to success," it recognized that the Army needed to look into postwar reconstruction as part of the process of staying connected to the pace of the events on the ground.[72] These changes were not confined to doctrine. For example, the planning and implementation of

Operation Fardh al Qanoon in February 2007 incorporated a number of key dimensions of the Counterinsurgency Field Manual.[73]

However, this new approach to speed in war was unevenly accepted and implemented. The Air Force and the Navy encountered difficulties in including these new findings in their understanding of war.[74] The battle successes enjoyed by both services through the use of technology have led to a greater focus on speed. Even in the Army and in the Marine Corps, some were reluctant to rethink the role of speed and address the challenge of strategic pace. For example, the Marines usually agree that victory is won by those with superior initiative and speed. Some Marines recognize that this is not conducive to "tactical patience," and that the notion that in stability operations the best action is no action is "counterintuitive" to enlisted Marines.[75] In the Army, this adaptation to a slower way of fighting proved challenging and more limited than initially expected.[76] Those who are adamant that the Army did adapt and learned to fight counterinsurgency, such as Janine Davidson, acknowledge that in state-building tasks, "a realm that often involves a number of nonmilitary actors and an environment in which 'lessons' are slow to emerge, the military's system of rapid tactical learning has limited utility."[77] These tasks are at the heart of most counterinsurgency campaigns.

British and French Adaptations

In Iraq and Afghanistan, the British Army faced serious challenges and there was a growing sense that its enemy was consistently faster because it possessed both the initiative and the greater capacity for surprise. The advantages of the British and American armed forces proved to be attritional, and their inadequate force-to-space ratio encouraged an attritional rather than maneuverist approach. This goes to show how a lack of focus on maneuver made the British slow to adapt to the wars in Iraq and Afghanistan.[78] Moreover the overarching preference for speed and quest for a short war meant that adjusting to the requirements of a much slower type of fighting proved difficult. For example, once the invasion of Iraq was completed, the deployed forces were "quickly reduced from a large division to a single fighting brigade."[79] This swift and significant drawdown made it impossible to control outlying tribal areas and to police the city of Basra.

The French Operation Serval in Mali illustrates the perceived civil–military tensions about the proper speed in operation.[80] In three months, from January to April 2013, a Franco-African combined armed force, with allied air and intelligence support, reconquered the north of Mali and significantly degraded the capacity of armed jihadi groups in that area. Heralded by the Army chief as a campaign of "lightning speed" (*fulgurance*), Operation Serval placed a strong emphasis on maneuver.[81] The operation illustrates that speed is not necessarily, or exclusively, the preference of the military, and that the political-military dialogue is an important aspect of the ultimate choice of operational tempo. Political and military leaders interact, and sometimes disagree, over the appropriate operational speed. In his account of the campaign, force commander General Bernard Barrera portrays an impatient political leadership that pushed for speed, while he claims that he favored a comparatively slower pace. In his view, moving as fast as possible was the key to political objectives and military strategy. According to Colonel Bruno Helluy, one of Serval's planners, President François Hollande urged the army to "get it done" as fast as possible. This was because the initial intelligence assessment predicted that "the enemy in Mali would not stand and fight, meaning that French forces would have to move as quickly as possible if they wanted to destroy the enemy before it successfully scattered or slipped out of reach."[82] Therefore, by moving at a high speed and attacking first and fast, the deployed force would achieve strategic surprise.

In his account, General Barrera repeatedly suspects that strong political pressure demanded quick action and retaking the initiative.[83] For example, as the progression toward Timbuktu and Gao started, the Paris headquarters ordered the force to accelerate and take both cities as promptly as possible, an order that he attributes to political pressure as well.[84] As his force approached Timbuktu General Barrera indicated that the General Staff was under strong pressure to take the city. Some claimed that his brigade, allegedly affected by the "Afghan syndrome," was too fearful of mines, which inhibited its leading elements and its leaders.[85] In consultation with headquarters, General Barrera decided to postpone taking the city by twenty-four hours, but he "quickly understood that this additional delay was not welcomed."[86] Moreover after taking the city he needed time to reorganize and reorient his force toward his next objectives.[87] This was due to the distances involved, the degraded infrastructure (especially energy and water), and the insecurity of the theater. Similarly, before the battle of the Ametettaï valley, he initially considered that the conditions for success were not met and that it was simply too soon to attack.[88] The preparation and coordination of simultaneous attacks on entrenched jihadi fighters from different directions was inadequate, and the fire support not fully available. After his tactical victory following two weeks of non-stop operations, he acknowledged on later reflection that it would have been preferable to exploit his success. However, in agreement with his subordinates on the ground, he decided instead that an operational pause was needed to allow his men to recuperate and regroup.[89] Following the tactical success of Operation Serval, Operation Barkhane was launched in 2014; it is still ongoing in 2020. This shows that the shift from swift but temporary achievements to a slower pace of operation and a protracted conflict in the Sahel region remains a serious challenge.

Conclusion: Balancing Fast and Slow Fighting—Mission Impossible?

Operational art is about much more than finding the right speed. The assessment of the enemy, the terrain, the mission, and the relation between time and space all contribute to operational performance. Speed should not be artificially isolated: it is intertwined with space and closely linked to the mission and its political and strategic context. Nevertheless time matters and fighting fast *and* slow proves easier said than done. One way in which the United States has sought to combine fast and slow fighting is through the utilization of one particular type of drone, the long-endurance remotely piloted armed aircraft such as the MQ-9A Reaper. For their users, the comparatively low human and financial cost of these drones helps to stay the course. Moreover, their nearly indefinite air persistence and relative effectiveness in counterterrorism show that in specific contexts it is possible to combine a gain in slowness (not speed) with retaining the capacity for surprise.[90]

Beyond long-endurance remotely piloted armed drones, two main policy recommendations stand out. First, when they face the issue of speed, war planners should acknowledge more systematically and comprehensively than they generally do that trade-offs are involved. At the very least they should take into account that their adversaries are likely to exploit tactically and strategically what they may see as a weakness in the preference for speed. Many of the efforts to broaden the understanding of the tempo of operations in response to the Iraq insurgency were on the right track and should not go to waste.

Second, the issues related to operational speed are bound to be intertwined with shifting political understandings of time and speed, which in turn are shaped by political preferences and goals. For example, the perceived need to preserve the "special relationship" drove the UK's policy aim to be at war in Afghanistan and Iraq if the US was at war.[91] As the British military strategy was embedded in this particular policy, this meant that the UK would be in combat for as long as the US was, which generated tensions regarding the need to fight fast and slow. This political-operational articulation of time is also influential at the theater level. In the aftermath of the invasion of Iraq, US leaders opted for a protracted handover of power while British diplomats argued strongly for early elections and a swift transition to the Iraqis, hoping to avoid discontent developing toward an occupying power.[92] In order to better calibrate speed at the operational level of war, war planners should continuously work out the articulation between their level of war and the expected role of speed (and time) at the political level. This is a lesson constantly forgotten and painfully relearned.

NOTES

1. An earlier version of this chapter was presented at the workshop on "The Pace of Modern War and the Erosion of Western Military Power" held at Chatham House, London, September 26–27, 2019. I thank the discussant Sir Jamie Shea, as well as Olivier Schmitt, Kenneth Kuniyuki, and the participants for their useful questions and comments. Wendy He and Nandini Patwardhan provided valuable research assistance. I gratefully acknowledge the support of the S. Rajaratnam School of International Studies (RSIS), Nanyang Technological University Singapore.

2. André Beaufre, *An Introduction to Strategy,* 1st ed. 1963 (London: Faber and Faber, 1965), pp. 35–36; Pierre Vendryès, *De la probabilité en histoire: l'exemple de l'expédition d'Egypte* (Paris: Albin Michel, 1952), p. 196; Jean Guitton, *La Pensée et la Guerre,* 1st ed. 1969 (Paris: Desclée de Brouwer, 2017), pp. 134, 216, 226–27.

3. Milan Vego, *Joint Operational Warfare: Theory and Practice* (Newport, RI: US Naval War College, 2009), p. 150; Jan Hanska, *Times of War and War Over Time* (Helsinki: National Defense University, 2017), pp. 209–25.

4. Daniel Kahneman, *Thinking, Fast and Slow,* 1st ed. 2011 (London: Penguin, 2012), pp. 79–88. The title of this chapter is, of course, borrowed from cognitive psychologist Kahneman's classic.

5. Solly Zuckerman, "Judgment and Control in Modern Warfare," *Foreign Affairs,* vol 40, no. 2 (January 1962), pp. 196–212; Thomas C. Schelling, "Comment," in *Limited Strategic War,* edited by Klaus Knorr and Thornton Read (London: Pall Mall, 1962), pp. 253–55.

6. E. L. Katzenbach, Jr., "Time, Space, and Will: The Political-Military Views of Mao Tse-Tung," in *The Guerrilla and How to Fight Him: Selections from the Marine Corps Gazette,* edited by T. N. Greene (New York: Praeger, 1962), pp. 13–15.

7. Theo Farrell, Sten Rynning, and Terry Terriff, *Transforming Military Power since the Cold War: Britain, France, and the United States, 1991–2012* (Cambridge University Press, 2013).

8. Pascal Vennesson, "Is Strategic Studies Narrow? Critical Security and the Misunderstood Scope of Strategy," *Journal of Strategic Studies,* vol. 40, no. 3 (2017),

pp. 372–77. The differences between US and UK military organizational cultures in counterinsurgency, for example, is a consistent finding of multiple inquiries: Deborah D. Avant, *Political Institutions and Military Change: Lessons from Peripheral Wars* (Cornell University Press, 1994); John A. Nagl, *Learning to Eat Soup with a Knife: Counterinsurgency Lessons from Malaya and Vietnam* (University of Chicago Press, 2005); Austin Long, *The Soul of Armies: Counterinsurgency Doctrine and Military Culture in the US and UK* (Cornell University Press, 2016).

9. Robert R. Leonhard, *The Art of Maneuver: Maneuver-Warfare Theory and AirLand Battle*, 1st ed. 1991 (Novato, CA: Presidio Press, 1994), pp. 8–9. On the limits of, and the problems associated with, the operational level of war, see Hew Strachan, *The Direction of War: Contemporary Strategy in Historical Perspective* (Cambridge University Press, 2013), pp. 210–34.

10. John A. Lynn, *Battle: A History of Combat and Culture. From Ancient Greece to Modern America* (Boulder, CO: Westview Press, 2003).

11. On time and timing in the art of war, see Richard E. Simpkin, *Race to the Swift: Thoughts on Twenty-first Century Warfare* (London: Brassey's, 1985); Robert R. Leonhard, *Fighting by Minutes: Time and the Art of War* (Westport, CT: Praeger, 1994); Hanska, *Times of War and War Over Time*; Andrew Carr, "It's About Time: Strategy and Temporal Phenomena," *Journal of Strategic Studies,* vol. 41 (October 15, 2018), https://doi.org/10.1080/01402390.2018.1529569.

12. Edward Luttwak, *Strategy: The Logic of War and Peace* (Harvard University Press, 1987).

13. On changes in force structures such as the creation of rapid reaction forces in Europe, see Anthony King, *The Transformation of Europe's Armed Forces: From the Rhine to Afghanistan* (Cambridge University Press, 2011).

14. Beaufre, *An Introduction to Strategy*, p. 28.

15. Colonel Jean-Baptiste Vachée, *Napoleon at Work*, 1st ed. 1913 (London: Adam and Charles Black, 1914), pp. 19–22.

16. Basil H. Liddell Hart, *When Britain Goes to War: Adaptability and Mobility* (London: Faber and Faber, 1932), p. 60.

17. Antulio J. Echevarria II, *Reconsidering the American Way of War: U.S. Military Practice from the Revolution to Afghanistan* (Georgetown University Press, 2014), pp. 18–19; Brian McAllister Linn, "The U.S. Armed Forces' View of War," *Daedalus,* vol. 140, no. 3 (Summer 2011), pp. 36–37. See also Keith L. Shimko, *The Iraq Wars and America's Military Revolution* (Cambridge University Press, 2010); Brian McAllister Linn, *The Echo of Battle: The Army's Way of War* (Harvard University Press, 2007).

18. Chad C. Serena, *A Revolution in Military Adaptation. The U.S. Army in the Iraq War* (Georgetown University Press, 2011), pp. 47–48, 52.

19. See, for example, Lieutenant Colonel John A. Nagl, *Knife Fights: A Memoir of Modern War in Theory and Practice* (New York: Penguin Press, 2014), p. 211, and the contrast with Anthony H. Cordesman and Abraham R. Wagner, *The Lessons of Modern War, Volume IV. The Gulf War* (New York: Westview Press, 1996), pp. 692–93, 955–56.

20. Tommy Franks, *American Soldier* (New York: Regan Books, 2004), p. 466.

21. Quoted in Anthony King, *Command: The Twenty-First Century General* (Cambridge University Press, 2019), p. 260.

22. Brian M. Linn, "The U.S. Armed Forces' View of War," in David M. Kennedy, ed., *The Modern American Military* (Oxford University Press, 2013), p. 45. See also Walter E. Kretchik, *U.S. Army Doctrine: From the American Revolution to the War on Terror* (University Press of Kansas, 2011), pp. 221–77.

23. Linn, "The U.S. Armed Forces' View of War," p. 46.

24. Ibid.

25. Headquarters, Department of the Army, *ADP 5-05 The Operation Process,* 1–17. See also in this volume chapter 10 by Nina A. Kollars, "War at Information Speed: Multi-Domain Warfighting Visions."

26. Hew Strachan, "Operational Art and Britain, 1909–2009," in John Andreas Olsen and Martin van Creveld, eds., *The Evolution of Operational Art: From Napoleon to the Present* (Oxford University Press, 2010). See also Shelford Bidwell and Dominick Graham, *Fire-Power: The British Army Weapons & Theories of War, 1904-1945,* 1st ed. 1982 (London: Pen & Sword, 2004); Simpkin, *Race to the Swift*; Markus Mäder, *In Pursuit of Conceptual Excellence: The Evolution of British Military-Strategic Doctrine in the Post-Cold War Era, 1989–2002* (Bern: Peter Lang, 2004); Austin Long, *The Soul of Armies. Counterinsurgency Doctrine and Military Culture in the US and UK* (Cornell University Press, 2016).

27. Strachan, "Operational Art and Britain, 1909–2009," p. 37.

28. Ibid., p. 41.

29. *Army Doctrine Publication (ADP) – AC 71940 Land Operations* 2017 (first published 2010), p. 79, https://assets.publishing.service.gov.uk/government/uploads/system/uploads/attachment_data/file/605298/Army_Field_Manual__AFM__A5_Master_ADP_Interactive_Gov_Web.pdf.

30. Ibid., p. 81.

31. Ibid., p. 80.

32. Ibid., p. 80.

33. Ibid., p. 25.

34. Ibid., p. 25.

35. Christopher L. Elliott, *High Command: British Military Leadership in the Iraq and Afghanistan Wars,* 1st ed. 2015 (London: Hurst & Company, 2017), pp. 144–45.

36. Ibid., pp. 151–52.

37. *ADP Operations* 2017, p. 17.

38. "Doctrine for the Employment of the French Armed Forces (FRA) JD-01 (A), no. 128/DEF/CICDE/NP as of 12 June 2014." For an overview of French military thinking, see Lars Wedin, *Marianne et Athéna. La pensée militaire française du XVIIème siècle à nos jours* (Paris: Economica, 2011).

39. Doctrine for the Employment of the French Armed Forces," p. 27.

40. Ibid., p. 26.

41. Ibid., p. 7.

42. Ibid., p. 35.

43. Ibid., p. 27.

44. Ibid., p. 31.

45. See, for example, Général Barrera, *Opération Serval. Notes de guerre, Mali 2013* (Paris: Seuil, 2015), p. 56.

46. Barrera, *Opération Serval,* p. 56.

47. "Doctrine for the Employment of the French Armed Forces," p. 28.

48. Ibid., p. 28.

49. Ibid., p. 36.

50. Barrera, *Opération Serval,* pp. 80–81, 84.

51. "Doctrine for the Employment of the French Armed Forces," p. 36.

52. Ibid., p. 57.

53. Michael Shurkin, *France's War in Mali: Lessons for an Expeditionary Army* (Santa Monica, CA: RAND Corporation, 2014), p. 33.

54. "Doctrine for the Employment of the French Armed Forces," p. 51.

55. Shurkin, *France's War in Mali,* p. 29; Barrera, *Opération Serval,* pp. 65–70. GTIAs and SGTIAs are task-organized combined forces designed to operate autonomously and independently according to their commanders' intent. SGTIAs and GTIAs have the same structure but differ in terms of scale, and their exact composition varies according to mission requirements and available resources.

56. Shurkin, *France's War in Mali,* p. 30; "Doctrine for the Employment of the French Armed Forces," p. 47.

57. "Doctrine for the Employment of the French Armed Forces," p. 47.

58. Shurkin, *France's War in Mali,* p. 39.

59. Ibid., p. 39.

60. Olivier Schmitt, "Wartime Paradigms and the Future of Western Military Power," *International Affairs*, vol. 96, no. 2 (March 2020), pp. 401–18.

61. Michael W. S. Ryan, *Decoding Al-Qaeda's Strategy: The Deep Battle Against America,* 1st ed. 2013 (Columbia University Press, 2017); Brian H. Fishman, *The Master Plan: ISIS, Al-Qaeda, and the Jihadi Strategy for Final Victory* (Yale University Press, 2016).

62. Ashton B. Carter, John D. Steinbruner, and Charles A. Zraket, eds., *Managing Nuclear Operations* (Brookings Institution Press, 1987). See also Paul Virilio, *Speed and Politics: An Essay on Dromology,* 1st ed. 1977 (South Pasadena, CA: Semiotext(e), 2006).

63. Linn, "The U.S. Armed Forces' View of War," pp. 46–47.

64. Ibid., p. 49.

65. Ibid., p. 49. (EBO is effects-based operations, and NCW is network-centric warfare.)

66. Ibid., pp. 49–50.

67. *The U.S. Army-Marine Corps Counterinsurgency Field Manual*, 1st ed. 2006 (University of Chicago Press, 2007), I-134, p. 43. At the tactical level, see Michael L. Burgoyne and Albert J. Marckwardt, *The Defense of Jis Al-Doreaa* (University of Chicago Press, 2009).

68. *The U.S. Army-Marine Corps Counterinsurgency Field Manual,* I-152, p. 49.

69. Linn, "The U.S. Armed Forces' View of War," p. 50.

70. Department of the Army, *FM 3: Operations* (Washington, DC: Department of the Army Headquarters, February 27, 2008), p. vii.

71. Ibid., p. vii.

72. Linn, "The U.S. Armed Forces' View of War," p. 51.

73. David H. Ucko, *The New Counterinsurgency Era: Transforming the U.S. Military for Modern Wars* (Georgetown University Press, 2009), p. 171.

74. Linn, "The U.S. Armed Forces' View of War," p. 53.

75. Quoted in Jeannie L. Johnson, *The Marines, Counterinsurgency, and Strategic Culture. Lessons Learned and Lost in America's Wars* (Georgetown University Press, 2018), pp. 118, 267–68.

76. Austin Long, *The Soul of Armies.* See also Isaiah Wilson III, *Thinking Beyond War. Civil-Military Relations and Why American Fails to Win the Peace (*New York: Palgrave, 2007).

77. Janine Davidson, *Lifting the Fog of Peace: How Americans Learned to Fight Modern War* (University of Michigan Press, 2011, first published 2010), pp. 190, 202.

78. Strachan, "Operational Art and Britain, 1909–2009," p. 38. See also Elliott, *High Command*; Theo Farrell, *Unwinnable: Britain's War in Afghanistan, 2001–2014* (London: Vintage, 2017).

79. Elliott, *High Command*, pp. 144–45.

80. Barrera, *Opération Serval*; General Patrick Brethous, "Le défi de la maîtrise du temps opérationnel," *Réflexions tactiques,* Special Issue, "Opération Serval: le retour de la maneuvre aéroterrestre dans la profondeur" (2014), pp. 59–62. See also Shurkin, *France's War in Mali.* On the case of Afghanistan, see Olivier Schmitt, "French Military Adaptation in the Afghan War: Looking Inward or Outward?," *Journal of Strategic Studies,* vol. 40, no. 4 (2017), pp. 577–99.

81. Shurkin, *France's War in Mali,* p. 11.

82. Ibid., p. 25.

83. Barrera, *Opération Serval*, p. 73.

84. Ibid., pp. 87, 90, 93, 146.

85. Ibid., p. 93.

86. Ibid., p. 93.

87. Ibid., pp. 101–02.

88. Ibid., pp. 181–82.

89. Ibid., pp. 237–38.

90. Patrick B. Johnston and Anoop K. Sarbahi, "The Impact of US Drone Strikes on Terrorism in Pakistan," *International Studies Quarterly,* vol. 60 (2016), pp. 203–19; Asfandyar Mir, "What Explains Counterterrorism Effectiveness? Evidence from the U.S. Drone War in Pakistan," *International Security,* vol. 43, no. 2 (Fall 2018), pp. 45–83.

91. Elliott, *High Command*, p. 150.

92. Ibid., p. 152.

TEN

War at Information Speed

Multi-Domain Warfighting Visions

NINA A. KOLLARS

As of 2020, each of the US military services is attempting to articulate its own vision of harnessing data and information across the domains of warfare. Whether it is the Army's Multi-Domain Battle/Operations (MDO), the Air Force's Multi-Domain Command and Control (MDC2), the Navy's Distributed Maritime Operations (DMO), or the ancillary support program to DMO, the Marine Corps' Expeditionary Advance Based Operations (EABO)—the central element is networked machinic data flows across air, sea, land, space, and cyberspace.

In this process, the physical battlespace is being re-imagined into a networked informatic system of systems: a kind of multi-dimensioned, semi-automated lethal information processor. It is a peculiarly narrow perspective. Future warfighting systems centered on information technology, in theory, achieve victory by equating the complexity of warfare with the complexity of data processing.[1] Such a system places the primary emphasis on data flows as the central problem of warfare to be solved. How can wars be won? By making smarter and faster choices through information processing. Battlefield dominance becomes synonymous with algorithmic dominance. It is a dream of war at information speed.

There are reasons to be skeptical. As many of the chapters in this volume demonstrate, the lure of faster warfare leading to faster victory is not only questionable but also a persistent techno-pathological obsession—particularly of techno-centric warfighting. Whether the concept is "network dominance," John Boyd's OODA loop (Observe, Orient, Decide, Act), or the current language of "distributed warfare," the notional promise is the same: technology increases speed, and speed is victory.[2]

These future warfighting concepts are not anchored by such elements as are described in Pascal Vennesson's chapter 9, in which actual battlefield metrics were compared to dreams of information and battle speed. Multi-domain concepts, despite the robust development of doctrine and white papers, remain fully imaginary. They are a vision of future warfighting not yet realized within any of the services' practices, not even as a functional exercise. Their timelines for realization remain unaligned across the military components, as well as between partners and allies.

If it works, the West's concept of future war will be realized through more secure and faster network connections, machine-learning algorithms, and distributed sensor networks creating new dynamic command-and-control capabilities. This transformative effort is being led by the United States and emulated actively by its partners.[3]

From an optimist's perspective, better and more data during warfare enable better and faster decisionmaking. The proliferation of cheap and expendable sensors has certainly increased the West's situational awareness. That much has been amply demonstrated in Iraq and Afghanistan with remotely piloted airborne machines.[4] The problem is, the services are leaping into information-centric systems with almost no concomitant consideration of the cross-service conflicts and multinational limitations that obstruct the realization of increased decisionmaking speed as the centerpiece of victory.

The conduct of war is a complex sequence of simultaneously unfolding decision processes—whom to kill or protect, what to order (Band-Aids or bullets), where to go (advance or retreat). Those decision chains are conducted in parallel at all echelons, from the strategic all the way down to the tactical. Which military leaders are empowered to make decisions, and when, affects how the military conducts the literal, physical process of warfighting—its pace and process are its politics. This chapter argues that the US military services differ in their vision of the value of speed of information, and that this is potentially problematic in two ways.

First, misaligned visions between services can result in incompatible systems in implementation. Incompatibility is no small matter if the services are intended to fight jointly as well as multinationally with US partners and allies. Currently there exists no cross-concept analysis to determine the trajectory of alignment. As a matter of inter-service rivalry, it is not even clear whether synchronizing future warfighting systems will be successful, since each of the services has longstanding cultural and organizational resources that it seeks to preserve.[5]

Second, fundamental changes to both the speed and the complexity of information systems carry implications for civilian leadership's decisionmaking and planning across the spectrum of peace and conflict. Politics may be made to serve war, as opposed to war being made to serve politics. Faster and more complex decision systems on the battlefield should be designed to clarify the relationships across the services in a joint warfighting environment, but most importantly to inform the civilian leadership's own pace and process more effectively, given the overall strategic ends of the conflict. Without those design considerations the end result may privilege a commander's decision speed at the tactical level, yet become bogged down in ownership of the decision-space between services, and ultimately override the civilian leadership's overall strategic primacy of decisionmaking.

Information as a tool of speed has real-world limitations that are not well represented by these visionary documents. Information speed cannot solve problems for which data are not collected, and the battlefield puzzle itself changes dynamically. As a case in point, the development of counter-improvised explosive devices in Iraq was theoretically sped up by research networks connecting the battlespace with the US research labs of JIEDDO— the Joint Improvised Explosive Device Defeat Organization. But in practice the pace of problem-solving was still significantly limited by data collection issues (US ground troops had other priorities immediately after explosions than conducting forensics on bombs), and the fact was that no matter how fast the research process could be, the construction of an IED was cheap and easily adapted to new designs.[6]

Replacing or adding new information systems to military operations is no simple endeavor. Networked intelligent systems, like machine learning architectures, are not condiments: they cannot be sprinkled on top of current systems and doctrine. Complex big data systems, like those imagined in the varied US future warfighting visions, must be systemically integrated into the command and control of all aspects of warfighting. Thus implementation of these future warfighting information systems entails far more than offering up good data for leadership to mull over; it requires the restructuring of the decision process itself. Bringing new information systems online therefore potentially changes the politics of war up and down the echelons, between the services, and can upset the balance of the civil–military relationship.

To date there has been no analysis of the changes to decision processes implied by the new US warfighting concepts and the way they will affect decisionmaking both on the battlefield and between the military and the state. This chapter holds up for interrogation the future operating concepts of the US Air Force, Army, and Navy, and analyzes their emphasis on speeding up decisionmaking processes. It examines several of the key documents and supporting interpretations of those documents released by the Department of Defense and each of the three service branches in turn. It provides an interpretation of the key structures and decision dynamics implied by each system, before briefly exploring the implications of those changes. The chapter ends with a plea for decision-process mapping to be developed alongside the development of future systems.

Within their current depictions of multi-domain information-centric future warfighting, the US service branches differ fundamentally in their respective perceptions of the purpose of information speed. Specifically, the Air Force's vision leverages speed to enhance its own cognitive capacity to speed up decisionmaking in command-and-control systems (operational agility), while the Army sees the value of information speed in a decentralized and influence-oriented system aimed primarily at the minds of others (convergence), and the Navy understands it as a literal decentralization of its physical assets within its domains (from ships to nodes).

Why Do These Documents Matter?

What makes these documents—these crystal ball–gazing imaginary versions of the future—worth studying? To be sure, there are obvious analytical caveats to any analysis of the military's discourse of future warfighting. It can be objected that, first, future warfighting concepts are deeply abstracted and so there can be nothing concrete to be learned from them; second, these documents are written with an eye to securing a portion of defense funding and thus are heavily biased to inflate threats or over-sell a new machine's value; and, third, these documents do nothing more than attempt to ensure a service's relevance to future warfighting.

Nevertheless, these documents matter. Future warfighting concept documents occupy a unique role in expressing and shaping the US military's thinking about threat trends and how to structure the overall organization to meet those threats. In terms of organization, future concepts for each of the services (Air Force, Army, Navy) tend to be developed within their respective force development directorates, which differ within each service's structure.

In terms of function, the purpose of producing future warfighting documents is to create an ideational pathway through arguments that, if successful, then become the physical pathway to military change. Thus future warfighting documents are a service's effort to turn words into new objects and systems. These documents are a peep into the pure ambition of an institution's efforts to change.

After a brief discussion of "domains" for those uninitiated in military technology and future warfighting jargon, the remaining sections examine the core documents associated with the future vision of each of the services, and highlight the key differences in implementation: the Air Force's "operational agility," the Army's "convergence," and the Navy's "from ships to nodes." Each section explains the respective service's interpretation of the future threat environment and the problem to be solved through faster information systems across domains, and analyzes the issues associated with its vision of multi-domain information speed.

What Is Multi-Domain?

The word "domain" represents the varied physical and conceptual spaces through which the military can conduct war. Those domains consist of air, sea, land, space, and cyberspace. The term "multi-domain," then, refers to the coordinated employment of military assets through two or more of those spaces to achieve an objective. Of course the concept of information systems as potentially transforming modern war has been around for decades. It is only recently, however, that the state of networked sensors and automated processing of the data that flow from them has advanced enough to produce what is ostensibly possible—at least in prototype—a digitally networked war across all the traditional domains of warfighting plus two new additions: space and cyberspace.[7]

The reader may ask, how is this new—surely the services have always conducted multi-domain warfare? The answer is, yes, sort of, but not exactly in the manner suggested by these future war visions. The desired end-state of these future visions is true integration of the elements that make up a military's assets. Currently each service or elements within a service that work in different domains (ground tanks versus fighter jets) have the capacity to cooperate and support others, and historically have done so. The most prominent cases in recent memory are in providing close air support (CAS)—armed helicopters, jets, predator unmanned aerial vehicles, and so forth—to protect transportation units en route to bases.[8] However, the complex coordination of these efforts has generally been left to different theater commanders, to battalion leaders on the ground, or to operations centers of a particular domain. For example, military assets that fly in a theater are generally coordinated through a CAOC (Combined Air Operations Center)—usually, but not always, operated by the Air Force. That CAOC prioritizes and provides flight coordination for all air assets in seventy-two–hour spans of time.[9] Whether those assets are from the Navy, the Army, or the Air Force, the operators and software in the CAOC make up the highly technical system that assigns flight areas, routes, and times of take-off and landing over an area of operations. It must do so because without a CAOC conflicts in air space will result in tragedy or failed missions. Insofar as a transportation convoy on the ground requires air support to protect it from potential ambush, that pairing process is one of cooperation between two leaders of different areas of control, rather than an actual integration in which a unified system would—in theory—combine the ground and air assets simultaneously. Just exactly how that integration through information systems occurs is significant for politics between (and within) the services and for the wider political processes of war.

Air Force Operational Agility through Multi-Domain Command and Control

The Air Force was the first of the services regularly to use the term multi-domain publicly. Its most thorough articulation of its unclassified vision for future war remains the *Air Force Future Operating Concept: A View of the Air Force in 2035* (hereafter referred to as 2035).[10] 2035's strategy for future war-fighting identifies key structural and demographic shifts in the warfighting environment as well as rising potential challenges to US supremacy, notably from China and Russia. The report also presents a broader systemic vision of the world derived from the Air Force Strategic Environment Assessment's 2014–2034 report, which identifies six trends:

> 1) adversaries' acquisition and development of capabilities to challenge the U.S.; 2) increasing importance or frequency of irregular, urban, humanitarian, and intelligence operations; 3) increasing challenges to deterrence; 4) energy costs; 5) exploiting new technology opportunities; and 6) challenges of climate change.[11]

Given this extremely complex future strategic environment, 2035 places singular emphasis upon what it refers to as "operational agility." This is defined as "the ability to rapidly generate—and shift among—multiple solutions for a given challenge."[12] The idea is not only to present the adversary with multiple dilemmas to induce a kind of strategic paralysis, though this may be a side effect; it is also to use technology to generate multiple solution sets in real time, updated rapidly, to offer to leadership. In the Air Force's eyes the problem of speed is not solely physical, but also cognitive. In the report's own terms: "Speed refers to the swiftness of a movement or action in both physical and cognitive ways. Physical speed is required to quickly execute changes or adjustments to provide a timely reaction. Cognitive speed is necessary to ensure information processing and reaction times provide timely inputs that drive physical action."[13]

Logically, from an Air Force perspective, this makes a fair bit of sense. Unlike ground troops, the pace at which air assets fly outpaces human decisionmaking capability. At a theater level on the ground it may take hours, if not days, for forces to reach their point of attack. In the air this is reduced to minutes. Decision speed must be increased to meet the challenges of airspace. Thus the promise of computer-processed complex decisionmaking—particularly in overcrowded airspace—is the solution to the existing bottlenecks hindering more dynamic operations. As such, it is fair to say that the Air Force's vision of future warfighting is very much a command-and-control vision.

The technological problem to be solved in 2035 is integration of air and ground systems into a solution-generating platform—a system that not only speeds up decisionmaking but offers the leadership multiple solutions across all domains that can be rearranged dynamically in real time. Instead of simply coordinating air assets in three-day planning cycles, a real-time sensor network tied across domains opens the Air Force to coordinating air assets more dynamically with ground, sea, cyber, and space effects. That is, rather than a cooperation across domains, the Air Force system envisions a highly complex but seemingly singularly managed system that can update itself in real time to provide leaders more rapidly with multiple options.[14]

Ultimately the limit to realizing this future agile vision is the technical architecture to be built. The Air Force has been developing a management system that underpins the resource and decision acrobatics implied by distributed assets but concentrated fire—named MDC2 (Multi-Domain Command and Control).[15] This MDC2 system in the 2035 vision replaces the prior CAOC system with an MDOC (Multi-Domain Operations Center). A former chief of staff for the Air Force, General David Goldfein, describes the MDOC concept as an improvement in communications and fighting. In Goldfein's eyes, multi-domain operations mean speed in all areas of Air Force operations—from warfighting tactics all the way back to education and technological acquisition. However, the crown of the Air Force system is MDC2. It is partly a provider of information to leadership about where assets and threats are, and partly a decisionmaker in identifying which assets can and should be used to resolve those threats.

In addition to the MDC2 system's value to theater-level leadership, the system is intended to provide aggregated data across all actors within a battlespace. This common operating picture gives commanders at the highest echelon unparalleled oversight of the tiniest details as a campaign unfolds. It is here that the inherent tension in the technological vision becomes apparent. In the Air Force's 2035 document it is argued:

> Rather than demanding "perfect" intelligence, military forces must be able to make accurate decisions at a rate that provides advantages over adversaries. In 2015, the Air Force has access to a wealth of data collected from a vast number of sources. However, it remains limited in its physical ability to process and integrate the sheer volume of data into actionable information in a timely manner. By 2035, the correlation of disparate bits of data will be even more critical to provide decision makers with the required information to make key decisions rapidly for operations. Collected data will be integrated in an open, adaptive information construct unburdened by unnecessary classification barriers. Air, space, and cyberspace ISR (intelligence, surveillance, and reconnaissance) assets will share information seamlessly and contribute to a Common Operating Picture (COP). A global COP will require advanced capabilities and various degrees of automation to unlock the power of Big Data and correlate diverse pieces of information more quickly. A User-Defined Operating Picture (UDOP) will provide the interface between the decisionmaker and the global COP. Human-machine interfaces will be engineered to deliver the right information and level of detail to the right person at the right time to make the right decision. This construct will balance speed with accuracy to deliver the ability to make risk-appropriate actionable decisions. Together, these elements will increase the speed and quality of decision-making to allow superior responsiveness.[16]

The language in the document appears to suggest that with additional data, decisionmaking is pressed downward regarding targeting, resourcing, or executing an attack. The key tension in the language is its reference to "the right information . . . to the right person," suggesting that this grid network of sensors is intended to provide situational awareness to all warfighters as well as the leadership—a kind of democratizing common operating picture. The subsequent vignettes and narratives provided in 2035 substantiate this conjecture: "Colonel Lee," a planner in the MDOC, upon observing changes in human patterns data, takes the initiative to convene a kind of cultural regional joint strategy team; "Captain Miller" flies her F-35 away from her intended target to refuel independently of her squadron; "Captain Deckard" observes space satellites and makes operational adjustments.[17]

In the language of the document the MDC2 is thus a democratizing decision tool that enables young officers to readjust their paths dynamically to meet the mission's objectives in the optimum way. In practice the lure of such high-resolution insights in real time offers an opportunity for dynamic updating across an entire campaign. That is, the generals, not the captains, will be the beneficiaries of operational and tactical decisions. Decisions in the narratives suggest that the speed and dynamism are intended to be part of decisionmaking by the lowest echelon. But simultaneously the lowest-level decisions will become available to the influence of those at the highest rank—the curse of the looming four-star general swooping in to manage battles. And for the joint operational environment across domains and services there is a similar blurriness. In replacing the CAOC with the MDOC the same ambiguity exists; the command and control of assets—though seemingly left to each of the services within its area of operations—cannot simultaneously be dynamically reordered at the real-time pace unless everything is unified under the direction of the Air Force CAOC model. In summary, what can be most clearly inferred from the 2035 concept is that speed and agility of operations will be enhanced with new big data control systems and networked sensors.

Two service-level political concerns about decision and control emerge from the Air Force picture. First, from an inter-service rivalry perspective, MDC2 appears as an unabashed attempt to unify the services under the Air Force's organizing umbrella—one system to rule them all. Thus regardless of the USAF's qualifications and capacity to manage such a network, in implementation the inter-service politics are likely to hamper actual integration of Army and Navy assets into the MDOC. In this sense there are political limits to realizing the 2035 vision as a joint cross-domain management system.

The second concern is about decision-making within the future vision framework. The Air Force's technological sensor network presents a decision-confused, if not Janus-faced, complex system that rhetorically appears to offer more choice and opportunity at the lower echelons, and yet simultaneously provides more command and control at the campaign level with the same ISR data. The tension is not resolved, and is ignored altogether in the document's supporting narratives, as well as in later supporting statements and documents about the concept. It is fundamentally unclear whether the Air Force networked sensor system is intended to empower fighters at the field level or to create a unified command system for a joint theater task force commander. If the answer is both, these documents do not explain how permitting increased warfighter independence at the tactical level is consistent with a dynamically updating theater-wide planning tool.

As for the connective tissue between military and state, the tactical design-level decisions will dictate the pace and frequency of opportunity for civilian leadership. If decisionmaking is brought upward, one risk is that an ongoing decision process for elites in the day-to-day activities may override the tempered process of allowing battles and campaigns to unfold before any shifts are made in the choice of staying at war or suing for peace. Additionally, more time spent managing the campaign by elites at a highly dynamic pace may leave less time for the kind of analytical relationship between the military and civilian leadership, in which measured political objectives are tied to a slower and more clearly unfolding theater of conflict.

Surprisingly, perhaps presciently, the document tantalizingly offers this insight without further development: "While war will remain an instrument of policy, with associated constraints/restraints and specified missions for military forces, navigating the relationship between policy and war will be even more challenging in the complex future."[18] That is, as faster and more complex information systems are brought online in the service of warfighting, the Air Force admits uncertainty over the relationship between policy and warfighting in a future with these complexities. Unfortunately, the document says little more about this.

The Army's Multi-Domain Battle/Operations (MDO) and Convergence

Despite the US Air Force's early capture and use of the "multi-domain" phrasing, it is the US Army that has taken on the primary role of pushing this vision upward to the all-encompassing joint staff in the Pentagon for implementation across the services. This is partially a matter of timing. Between the 2015 Air Force 2035 concept document and the Army's vision, the National Defense Strategy was published in 2018. In an ambitious effort later that year to shape the future national vision, the US Army published its most thorough articulation of how to conduct future warfare in *The Army in Multi-Domain Operations 2028*.[19] This fully incorporated many of the scoping elements associated with the US shift in strategic vision. In the 2018 National Defense Strategy there was a marked shift in emphasis, from considering the broader systemic changes in the international system to the much narrower scoping of Russia and China as adversaries and the branding of the character of those threats as "great power competition" rather than conflict.[20]

Taking its lead from the 2016 National Defense Strategy, the Army's vision of MDO is unique in spanning the entire spectrum of competition and conflict. That is, unlike the Air Force's largely battle management view of networked warfare via the MDC2, the Army's document spends just as much time addressing competition—that is, activity below the use of force and for creating anti-escalatory ramps to avoid conflict—and the development of interoperability and capacity building for partners and allies.[21]

MDO's conceptual roots lie in a decades-long modernization attempt by the Army to integrate its own operations across its air power and land power assets. Nevertheless the document expands the concept well beyond prior future warfare visions like AirLand Battle through its emphasis on cyberspace impacts, and, as noted, the addition of competition to the multi-domain networks challenge. The Army's vision significantly raises the technological complication bar, not simply to create an integrated picture but to expand the conditions under which those systems are to be applied, particularly in terms of information operations. The term of art for the Army is "convergence." Convergence "achieves the rapid and continuous integration of all domains across time, space and capabilities to overmatch the enemy."[22]

The Army's 107-page pamphlet is exhaustive; it directly addresses not only the tactical and operational integration of the different capabilities in each domain, but also information influence and cross-domain integration of those effects in an area of operations. Speed is seen as a matter not simply of creating a common operating picture in the Army's mind, but also of affecting the mind of the adversary, the adversary's public, and the US public. This is why convergence is a much larger umbrella for a whole set of information processing systems and sensors beyond Air Force MDC2.

For the Army, convergence addresses the question of information speed not as a single battle management system but as an interoperability problem across domains below the use of force:

> Convergence has two advantages over single domain alternatives: cross-domain synergy creates overmatch and multiple forms of attack create layered options across domains to enhance friendly operations and impose complexity on the enemy . . . but [the services] will have to conduct continuous and rapid integration of multi-domain capabilities enabled by mission command and disciplined initiative against near-peer threats in the future.[23]

Moreover convergence extends into peacetime efforts to compete with Russian and Chinese information manipulation. Thus multi-domain efforts are seen not simply as a capacity of the US, but also as one that its adversaries are already conducting:

> In competition, both states seek to fracture U.S. alliances and partnerships through a combination of diplomatic and economic actions; unconventional warfare; information warfare; exploitation of social, ethnic, or nationalistic tensions in a region; and the actual or threatened employment of conventional forces. By generating instability within countries and alliances, they create political separation that results in strategic ambiguity, reducing the speed of friendly recognition, decision and reaction.[24]

In short, the Army's articulation is broader and far more ambitious, uses more machines, and introduces far more complexity into the conduct of MDO. In the words of Naval Submarine Commander Will Spears, "They aspire to a cycle of cross-domain perception, decision-making, and action that is accelerated to the point where these functions occur almost instantly and simultaneously, a sort of operational nirvana the Army's theorists call convergence."[25]

Ironically, bringing together domains to create complexity for the adversary is itself complicated. Decisionmaking within the Army's MDO construct for warfighting carries with it the same weaknesses in presuming that choice can easily be democratized up and down echelons, but it also expands the scope into the minds of others, as well as across the entire spectrum of competition and conflict. Much like the Air Force, MDO also incorporates adaptive battlefield responses through information processing, and real-time updates to leadership for modifying the overall theater campaign. Thus the Army's vision essentially encapsulates the Air Force's more technical solution. According to some recent reports, the Air Force and the Army are actively collaborating to incorporate the former's narrowly technical conceptualization into the latter's broader MDO landscape.[26]

However, the bigger domestic political and wider geopolitical implications for information speed across domains in MDO are operationally and politically challenging for the US leadership and its operations with its military partners and allies.

To its credit, the Army pamphlet recognizes the role of civilian political decisionmaking under conditions of competition. "The Joint Force succeeds in competition by defeating the adversary's efforts to achieve their strategic goals and deterring military escalation; it does this by expanding the competitive space for policymakers through multiple options for employing the elements of national power."[27]

Conversely, under conditions of conflict, it is unclear just how much control the civilian leadership would have over the wildly complicated, dynamically updating rhythm of warfighting. If the Air Force vision of information speed through MDC2 was unclear about facilitating civilian negotiation capabilities during conflict, the Army MDO appears even more unruly, with a heavy emphasis on parallel routes of attack and continuous contact with the adversary. This means that the temptation for the higher-echelon leadership to try to manage below its level of responsibility will only increase.

Additionally, despite the pamphlet's clear statement about facilitating the civilian leadership's political objectives under competition, that language disappears when the use-of-force threshold is reached. In its place is the unhelpful jargon "return to competition"—to "re-compete." This language introduces the potential sidelining of the civilian leadership's decision processes during a high-end fight. It is unclear whether the Army's vision is explicitly designing room for civilian bargaining in the conflict process or simply taking over to win the fight first and making time to talk later. Ultimately the language of the document reflects the relative immaturity of MDO in considering what additional speed and complexity in battle will do for the civil military relationship.

Moreover the international political realities of MDO also go unresolved in its vision of information-speed future warfighting. In the context of a counter-Russian campaign, the Army's fight is a ground fight. While networked warfare across domains could be part of a fight against Russia as it currently stands, NATO allies have neither the resources nor the interoperability to realize MDO. As RUSI's Jack Watling and Daniel Roper painfully point out, the United States' investment in networked warfighting capabilities has outrun that of both its adversaries and its allies.[28] While much of this mismatch stems from the US Army–centric development of the concept—from the bottom up—without close coordination with partners and allies, a land-based fight in Europe will not be coordinated in a manner that is even remotely close to the Army's MDO vision unless the US wants to increase such investment to help its allies develop that capability. Thus speed and integration across domains—despite rhetorically including joint and multinational operations—is unlikely outside US regions of control.

Navy Distributed Maritime Operations—From Ships to Nodes

The Navy's effort is referred to as "distributed maritime operations" (DMO). In contrast to the Air Force's cognitive speed and the Army's integration speed issues, the Navy is leveraging information speed to operate literally as a distributed force—Navy assets, spread across an area of operations, continuously operating in support of one another.

DMO is the youngest and publicly least well-articulated concept. What is known is that portions of the DMO concept are linked in development from a prior concept referred to as "distributed lethality" (DL), which emphasized increased dispersion of forces across the fleet.[29] Despite the fact that neither DMO nor DL has unclassified concept guidelines, a significant amount of public discussion and writing indicates that the Navy is actively working to resolve its internal debates about DMO while simultaneously attempting to catch up with the Air Force and the Army's efforts, and to synchronize its future vision with theirs. The Navy's domain—water—presents significant constraints with regard to its future warfighting vision, as well as its primary framing of threats.

Unlike the hallmark publications on future operating concepts published by the Army and the Air Force, the Navy has proceeded more carefully in issuing unified statements about how to structure its future fleets by leveraging information speed. So far in its articulation the Navy's integration of information speed is to increase the pace of firing on targets by turning the entire fleet into its own literal network—from ships to nodes. Though there are no major unclassified doctrines that explain the Navy's future operating concept, numerous analyses of public unclassified talks, short white papers, and GAO (Government Accountability Office) reports can be used to triangulate its vision of distributed maritime operations. The DMO concept pivots upon two main elements: the robust layered defense capacity of the Chinese (generally referred to as A2AD—Anti-Access/Area Denial), and the lure of cheaper unmanned systems that may be able to suffer fewer losses with smaller surface profiles than standard Navy cruisers and destroyers. These two ongoing debates over the future fleet structure converge into an increasingly more coherent DMO. Ultimately the idea behind the distributed and smaller networked systems for a China scenario is to shift the Navy's thinking from large "ship-centric" forces to a "net-centric" force.[30]

In January 2016, then Chief of Naval Operations (CNO) Admiral John Richardson published a document entitled "A Design for Maintaining Maritime Superiority." Richardson's premise mirrored the overall shift in the NDS vision—that all the services were readjusting their force posture to reflect the new challenges of great power competition.[31] For the Navy the challenge is clearly in the Asia-Pacific region and China's growing naval capabilities. Not only is its numerical capacity increasing, but China has increased its capacity to control the shipping lanes in the Pacific, and it has bolstered its layered defense system, making the first inner island chain off Southeast China the center of many debates.[32] The China challenge is coupled with the US Navy's ship-building woes under limited resources, a decaying supply chain that limits the pace of production of new ships, and the jaw-dropping costs of maintaining the existing fleet.[33] On top of all these challenges, there remains a structural/technical debate over what exactly a winning strategy with China might look like, with competing interpretations of "outside in," inside out, hedgehog, or distant interdiction approaches.[34] This is problematic for the Navy since each of these approaches requires a different alignment of relationships, technologies, and joint forces.

The conceptual core emphasis of the Navy's DMO appears to be that of physical networks but leveraged with a decidedly Navy perspective on warfighting. If the *leitmotiv* for the Air Force is operational agility (cognitive speed), and for the Army is convergence, then the Navy could be understood as a network of ship nodes.[35] Thus it is narrower in scope than the Air Force's vision, and jettisons the Army's emphasis upon partners and allies. In Richardson's view a node formation has the benefit of creating a resilient grid of communications and sensors linking all ships simultaneously—but it differs in function and purpose from the current systems.

In political terms, going from ships to nodes is no small intraservice feat. Current naval power projection at sea is largely centered upon the formation of clusters of mutually supporting ships assembled into carrier battle groups. In each of those groups the different ships have differing supporting tasks— communications, defense, offensive firepower, transportation of air assets, and so on. Not only are some of those assets extremely large—carriers, cruisers, destroyers—and therefore easily targeted from land, but within each clustered group there is mutual security and support since not all ships have both offensive and defensive capability. This is not so in the future warfare vision.

The DMO concept demands a significantly different future fleet architecture. It also articulates a decentralized system of tasking, implying that each ship must be able to conduct defensive as well as offensive tasks. Imagine a deconstruction of tasking for the main organizing concept for power projection—the carrier battle group. Instead of its current construct of mutually supporting ships with specialized duties operating as a dedicated team, the grid-enabled situational awareness software will provide asset-agnostic (that is, any ship, sub, or jet) assessments pinned to a commander's objective. This means that Navy assets—whatever ships, guns, or planes will work—will be called into a mission on the basis of their suitability for the objective, irrespective of the entire grouping's movement. If this is an accurate interpretation, then in real terms all assets will operate more independently and will be able to defend as well as fire on targets. In addition, the information system that will create the common operating picture for leadership—sometimes referred to as the fleet tactical grid—will use all Navy assets (sensors, ships, planes, undersea elements) to build and share in a networked grid that is resilient and resistant to single points of network failure.[36]

Of the three visions of distributed multi-domain future warfare, the Navy's is far behind those of the other two services. This is unsurprising given that DMO works most aggressively against the current structure of the Navy, leading to much bigger debates and a much more complex transition to the new way of warfighting. Ship commanders have historically had control over their own fire power. As part of what is referred to as mission command, ships' captains under current practice are tasked with an objective and are expected to use their own judgment in achieving it.[37] The networked system—the fleet tactical grid—is expected to feed the Maritime Operations Center not only with ship location sensor data, but also with arms supply levels. Again, as in the case of the Air Force's MDC2, this introduces ambiguity over who has control over what. The grid information system suggests that ships' captains could lose that freedom. Instead they would be releasing firing control and positioning to a higher artificially intelligent information system. This will be not only technologically difficult but highly unpopular among existing commanders.

Overall, like both the Air Force and the Army examples, DMO is confused in terms of decisionmaking responsibility, particularly when the leadership continues to discuss the common operational picture as intended for "empowerment of commanders . . . [to] push decision downward."[38] In none of the visions is it clear who is losing control, whose choices are becoming automated, and just how much more control the higher echelon has over the smallest elements of the battle.

Moreover the proliferation of unmanned surface water vessels as a component of DMO presents the Navy with very complex manning decisions at sea. Unlike the air and ground visions, the ships-as-nodes vision is the network itself. Having ships as nodes on the sea domain means more oversight and management at sea for all of the Navy's unmanned assets by the remaining manned ships. With current staffing, the maintenance and oversight of those additional units would be impossible. Until the Navy can articulate a clearer understanding of the human-operated to unmanned ratio in the ships-as-nodes network, it will not be able to progress significantly in operationalizing DMO.

Of the three visions of the future, the Navy's DMO is also the least clear from the civil–military perspective. The Navy's primary area of responsibility remains the sea—and the sea's surface is the transportation highway for global trade. It is littered with the goods being transferred from continent to continent. These trade routes represent a potential distal hurt point, or a bottleneck in a country's capacity to endure a long war at full strength, but such economic levers on the surface of the sea do not occupy quite the same primacy in the minds of publics as land-based operations. Thus if new information systems give rise to potential tears in the civil–military fabric, it is hard to imagine the Navy being at the forefront.

Having said that, perhaps the cognitive difference between sea and land attacks will have an effect not on the US civilian leadership's decisionmaking but on the adversary's. That is, if attacking unmanned nodes at sea is hard to perceive as grounds for war, then the expansion of the Navy's networks at sea may become de facto targets of opportunity under conditions of competition. Certainly the Iranian downing of the US UAV and other instances of clashes at sea would prove to be important case studies for determining whether this is the case.[39] Analyzing the cognitive differences between sea and land-based attacks, and between robotic and manned systems, is beyond the scope of this chapter, but is definitely an important next step for research in this area.

Conclusion: Information, Data, Speed, and the Politics of Decision

Despite the variations in the future warfighting visions of the US Air Force, Army, and Navy, each of the services associates victory with information speed—the implementation of information processing networks to bring about conditions for success. The Air Force's operational agility, the Army's convergence, and the Navy's ships-to-nodes vision all leverage information technologies as core to their theories of victory. However, they are implementation solutions to very different problems that are specific to each service perspective or vision. As with any technological system, the devil is in the design detail. It is not enough simply to link the anticipated speed of information processing and big data with the execution of war, and to declare innovation—there must be an ability to synchronize these data, not simply across services but with external partners and allies. Thinking clearly about the speed of machines and information systems on the battlefield without articulating what kinds of decisions will be made by whom is a fundamentally false and dangerously anti-intellectual scoping of the complex entities that design, plan for, and execute the mechanisms of war.

Moreover it cannot be assumed that these considerations will be resolved later in implementation. Developing these systems without paying concomitant attention to politics risks several adverse outcomes. First, the services will eventually need to synchronize these systems in order to conduct joint warfighting efforts. Information systems that are developed independent of the overall joint force (Army, Navy, Air Force, Marine Corps) are likely to suffer interoperability friction or, worse, incompatibility issues, in an actual cross-domain/multi-domain warfight. And this is to say nothing about synchronization with US partners and allies. Furthermore waiting to synchronize those systems not only risks conflicting accounts of decision processes that will require wasteful redesign but is also likely to incur implementation delays, with each of the services vying to make its system the dominant one.

Besides investigating these significant variations between the visions of the different services, this chapter explored the implications of information speed on civilian leadership decision opportunities. This is premised on the idea that changes to the speed and character of warfighting can have knock-on effects on the connective tissue between civilian leaders and the military machine. Admittedly the documented elements of foresight for the civil–military relationship are hardly intellectually satisfying. The overall design—or non-design—of the system will ultimately dictate how much tension it places upon civil–military relations. The current language suggests that most authors (including this one) are on thin speculative ice. What can be said is that the documents (apart from portions of the Army's vision) have nothing to say about civilian leadership decisions during war. Instead there is elevated emphasis on faster, better, smarter military positioning. Insofar as this is the case, it is appropriate to voice concerns regarding lagged and reduced civilian opportunities to intervene. And given the increasing coherence of the visions for each of the services, the time for taking up the pen is now. Increased speed of decisionmaking at the tactical, operational, and military strategic levels risks changing how and when civilian leadership intervenes. State leaders do not stop making decisions when war begins; they are (at least in Western models of warfighting) part of the process, ideally overseeing it: this is at the core of the "civic militarism" discussed in part I of this volume.[40] Bargaining during war has a purpose, and it is the civilian leadership's role to shape those higher-level political outcomes.[41] State leaders make use of the war machine's pace and data in order to make choices such as determining the necessity of continued violence; signaling to the adversary; negotiating terms of surrender; engaging in cessation talks; and planning postwar settlements; or even assessing the necessity of escalating the conflict further.[42] Changes to the speed and pace of how wars are fought carry the potential to change how and when states engage in war, and the bargaining over the terms of war itself.[43] The tether between the state and military leadership matters most in the execution of warfare.[44] Information speed will matter when the services finally manage to produce a prototype that works. The question is, what are the appropriate decision entry points for aligning military efforts to national objectives? This is not the first time such anxieties have been expressed. In his 2012 book *Supreme Command*, Eliot Cohen reflects on the decisions of Lincoln, Clemenceau, Churchill, and Ben-Gurion. He is prescient in writing:

> These four statesmen conducted their wars during what may come to be seen as the time of the first communications revolution, when it became possible to communicate useful quantities of information almost instantaneously and to move large quantities of men and war materiel at great speed by means of mechanical transportation. . . . One might suggest that a second communications revolution is now upon us, in which a further quantum increase in the amount of information that can be distributed globally has occurred, and the role played by that information in all of civilized life will again transform society and ultimately the conduct of war.[45]

The conduct of war is a matryoshka doll of decision processes, and those processes are shot through with politics. Networked information management systems (intelligent software agents, big data science, distributed processing, and rapid communications) will alter the speed, and therefore the politics, of decision processes. Thus, insofar as the linchpin of Western future warfighting speeds up complex decisionmaking, we must insist upon the simultaneous design of decision routes that ensure the primacy of civilian control before, during, and after the use of the military tool.

Michael Horowitz's work on fully autonomous warfighting systems is also relevant here in information networked warfare. There is a danger that the speed of automated decisionmaking may outrun the military's own capacity to understand and therefore intervene meaningfully when and where it matters.[46] Complex warfighting systems that rely upon near-continuous unceasing battle rhythm, as is suggested by multi-domain battle, may leave civilian leaders without clear opportunities to engage in the kind of negotiations during conflict that are an essential part of the Western tradition of political oversight of the conduct of war.

We would do well to recall that, historically, speed has not led to decisive wars, and yet here we are again. Overall, the exuberance in inviting operational complexity at the pace of data flows needs to be checked, with close inspection of who will make decisions, and how. Rather than racing headlong into speeding up decision chains to enhance lethality, the implementation of networked information as a part of future warfare should serve primarily to make the melee of warfare more comprehensible to both military and civilian leadership—not, as so many of the documents seem to suggest, to envelop the adversary in a confounding, cataclysmic swarming attack which could, incidentally, prove fundamentally escalatory. At a minimum, what is needed going forward is: (1) explicit and careful articulation of when and how the implementation of information speed will be leveraged; then (2) a thoughtful reflection on how this affects opportunities for civilian decisionmaking in conflict; and finally (3) a clearly worded justification of the necessity for removing those chains of decision.[47]

Finally, if we were truly attempting to be innovative, to be responsible with the leveraging of information in war, I would suggest the following. Information speed—the complex merging of sensors and knowledge—does not need to increase war machine speed; it could be designed simply to make us smarter. It could also be designed to introduce periods of strategic pause; to present leadership with more opportunities to delay, to buy time, and to ensure the enemy's intent is understood. Machinic systems can be made to buy time, which also arguably reduces the risk of imprudent or accidental loss of blood and treasure. Information speed can do more than make us faster and more lethal, it can also make us more rational. But we would have to start now to design that.

NOTES

1. Robert Mandel, *Global Data Shock: Strategic Ambiguity, Deception, and Surprise in an Age of Information Overload* (Stanford University Press, 2019).

2. Bob Work, "The Third U.S. Offset Strategy and Its Implications for Partners and Allies," Deputy Secretary of Defense Speech, Washington, January 28, 2015 (US Department of Defense); Michael T. Plehn, "Control Warfare: Inside the Ooda Loop" (Maxwell AFB, Montgomery, AL: Air University Press, 2000).

3. Over the Horizon, "NATO Planning and Multi Domain Operations: A German Perspective," OTH, September 17, 2018, https://othjournal.com/2018/06/27/nato-planning-and-multi-domain-operations-a-german-perspective/.

4. Kelley Sayler, *A World of Proliferated Drones: A Technology Primer* (Washington, DC: Center for a New American Security (CNAS), June 10, 2015).

5. Adam Grissom, "The Future of Military Innovation Studies," *Journal of Strategic Studies,* vol. 29, no. 5 (2006), p. 908.

6. Kelsey D. Atherton, "When Big Data Went to War—and Lost," Politico, October 12, 2017, https://www.politico.eu/article/iraq-war-when-big-data-wentto-war- and-lost/.

7. Mark Pomerleau, "The Network Will Underpin Army's Multi-Domain Battle Concept," C4ISRNET, March 10, 2018, www.c4isrnet.com/it-networks/2018/03/09/the-network-will-underpin-armys-multi-domain-battle-concept/.

8. Derek O'Malley and Andrew Hill, "The A-10, the F-35, and the Future of Close Air Support," War on the Rocks, August 10, 2015, https://warontherocks.com/2015/05/the-a-10-the-f-35-and-the-future-of-close-air-support-part-i/.

9. M. V. Schanz, "Room with a View: It's Just a Nondescript Building in a Gulf Country, but Inside You Get a Superb View of the War on Terror," *Air Force Magasin,* vol. 90, no. 8 (2007).

10. US Air Force, "Air Force Future Operating Concept: A View of the Air Force in 2035," September 2015, https://www.af.mil/Portals/1/images/airpower/AFFOC.pdf.

11. Ibid., p. 3.

12. Ibid., p. 9.

13. Ibid., p. 7.

14. Tech. Sgt Robert Barnett, "Goldfein: Future of War Is Networked, Multi-Domain," U.S. Air Force, March 22, 2017, https://www.af.mil/News/Article-Display/Article/1127212/goldfein-future-of-war-is-networked-multi-domain/.

15. David Goldfein, "Enhancing Multi-Domain Command and Control," *CSAF Focus Area Paper* (2017).

16. US Air Force, "Air Force Future Operating Concept," p. 14.

17. Ibid., p. 15.

18. Ibid., p. 5.

19. U.S. Army Training and Doctrine Command, *The U.S. Army in Multi-Domain Operations 2028*, Tradoc Pamphlet 525-3-1 (Ft. Eustis, VA: U.S. Training and Doctrine Command, 6 December 2018), pp. viii–x.

20. Jim Mattis, "Summary of the 2018 National Defense Strategy of the United States of America" (Department of Defense, 2018).

21. MDO, p. 7.

22. MDO, p. iii.

23. Training and Command, p.14.

24. Ibid., p. 14.

25. Will Spears, "A Sailor's Take on Multi-Domain Operations," War on the Rocks, May 21, 2019, https://warontherocks.com/2019/05/a-sailors-take-on-multi-domain-operations/.

26. Ibid.

27. Training and Command, p. 25.

28. Jack Watling and Daniel Roper, "European Allies in US Multi-Domain Operations," in *RUSI Occasional Paper* (London: Royal United Services Institute, 2019).

29. Jeffrey Kline, "A Tactical Doctrine for Distributed Lethality," *Center for International Maritime Security*, vol. 22 (2016).

30. Ronald O'Rourke, *Navy Force Structure and Shipbuilding Plans: Background and Issues for Congress*, CRS Report (Washington, DC: U.S. Congressional Research Service, 2019).

31. John M. Richardson, "A Design for Maintaining Maritime Superiority," *Naval War College Review*, vol. 69, no. 2 (2016), article 4, https://digital-commons .usnwc.edu/nwc-review/vol69/iss2/4.

32. David Fouse, *US–Japan Alliance Confronts the Anti-Access and Area Denial Challenge: Toward Building Capacity, Cooperation and Information Sharing in the Western Pacific,* Asia-Pacific Center for Security Studies, Honolulu, 2015.

33. "Comparing a 355-Ship Fleet with Smaller Naval Forces," Congressional Budget Office, March 14, 2018, www.cbo.gov/publication/53637.

34. An excellent summary of the differences between the strategic approaches is available online via CIMSEC: Jeremy Renken, "Strategic Architectures," Center for International Maritime Security, February 13, 2014, http://cimsec.org/strategic -architectures/9941.

35. Megan Eckstein, "Navy Planning for Gray-Zone Conflict; Finalizing Distributed Maritime Operations for High-End Fight," *USNI News*, December 19, 2018, https://news.usni.org/2018/12/19/navy-planning-for-gray-zone-conflict -finalizing-distributed-maritime-operations-for-high-end-fight.

36. Sydney J. Freedberg, "Navy in Midst of High-End War 'Renaissance': Vice Adm. Rowden," *Breaking Defense*, January 8, 2018, https://breakingdefense.com /2018/01/a-renaissance-for-navy-warfighting-despite-collisions-admiral/.

37. Patricia Kime, "Navy to Embrace 'Mission Command' Concepts to Match Adversaries," Military.com, January 15, 2019, www.military.com/daily-news/2019 /01/15/navy-embrace-mission-command-concepts-match-adversaries.html.

38. Christopher H. Popa, Sydney P. Stone, Ee H. Aw, and others, "Distributed Maritime Operations and Unmanned Systems Tactical Employment," Naval Postgraduate School Monterey, United States, 2018.

39. Oxford Analytica, "Caution Will Probably Prevail after Iran Downs US UAV," June 20, 2019, *Emerald Expert Briefings*, oxan-es.

40. See, for example, R. Harrison Wagner, "Bargaining and War," *American Journal of Political Science,* vol. 44, no. 3 (2000); Branislav L. Slantchev, "The Principle of Convergence in Wartime Negotiations," *American Political Science Review,* vol. 97, no. 4 (2003).

41. Eric Min, "Negotiation as an Instrument of War," Working Paper, Stanford University, 2017.

42. Paul R. Pillar, *Negotiating Peace: War Termination as a Bargaining Process*, 1st ed. 1983, vol. 695 (Princeton University Press, 2014).

43. See Michael C. Horowitz, "When Speed Kills: Lethal Autonomous

Weapon Systems, Deterrence and Stability," *Journal of Strategic Studies,* vol. 42, no. 6 (2019). Although Horowitz does not address war termination, he does address potential escalation and uncertainty with autonomous weapons systems.

44. Eliot A. Cohen, *Supreme Command: Soldiers, Statesmen and Leadership in Wartime* (New York: Free Press, 2012).

45. Ibid., p. 6.

46. Horowitz, "When Speed Kills."

47. I am likely not alone in skepticism that this will occur—but it needs to.

ELEVEN

The Limits of Technology

The Impact of Speed and Innovation on Western Military Primacy

HEATHER WILLIAMS

In 1988, the first undersea fibre optic cables were laid.[1] Twenty-five years later, in 2013, British intelligence's Tempora program had access to 5 petabytes of data *every 24 hours* from bulk fibre optic cables, approximately 44 times the content of the entire the British Library.[2] In 1991, the Tomahawk cruise missile was first used in Operation Desert Storm, reaching a top speed of approximately 550 miles per hour.[3] The hypersonic missiles currently under development, such as Russian's Avangard, may reach speeds of 15,345 miles per hour, Mach 20, in the next 25 years.[4] Emerging technologies such as hypersonics and artificial intelligence (AI) allow militaries to move faster than ever before, but also create uncertainties about their short-, medium-, and long-term impact on conflict escalation and military balances.

This era of technological advancement is not happening in a political vacuum, of course. The 2017 US *National Security Strategy*, for example, defined the current environment as a "competitive world," with Russia and China, in particular, challenging American power. At the same time, it asserted, "access to technology empowers and emboldens otherwise weak states," such as North Korea,[5] and technological advances highlight the role of non-traditional actors, such as the private sector, in military competition.

These three converging trends—emerging technology, geopolitical competition, and a growing role for non-traditional actors—raise fundamental questions about international security and world order: do advanced technologies provide Western military powers with a strategic advantage? If so, how might those militaries use technological advantage to avoid conflict and escalation? If not, why do non-Western actors have a strategic advantage, and what are the implications for the future of military competition?

This chapter aims to open new intellectual space for thinking about speed, technology, and Western military power. With a few important exceptions,[6] scholarship on the impact of emerging technology on Western military primacy treats technology, or a single category of technology, as a whole with little granularity. For example, much of the literature looks at "cyber" as a monolith, rather than examining specific applications. This approach is particularly challenging for dual-use technologies, and therefore conflates a variety of activities, muddying the waters of strategic analysis. To offer another example, the use of AI in pattern recognition is likely to have a different impact on a crisis from its use in drone targeting.

In trying to fill this gap in scholarship, the chapter starts by outlining the reasons for choosing three major lenses for evaluating the impact of technology on military balancing: strategic stability, offense–defense balance, and technological opportunism. It then applies these lenses to two fast technologies: hypersonic missiles as a technology still under development with purely military applications; and the use of AI in pattern recognition for intelligence purposes, as an example, with an indirect military application that is already widely used by a number of countries, including the United States and China.

In arguing that the impact of increasingly fast technology is limited and does not inherently undermine Western military primacy, the chapter reinforces scholarship by Keir Lieber[7] and, more recently, Caitlin Talmadge[8] showing that technology and speed alone do not necessarily increase the likelihood of conflict; rather, it depends on the political context. Whether or not they give Western powers a unique advantage, therefore, depends on how these fast technologies are situated both within a wider array of military capabilities and postures, and within the geopolitical context or crisis scenario. Where speed may have tactical implications, however, is by reducing decision-making time during crises and thickening the "fog of war." These implications point to at least four policy recommendations, which are detailed at the end of the chapter: expansion of crisis communication channels; a stronger normative framework around risk reduction; involving the private sector; and promoting dialogue with the potential to reduce risks associated with emerging technologies, but recognizing that opportunities for arms control around emerging technology will be limited while states play "catch-up."

Three Approaches to Technology: Stability, Balance, and Opportunism

Much of the current scholarship on speed and emerging technology takes an alarmist view: faster weapons reduce decisionmaking time and increase risks of misperception, incentivize first-strikes, and create moral quandaries around keeping a human "in the loop."[9] Fear of speed is understandable on the part of military planners. A fast attack threatens to limit situational awareness and increase uncertainty, thickening the "fog of war." As a result, states could inadvertently escalate a crisis in a perceived "use-it-or-lose-it" scenario. Additionally, the threat of a fast attack necessitates either managing vulnerability and coping with the inevitability of attack, or a constant sense of vigilance and defense in preparation for a rapid assault. While the former is inconceivable for many Western strategic cultures, the latter is impossible for financial and technological reasons. For example, cyberattacks cannot be defended against 100 percent of the time, and many Western states have instead adopted a limited deterrence approach, which requires accepting *some* vulnerability and attacks.[10] The implications of this fear include offensive and defensive arms races, along with distrust within an alliance about the credibility of security guarantees.

But emerging technologies may also have a stabilizing effect, which has received less attention. Questions about the impact of technology and stability have already been posed in relation to cyber technologies, for example, and offer an example of their multiple effects. In contrast to some of the alarmist literature on the impact of cyber technologies, Martin Libicki argues that "the continued existence of nuclear weapons limits the ability of cyberspace to cause strategic destabilization,"[11] and Erik Gartzke and Jon Lindsay see it as beneficial not only to offense but also to defense: "defenders can also employ deceptive concealment and ruses to confuse or ensnare aggressors. Indeed, deception can reinvigorate traditional strategies of deterrence and defense against cyber threats, as computer security practitioners have already discovered."[12] Similar consideration is gradually being given to other emerging technologies defined by their speed.

Three existing frameworks offer insights on how to conceptualize the impact of speed and emerging technology on Western military primacy and the future of military competition: strategic stability, offense–defense balance, and technological opportunism. These three concepts are by no means exhaustive; rather, they have been selected as three of the most prominent in international relations scholarship that specifically take into account technological innovation.

Strategic Stability

Strategic stability is a concept typically associated with the Cold War bilateral nuclear balance, wherein the United States and the Soviet Union held each other hostage in what was assumed to be a stable deterrence relationship. This balance was defined by their ability to survive a nuclear first strike and retaliate. Nuclear forces, therefore, needed to be "sufficiently invulnerable" to withstand a pre-emptive attack, but also to be sufficiently vulnerable for decisionmakers to be deterred from striking pre-emptively for fear of retaliation.[13] For Thomas Schelling and others, strategic stability had two components: crisis stability, wherein escalation was unlikely, and arms race stability, whereby neither side sought a significant military advantage so as to be able to launch a decapitating first strike through the use of a new offensive capability, or to be completely invulnerable to attack, such as through advances in defenses.[14]

Since the end of the Cold War the concept of strategic stability has evolved beyond definitions of a survivable second strike, in two important ways. First, recent scholarship by Dmitry Adamsky,[15] Kristin Ven Bruusgaard,[16] and others has highlighted that strategic stability means different things to different actors: Russia's conceptualization of stability has always differed from that of the United States, using a broader interpretation that includes conventional, diplomatic, and even psychological components. Second, strategic stability is no longer solely defined in nuclear terms. Indeed the 2018 US "Nuclear Posture Review" took an important step in moving closer to a Russian definition of strategic stability to include non-nuclear capabilities.[17] The declaratory policy reads:

> The United States would only consider the employment of nuclear weapons in extreme circumstances to defend the vital interests of the United States, its allies, and partners. Extreme circumstances could include significant non-nuclear strategic attacks. Significant non-nuclear strategic attacks include, but are not limited to, attacks on the U.S., allied, or partner civilian population or infrastructure, and attacks on U.S. or allied nuclear forces, their command and control, or warning and attack assessment capabilities. . . . Given the potential of significant non-nuclear strategic attacks, the United States reserves the right to make any adjustment in the assurance that may be warranted by

the evolution and proliferation of non-nuclear strategic attack technologies and U.S. capabilities to counter that threat.[18]

This brings non-nuclear systems into the strategic stability equation. Such a broader interpretation is not wholly new. For example, in 1978 John Steinbruner highlighted the importance of organizational issues and command and control for stability, whereby it was not simply a technical matter of counting,[19] and in 2014 Nancy Gallagher argued for a more holistic approach to strategic stability, based on mutual security and cooperation, and reviving the work of Hedley Bull.[20]

Taking into account both the traditional definition of strategic stability (survivable second strike) and the broader contemporary interpretation, what is the impact of technological innovation and speed on stability? From a traditional perspective, the impact of a new technology will depend on whether or not it gives one side an offensive advantage in striking first, enabling it to decapitate an adversary's ability to respond. With regard to nuclear stability, this may not be particularly destabilizing as long as the main nuclear actors have, for example, nuclear-armed submarines that are highly survivable and stealthy. A more contemporary approach to strategic stability, incorporating various domains, is more complex; here emerging technologies might increase the vulnerability of nuclear arsenals[21]—for instance, cyberthreats to command and control, or the entanglement of conventional and nuclear forces in a crisis escalation.[22]

Offense–Defense Balance

Another conceptual lens rooted in the Cold War is the offense–defense balance, which has already received some attention in scholarship on emerging technology.[23] The original tenets of offense–defense theory were that war is more likely when the offense has the advantage and less likely when defense does.[24] Additionally, arms races and competition are driven by the risks of misinterpreting a defensive weapon as an offensive one, often entailing the danger of nuclear escalation, in the classic security dilemma.[25] When offense has the advantage, cooperation and negotiation are less likely,[26] further increasing the risks associated with emerging technologies that might give an offensive advantage or the *perception* of one.

According to Robert Jervis, technology and geography are the main factors determining whether the offense or the defense has the advantage.[27] Technology has an impact not only by improving capabilities, but also in terms of their *cost*. Two types of technological changes affect the offense–defense balance. In the most simplistic interpretation, therefore, speed would be either stabilizing if it improved defenses, or destabilizing if it improved offensive forces. But this traditional approach to the offense–defense balance presents three challenges for strategy: the emphasis on geography, ambiguity about technology, and treating offense and defense as a binary.

Territory can no longer be defined in purely military or physical terms. In an *International Security* correspondence from 1995, Stacie Goddard argues: "The balance cannot be represented as the probability of taking territory, and should not incorporate the absolute value of an attack. . . . it says nothing about the ultimate outcome of a war, and thus avoids incorporating power into the concept."[28] Whether a side is offense-dominant or defense-dominant, whether it can gain or hold territory, does not necessarily determine the outcome of a conflict. Offense–defense balance theory must therefore take into account non-territorial gains and the political goals of either side. Additionally, in a potential future conflict involving highly sophisticated technology, such as cyber or AI, the battlefield is likely to be virtual and territorial gains will not necessarily be a deciding factor, if they are relevant at all.

Second, offense–defense balance scholars often treat technology as a monolith, or categorize a capability as either "offensive" or "defensive." But more contemporary interpretations of the offense–defense balance attempt to recognize the complexity of the relationship and the importance of political factors. Keir Lieber, for example, argues that it is flawed because, "it mistakenly views technology as a powerful and largely autonomous cause of war and peace."[29] Returning to the cyber example from Gartzke and Lindsay, "the cyber offense-defense balance is likely conditional on the complexity and severity of the attack and the resolve of the opponents."[30] The impact of speed and technology on the offense–defense balance therefore depends on the application of the technology. In addition Sean Lynn-Jones identifies numerous conceptual flaws with this balance in failing to take into account the political intentions of states, the distribution of power, and the domestic context.[31]

These criticisms suggest such a balance is a continuum, rather than a set of scales. Lynn-Jones argues it is misleading to describe an international system as being either "offense-dominant" or "defense-dominant."[32] If we think of it as a continuum, rather than a binary favoring one side or the other, additional implications for the impacts of technology emerge. If an adversary *perceives* an offensive advantage owing to a new technology, this may embolden it to act recklessly. Moreover allies will also *perceive* the technological advantages of an adversary with implications for extended deterrence and military cooperation.[33] The importance of perception is not limited to fear of aggression, but rather also links to the risks of a potentially costly arms race.

For Lynn-Jones and others, the costs associated with technological innovation and advantage are as important as any advances in capabilities. Specifically, "when a technological innovation changes the relative costs of offensive and defensive capabilities, the offense-defense balance shifts. Because the offense-defense balance is a continuum, the magnitude and direction of such shifts are more important than whether the balance simply favors the offense or the defense."[34] Technological innovation may make a strategy more effective at a lower cost, and it may also reduce the costs of production.[35] The importance of investment to the offense–defense balance was recently examined in the context of emerging technology by Ben Garfinkel and Allan Dafoe, who introduced the concept of "OD scaling," whereby scaling up investments initially benefits offense, but eventually and ultimately will give an advantage to defense.[36]

Technological Opportunism

Among the many critics of the offense–defense balance, Lieber offers an alternative framework that is particularly useful in evaluating the impact of technological innovation and speed—"technological opportunism." Lieber describes this as follows:

> The basic imperative to maximize relative power is compounded by the fact that leaders face enormous uncertainty when it comes to evaluating the offense-defense balance and predicting technological change. Even if leaders could measure an offense-defense balance, they would have trouble determining how much defense dominance was enough to preserve national security at any given time. . . . To the extent that technology does play a role in determining winners and losers in battle, the impact arises when one state has a technological edge over an adversary based on the array of weapons at its disposal, not when the nature of technology favors either offense or defense.[37]

The key factor is not necessarily the technology itself, but the uncertainty generated by technological innovation and the intersection of that uncertainty with the political context. This uncertainty not only inspires states to take advantage of technological advantages where they exist for political gains, but also to pursue technological change for maximum "relative power."[38] In the nuclear realm, Mark Bell refers to "nuclear opportunism," whereby "states use nuclear weapons in an opportunistic way to improve their position in international politics and to help them achieve political goals that the state cares about."[39]

Lieber's approach also challenges many of the tenets of strategic stability, mainly by arguing that the survivability of nuclear weapons should not be taken for granted; rather, as he argues in an article with Daryl Press, "one should expect countries to act as they always have when faced with military threats: by trying to exploit new technologies and strategies for destroying adversary capabilities."[40] A recent study by Caitlin Talmadge, drawing on Cold War examples of emerging technology, found that "the findings largely cast doubt on the idea of emerging technologies as an independent, primary driver of otherwise avoidable escalation, suggesting instead that technology more likely functions as an intervening variable—a sometimes necessary, but rarely sufficient, condition for escalation."[41]

Technological opportunism, therefore, means that a new technology must be evaluated according to a variety of factors, not simply by whether or not it undermines survivable second strike or gives advantage to offense or defense. Its impact depends on or is determined by, first, the technology itself, particularly its military application; second, how the technology is embedded in a country's suite of military capabilities, rather than as a stand-alone; third, the political context and whether or not a country will use it for military competition; and, finally, a country's ability and willingness to use it as a signaling tool.

Technology and Western Military Primacy

As outlined in the Introduction to this volume, Western warfare is defined by liberal institutions, particularly civilian leadership of military affairs; the concept of a culminating point and the "ability to endure and deliver fatal blows"; and that war is ultimately a test of political wills. At the outset, we can conceive of scenarios that would challenge these premises and potentially undermine Western military primacy. With shortened decisionmaking time, authority could be removed from civilian authorities and transferred to military leaders. The culminating point may be reached months in advance but remain dormant, such as a zero-day vulnerability, increasing the "fog of war" during a crisis if at least one actor does not know that such a vulnerability exists but can be activated in a matter of seconds. And AI may negate fatigue in wars of attrition, such as providing round-the-clock surveillance or alternatives to human warfighters. The above concepts can help to understand these and other scenarios by highlighting three themes.

First, avoiding nuclear use and crisis escalation is increasingly complex because of a more diverse range of technologies. The intersection of these technologies is poised to increase confusion, particularly during a crisis, and creates military asymmetries on an unprecedented scale across domains. This is particularly evident in more contemporary thinking about strategic stability along with the concept of technological opportunism, but it also relates to Lynn-Jones's idea of offense–defense as a continuum. States that previously had a nuclear disadvantage might hope to compensate in conventional capabilities and vice versa, but in the current environment some states have a host of options in trying to compete with Western powers. Whereas in the past the offense–defense continuum was a two-dimensional spectrum, it is now multi-dimensional and defined by complexity.

Second, technology cost matters. Historically, according to the rationale of strategic stability, states refrained from arms races during times of limited competition; today, however, peer competitors, smaller states, and even non-state actors are investing in technologies defined by speed that could undermine Western military primacy. Particularly in democratic societies, militaries cannot spend without limit and must instead make strategic choices about which technologies to invest in so as to balance other, rising powers. Costs may prove a comparative *disadvantage* for Western countries, relative to more authoritarian countries such as China or Russia, where government demand and producer supply are linked. This again reinforces the need to disaggregate types of technology, given that some are relatively inexpensive and others, such as hypersonics, are proving costly.

Third, perception of technology matters. Some emerging technologies, such as hypersonics, could fit in with traditional concepts of security challenges. Others, however, raise difficult questions about how technologies are perceived across a diverse range of actors. One set of uniquely affected actors will be allies that underpin many Western military institutions, such as NATO. But other groups will be affected as well, including smaller states that may not be able to compete in developing advanced technologies—how might they perceive the military applications of AI, for example? Perceptions of fast and novel technologies will influence the ability of Western states to maintain military advantages and avoid conflict.

Case Studies in Speed: Hypersonic Missiles
and AI Pattern Recognition

These themes of complexity, cost, and perception can now be applied to two case studies. As highlighted by all three concepts, scholarship on emerging technologies must disaggregate types of technology, specifically their military applications, and how they fit into the broader geopolitical context. To address this, the case studies below focus on two specific military applications of an emerging technology defined by speed: hypersonic missiles and AI used for intelligence analysis.

These cases differ in three important ways in terms of examining the utility of various approaches to Western military primacy and the potentially destabilizing impact of emerging technologies. First, the use of hypersonic missiles is a direct military application with no possible civilian use, whereas AI is largely being developed by the private sector and has both military and civilian applications. Second, while hypersonic weapons are still being developed and have not yet been deployed to their fullest extent, as of mid-2020, AI is already in use by intelligence agencies for pattern recognition. And third, hypersonic missiles are clearly defined as "hardware," whereas AI is typically defined as "software"—though, as will be discussed, AI presents unique definitional challenges.

Hypersonic Missiles

Hypersonic weapons are being designed to travel at speeds of Mach 5 or faster by at least five countries: China, France, India, Russia, and the United States. While US investment in hypersonics has been of a "stop-start" nature,[42] Russia and China have been gradually building and testing their own hypersonics programs to compete with the United States. In March 2018, for example, President Putin announced the development of the "Avangard" missile, which will carry a hypersonic glide vehicle (HGV) and was deployed in late 2019.[43] On November 26, 2019, Russia demonstrated its Avangard system with a hypersonic boost-glide vehicle to the United States.[44] China has conducted at least seven tests of its hypersonic missile, which is also likely to be nuclear-capable. The United States has said it hopes to develop a hypersonic missile capable of traveling 8,000 km, but at present no country is believed to have achieved or to be anticipating in the near future a range beyond 2,200 km.[45]

At first glance it would seem that HGVs will be treated in a similar way to intercontinental ballistic missiles (ICBMs) and therefore do not necessarily increase cross-domain complexity. According to strategic stability logic, an HGV might have the ability to conduct a decapitating strike on a small nuclear actor, but likely not on a peer competitor among the United States, Russia, and China. Therefore HGVs would simply reinforce existing deterrence paradigms. They could potentially be used offensively as a first-strike weapon, but could also be perceived as defensive if nuclear-armed and contributing to overall deterrence—as such, this proves a useful contemporary example of Lynn-Jones's argument that offense–defense is a continuum rather than a simple balance. Where HGVs could play a destabilizing role is by incentivizing a pre-emptive nuclear strike. A smaller nuclear actor, such as North Korea, would have an incentive to use its nuclear weapons before a decapitating and fast strike in a "use it or lose it" situation if attacked. And a broader interpretation of strategic stability, to include multiple domains, points to the additional vulnerabilities in HGVs. For example, James Acton suggests a scenario in which the United States would destroy China's anti-satellite capabilities with HGVs to disarm its navigation and anti-access/area-denial: "The result could be rapid escalation that both sides might rather avoid."[46]

HGVs raise concerns about a costly arms race. Arguably, the United States, Russia, and China are already in a hypersonics arms race as they continue to invest heavily in their respective development programs. According to Thomas Schelling and Morton Halperin, an arms race is defined as "the interaction between two or more adversaries' military programs, . . . a tendency for each side's program to respond to what the other is doing."[47] This is often seen in technological advances, which turn into "insatiable programs."[48] Based on this logic and broader contemporary understandings of strategic stability, a hypersonics arms race would not merely be investment in the technology but also a pursuit of strategic superiority amid a suite of capabilities. For example, while China may ultimately achieve an advantage in HGVs, its smaller nuclear arsenal puts it at a relative strategic disadvantage. Additionally, declaratory statements such as the US "Nuclear Posture Review" are intended to clarify that non-nuclear attacks, such as those potentially carried out by conventional HGVs, will still be subject to the logic of retaliation and deterrence that arguably maintained strategic stability and prevented nuclear use for seventy-five years.

The majority of literature on HGVs points to their potential to increase misperception and risk escalation during crises. Acton has highlighted risks associated with warhead ambiguity, whereby it is unclear if an HGV is carrying a nuclear or conventional warhead, and destination ambiguity, since the maneuverability of HGVs makes it difficult to predict the point of impact.

During a crisis these uncertainties could prompt a launch-on warning; but given that the impact and destination are unknown, decisionmakers will be in the dark as to whether their retaliation is proportionate. For example, if presented with intelligence about an incoming HGV, a decisionmaker may be forced to respond quickly and opt for nuclear retaliation, assuming the incoming missile is nuclear-armed. Should the incoming HGV prove to be armed with a low-yield conventional weapon and be detonated in a remote area, the decisionmaker will have responded in a decidedly, though unintentionally, escalatory way. Moreover the speed of HGVs suggests they are intended as a first-strike weapon to destroy an adversary's ability to respond.

An alternative interpretation, however, is that HGVs will ultimately play the same role as ICBMs and deter escalation. Indeed according to the traditional logic of strategic stability, this ambiguity could potentially have a stabilizing effect. Corentin Brustlein, for example, has argued that "the specific added value of conventional prompt strike should remain limited to the most demanding missions (decapitation strikes, preemptive or preventing strikes on a very small set of targets in A2/AD environments, etc.) that the U.S. could have to conduct against regional powers such as North Korea or Iran."[49] This would shift the "burden of escalation" to the disadvantaged adversary, who would have few options short of risking annihilation.[50]

AI and Intelligence Pattern Recognition

While HGVs fall into traditional concepts of strategic strike capabilities, AI suffers from a variety of definitional problems. Is it hardware or software? In a useful study on potential applications of AI to intelligence analysis, James Regens defines AI as "a branch of computer science that deals with developing hardware and software systems [to] operate autonomously, perform tasks or discern solutions to complex problems in a human-like fashion, and mirror natural intelligence by emulating neurobiological processes functions."[51]

Artificial intelligence is increasingly used in a variety of applications, from targeting to facial recognition. Kenneth Payne argues that its applications are largely tactical, but with the potential to shape strategy and "increase fighting power."[52] One of its most prevalent uses is in pattern recognition, whereby it can consume massive amounts of data, more than any human possibly could, to identify trends and anomalies. This includes machine learning and computer vision to process both structured and unstructured data much as a human would.[53] The Department of Defense is sponsoring development of algorithms for multilingual speech recognition and translation in noisy environments, creating 3-D models, and "building tools to infer a building's function based on pattern-of-life analysis."[54] Additionally, machine learning could assist in "predicting what responses are likely under given circumstances by identifying patterns that were previously undefined or unknown," according to Regens.[55]

One example of the common refrain around the risks of AI is: "left unchecked the uncertainties and vulnerabilities created by the rapid proliferation and diffusion of AI could become a major potential source of instability and great power strategic rivalry."[56] These risks are of concern in a nuclear context—for instance, if AI is used in early warning and creates a false alarm,[57] or in some way undermines the credibility of a nuclear deterrent.[58] This is indeed one interpretation of the risks associated with AI; given its newness, in particular, further scholarship can explore alternative approaches and manifestations through specificity of applications and definitions of stability.

The speed of AI development is not being driven by the military but rather by companies that are the main investors in and developers of the technology. For example, US technology companies are likely to increase investment in AI from $20–30 billion in 2016 to $126 billion by 2025.[59] In the military, by contrast, the US Department of Defense increased (unclassified) spending on AI from $600 million in 2016 to $800 million in 2017.[60] Other experts, including Michael Horowitz and Elsa Kania, have pointed out that owing to the relationship between its government and economic entities, China may have an advantage in AI development and military applications.[61]

The application of AI to intelligence analysis has a particularly important effect on the speed of decisionmaking and risks of misperception during a crisis. Drawing on vast amounts of data across a variety of sources, AI devices can present their human counterparts in intelligence analysis with trends and anomalies in record time. The risks of this, of course, are that the machine misses important contextual factors and could inadvertently suggest an escalatory scenario, such as missile deployments, or indicate a crisis where one does not exist. This could prompt a military or political response based on misperceptions due not to human psychology, as was a fear throughout the Cold War and in the offense–defense balance, but rather to *machine* misunderstanding. An additional, though under-explored risk, is that AI intelligence analysis may be generating more information than current intelligence organizations can process reliably with a human "in the loop." Horowitz and others, for example, have argued that the impact of AI will largely depend on how it is incorporated into existing economic, political, and military systems; the technology itself is not necessarily the risk to stability.[62]

The alternative to this, of course, is that AI-informed intelligence analysis would have a stabilizing effect by giving decisionmakers richer and more accurate information, free of any potential human biases. Greater understanding of an adversary's capabilities or political motives, for example, would contribute to what Ken Booth and Nicholas Wheeler label "security dilemma sensibility," defined as "an actor's intention and capacity to perceive the motives behind, and to show responsiveness toward, the potential complexity of the military intentions of others."[63] The faster pace of intelligence collection and analysis would also afford decisionmakers *more* time, not less, which could have a stabilizing effect. Ultimately, whether faster and more diverse intelligence has a stabilizing or destabilizing effect depends on the intersection of AI and human analysts and the political context.

Artificial intelligence cannot be readily categorized as "offense-dominant" or "defense-dominant"; rather, where it falls on the continuum depends on its application. In the case discussed here, AI-assisted intelligence and pattern recognition, AI could be used for offensive purposes to assist in identifying a target for a covert military strike, or defensively as a warning of an imminent threat. Arguably, pattern recognition could have a stabilizing impact during a crisis by reducing risks of misperception and increasing decisionmaking time. And finally, the advantages of AI will be largely felt by countries with robust private sectors involved in AI development—mainly in peer competitors such as Russia, China, and the United States, along with developed countries such as Japan and South Korea.

Implications: Keeping Up with the Competition

Do these fast technologies make conflict more or less likely? This analysis of speed and stability suggests that moving fast does not always break things, to misquote Mark Zuckerberg. Rather, whether or not speed has a destabilizing effect depends on a variety of factors; it may actually reduce the likelihood of conflict in some circumstances. This challenges much of the alarmist conventional wisdom on emerging technology as ultimately having a negative impact on international security and Western military primacy.

Turning back to the themes of our earlier models, these case studies offer insights into how the complexity, cost, and perceptions associated with fast technologies could undermine Western military primary.

First, as was particularly evident in the case of HGVs, domains are increasingly blurred and there are not always clear divides between "nuclear" and "conventional." This blurring of domains could present unique challenges for escalation management for Western militaries and strategic thinkers, which still often tend to think in terms of a "ladder" or a clear divide between conventional and nuclear. Fast technologies also create complications with additional actors—in the case of HGVs this was evident with smaller nuclear states, and with AI a key actor is the private sector.

Escalatory effects will in addition continue to rely on political dynamics. Both of the cases examined here reinforce Lieber's concept of technological opportunism, whereby neither creates a first-mover advantage. Talmadge's recent study concludes that "policymakers might develop technologies expressly for the purpose of being able to manipulate escalatory risk in new ways, or may look opportunistically to technology to help them implement escalatory military campaigns or strategies that they already want to pursue for other reasons."[64] An HGV threat to a small nuclear-armed country could have a destabilizing effect by prompting a use-it-or-lose-it situation; alternatively, an HGV threat to a peer competitor, such as between the United States and Russia, could reinforce the strategic status quo and encourage stable deterrence relations. It is important to reiterate that the impact of technology on stability depends as much on the political context in which it is used as on the application.

Second, fast technologies are indeed expensive, and peer competitors have a more direct means of controlling supply and investment. The increasing speed of conflict due to technological innovation increases incentives for investing in new capabilities and has the potential to incite arms races. Garfinkel and Dafoe suggest that technological innovation will not only inspire a like-for-like arms race, as is currently being seen in HGVs, for example, but may also cross domains: "We note that progress in artificial intelligence and in robotics will, in effect, scale up the number of weapons platforms that actors deploy, as well as the number of software vulnerabilities that they can discover."[65] The costs of the technologies discussed here are largely prohibitive for the majority of international actors, potentially creating an asymmetry whereby the major military powers—the United States, China, and Russia—maintain an ever-widening technological advantage. This does not necessarily translate into stability, of course, as smaller states and non-state actors will resort to other means of undermining Western advantages, as discussed by Amelie Theussen and Peter Viggo Jakobsen in chapter 7. But this asymmetry has been a constant trend of warfare and is unlikely to change with the emergence of ever-faster weapons.

The need for sustained funding was particularly evident in the case of HGVs. Western investment in AI is particularly hard to track because of the definitional issues discussed, but requires further study, although new initiatives such as the US Project Maven suggest some Western states are attempting to stay competitive by working with the private sector. An additional major funding challenge for Western democracies will be sustained funding as technologies continue to emerge, and deciding where and how to invest. This is one area in which the West may be at a disadvantage relative to more state-driven military industrial complexes. Sustained military investment will depend on a combination of factors, most notably public support. One potential opportunity created by emerging technologies and increasing complexity is for Western countries also to adopt low-cost solutions and an asymmetric model. However, this would require abandoning the practical and symbolic attachment to quantitative parity and taking an ever-broader approach to stability—which seems unlikely in the near future, particularly for the United States.

Finally, fast technologies may have the potential to improve awareness, help political leadership make better-informed decisions, and reduce misperceptions, as in the case of AI, but they simultaneously decrease decision-making time in crises. As demonstrated in this example, "AI" could refer to nuclear early warning and have a destabilizing effect by generating a false alarm. This would be a twenty-first-century version of the incident in 1983 when Lieutenant Colonel Stanislav Petrov of the Soviet Union concluded, correctly, that the Soviet early warning system was malfunctioning when it reported six incoming US nuclear ICBMs.[66] Ultimately the impact of speed and technology on stability is limited and depends not only on the technology but also on its specific application.

Policy Recommendations

These implications point to four recommendations on how Western military powers can remain competitive in the face of increasingly fast technologies. Complexity works both ways, and the West can be just as effective as its adversaries in capitalizing on asymmetric advantages.

The first recommendation, therefore, is that Western states should incorporate emerging technologies into their strategic doctrine reviews not only as potential threats, but also as opportunities for gaining a strategic advantage. The upcoming Integrated Review in the United Kingdom, for example, could explore Britain's asymmetric advantages in technology as part of a broader suite of capabilities, rather than simply seeing it as a threat. In evaluating the role of fast technology in strategic doctrine, Western powers can delineate where they have a comparative advantage that is also cost-effective. It is possible these analyses are already underway; however, they were noticeably absent from documents such as the US *National Security Strategy*, which primarily framed technological uncertainty as a risk rather than an opportunity.

Second, the budget process should allow for sustained long-term funding in emerging technologies, potentially in partnership with the private sector. Again, this investment does not need to include the entire suite of fast technologies, but rather can be tailored to states' areas of advantage and interest to develop an asymmetric response to asymmetric threats. This should not be done at the expense of an open and transparent defense budget review process, but rather requires increased engagement with decisionmakers to boost education about the opportunities provided by specific technologies. One practice that seems successful and can be continued is collaboration with the private sector in competitions to develop technology with military applications, such as the Red Balloon Challenge; however, this could be further developed to include a cost savings component.

Third, using the lenses of strategic stability, the offense–defense balance, and technological opportunism, the difficult cross-cutting theme of perception needs to be addressed. Any advances in Western military technology could be perceived as offensive by an adversary and the start of an arms race. Such technologies could unintentionally send escalatory signals during a crisis, as in the North Korea example offered above. Two specific recommendations can help here. First, the nuclear possessors, which are also the highest investors in emerging technology, can continue to provide transparency about their strategic doctrines. At present this is done through a "P5 Process" in the context of the Nuclear Non-Proliferation Treaty review cycle, but it could be expanded to include discussion of emerging technology in bilateral "strategic security" dialogues. A key component of these dialogues would be engagement by military officials. Second, to mitigate the risks of crisis escalation, the relevant states should develop additional crisis communication channels focused on the need for speed. China could be incorporated into the Nuclear Risk Reduction Center networks between the United States, Russia, and the Organisation for Security and Co-operation in Europe (OSCE), for example.

Finally, in addition to the potentially destabilizing impact of some technologies, there are opportunities for managing them through arms control and other risk reduction measures, but these will have to adapt to a post–Cold War environment with multiple actors and across domains. Jervis identifies an important precondition for arms control in an era of technological innovation: "A state can be relaxed about increases in another's arms if it believes that there is a functioning collective security system. By contrast, the security dilemma is insoluble when each state fears that many others, far from coming to its aid, are likely to join in any attack."[67] Therefore, in the absence of more collective security arrangements and the breakdown of historical arms control mechanisms such as the 1987 Intermediate-range Nuclear Forces Treaty, states are likely to see technological developments as undermining their security and to resist arms control efforts. Instead, they will prefer to play catch-up or develop their own technological capabilities and advantages. As such, the prospects for arms control in the short term are bleak. But as political circumstances evolve and the costs of an arms race increase, arms control becomes increasingly attractive. This chapter's approach is particularly useful in identifying ways in which emerging technology and speed could be destabilizing, as this analysis can help to focus future arms control efforts, along with seeing technology as an opportunity that may directly or indirectly contribute to arms control.

Conclusion

The implications of speed and emerging technology extend, of course, well beyond the military sphere to include organizational issues, moral questions, and the role of the private sector. Steinbruner, for example, challenges the concept of strategic stability as being too technical because it needs "to account for organizational factors."[68] Accordingly, he argued, "the conceptualization of national strategy should be organized not around deterrence but rather around the much broader issues of managing modern strategic operations."[69] In the contemporary context of rapid technological innovation and increasing speed of warfare, Horowitz has similarly argued that,

> inventing technologies or even being the first to use them does not guarantee advantages in international politics. There is a big difference between the introduction of a technology onto the battlefield and the full integration of that technology into national strategy, including warfare and coercive diplomacy. It is the difference between the two, in fact, that often determines success or failure in international politics. It is the employment of technologies by organizations, rather than the technologies themselves, that most often makes the difference."[70]

The preceding discussion of AI use in intelligence, for example, flagged the potential challenge of maintaining a *human* capacity to interpret and integrate AI-generated intelligence findings. This will rely on organizational evolution and the relationship between political and military decision-makers, among a variety of other factors.

In addition the impact of emerging technology and speed on military balancing raises challenging moral questions. John Yoo, for example, has argued that emerging technologies can advance humanitarian aims by avoiding civilian casualties through improved targeting and intelligence.[71] Conversely, activists continue to call to "Stop Killer Robots" and scholars such as Lucas Kello point to technology as a first-order revolution against the "building blocks" of the international system and a major challenge to the moral order.[72] The complexity and secondary and tertiary impacts of these technologies reinforce the main argument of this chapter: a need for specificity in the technology's *application* as a precursor to useful analysis.

This chapter has aimed, in particular, to highlight the intersection of technology and political outcomes. Other chapters in this volume reinforce Antulio Echevarria's observation that the West struggles to convert military victory into positive political outcomes.[73] Owing to the high entry costs in many fast technologies, the great powers can be expected to maintain a military advantage in *speed*; whether they can convert this to political stability, however, particularly for the West, is the bigger challenge. The revolution in speed has become unavoidable, and in many instances the West is already locked in an arms race for the latest *fast* weapon. But there are certain steps Western powers and military planners can take to sustain military primacy and at least reduce the risks associated with speedy technology.

NOTES

1. Stuart Abbott, "Review of 20 Years of Undersea Optical Fiber Transmission System Development and Deployment since TAT-8," 34th European Conference on Optical Communication, Brussels, 2008, pp. 1–4, https://ieeexplore.ieee.org/abstract/document/4729162.

2. Calculation based on figures from Ewan MacAskill, Julian Borger, Nick Hopkins, and others, "GCHQ Taps Fibre-optic Cables for Secret Access to World's Communications," *The Guardian*, June 21, 2013, www.theguardian.com/uk/2013/jun/21/gchq-cables-secret-world-communications-nsa.

3. U.S. Navy Fact File, "Tomahawk Cruise Missile," April 26, 2018, www.navy.mil/navydata/fact_display.asp?cid=2200&tid=1300&ct=2.

4. Michael Peck, "Moscow Fears America's Missile Defenses. But Does It Really Need To?," *National Interest*, November 7, 2018, https://nationalinterest.org/blog/buzz/russia-says-it-will-soon-deploy-mach-20-avangard-hypersonic-weapon-35377.

5. U.S. *National Security Strategy*, 2017, p. 3.

6. See, for example, Michael Horowitz, Elsa B. Kania, Gregory C. Allen, and Paul Scharre, "Strategic Competition in an Era of Artificial Intelligence," *Center for a New American Security*, July 25, 2018; and Todd S. Sechser, Neil Narang, and Caitlin Talmadge, "Emerging Technologies and Strategic Stability in Peacetime, Crisis, and War," *Journal of Strategic Studies*, vol. 42, no. 6 (2019), pp. 727–35.

7. Keir A. Lieber, *War and the Engineers: The Primacy of Politics over Technology* (Cornell University Press, 2005).

8. Caitlin Talmadge, "Emerging Technology and Intra-war Escalation Risks: Evidence from the Cold War, Implications for Today," *Journal of Strategic Studies*, vol 42, no. 6 (2019), pp. 864–87.

9. See, for example, James Johnson, "Artificial Intelligence & Future Warfare: Implications for International Security," *Defense & Security Analysis*, vol. 35, no. 2 (2019), pp. 147–69.

10. Dmitry Adamsky, "Cross-Domain Coercion: The Current Russian Art of Strategy," *IFRI Proliferation Papers*, 54, November 2015.

11. Martin Libicki, "The Nature of Instability in Cyberspace," *Brown Journal of World Affairs*, vol. 18, no. 1 (Fall/Winter 2011), p. 72.

12. Erik Gartzke and Jon Lindsay, "Weaving Tangled Webs: Offense, Defense, and Deception in Cyberspace," *Security Studies*, vol. 24, no. 2 (2015), p. 316.

13. John D. Steinbruner, "National Security and the Concept of Strategic Stability," *Journal of Conflict Resolution*, vol. 22, no. 3 (September 1978), p. 413.

14. See, for example, Thomas Schelling and Morton Halperin, *Strategy and Arms Control* (New York: Twentieth Century Fund, 1961).

15. Adamsky, "Cross-Domain Coercion."

16. Kristin Ven Bruusgaard, "Russian Strategic Deterrence," *Survival*, vol. 58, no. 4 (2016), pp. 7–26.

17. Heather Williams, "Strategic Stability, Uncertainty and the Future of Arms Control," *Survival*, vol. 60, no. 2 (2018), pp. 45–54.

18. U.S. "Nuclear Posture Review," 2018, p. 21.

19. Steinbruner, "National Security and the Concept of Strategic Stability."

20. Nancy W. Gallagher, "Re-thinking the Unthinkable: Arms Control in the Twenty-First Century," *Nonproliferation Review*, vol. 22, no. 3–4 (2015), pp. 469–98.

21. Keir A. Lieber and Daryl G. Press, "The New Era of Counterforce: Technological Change and the Future of Nuclear Deterrence," *International Security* (Spring 2017), pp. 9–49.

22. James M. Acton, "Escalation through Entanglement: How the Vulnerability of Command-and-Control Systems Raises the Risks of Inadvertent Nuclear War," *International Security*, vol. 43, no. 1 (Summer 2018), pp. 56–99.

23. See, for example, Gartzke and Lindsay, "Weaving Tangled Webs."

24. Sean M. Lynn-Jones, "Offense-Defense Theory and Its Critics," *Security Studies*, vol. 4, no. 4 (1995), pp. 660–91.

25. Lieber, *War and the Engineers*, p. 6.

26. Stephen Van Evera, "Offense, Defense and the Causes of War," *International Security*, vol. 22, no. 4 (Spring 1998), pp. 5–43.

27. Robert Jervis, "Cooperation Under the Security Dilemma," *World Politics*, vol. 30, no. 2 (January 1978), p. 194.

28. Stacie E. Goddard, "Letter to the Editors Correspondence: Taking Offense at Offense-Defense Theory," *International Security*, vol. 23, no. 3 (Winter 1998/99), p. 194.

29. Lieber, *War and the Engineers*, p. 2.

30. Gartzke and Lindsay, "Weaving Tangled Webs," p. 343.

31. Lynn-Jones, "Offense-Defense Theory and Its Critics."

32. Ibid.

33. Ted Hopf, "Polarity, The Offense-Defense Balance, and War," *American Political Science Review*, vol. 85, no. 2 (June 1991), p. 478.

34. Lynn-Jones, "Offense-Defense Theory and Its Critics," p. 667.

35. Ibid.

36. Ben Garfinkel and Allan Dafoe, "How Does the Offense-Defense Balance Scale?," *Journal of Strategic Studies*, vol. 42, no. 6 (2019). This is anticipated to be particularly significant for drone swarm warfare and automated vulnerability discovery.

37. Lieber, *War and the Engineers*, p. 5.

38. Ibid., p. 6.

39. Mark S. Bell, "Nuclear Opportunism: A Theory of How States Use Nuclear Weapons in International Politics," *Journal of Strategic Studies*, vol. 42, no. 1 (2019), p. 8.

40. Lieber and Press, "The New Era of Counterforce," pp. 15–16.

41. Talmadge, "Emerging Technology and Intra-war Escalation Risks," p. 864.

42. Acton, "Escalation through Entanglement."

43. See, for example, "Russia Proceeds with Avangard Hypersonic Missile Production According to Schedule," Tass, July 2, 2019, https://tass.com/defense/1066695.

44. "Demonstration of Russia's New Avangard System to US Specialists was Expected—Expert," Tass, November 28, 2019, https://tass.com/world/1093045.

45. Heather Williams, "Asymmetric Arms Control and Strategic Stability: Scenarios for Limiting Hypersonic Glide Vehicles," *Journal of Strategic Studies*, vol. 42, no. 6 (2019), pp. 789–813.

46. Acton, "Escalation through Entanglement," p. 5.

47. Schelling and Halperin, *Strategy and Arms Control*, p. 34.

48. Ibid., p. 35.

49. Corentin Brustlein, "Conventionalizing Deterrence? U.S. Prompt Strike Programs and Their Limits," *IRI Proliferation Papers*, no. 52 (January 2015).

50. Ibid., p. 45.

51. James L. Regens, "Augmenting Human Cognition to Enhance Strategic, Operational, and Tactical Intelligence," *Intelligence and National Security*, vol. 34, no. 5 (2019), p. 678.

52. Kenneth Payne, "Artificial Intelligence: A Revolution in Strategic Affairs?," *Survival*, vol. 60, no. 5 (2018), p. 11.

53. Regens, "Augmenting Human Cognition," p. 676.

54. Kelley M. Sayler, *Artificial Intelligence and National Security*," Congressional Research Service Report, January 30, 2019, p. 8.

55. Regens, "Augmenting Human Cognition," p. 678.

56. Johnson, "Artificial Intelligence & Future Warfare," p. 147.

57. Ibid., p. 152.

58. Payne, "Artificial Intelligence."

59. Sayler, *Artificial Intelligence and National Security*.

60. Ibid.

61. Horowitz and others, "Strategic Competition in an Era of Artificial Intelligence."

62. Ibid.

63. Kenneth Booth and Nicholas Wheeler, *The Security Dilemma: Fear, Cooperation and Trust in World Politics* (Palgrave Macmillan, 2007).

64. Talmadge, "Emerging Technology and Intra-war Escalation Risks," p. 869.

65. Garfinkel and Dafoe, "How Does the Offense-Defense Balance Scale?"

66. See, for example, Patricia Lewis, Heather Williams, Benoit Pelopidas, and Sasan Aghlani, *Too Close for Comfort: Cases of Near Nuclear Use and Options for Policy*, Chatham House Report (Royal Institute of International Affairs, April 2014).

67. Jervis, "Cooperation Under the Security Dilemma."

68. Steinbruner, "National Security and the Concept of Strategic Stability," p. 424.

69. Ibid.

70. Horowitz and others, "Strategic Competition in an Era of Artificial Intelligence," p. 2.

71. John Yoo, "Embracing the Machines: Rationalist War and New Weapons Technologies," *California Law Review*, vol. 205, no. 2 (April 2017), pp. 443–500.

72. Lucas Kello, *The Virtual Weapon and International Order* (Oxford University Press, 2017), p. 13.

73. Antulio J. Echevarria, *Toward an American Way of War* (Carlisle, PA: Strategic Studies Institute, 2004).

TWELVE

Military Operations

What If Digital Technologies Fail on the Battlefield?

JOSEPH HENROTIN
STÉPHANE TAILLAT

General, Ladies, and Gentlemen,*

I would like to thank the organizers for giving me the opportunity to make this presentation entitled: "Does the Digitalization of Armed Forces Enable or Disrupt Military Operations?" This is the perspective from which we must address the question of "the temporality and the decline of Western military power." The digitalization process is the backbone of the changes in equipment, force structures, and operational concepts they have experienced since the end of the Cold War. According to its rationale, leveraging digital technologies would improve operational efficiency and make the internal functioning of our organizations more fluid.

Thus the purpose of digitalization would be to accelerate the operational tempo through more appropriate and timely decisions and actions. Digital technologies would indeed allow the battlefield to be put into data ("datafication") and forces to be networked ("networking"). Upstream the battlefield would become more transparent. Downstream this information superiority

---

* Transcript of the presentation given by Lieutenant-Colonel N., Future Warfare Division, French Army Doctrine and Leadership Training Centre, Paris, Ecole Militaire, December 12, 2025.

would result in more collaborative command and combat modes. Better and faster fighting would thus make it possible to be more tactically decisive and more strategically relevant, especially when the nation's vital interests are not at stake. In short, digitalization is the necessary and sufficient condition for this transformation toward more expeditionary, more professional, more lethal forces and therefore toward forces capable of carrying out all the missions assigned to them.

However, I would like to show you how reductive and biased this vision is. Reductive because digitalization is far from being limited to transformation programmes initiated within the armed forces, such as the SCORPION programme within the French Army. Biased because trapped in a torn relationship to time, between our preferences for decisive and rapid actions on the one hand and longer-lasting conflicts on the other. We have become dependent on digital technologies because they are at the heart of unit *cohesion* and of the *coordination* of missions and tasks. Being deprived of those technologies, or seeing them disturbed, exposes us to the worst scenario: being slowed down (friction) or even blocked (paralysis) while the opponent continues to maneuver at his speed and according to his pace.

I will illustrate my point with the experience of the 3rd Company, Regiment X. I was the executive officer of the Battle Group within which it was deployed in Mali. Then I became liaison officer in the staff of the EFP (Enhanced Forward Presence) in Rukla during the company's deployment as its French component in Lithuania. This case study will analyze the effects of disruptions or denial of our forces' digital capabilities. I will conclude by referring to the lessons I have learned and the need to adapt our perception of time as a result.

Tessalit, Mali, January–March 2024

In retrospect, we should have been aware of these problems as soon as the company deployed in Mali during Operation Barkhane—which, as you probably know, forms the framework for the French armies' operations against jihadi organizations in western Sahel. Our force structure includes several Battle Groups, one of which is based in Gao, Mali, with detachments in Forward Operating Bases (FOB) in Tessalit and Kidal.

The unit's officers and NCOs were at that time concerned about recent intelligence analyses of the strikes carried out by the Ansar Al-Dine organization using drones purchased on Amazon. Focused on the jihadists' ability to use social media and e-commerce applications, they paid little attention to the online behavior of their own soldiers. Two incidents reminded us how the development of digital social media blurs the distinctions between private and professional life, and how much this has consequences for our armed forces.

At the beginning of March a platoon of the company had to be redeployed to ensure the security of logistics convoys between Gao, Kidal, and Tessalit. During a patrol conducted at the end of our mandate, it was to join another platoon of the company, based in Kidal. Before it arrived at the crossroads of the Route Nationale 18 and Route Nationale 19, an IED exploded as the second vehicle of the convoy passed by, while the rest of the unit came under attack by small arms and mortar fire. Initially immobilized, the platoon managed to clear itself without losses, although it was the most serious skirmish in the area since 2015. Patrols along this axis were suspended for several days, with several units mobilized to secure the area. However, the most important consequence was not the claim of the attack on social media platforms (with video footage released online) but the revelation that its accuracy owed everything to the recklessness of several soldiers in the platoon. In anticipation of their mission's end, several of them had consulted online applications to prepare for enjoying their free time once in Gao. Some had been approached in this way by individuals posing as young Malians supporting our soldiers. Without revealing anything about their itinerary, several of them had neglected to set up the geolocation options in a confidential mode, allowing the convoy to be monitored in real time. Using this information, the jihadists were then able to strike the column, not so much to publicize an attack—in a context of questioning the relevance of the action of French forces in the Sahel—as to deny the circulation of logistics supplies for over a week. This event undoubtedly contributed to the subsequent decision to concentrate the main forces on Gao, to the detriment of Tessalit. At that time, Ansar Al-Dine's actions over there made it more difficult to remain in this temporary advanced base.

A second event, unfortunately ignored by the main people involved at the time, would have greater consequences in the long term. Several officers and non-commissioned officers had become accustomed to an exercise routine that involved running around the camp, particularly during the company's operational break in mid-January. To do this, they all used the same app to geolocate the routes in order to measure their performance. On March 25, all but one of them received threatening text messages disclosing the identities and whereabouts of their family members. One of them, an NCO, even received a frightened call from his son, who had been contacted on WhatsApp by a stranger threatening to harm him because of his father's activities; the

NCO's GPS coordinates were specified in the message. The mysterious trans-mitters had in fact taken advantage of careless behavior: not only had officers and NCOs forgotten to opt out of data-sharing with other users, but most had also used their personal account to identify themselves during their runs around the FOB in Tessalit. Some open source (OSINT) research had enabled jihadists to find the addresses and contact details of their family members. It turned out that the sole NCO spared from these intimidation maneuvers was the one who had created an account for professional use only and who had set up his data-sharing parameters on secure mode.

Lessons learned from these incidents are far from simple. I suppose we can define the actions of our opponent as irregular warfare. But in this case our addiction to social media provided valuable information enabling us to be targeted either kinetically or through psychological pressure. Tactically this increased the opponent's ability to take the initiative, allowing him to harass us in order to discourage us. More importantly, our temporary paralysis (es-pecially since we focused on ourselves more than on the opponent, and then finally reacted after a delay) had an impact on our freedom of action in the area of operation. Strategically this harassment has increased the questioning of the French military presence in this part of the Sahel by local media outlets keen to criticize our actions (or, in this case, temporary lack of action).

Paphos, Cyprus, April 2024

During the post-operational decompression period none of the officers and NCOs who were victims of these intimidation attempts mentioned that the anguish they felt about their families had seriously hampered their ability to carry out their mission in the days following the receipt of the text messages. The NCO whose son had phoned was actually unable to do anything serenely during the rest of the deployment. But he preferred not to tell the psycholo-gists and not to report to his superiors. Considering himself a good leader, he did not want to show how weak and paralyzed he had been by the event.

In retrospect the post-operational management period in Cyprus was also the moment when suspicions began to develop among these officers and NCOs that the Russian tourists they met from time to time were not what they seemed to be. This state of mind had the effect of weakening the unit in its cohesion, but it also showed to what extent friction emanating from social media could have consequences if it was properly exploited by the adversary.

Rukla, Lithuania, September 2025

The company's experience in Africa and Cyprus was a warning shot. What we were going to suffer next in Lithuania—a few weeks ago, as you know—would show much more complex patterns of adverse action, not only in their application, but also in the effects on our forces and alliances, and even on our thinking about combat and warfare. The problems were all the more acute because the scale was not the same. Where the experience in Barkhane illustrates the vulnerabilities and risks of our dependence at the individual level, what has just happened in Lithuania includes systemic effects and relates rather to our ability to operate in the contemporary battlefield.

As you know, France has been deploying forces in the Baltic states as part of the Lynx mission since 2015, as a reassurance measure within the framework of NATO's Enhanced Forward Presence (EFP). Typically we deploy an augmented company comprising 300 to 350 men, around thirteen or fourteen Infantry Fighting Vehicles, and four Leclerc tanks, and their support. During the "incidents"—to put it mildly—on September 17, 2025, I was the French liaison officer to the battalion in the Rukla headquarters. As usual for the past four years, the Russians conducted a large part of their Zapad exercises in Belarus. This year, less than a dozen brigades were involved, on their usual exercise grounds, with relatively few airborne units. The situation seemed much less tense than in 2017, for example. We were a few weeks away from the end of our mandate. A significant part of public opinion in France seemed to feel that the mission was no longer necessary.

Many of our elements operated relatively close to the border, between Lavoriškės and Medininkai, about 100 kilometers from Rukla. For some years now our forces have been digitalized through SCORPION, which allowed us to build data gateways with the other two countries that formed the reinforced battalion, namely the Netherlands and a former partner but nevertheless an ally that I will not mention here to avoid offending sensitivities. Classically we planned to take advantage of Zapad to observe the Russian radio and data traffic in real time and transmit the incoming intelligence to our higher echelons and to the Lithuanians. At first everything went very conventionally. Since 2013 the Russians have been jamming GPS signals before their exercises and they did not deviate from this: so far, no surprises. But two days after we started, on September 13, the interference also affected our bandwidth. Over the next few days we ended up losing fifty percent of the bandwidth. Among our partners it was even worse. One of them lost ninety percent.

This interference did not only concern our subordinate units. The links

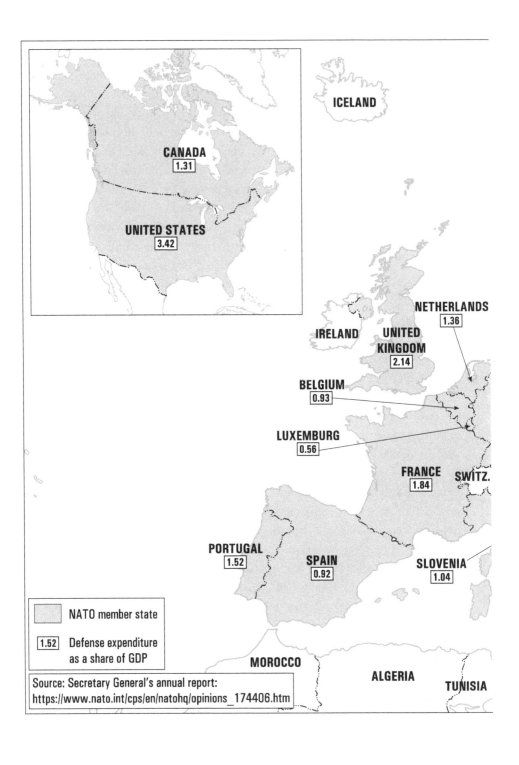

ICELAND

CANADA
1.31

UNITED STATES
3.42

NETHERLANDS
1.36

IRELAND
UNITED KINGDOM
2.14

BELGIUM
0.93

LUXEMBURG
0.56

FRANCE
1.84

SWITZ.

PORTUGAL
1.52

SPAIN
0.92

SLOVENIA
1.04

MOROCCO

ALGERIA

TUNISIA

NATO member state

1.52 Defense expenditure
      as a share of GDP

Source: Secretary General's annual report:
https://www.nato.int/cps/en/natohq/opinions_174406.htm

NATO Membership and Contributions as a Percentage of GDP

NORWAY
1.80

FINLAND

SWEDEN

ESTONIA
2.14

LATVIA
2.01

RUSSIA

DENMARK
1.32

LITHUANIA
2.03

to Rus.

BELARUS

GERMANY
1.38

POLAND
2.00

CZECH REP.
1.19

SLOVAKIA
1.74

UKRAINE

AUSTRIA

HUNGARY
1.21

MOLDOVA

CROATIA
1.68

ROMANIA
2.04

GEORGIA

BOS. SERBIA

KOS.
MAC.

BULGARIA
3.25

ITALY
1.22

MONTENEGRO
1.66

ALBANIA
1.26

GREECE
2.28

TURKEY
1.89

SYRIA

0   300 miles

0   300 kilometers

between our battalion and Supreme Headquarters Allied Powers Europe (SHAPE) also suffered. The Russians traditionally attack a few servers, so we compensated by switching to satellite links. What we did not know, on September 17, was that some of the information provided by SHAPE had not reached us. The latest unencrypted messages indicated that two Russian brigades had left their training area and were heading west on the Belarusian road P45 at 2:00 a.m. We immediately warned the Dutch company of this very unusual movement and of the risk of ending up with Russian tanks near the border and therefore a few kilometers from Lavoriškės. The company's tactical drones didn't help us either: three were launched but the line-of-sight links were jammed. Two were lost in the forests.

We knew that the Russians could perform shows of force, with two brigades offering them many options. But we had not expected to see just one battalion of motorized riflemen enter Lithuanian territory in Šumskas, twenty kilometres south of Lavoriškės, around 9:30 a.m. At that time, we had no one on site. We knew that three platoons of the Lithuanian National Guard were conducting an exercise nearby, but these reserve units were not digitalized and had no direct connection to our battalion. In fact it was thanks to Twitter that we learned the Russians had crossed the border! Surprised Lithuanian civilians had used their smartphones to film a column of tanks flying the Russian flag. At HQ this movement caused confusion: it looked like a battalion, but where was the rest of the two brigades? Was it a diversion? Where, then, should we lead the effort? Why didn't we have more information?

Immediate Reactions

Our first reflex was to forward the information: to SHAPE, to the other EFP battalions in the Baltic states, to the American forces in Poland, to the Lithuanian army. We are in the Baltic states first as a tripwire, to establish the facts. Connections worked with difficulty. It was finally understood that SHAPE and the American forces already knew what was going on and we were ordered to deploy our companies and squadrons as soon as possible to the south, toward the Suwalki gap, in order to protect this vital link between the Baltic countries and Poland. But we still had to reach our units. . . . The French and Dutch reacted quickly. Many of their platoons were too far from their FUPs (Forming Up Places), and the connections between them within the companies were not easy. Moreover, going south could make them cut across the route of Russian units. . . . Our third partner, the southernmost one, was unreachable: the messages seemed to get lost in the electronic ether. Whatever the means used, you never knew if the message had been understood. Luckily a Lithuanian courier agreed to place his motorcycle under the battalion's command. One of our sergeants left with written orders. . . . But at best he would not reach his destination for two and a half hours. We had the unpleasant feeling that we no longer had control over our forces; and that there was not much we could do for them.

The HQ had several televisions and these became our window on the world. But only CNN and Russian news channels were still on cable. It was later learned that the main Lithuanian TV operators had been hacked. For us, the surprise was huge: the Russia-1 programme opened its special edition on the fact that NATO was attacking Russian tanks! The close-up images only showed part of the truth: BTR-80s burning. Impossible to know where this had happened: these images were made to shock public opinions, just for a few hours. In fact, at 10:10 a.m., two of the three Lithuanian reserve platoons, alerted by their HQ in Vilnius, arrived at the edge of a wood on the outskirts of Šumskas. Three Javelin anti-tank missiles were fired and hit the mark. The images on Russia-1 were those posted on Facebook by a local farmer and also those taken by a Russian army drone.

Less than three minutes after the Russian BTRs were destroyed, around 10:15 a.m., thirty 152 mm shells struck Lithuanian positions. After firing their missiles the reservists had certainly dispersed, but the Russians had taken this into account in their calculations. Both Lithuanian platoons had been destroyed but, miraculously, only three civilian houses had been damaged. We had more information around 10.30 a.m. when the secured connections saw contradictory messages pass through: the Lithuanians had counterattacked, Šumskas was under artillery fire, and Russians were said to have been observed in Marijampolė, less than 25 km from the Suwalki gap. Actually, they were not there. In the panic, rumours had started to spread among the population—one of our micro UAVs was even downed with a shotgun because a local farmer thought it was Russian. The "Marijampolė Russians" were actually the company of our former battalion partner.

In fact we were missing the real problems. Focused on moving our HQ to the Suwalki gap, maintaining our links with our subordinate units, and monitoring their progress, we lost sight of the big picture . . . as well as losing the initiative. This was only known after our redeployment to the south, but very soon after the Russian strike on Šumskas, the Lithuanian PzH2000 howitzers responded: the third Lithuanian reserve platoon, set back from the village, had provided the firing coordinates. It seems that this good old friction still exists: shells hit the Russians who were withdrawing from the city, but also on the Belarusian side. On our side, by a stroke of luck, the sergeant who had left on his motorcycle was able to liaise with two platoons of our former battalion partner around noon and provide them with satellite phones. By 4:00 p.m. nearly the entire battalion had taken up positions on the Suwalki gap and links were established with the Poles on the other side of the border. According to the Lithuanians, the last Russian elements had left the territory around 1:00 p.m., but Russian TV stations continued to operate there for three days.

As a result the Russians withdrew from Lithuania; the gap was secure—although potentially under Russian artillery fire from Kaliningrad and Belarus—and no EFP units had been hit. On the one hand, we can say that we have done a good job. But on the other hand, keeping our tactical and operational cohesion has been a real problem and commanding under these conditions in the event of a real war would have been hellish. We found ourselves virtually paralyzed. When we reported to SHAPE, everyone considered this issue of cohesion and command exercise to be a technical one. But it ended up having consequences on the real battlefield, where the worst happened. I am not talking about the Šumskas area, but in the chancelleries. As you know, these consequences have been twofold. First, Lithuanian artillery strikes frightened the Belarusians. Moscow, which had been hoping for years to strengthen its positions on the spot, was therefore asked to position units there. The two countries seem to have resumed their discussions on joint commands. In the end, our position in the Baltic states remains dependent on a Suwalki gap that is now more vulnerable.

Longer-term Consequences and Implications

And then there are the longer-term consequences. At the time of the incidents our former battalion partner was less than a week away from a general election. The rumour of the "Marijampolė Russians" had made the pro-Russian opposition there say that their forces could have come face to face with Moscow's, and that NATO had not hesitated to shoot at Russian tanks. Russia-1's images were widely used to support their narrative. Both Russia and the opposition explained in every language that their battalion's entry into Lithuania was only an unfortunate navigational error. . . . After all, why would they invade a country with less than one brigade? The ruling majority decided not to make the incidents a domestic political issue, so two days later, on September 19, they announced the suspension of their participation in the battalion, ordering the repatriation of their unit. The battalion lost a third of its strength.

But the matter was not over. The breakdown in communications between the battalion and our other partner was reported in the local press. A debate began on the modernization of the forces and the fact that the NATO model imposed budgetary costs that were incompatible with the country's finances. Others said that, as a result, units would no longer have been able to defend if attacked—which was not completely false. Both pro-Russian and pacifist political parties took advantage of the revelations to question publicly the relevance of their country's participation in the Atlantic Alliance. According to them, the defence of the Baltic states is not a vital security issue and the positioning of a company in Lithuania has only made relations with Russia a little more tense, unnecessarily for some. As you know, since then the result of the elections has become known, with a clear rise in the numbers voting for populist and pro-Russian parties. This should quickly lead to a coalition whose objective will be to leave NATO and achieve neutralization status . . . oh, sorry for this slip of the tongue, of course I meant neutrality. The subsidiary question is obviously whether other countries in the region might not adopt the same position. . . .

As we are at the Ecole de Guerre, I will not avoid the combat analysis. In this case, we experienced a hybrid war situation in the NATO sense of the term. But the fact is that it could have been a high-intensity fight. Our ability to command in a nominal way has clearly been called into question and the very maintenance of the cohesion of our units over the distances that separated them cast into doubt, despite virtually zero adverse kinetic engagement. We ended up executing our mission in more or less good order in less than a day, but what would have happened if our HQ had been the target of direct strikes?

So much for the tactical plan. Operationally, links with the host nation have been erratic and the distribution of intelligence has been random. . . . Digitalization clearly does not eliminate friction either. . . . It is obviously at the strategic level that the effects are most noticeable. NATO has probably lost a member. The position of the Baltic states, so symbolic for the credibility of Article 5—if they are not defended in the event of an attack, what will be the value of the "most powerful alliance of all time?"—is a little more fragile.

Facing the Emerging Battlefield: Paradox
and the Need to Change Our Praxis

What about our armed forces? Their situation is paradoxical. On the one hand, digitalized capacities should enable them to act more quickly and efficiently. On the other hand, these capabilities are also an Achilles' heel, in that depriving our forces of them can slow them down or even paralyze them, which could lead to a strong military and political de-cohesion. Not only have our armed forces become dependent on these technologies, but they cannot control all their developments, since digitalization also results from practices and technologies that developed at societal level. Units like the 3rd Company are thus subject to a double dependence: dependence on military network-centric technologies, and dependence on the emerging uses of digital tools. However, traditional solutions—partitioning digitalized forces in order to isolate them on the one hand and regulating practices within the organization in order to limit security risks on the other —seem doomed to failure. There are two main reasons for this.

First, the battlefield is no longer (if ever) an enclosed space impervious to external factors. Like it or not, it is a socio-cultural product. But contrary to the highest hopes and the worst fears, it has not become transparent either. On the one hand, digital tools and datafication have produced a clearer battlefield, but this partial lifting of the "fog of war" has yet to translate in to higher operational speed. Actually it seems that there is no linear relationship between the degree of transparency resulting from datafication and an increase in operational tempo. By contrast this partial unveiling of military operations and forces has had a severe impact on operational security at the unit and individual levels. From being an opportunity to pursue, transparency has become a vulnerability to mitigate.

On the other hand, the dual process of top-down and bottom-up digitalization has increased the complexity of the battlefield, both in scale and in scope. There are four aspects to this. First, the amount of data processed by traditional command-and-control structures has increased by an order of magnitude. Second, these data come from increasingly heterogeneous sources whose authenticity and truthfulness remain highly questionable and dubious. Third, the capabilities to intercept, jam, and manipulate these data have become more and more common and evenly distributed across a broad range of actors and adversaries, especially in and through traditional and social media. As a result digitalization has thickened the fog of war. And finally, the battlefield has been enlarged to include a heterogeneous set of actors—

adversaries, partners, and spectators alike—located at multiple levels and across a geographical range. This new geometry of the battlefield is further compounding the complexity of managing an equally heterogeneous set of units in both combat and command.

The second main reason why traditional solutions will not work is that military organizations operate within a complex system both in their managerial dimension (to achieve a given effect) and in their strategic dimension (to achieve a given effect *when facing an adversary*). The nature of war has not changed: one can try to be more effective and efficient, including through digitalization, but the adversary remains a veto player. So to the heterogeneity of the organization must be added the heterogeneity of the battlefield. The inner core of military organizations is increasingly cyber- and thus digitally dependent command-and-control (C2) systems. Their primary function, even before generating orders, is taming the complexity of battlefields and conflicts, including political complexities arising from much more coalition-centric operations. Command posts and their C2 systems are compensating actors/factors for the complex and rapid shifts that are ontologically linked to the pace and the rhythm of battle. In any complex system, the first factor of speed and pace is not the "muscles"—in our case, the forces by themselves—but cognitive and decisional agility, giving command systems a much more central role than previously.

Organizational Implications

Dealing with this paradox needs a change in our practices. In the French army, the promotion of a "warrior spirit" sometimes seems to serve as a mechanism *to compensate for* technological vulnerabilities.[1] By assuming the major role of "moral forces" in war relative to material aspects, this "warrior spirit" can effectively contribute to reducing the risks linked to technological vulnerabilities and increase the resilience of individuals and units. But it also requires us to go beyond some of its limits. Let me emphasize three aspects in relation to these lessons learned.

First, "militariness." This concept refers not only to a strong military identity but also to the procedures associated with it. This implies the ability to return to the basics in order to be able to operate in an alternative mode, without waiting for the digital network to work normally. Initial education and professional training thus make it possible to revert to skills and know-how such as compass navigation or the emphasis placed on the basics of combat (by focusing on mobility rather than protection). This translates into an operational culture that values the ability to operate in austere environments and with limited resources. In a way, "militariness" makes it possible to free oneself from the constraints and risks resulting from an excessive dependence on material and logistical aspects. We are not system operators or managers; we must remain soldiers and warriors.

Second, mission command. The ability to delegate decisionmaking authority is crucial to pursue the mission if organizational cohesion is lost. The ability of junior officers to take initiative is primarily a result of their training and therefore also a result of the organizational culture. Here digitalization is ambiguous. On the one hand, it should make it possible to further decentralize decisionmaking and, through collaborative action, permit simultaneous and distributed actions. On the other hand, it tends to shorten chains of command and therefore centralize information. It is therefore important to take mission command seriously and give even more authority and initiative to the lower levels in order to reduce network dependency and the resulting vulnerability. But tipping the scales toward micromanagement must not go too far, at the risk of further de-cohesion between command echelons. Hence a trade-off is to be made between distributed command and hierarchical leadership. A balanced approach could envision a two-tier command model encompassing hierarchical procedures for planning and conducting the operations, and a distributed network of autonomous units to execute them. Here national choices matter. I know that there are many debates surrounding this issue, especially when it comes to fighting within a coalition involving a large number of actors whose action must be coordinated. But we will not eschew a debate on these subjects.

So much for the compensation mechanisms: a return to fundamentals and the development of a broader culture of initiative in command. But if digitalization is an enabler (of speed) that nevertheless generates dependency and vulnerabilities (friction, paralysis, and de-cohesion), is rebalancing enough? We have already had to adapt our combat and command practices to the changing character of warfare accompanying digitalization. Now we must also rethink our relationship to time and learn to manage the risks posed by digitalization in terms of uncertainty. In short, we must change the cultural foundations underpinning our practices in warfare.

The third aspect of change needed is therefore the development of a mindset compatible with another perception of time, where we must operate in a permanently contaminated environment, and where we understand command and control as a continuum rather than compartmentalized times and spaces. This aspect is by far the most complex to implement. It requires not only cultural changes and adapted training and education, but also a rethinking of the articulation within organizations that often operate in silos and are tied to their bureaucratic procedures as much as to their hierarchical structure. Two points should be highlighted. First, the main obstacle remains the specific organizational culture inside the Army regarding technology and technological assets. Far from rejecting technology—or idolizing it—it is rather a question of exploring how it results from our uses, practices, and representations. It is about embracing technological change while assuming its risks. But second, such a change requires above all a move away from a perception of time where speed is the key factor to be sought. There is no point in going too fast when the pace of war is asynchronous and perceptions of time and space among the various actors differ according to their individual perspectives. In other words, the challenge is to adopt a conception of time that, because it no longer separates the different temporalities and rhythms so rigidly, makes it possible to resolve the tensions and contradictions between them. It is no longer a question of maintaining coherence and cohesion but rather, by playing with uncertainty, of making oneself capable of adapting and evolving.

Thank you for your attention. I am ready to answer your questions.

NOTES

1. In reorganizing the French Army's structure from 2016 on, the chief of staff decided to insist on the moral and ethical values permeating the organization. "Warrior spirit" (*"Esprit guerrier"*) embodies this move insofar as it is supposed to associate military traditions with new technologies and battle hardening based on resilience, combativeness, and robustness as its core principles.

Conclusion

STEN RYNNING
OLIVIER SCHMITT
AMELIE THEUSSEN

The West did not so much win the Cold War in the late twentieth century as lose its way, writes Kishore Mahbubani. The Tiananmen Square protests in Beijing in 1989 triggered a conviction that was always latent in the West, namely that Western societies "had found the magical formula for economic growth and political stability." What followed were two decades of Western "hubris" that blinded Western governments to the "return" of China and India to world politics; led them into a bitter conflict with the Islamic world, notably with the 2003 war in Iraq; led them to humiliate Russia with NATO's geographical expansion; and led them, finally, to pursue "thoughtless intervention" in the internal affairs of several countries.[1]

Mahbubani's goading of the West to settle down and become part of the human tribe, as he puts it, proceeds from the fractures around which the present volume is also organized: a fracture inside Western institutions between civil and military communities, a fracture between Western political ambitions and international norms of restrained behavior, and a fracture between Western military fighting power and strategic abilities. These fractures combine to define a Western decline in world politics, but the lingering question is whether time is indeed up for the West in world politics writ large, and in the brutal but critical business of warfare more specifically. The answer may be less straightforward than Mahbubani and other skilled observers are inclined to think.

The sense that the West has had its time builds on a certain understanding of temporality—of how past, present, and future come together. The mainstream reading of the West is that its rise was the result of a combination of Chinese reticence, as evidenced by the arrested adventures of Admiral Zheng He in the fifteenth century, and European entrepreneurial spirit displayed by budding capitalists as well as explorers such as Christopher Columbus, Ferdinand Magellan, and Amerigo Vespucci. For some 200–300 years the West could rule the world on account of industrial and geographic advantage, but it is now at a culminating point where its future is either normal or bleak, but in no way extraordinary, with the rise of "the rest." This understanding of Western temporality is widespread and often associated with criticisms of Western warfare that depict battlefield advantages as incidental to greater political flaws and declining economic muscle.

This book does not seek to follow in these footsteps, nor in those of critics whose sense of temporality is the exact inverse, seeing a West that was crafted politically and institutionally in ancient Greece and Rome, the principles of which have endured ever since, even if their application at times has been calamitous. The book steers clear of the Scylla and Charybdis of such firm and fixed temporal boundaries, analyzing instead distinct Western temporalities and their political implications. It asks what the Western experience is like in terms of trajectory, perception, and pace—three critical dimensions of temporality. It investigates fractures and tensions associated with each dimension, laying bare the confusion of thought and problematic practice that each of them brings. But in so doing it also derives insight not only into a decline of fortunes but also into the potential for political and institutional renewal. It is to this balance sheet that we now turn.

A Western Condition?

Throughout the chapters of this book we do encounter a perspective of continuity, though not one of political triumph or a similar facet of superior principle. Rather, at issue is a condition of paradoxical power. On the one hand, the West harbors and commits to political principles purportedly of universal reach and timeless duration—principles that define an enduring source of energy and inspiration. On the other hand, it is beset by short-term crises and an often overwhelming sense of impending defeat that only extraordinary efforts can stave off. The Western condition is paradoxical because it has faith in the long run but is fearful of the short run. Faith in the long run inspires investment in political and military institutions; fear of the short run provokes efforts to circumvent institutions in an appeal to heroic action.

We recognize this condition with respect to all three sections of the book. In terms of trajectory and thus the grand destiny of the West, Rebecca R. Moore perceptively links NATO's commitment to liberal principle and an international order of democracy to a frantic and sometimes ill-conceived policy of drawing in illiberal partners for operational gain. NATO's ability to balance long- and short-term commitments is difficult by nature, perhaps, but its crisis management operations may in this regard not have been the Alliance's finest hour. As Tobias Bunde warns in his scenario chapter, this inability to choose between the long and short horizon, or to clarify the nature of NATO's trajectory, has led the allies to a point where their basic political cohesion is at risk.

Perceptions of time during operations reveal the same paradoxical condition. Natasha Kuhrt details how the West is torn between two temporalities, one calling for swift action to protect civilians and the other feeding a reluctance to return to wartime. Both temporalities emerge from the same set of underlying Western liberal principles, urging protection of the innocent while also shaping the view that war is a brutal affair and that humankind should move beyond it. In Kathleen McInnis's chapter we see how this paradoxical condition drove the West to engage in a long war in Afghanistan to protect the population, but also resulted in poorly thought-out campaign plans. Campaign plans go to the heart of war as they grapple with the enemy, shaping operations, and battle, but if governments are predisposed to dislike, or move beyond, war, they cannot define such plans. In the end the paradoxical condition prolonged the Afghan war at great cost, and today, as Amelie Theussen and Peter Viggo Jakobsen make clear, it shapes a reluctant and often incoherent Western approach to gray zone conflicts that adversaries are all too willing to exploit.

Technology has become the facet of this paradox in relation to the pace and speed of war. In terms of command-and-control systems, Nina Kollars writes, Western militaries have been so committed to minimizing the loop running from observation over orientation and decision to action—all in order to gain speed—that they have come to ignore adverse effects on command authority, to their own detriment. Among the benefits of authority are experience and a grasp of the overall conflict, which feed into an ability to master not speed but the pace of war. In this regard Kollars's observation links back to the enduring need for "civic militarism"—as an equilibrium between liberal and civilian institutions and martial military institutions—because civilian leadership is integral to such command authority. Heather Williams builds on this analysis as she argues that technologies tend to escape institutional capture in the West, because particular technologies are seen either as a looming threat or as a must-have tool in the Western political-military toolkit. In either case, advocates of new technologies argue outside the institutional channels that would normally select, procure, and apply new technology. Speed, once again, becomes an enemy of enduring principles of institutionalized governance.

Rather than invoking a West of either boom-and-bust or triumphalism, the analysis in this book suggests an enduring internal struggle for equilibrium. In his famous essay on *The Three Types of Legitimate Rule,* Max Weber conceptualized traditional, charismatic, and legal-rational authority and suggested that government could shift over time from the former to the latter, in what would in effect be a pattern of historical improvement in governance capacity. Later in the twentieth century Western thinking would explore this perspective by means of various theories of modernization and development that lost credence in the late stages of decolonization and the last phase of the Cold War, regaining some of their luster in the immediate post–Cold War years, only to founder in Bosnia, Kosovo, Afghanistan, and Iraq. War—perhaps especially war tethered to progressive ambitions—patently has a power to destroy such trust in progress. We thus return to the equilibrium that Carl von Clausewitz also sought to conceptualize, namely between ideas of enlightenment and romanticism. The former offers control by way of knowledge and insight; the latter survival by energy and heroism. In the history of military thought, perhaps Clausewitz misread the balance of these forces and became too engulfed by the need for speed and the annihilation of enemy forces as war's final act.[2] But maybe Clausewitz grasped something of enduring value—namely that Western governance is struggling, perhaps permanently, to reconcile these two impulses.

In the best of lights, this condition commits the West not to international mastery but to political struggle inside its own polities. When the struggle results in equilibrium, as in a government able to defend itself and uphold democratic standards, it holds the potential to become "a pattern to others," rather than "an imitator," by way of its laws, equal justice, social advancement by merit, and open societies. Such were the words spoken by Pericles in the early stages of the Peloponnesian war when his state, Athens, had both power and political legitimacy. But the struggle may also fail, in which case the political fate of Western governance may resemble that of Athens as traced by Thucydides, one of eroding equilibrium, increasing corruption, brutal warfare, and strategic loss.[3]

This paradoxical condition relativizes the fixed and firm temporalities that surround much of the debate over the West. It suggests that the West is neither destined to rule nor doomed to fail but rather condemned to struggle to balance its disparate politico-military institutions and the temporalities they harbor.

A Changing Condition?

If the West represents a struggle to balance institutions and their temporalities, then it remains possible that at some point the West will lose its balance forever. This is the sense of Mahbubani, and it is a predominant concern running through the book's three scenario chapters. All three aim to provoke the reader to revisit presuppositions about Western power, but all three also play with the idea that perhaps this time around, the West is at a loss.

In zooming in on a NATO without the United States, Tobias Bunde questions the political and ideological cohesion of the West. Ernst Dijxhoorn chooses to engage Djibouti and the prospect that an emboldened China will present the West with a land grab *fait accompli*. In Dijxhoorn's assessment, the West is so caught up in political concerns about war's costs and legal constraints that it will fail to respond. Stéphane Taillat and Joseph Henrotin look to Mali, Cyprus, and Lithuania to depict a gloomy future in which Western forces have become so reliant on vulnerable digital technologies that they will be both slowed down and blocked in their actions. In their scenario, the West might be about to hand control of the speed and pace of war to future adversaries.

The chapters of the book indicate how such a change of fortunes could come about. In its strongest form, this outcome would depend on a multitude of factors rather than any single factor, such as technology. When combined, these factors indicate how Western temporalities could come together—could conspire—to fundamentally disrupt the ability of Western governments to think and act coherently in matters of war.

One such factor is a long-term disconnect within Western institutions. Sarah Kreps and Adi Rao effectively debunk the idea that the modern Western state builds on an enduring approach to war financing. Rather, aligning with the literature on a short-lived military revolution, they argue that through much of the nineteenth century, and into the twentieth, the modern state was (relatively) strong in terms of both financial muscle and democratic engagement. Taxation for war purposes was the key, they argue, because—unwieldy and contested as taxation may be—it forced political and military institutions to think through the objectives of war and restrain its duration, keeping society mobilized behind it. As states turned to debt financing instead of taxation, politicians gained freedom of maneuver but, critically, lost institutional commitment and engagement. The modern Western state thus remained strong financially but weakened democratically. With the loss of restraint, a downward trajectory began, and forever wars became possible.

According to Paul Brister, the loss of institutional restraint opened a vacuum that strategists and political enthusiasts were only too happy to fill with the allure of technology. This happened gradually and along distinct trajectories in different Western countries, but the trend is nevertheless clear, Brister argues: a clear Western proclivity to think in terms of offense, quick-win strategies, and the possibility of dominance by way of heavy engagement.

One of the brutal inflection points within this trend was World War I, which started with a "cult of the offensive" but ground to a halt in defensive-dominant trench warfare that not even the most dedicated artillery-led offensives could break. In response, Germany spearheaded the "operational art" of coordinating across tactical engagements, a critical measure enabling it to gain the speed necessary to outwit adversaries on both its geographical flanks. Since then, "operational art" has been a key concern of Western combined arms warfare. As Pascal Vennesson details, this may not have resulted in a uniform commitment to Western-style *blitzkrieg* but has nonetheless focused Western military thinking around speed and how to leverage it to Western advantage. The United States, Britain, and France have sophisticated doctrinal thinking in this respect, Vennesson demonstrates, but this thinking has matured at the cost of perceptions of space and political context. Western forces are thus superior at operational maneuver, yet also strategically challenged.

The loss of institutional restraint and strategic foresight at home is reinforced by the character of the international institutions developed and supported by Western states since World War II. These institutions do not seek to eliminate war but rather limit war to just purposes and conduct. The "just war" tradition is one critical step away from the "absolute pacifist tradition," whereby war can never be justified, and it emerges from "classical Greek and Roman thought," "Christian theology," and then the "changing circumstances of the church under the Roman Empire."[4] In the early modern years, the tradition of just war rubbed up against sovereigns' claimed right to initiate wars at will, but in the twentieth century Western powers reinvented the tradition by replacing the heavenly reward of virtue with the punishment of transgression. Deterrence became the pivot that the Church once was, enabling the West to find a new equilibrium for being both civic (liberal) and militarist (deterring).

The character of this equilibrium has become a challenge for the West, as several chapters indicate. The trouble is that it was founded on an abhorrence of war, related to the carnage of the two world wars including the use of atomic bombs, and hence a consensus that those who *choose* war are illegitimate and therefore liable for collective punishment. Today, as a consequence of new technologies and precision warfare along with the limited character of protracted warfare against terrorists, insurgents, and other asymmetrical adversaries, the choice of war is less obviously condemnable. The international institutional restraint remains, but the de facto political temptation to conduct limited war has grown. In consequence, as Natasha Kuhrt, Nina Kollars, and Heather Williams all demonstrate, the political temptation is to circumvent institutional restraint and instead appeal to new technology and the promise of quick-fix victories. This biased perception that time can be accelerated at will in turn engenders resistance both within and outside the West by political forces committed to either peacetime or alternative visions of governance.

Stéphane Taillat and Joseph Henrotin suggest that instead of engendering a Western military dependency on digital technologies, the West should foster a military culture of mission command and warrior spirit. True warriors, they imply in their scenario, will not be bewildered by the loss of GPS signals but adapt to a non-digital battlefield and the effort of adversaries to control the pace of war. This appeal to the martial side of the Western tradition is up against strong opposition, however, in the shape of Western civil society aligning with the distinct normative restraint of international institutions, and political leadership able to design war outside institutional restraints of the past, notably through taxation but also councils of grand strategy-making.[5] In effect, where the warrior would go with the flow of wartime, civilians eyeing a distant horizon of progress would turn their back on it, while political leadership would pretend to be able to accelerate it at will. Such trends seem a recipe for Western decline beyond the vagaries inherent in the paradox of power outlined above.

What Is to Be Done?

The challenge for Western societies is to regenerate the equilibrium of democratic government and military ability, or else face the prospect that permanent decline could set in. In all this the prospect is not of a mythic return to glorious days of global command, but simply, and certainly less glamorously, of a return to political cohesion and a capacity to employ military means for political objectives in the international arena. This need not imply war-war, as the saying goes, but relative to the present it does imply an enhanced capacity for managing political antagonisms, broadly conceived, and for averting war by means of defense and deterrence.

We cannot offer a cookbook recipe in this respect, but we can identify a number of key themes and delineate their policy implications. The political operator may wish that we had gone further in defining *how* all this can happen, but our focus is on *what* needs to happen and thus the key issues to which decisionmakers and their advisers must give particular attention. Five such key issues, all facets of the challenge of managing tensions within the West between liberal thought and military practice, and between sovereignty and togetherness, emerge from our analysis in this book.

Political Restraint

As Tobias Bunde writes, the West is at risk of disappearing because it has no answer to the question of what the West is. Instead, a culture of partisanship has taken hold in most Western capitals, whereby political opponents are seen not as future officeholders but as adversaries who must be kept out of office by almost any means. The return of nationalism to Western politics has thus not brought Western polities together, as nationalism would otherwise pretend to do, but has fractured the polities into political tribes. The trajectory of time that once implied a shared Western fate has in turn become nationalized and tribalized. First and foremost, therefore, Western governments must invest in the values that engender consensus. Such values in the West will be liberal. Each Western society must define for itself how it can best limit tribalism or partisanship at home, but it remains a collective task to engage the "next horizon" of liberalism that can inspire mutual cooperation, and that does not exclude wider global cooperation. Natasha Kuhrt speaks of the West's "normative indeterminacy" as a distinct vulnerability, which is another way of framing the West's inability to define a normative core to which it is committed and around which it defines its political contours.

New Political-Legal Doctrine

Western militaries, and perhaps especially land forces, are experts at writing military doctrine, but what we have in mind is a broader derivative of the above-mentioned "normative core," namely political-legal doctrine and its military implications. As Stéphane Taillat and Joseph Henrotin write, if political-legal restraints are emptied of political purpose and become mere obstacles, military doctrine will deteriorate in quality as it substitutes technology for warrior ethos. To avert this development, we must look to the political-legal order under consideration by Amelie Theussen and Peter Viggo Jakobsen. As they emphasize, there can be no questioning the desirability of the West's operating within normative boundaries, but these boundaries are being tested by multiple actors, including Russia and China. The West should therefore invest in debates on such normative boundaries. Its ambition should be to challenge actors that exploit Western wartime/peacetime distinctions to the detriment of current international norms. To overcome its inhibition over pondering conflict in the gray zone between these distinctions, the West could insist on new standards of reciprocity, the absence of which would be considered hostile intent: it could clarify the stakes at issue in Ukraine, the South China Sea, and elsewhere. Like the rest of the advice offered here, this would not be a straightforward undertaking, and it would not be the answer to every armed conflict across the globe. However, it would reconcile clashing temporalities inside the West, between a military ethos abiding by war time and a civilian ethos committed to time's progress; it would diminish the ability of others to exploit this divide; and it would enhance Western thinking on the values at stake in the international order—values that in turn could reinforce the drive for political restraint at home.

Visible Costs of War

War time ought to involve a change of societal and government priorities reflecting the cost of war. As Sarah Kreps and Adi Rao make vividly clear, to pretend otherwise is to corrupt and indeed eliminate the political bargaining on which strategy depends. Political bargaining defines ambitions for war, with due respect for adversaries and operational conditions, and then also the cost imposed on society. If financial borrowing disrupts this logic, decision-makers will be tempted to skip the bargaining and insist on their ambitions for war, short-circuiting intelligence and political advice as well as public engagement. This engenders another clash of temporalities, between political leaders for whom wars are intense and in need of speed, and society for which it is essentially peacetime. Taxation was once a primary means for bringing the cost of war to the political table, but even if taxation could be a tool for correcting course, it would be futile to imagine a simple return to "the good old days." Rather, the guiding principle must be that since war is extraordinary, it should be associated with extraordinary measures in government policy that attract societal attention and engagement. It will be politically inconvenient, but it would reconcile clashing temporalities and thus enhance the capacity of Western governments to reconcile ends, ways, and means.

The Future Is Now

As is eminently clear in the chapters by Heather Williams and Pascal Vennesson, Western governments and militaries tend to employ speed to win in the present and stave off future adverse developments. Inherent in this approach is thus an anxiety about temporality, a fear that time is not on the West's side. Western thought is generally optimistic about a progressive future, but when engaged in war it becomes anxious and obsessed with the short term. To the extent that they can, governments and funders of think tanks and university research should stimulate thinking that adopts an inverse mindset. Such thinking, anchored in a renewed tradition of war studies, should be dedicated to "the future is now" and thus war as defense-dominated, drawn-out affairs that last beyond any one claim to victory. It should be committed to contextualizing the impact of technology on war, drawing on all the historical evidence that indicates how, in the clash between speed and pace, pace tends to win. Such thinking should not only be institutionally nourished; it also must be brought into the political arena for robust debate.

A Grand Debate on History and Culture

The West by definition extends beyond any one state or nation, and by definition it thus involves a tension between sovereignty and togetherness. War is a source of stress that can cause governments and societies to give up on managing this tension and to search for more wholesome national options, but war is not the only source of such stress. The COVID pandemic likewise caused a breakdown of Western cooperation and fanned the flames of national self-sufficiency, or, alternatively, the idea that Europe and North America were not in this fight together. The pandemic thus energized the transactionalist impulse in transatlantic affairs—the idea that the transatlantic quid pro quo, whether in terms of defense spending, trade surplus, or medical devices, must be visibly and immediately balanced. And the problem with transactionalism, as Michael Kimmage has underscored, is that it lacks the historical and cultural content that gives enduring meaning to political relationships.[6] The proper counter to such corrosive transactionalism is a vigorous and critical debate on the history of how the West has balanced and will continue to balance human and state security, and how the West has balanced and will continue to balance liberty and defense. Put differently, if the linear "mono-chronistic" story of the West—containing a beginning, middle, and end—is not to fast forward to a tragic ending, the West must make room at the table typically dominated by decisionmakers, generals, strategists, and engineers for humanists who understand the pace of history and the meaning it confers.

Striking a Balance

Paraphrasing Henry Kissinger's dissection of the American challenge in the post–Cold War environment, we might in conclusion venture that the challenge for the West is to strike a balance between the twin temptations of seeking to remedy every wrong and stabilize every dislocation, and of following the instinct to withdraw and refine domestic values in a post-political world of sustainable development goals.[7] If it were eventually to discard the need for politico-military thinking, the West would be clearly signaling it is failing in this balancing act and quite possibly has entered a phase of terminal decline. Conversely, making the effort to wrestle with the issues and problems outlined here would suggest that the West could perhaps remain in a condition of paradoxical power and contribute to the evolution of international order. Such a Western contribution to order would not represent a return to the past of European, American, or transatlantic leadership. It would instead emerge from a reinvention of the Western practice of balancing liberty and defense inside institutions of government, which quite possibly could enhance the global character of the West or perhaps involve a shift of Western practice away from the old transatlantic heartland. The future of the West will thus be defined not only by its ability to withstand the competition offered by non-Western governments and societies, but just as much by the West's own ability to invest in its dynamic vision of temporality, meaning, and leadership.

NOTES

1. Kishore Mahbubani, *Has the West Lost It? A Provocation,* 1st ed. 2018 (London: Penguin, 2019).

2. Azar Gat, *A History of Military Thought: From the Enlightenment to the Cold War* (Oxford University Press, 2001); Thomas X. Hammes, *The Sling and the Stone: On War in the 21st Century* (St. Paul, MN: Zenith Press, 2004); Thomas X. Hammes, *Deglobalization and International Security,* Rapid Communications in Conflict and Security Series (Amherst, NY: Cambria Press, 2019).

3. Thucydides, *The History of the Peloponnesian War* (Project Gutenberg, 2013), https://www.gutenberg.org/files/7142/7142-h/7142-h.htm#link2H_4_0007.

4. Inis L. Claude, "Just Wars: Doctrines and Institutions," *Political Science Quarterly,* vol. 95, no. 1 (1980), pp. 83–96, https://doi.org/10.2307/2149586.

5. Hew Strachan, "Strategy in the Twenty-First Century," in *The Changing Character of War*, edited by Hew Strachan and Sibylle Scheipers (Oxford University Press, 2014), pp. 503–21.

6. Michael Kimmage, *The Abandonment of the West: The History of an Idea in American Foreign Policy* (New York: Basic Books, 2020).

7. Henry Kissinger, *Diplomacy* (New York: Simon & Schuster, 1994).

Contributors

STEN RYNNING is professor of war studies and vice dean for research in the Faculty of Business and Social Science, University of Southern Denmark.

OLIVIER SCHMITT is professor (with special responsibilities) in the Center for War Studies, University of Southern Denmark.

AMELIE THEUSSEN is assistant professor in the Center for War Studies, University of Southern Denmark.

PAUL BRISTER is a visiting professor in the Security Policy Studies Program at the Elliott School of International Affairs, George Washington University.

TOBIAS BUNDE is a post-doctoral researcher in the Centre for International Security, Hertie School, and director of research and policy at the Munich Security Conference.

ERNST DIJXHOORN is assistant professor in the Institute of Security and Global Affairs, Leiden University.

JOSEPH HENROTIN is a research fellow at the Institute for Comparative Strategy.

PETER VIGGO JAKOBSEN is associate professor in the Department of Strategy at the Royal Danish Defence College.

NINA A. KOLLARS is a nonresident fellow at the Modern War Institute, West Point, and assistant professor in the Strategic and Operational Research Department at the U.S. Naval War College.

SARAH KREPS is the John L. Wetherill Professor of Government, Cornell University.

NATASHA KUHRT is lecturer in international peace and security in the Department of War Studies, King's College London.

KATHLEEN J. MCINNIS is a nonresident senior fellow with the Scowcroft Center for Strategy and Security at the Atlantic Council.

REBECCA R. MOORE is professor and chair of the Political Science Department, Concordia College.

ADI RAO is a graduate fellow in the Reppy Institute for Peace and Conflict Studies, Cornell University.

STÉPHANE TAILLAT is associate professor of war and strategic studies at the French Institute of Geopolitics, University of Paris-Saint Denis.

PASCAL VENNESSON is senior fellow and professor of political science, S. Rajaratnam School of International Studies, Nanyang Technological University.

HEATHER WILLIAMS is a lecturer in the Centre for Science and Security Studies at King's College London.

Index

Abhkazia, 147–148, 193

absolute war, 9

Acton, James, 263

Adamsky, Dmitry, 256

Addis Ababa Annan Plan, 151

Afghanistan, 111, 293; campaign coherence in, 124–126; civilian casualties in, 115–117, 122, 125, 133n22; concept of speed in Afghanistan war, 220–222; funding of US war in, 36, 38; as global partner to NATO, 65–66; NATO operations in, 12, 59–66, 68, 74, 77–78, 81n30, 116, 123–130; temporality and, 115, 122–123, 127, 131

Afghan National Defense and Security Forces (ANDSF), 125, 129–130, 136n63, 137n68

Af-Pak Hands, 127

African Union, 148–149

Air Force Future Operating Concept:

A View of the Air Force in 2035 (USAF), 235–239

AirLand Battle doctrine, 208, 240

Allen, John, 49

Allvin, David, 208–209

American hegemony, 23

American War of Independence, 28, 30

Ansar Al-Dine, 276–277

anti-access/area denial (A2/AD) capabilities, 13, 212, 243, 264

Arab League, 69, 153

Arab Spring, 72, 152

Arhran, Ariel, 63

Aristotle, 19

Armenia, 63

arms races: hypersonic missiles and, 262–264; perception and, 269; stability and, 256, 261

Army Doctrine Publication (ADP) Land Operations (UK military, 2017), 215

Article 5 (NATO), 75–76, 95, 101n11, 139, 166–167, 175, 199, 285; gray zone conflict and, 162, 165, 167, 175
artificial intelligence (AI), 48–49, 53, 253–254, 260, 262, 264–268, 270–271; private investment in, 265
Assad, Bashar al-, 149, 153
asymmetric war, 168, 178, 268–269, 297
Aurora 17, 76
Australia, 64, 67, 78
"Avangard" missile, 253, 262
Azerbaijan, 63

Ban Ki-moon, 154–155
Barbary Wars, 30
Barrera, Bernard, 217, 223
Bell, Mark, 259–260
Belt and Road Initiative (BRI), 173, 185, 195
Berdal, Mats, 145
Bergson, Henri, 2
Bismark, Otto von, 8
Blair, Tony, 142–143
Bodganov, Sergei, 168
Boer War, 45
Boko Haram, 137n65
Bolton, John, 153, 190, 192
Boot, Max, 29
Booth, Ken, 266
Bosnia, 59, 141, 194
Boyd, John, 47, 208, 231
Brexit, 90, 95–96
Brims, Robin, 216
Brister, Paul, 21–22, 296
Britain. *See* United Kingdom
Brown, Daniel, 63
Brustlein, Corentin, 264
Bunde, Tobias, 23, 293, 295, 298
Bush, George W., 145
Byers, Michael, 143–144, 155

campaign coherence, 118, 124–125, 128

campaign continuity, 126–128
Canada, 123, 127
Central African Republic (CAR), 140, 149, 153
Chekinov, Sergei, 168
Chin, Gregory, 151
China, 150–152, 161, 170–173, 184–185, 195–197; conflict in South China Sea, 50–51, 172–173, 184, 197, 299; Djibouti and, 13, 112, 173, 184–185, 188–192, 194–200, 295; *fait accompli* strategy and, 150–152, 184–185, 195–200; gray zone conflict and, 161–162, 171–173; Hong Kong and, 184; international legal norms and, 110, 112, 139; military strength of, 5, 197; military technology and, 262–263, 265–266; non-interference and, 150–152, 185, 191; perception of time in, 171, 212; perception of war, 170–173; PNA doctrine and, 185, 191, 192–193, 198; R2P and, 146, 150–151, 155–156; relationship with Russia, 97, 151–152; relationship with "the West," 194–200, 291–292; relationship with UN, 141; relationship with US, 243–244, 253; South China Sea conflicts and, 50–51, 172–173, 184, 197, 244, 299
Chivvis, Chris, 70, 74
Christianity, 2
Churkin, Vitalii, 147
Cicero, 28, 165
civic militarism, 19–21, 293–294; civilian leadership and, 247–248; decline of, 34, 36, 88–89; defined, 19; limited war and, 26; NATO and, 68, 78–79; taxation and, 30, 33, 38–39
civilian casualties, 12, 116–122, 125, 133n22, 134n26, 293; accounting for, 132n9; artificial intelligence and, 271; China and, 151; humanitarian intervention and, 142; international

legal norms and, 118–122, 131, 145; R2P and, 145, 156

civilian leadership, 7, 242, 246–249, 260, 293–294

civil-military relationship, 7, 45, 232, 242, 247

Civil War (USA), 30–33, 45

Clark, Christopher, 8

Clausewitz, Carl von, 9, 22, 50, 163, 167, 196, 294

closing of war, 21

Coats, Dan, 172

cognitive slippage, 145

Cohen, Eliot, 213, 248

Cold War, 10–11, 256–257, 291

colonialism, 6

Columbus, Christopher, 292

Combined Air Operations Center (CAOC), 235–236, 238

Combined Arms Tactical Groups (GTIAs), 218, 228n55

Combined Joint Expeditionary Force (CJEF), 218

command and control (C2) systems, 287

contingent pacifism, 20

convergence, 240–241, 244, 246

cooperative security, 60

countering violent extremism (CVE) operations, 130, 137nn65–66

counterinsurgency operations, 140, 220–222; in Afghanistan, 62, 64, 124–125

counterterrorism operations, 61, 65, 121, 125, 128–130, 154, 224

COVID pandemic, 300

Crimea, 50–51, 68, 75, 76–77, 147–148, 155, 192–194, 198

crisis stability, 256

"cult of the offensive," 44–45

cyber technologies, 255, 258, 287

cyber warfare, 110, 164, 166–167; China's use of, 172–173; gray zone conflict and, 173, 176–177

Cyprus, 278

Dafoe, Allan, 259, 267

Darfur, 144–145

Davidson, Janine, 222

Davidson, Philip S., 172, 197

debt, 28–29, 37–39, 296

decolonization, 6, 294

Defense and Related Security Capacity Building Initiative, 67

Democratic Republic of Congo (DRC), 140

Deng Xiaoping, 184–185

Deptula, David, 213

Dhuule, Axmed Liibaan, 189

digital communications, 14, 209–210. *See also* digitalization process

digitalization process, 275–276, 286–288, 295

Dijxhoorn, Ernst, 112, 295

disinformation campaigns, 168, 172–173

Distributed Maritime Operations (DMO), 230, 243–246

Djibouti, 13, 112, 184–200, 295; Chinese operations in, 173, 189–192, 194–200; maps of, 186–187; Western response to China in, 192–195

Driant, Emile, 44

drone warfare, 50, 139–140, 164, 224; civilian casualties and, 81n30, 117, 119; gray zone conflict and, 162

Dudziak, Mary, 167, 177

Edelstein, David, 8

Egnell, Robert, 73

Elliott, Christopher, 216

endless war, 167, 180n36

Estonia, 75, 87

ethnic cleansing, 142

Euhus, Brandon, 50

Euro-Atlantic Cooperation Council (EAPC), 60, 62

European Union (EU), 95–96, 176, 199

Expeditionary Advance Based Operations (EABO), 230

extraction. *See* taxation
extraction-coercion cycle, 27

Facebook, 170
fait accompli, 13, 42, 50–51, 172, 188,
   194, 196, 198–200; Chinese operations in Djbouti as, 13, 184, 188,
   194–200; Russian annexation of
   Crimea as, 198
Fazal, Tanisha, 110
Ferdinand, Peter, 150
financial technologies, 29
financing of war. *See* war financing
Finland, 60, 67, 75–78
Finnemore, Martha, 111, 119
France, 96–98; military speed and,
   216–219, 222–224; military technol-
   ogy and, 262, 276, 279, 286–289;
   operations in Mali, 217–218,
   222–224, 276–278; participation in
   NATO operations, 72, 279; peace-
   keeping missions and, 153
Frank, Barney, 36
Franks, Tommy, 143, 214
Frederick II, 8, 213
Freedman, Lawrence, 10, 21, 196
Fuller, J. F. C., 4

Gallagher, Eddie, 119
Gambari, Ibrahim, 151
Gareev, Makhmut, 168
Garfinkel, Ben, 259, 267
Gartzke, Erik, 255, 258
Gates, Robert, 71
Gaub, Florence, 71
Gauck, Joachim, 89, 101n12
Geneva Conventions, 109, 179n23,
   179n26, 180n29
Georgia, 63, 67, 147
Gerasimov, Valery, 168–169
Germany, 8, 101n15, 145; NATO
   and, 89–92; World War II and,
   51–52
Giles, Keir, 148, 169

Gladstone, William, 31
Goldfien, David, 236–237
Goldgeier, James, 92
Gow, James, 194
Gray, Christine, 145–146
Gray, Colin, 197
gray zone conflict, 13, 112, 155,
   161–178, 293, 299; challenges to
   West posed by, 173–175; China and,
   170–173, 197; declining importance
   of military force and, 164–165;
   defined, 161; efforts to counter,
   175–178; NATO and, 162, 175–176;
   Russia and, 145, 168–170; Western
   understandings of war and, 163–168
Great Britain. *See* United Kingdom
Greece, ancient, 1–2, 6, 19–20
Gregorian Reform, 2
Grotius, Hugo, 165
Gulf War (1st Iraq War), 46–47,
   163–164; military speed and, 10, 51,
   214–216, 253
Gulleh, Ismail Omar, 189–190

Haiti, 140–141
Halperin, Morton, 263
Hammes, T. X., 49
Hanson, Victor Davis, 6, 26, 28, 30,
   35, 38
Harrison, George, 128
Harriss, Gerald, 28
Hart, Basil Liddell, 208
Hehir, Aidan, 139, 144
Helluy, Bruno, 217, 223
Henrotin, Joseph, 295, 297, 299
Hoffman, Frank, 164
Hollande, François, 217, 2233
Hong Kong, 184
Horowitz, Michael, 248–249, 265, 270
Howard, Michael, 21
humanitarian intervention, 141–146,
   152, 156, 202n36; Chinese attitudes
   towards, 150–152; contrasted with
   R2P, 143, 145–146; Russian at-

titudes towards, 146–149. *See also* non-intervention; Responsibility to Protect (R2P)

human rights, 20, 74, 141–143, 145–146, 149, 151

Husain, Amir, 49

hybrid warfare, 110, 164, 175–176

hypersonic missiles/ hyper glide vehicles (HGVs), 13–14, 53, 253–254, 261–264, 266–267

hyperwar, 43, 48–50, 53

Ignatieff, Michael, 148, 213

illiberal democracy, 37

income taxes, 30–31

India, 7, 110, 152–153, 164, 262

information speed, 230, 232–234, 240–243, 247–249

information technology, 230–235, 246–250; digitalization process, 275–276, 286–288; US Air Force and, 235–239; US Army and, 239–242; US Navy and, 243–246

information warfare, 170

international cooperation, 22, 59, 199. *See also* NATO

International Security Assistance Force (ISAF), 59–69, 77–78, 123–131; campaign coherence and, 124–126; campaign continuity and, 126–128; civilian casualties and, 116; strategy coherence of, 128–131. *See also* Resolute Support Mission (RSM)

Iran, 25, 139–140, 172, 199, 246; Stuxnet attack on, 162, 167

Iraq, 47, 142–144; civilian casualties in, 117, 122; concept of speed in Iraq war, 10, 51, 214–216, 219, 220–222, 224–225, 253; first Gulf War in, 10, 46–47, 51, 163–164, 214–216, 253; funding of US war in, 36, 38; NATO operations in, 67; second Gulf War in, 214, 219; strategic pace and, 43, 47; UNSC and, 139, 155

irregular war, 164, 220, 278

Israel, 162, 167, 193

Istanbul Cooperation Initiative (ICI), 60, 63, 67, 71

Italy, 52, 72

Jackson, Aaron, 64

Jakobsen, Peter Viggo, 196, 293, 299

Japan, 38, 64–65, 67, 78, 266

Jervis, Robert, 257–258

Johnson, Lyndon, 34–35

Jokobsen, Peter Viggo, 112

Jomini Baron de, 44

Jones, Patricia, 95–96

Jones, Seth, 61–62

Jonsson, Oscar, 169

Jordan, 58, 63, 67, 69–70, 74

Just War theory, 149, 296–297

Kahl, Colin, 119–120

Kania, Elsa, 265

Karlsrud, John, 145

Karzai, Hamid, 116

Kazakhstan, 62

Kello, Lucas, 271

Kelton, Maryanne, 64

Kimmage, Michael, 300–301

Kissinger, Henry, 301

Kofman, Michael, 154

Kolenda, Chris, 117

Kollars, Nina, 52, 293, 297

Korean War, 25–26, 30, 34

Kosovo, 147–148, 153; humanitarian intervention in, 141–142, 154

Kouchner, Bernard, 141

Kreps, Sarah, 21–22, 38, 295, 299

Kuhrt, Natasha, 112, 191, 293, 297–298

Larson, John, 36

Latvia, 75, 87

lawfare, 148, 165, 170, 171–172

legal warfare, 51, 171–172

Lewis, Jerry, 36

liberalism, 2; NATO and, 59–60, 69, 74, 77–79, 104n41, 293; pace of war and, 9; post-war increases in, 33

Libicki, Martin, 255

Libya: humanitarian intervention in, 139, 145–146, 155–156; NATO operations in, 58–60, 68–75, 77–78; Russia and, 146–147

Lieber, Keir, 254, 258–260, 267

limited war, 26, 36, 51; funding of, 27, 34–35

Lindsay, Jon, 255, 258

Linn, Brian, 220

Lithuania, 75, 87, 279, 282–285

Lute, Doug, 129

Luttwak, Edward, 47, 54

Lynn-Jones, Sean, 258–259, 261

Lynx mission, 279

Macron, Emmanuel, 96–98, 103n35, 199

Magellan, Ferdinand, 292

Mahbubani, Kishore, 291–292, 295

Major Joint Operation Plus (MJO+), 88

Malaysian Airlines Flight 17, 174

Mali, 140, 150, 217–218, 222–224, 276–278

Mao Zedong, 212

Mattis, James, 121, 164, 208, 214

Mattox, Gale, 66

McCain, John, 154

McChrystal, Stanley, 116, 125, 129

McInnis, Kathleen J., 111, 293

McKiernan, David, 116

Mediterranean Dialogue (MD), 60, 63, 67, 71

Merkel, Angela, 89, 101n12

Mesquita, Bruce Bueno de, 30

military efficiency, 28

Military-Related Intelligence (MRI), 218

military technologies, 21–22, 294; AI and, 48–49, 53; arms race and, 54;

artificial intelligence (AI), 48–49, 53, 253–254, 260, 262, 264–268, 270; costs of, 259, 261, 267–269; destabilizing impact of, 255, 258, 263, 266–270, 269–270; digital communications, 209–210; digitalization process, 275–276, 286–288; drone warfare and, 119, 162, 224; French military and, 286–289; hypersonic missiles, 253–254, 262–264; hyperwar and, 43, 48–50, 53; individual wars and (*See* individual wars); information technology, 230–235, 246–250; likelihood of conflict and, 266–268; malfunctions and, 268; modularity and, 54; offense/defense balance and, 45, 48–50, 54–55, 254, 257–259; perception and, 269; policy primacy and, 54; policy recommendations and, 268–270; private funding of, 253, 254, 262, 266–270; speed and, 209, 253–255, 293; stability and, 255–257, 268; strategic pace and, 42–43, 45–48; technological opportunism, 254, 256, 259–261, 267, 269; unmanned surface water vessels, 245–246; Western military primacy and, 260–261

Miller, Jorge, 92–93, 97

Mills, Wilbur, 35

modularity, 54

Mongolia, 64

Moore, Rebecca R., 22, 293

Morocco, 58, 69, 74

Müller, Thomas, 89–92, 98

Multi-Domain Battle/Operations (MDO), 209, 230, 234

Multi-Domain Command and Control (MDC2), 230, 236–238, 240, 242, 245

Multi-Domain Operations Center (MDOC), 236–238

multi-domain warfighting, 230–231, 233–235; US Air Force and,

235–239; US Army and, 239–242; US Navy and, 243–246

Murphy, Sean, 154

Murray, Williamson, 54

Murtha, John, 36

Myanmar, 146, 151

Napoleonic wars, 12, 21, 44; income tax and, 30–31

Nardulli, Bruce, 70–71

nationalism, 298

NATO (North Atlantic Treaty Organization), 12, 22, 58–79, 85–99; Arab partners of, 69–72, 74; Article 5 of, 75–76, 95, 101n11, 139, 166–167, 175, 199, 285; Central Asian governments and, 62–63, 65–66; China and, 195–196; civic militarism and, 78–79; civic military balance and, 22–23; civilian casualties and, 121; defense expenditure as share of GOP, 280–281; Enhanced Opportunities Partners of, 67; *fait accompli* strategies and, 199; France and, 96–98; Germany and, 89–92; global partnerships and, 60–61, 64–68, 72; gray zone conflict and, 162, 175–176; Great Britain and, 95–96; hybrid warfare and, 175–176; ISAF and, 61–68; liberal values and, 59–60, 69, 74, 77–79, 104n41, 293; major Non-NATO allies, 75–77; operations in Afghanistan, 12, 59–66, 68, 74, 77–78, 123–131; operations in Libya, 58–60, 68–75, 77–78; operations in Lithuania, 279; Poland and, 94–95; post-2025 future of, 98–99; potential future conflict with Russia, 279, 282–285; potential US withdrawal from, 12, 85–86, 88, 92–94, 102n20, 295; Russia and, 68, 75, 78–79, 91–93; Swedish participation in, 72–74; threshold of war and, 166–167

Nemo, Phillipe, 1–2

Netherlands, 199

network-centric warfare, 4, 10, 171, 209, 221 (NCW), 286

New Zealand, 64, 78

non-intervention/non-interference, 12–13, 138, 188, 192; China and, 150–152, 185, 191; India and, 152; Iraq and, 144; R2P and, 142, 155; RIC states and, 153

non-state actors, 13, 79, 139, 149, 261, 267; gray zone conflicts and, 162, 164, 166–167, 174; international legal norms and, 110

normative indeterminacy, 298

norms, international legal, 12, 109–112, 299; civilian casualties and, 118–122, 131, 145; *fait accompli* strategy and, 188; Geneva Conventions, 109, 179n23, 179n26, 180n29; gray zone conflict and, 176–178; humanitarian intervention and, 141–144; normative indeterminacy, 298; R2P and, 139; sovereignty norms, 151–152; temporality and, 111, 138, 207; use of force and, 138–141

North Atlantic Cooperation Council (NACC), 60

Northern Wind, 75–76

North Korea, 25, 253, 269

nuclear weapons, 196, 211; AI and, 265, 268; blurring of domains and, 266–267; deterrence and, 34, 90; France and, 96–98, 103n35; HGVs and, 262–264; Iran and, 162, 167; just war theory and, 297; non-proliferation treaties, 269–270; nuclear opportunism, 259–261; offense-defense balance and, 220; Russia and, 91, 104n41; speed and, 220; stability and, 255–257

Obama, Barack, 128

Obama effect, 93

Obey, David, 36

offense/defense balance, 254–255, 257–259, 261, 263, 265, 269, 296; artificial intelligence and, 266; military technology and, 45, 48–50, 54–55; perception and, 258–259

On War (Clausewitz), 50

OODA (observe, orient, decide, act) loop, 49, 208, 231

Open Source Intelligence (OSINT), 218, 278

operational agility, 233–235, 244, 246

operational pace, 44, 51–52

operational speed, 212, 214, 218–220, 223–224. *See also* speed

Operation Barkhane, 224, 276, 279

Operation Desert Storm, 253

Operation Enduring Freedom (OEF), 61, 62, 65, 125

Operation Fardh al Qanoon, 221–222

Operation Freedom's Sentinel, 129

Operation Odyssey Dawn, 58, 68

Operation Serval, 217–218, 222–224

Operation Unified Protector (OUP), 58–60, 68–75, 77–78

Orbán, Viktor, 98

O'Rourke, Beto, 37

pace of war, 9–11. *See also* operational pace; speed; strategic pace

Pakistan, 65, 81n30

Papal Revolution, 2

paradoxical power, 292–293, 301

Parker, Geoffrey, 5–7, 28, 38

Parrott, David, 29

Partnership for Peace (PfP), 60, 62, 67, 73, 75

Partnership Interoperability Initiative (PII), 66, 82n40

Payne, Kenneth, 264

peacekeeping operations (PKOs), 140, 150, 152–154, 191; Chinese participation in, 150, 191; Indian participation in, 152; Russian participation in, 148–149

Peel, Robert, 31

Peloponnesian war, 294

People's Liberation Army (PLA) of China, 150, 171–172; in Djibouti, 185, 191

perceptions of time. *See* time, perceptions of

Pericles, 294

Petraeus, David, 116

Petrov, Stanislav, 268

Pitt the Younger, William, 30–31

Plato, 19

Poland, 75, 94–95

policy primacy, 52–53

political bargaining, 299

political-legal doctrine, 298–299

political restraint, 298–299

poll taxes, 28–29

"porcupine strategy," 49–50

Pothier, Fabrice, 71

Press, Daryl, 260

privatization of war, 21

Protection of Nationals Abroad (PNA) doctrine, 184–185, 192–194, 198, 202n30, 202n36

psychological warfare, 168, 171–172

public opinion warfare, 51, 171

Putin, Vladimir, 91–92, 94, 122, 148

Qaddafi, Muammar, 58–59, 69–72, 74

Qatar, 58, 64, 69–72

Qiao Liang, 171

Rao, Adi, 21–22, 295, 299

Rapid Dominance strategy, 47

Rasmussen, Mikkel Vedby, 99

Readiness Action Plan (RAP), 75

Red Balloon Challenge, 269

Regens, James, 264

Resolute Support Mission (RSM), 63, 65, 75, 129–130

Responsibility to Protect (R2P), 74, 141–146, 154–156, 157n14; after 2005 World Summit, 144–146;

China and, 146, 150–152; contrasted with humanitarian intervention, 143, 145–146; India and, 152–153; as international norm, 139–140; Iraq war and, 142–144; Libya and, 139; Russia and, 146–149

restrained warfare, 20

Revolution in Military Affairs (RMA), 10

Richardson, John, 243–244

RIC states, 153–154

Ridgway, Matthew, 26

risk management, 10–11

Roberts, Adam, 142

Roberts, Michael, 5–7, 20–21

Rodin, David, 20

Rome, ancient, 2, 6

Roosevelt, Franklin, 32

Roper, Daniel, 242

Russia, 146–149, 153–154, 161, 168–170; China and, 97, 151–152; conception of stability, 256; Crimea and, 50–51, 68, 75, 76–77, 147–148, 155, 192–194, 198; gray zone conflict and, 161–162, 169, 174; humanitarian intervention and, 143, 146–149, 155–156; international legal norms and, 110, 112, 139; military technology and, 262–263, 266; NATO and, 68, 75, 78–79, 91–93, 279, 282–285; nuclear weapons and, 91, 104n41; perception of war, 168–170; PNA doctrine and, 193–194, 202n30; Syria and, 142, 149, 153–154, 199; Ukraine and, 68, 75, 76–77, 147, 155, 169–170, 193–194; UN and, 140–141; US 2016 election and, 169–170, 181n51; World War II and, 52

Rwanda, 140, 145

Scales, Robert, 208

Schelling, Thomas, 256, 263

Scheve, Kenneth, 32

Schmitt, Jean-Claude, 3

Schmitt, Olivier, 10

SCORPION programme, 276, 279

September 11 terrorist attacks, 59–60, 139

Serbia, 147

Shanahan, Patrick M., 93

Sikkink, Kathryn, 111, 119

small-scale military ventures, 29–30

Smith, Adam, 28

Soleimani, Qasem, 140

Somalia, 140

South China Sea, 50–51, 172–173, 184, 197, 299

South Korea, 64, 67, 78, 266

South Ossetia, 147–148, 193

sovereignty norms, 151–152

Soviet Union, 256, 268. *See also* Russia

speed, 9–11, 13, 42–43, 208–213, 293, 300; counterinsurgency and, 220–221; drone warfare and, 224; "fighting slow" and, 220–224; French military and, 216–219, 222–224; "hyperwar" and, 48–51; information speed, 230, 232–234, 240–243, 247–249; Iraq wars and, 51, 214–216, 219, 220–222, 224–225; likelihood of conflict and, 266–268; limits of, 219, 249; multi-domain warfighting and, 231–235; Napoleonic warfare and, 44; offense-defense balance and, 44–45, 258; operational speed, 212, 214, 218–220, 223–224; perceptions of time and, 14, 78, 289; policy recommendations and, 53–55, 224–225, 268–270; risks of, 211–212; strategic stability and, 209, 271; tactical speed, 43, 44, 46, 50–52; technological innovation and, 253–255, 262–266; UK military and, 215–216, 219, 222–224; US military and, 46–47, 213–214, 219, 220–222, 235–246; World War I and, 45, 296. *See also* strategic pace; temporality; time, perceptions of

Sri Lanka, 146
Stasavage, David, 32
Steinbruner, John, 257, 270
Steinmeier, Frank-Walter, 99
Stevenson, Adlai, 34
Strachan, Hew, 21
strategic pace, 22, 42–43, 46, 51–53, 55, 221–222, 293; civil-military relations and, 45; difficulties in predictions, 44, 47–48, 55; *fait accompli* concept and, 50–51; hyperwar and, 49; importance of speed, 208–210; military technology and, 45–46; Napoleonic wars and, 44; policy primacy and, 52–53; tactical speed and, 43, 44, 46, 50–52. *See also* operational pace; speed
strategic security dialogues, 269
strategic stability, 14, 209, 254–257, 260–261, 263–264, 269–270
Stryker Brigade Combat Team, 213–214
Stuxnet attack, 162, 167
Sudan, 151
Surkov, Vladislav, 169
Svoboda, Karel, 86, 889
Sweden, 58, 60, 67, 69, 72–78
Syria, 139, 153; Russian intervention in, 149, 153–154; US operations in, 142, 146, 154, 199

tactical speed, 43, 44, 46, 50–52. *See also* speed
Taillat, Stéphane, 295, 297, 299
Talmadge, Caitlin, 254, 260, 267
taxation, 21–33, 38–39, 295–296, 299–300; historical evolution of, 27–29; income taxes, 30–31; limited war and, 34–37; poll taxes, 28–29; in United States, 30–37
technological opportunism, 254, 256, 259–261, 267, 269
temporality, 2–4, 111–112, 292, 299–300; Afghanistan intervention and, 115, 122–123, 127, 131; civilian

protection and, 13, 138, 293; gray zone conflict and, 161, 173; international legal norms and, 111, 138, 207; pace and, 3, 9–11; perception of time and, 3, 8; Western military power and, 5–7, 275, 292, 295. *See also* speed; time, perceptions of
terrorism, 2, 130, 220; civilian casualties and, 117; counterterrorism operations, 61, 65, 121, 125, 128–130, 154, 224; September 11 attacks, 59–60; US "War on Terror," 167
Teutt, Sarah, 151
Thakur, Ramesh, 151
Theussen, Amelie, 112, 196, 293, 299
threshold of war, 13, 161–162, 165–167, 170–178
Tibet, 150
Tienanmen Square protests, 291
Tilly, Charles, 5, 26
time, perceptions of, 2, 12, 207–210, 288, 295, 297; Chinese, 171, 212; Christianity and, 2; nationalization and, 299; speed and, 14, 78, 289; temporality and, 8; UK military and, 215–216. *See also* speed; strategic pace; temporality
transactionalism, 300–301
Trident Juncture, 75–76
Truman, Harry, 34
Trump, Donald, 25; "America First" policy of, 110; Chinese occupation of Djibouti and, 190; consequences of potential reelection of, 85–86, 88, 94; Poland and, 94, 105n51

Ukraine, 299; Russian intervention in, 68, 75, 76–77, 147, 155, 169, 193–194
Ullman, Harlan, 47
UN High-level Panel Report on Threats, Challenges and Change, 143
United Arab Emirates (UAE), 58, 63, 69–72

United Kingdom, 95–96; Brexit and, 90, 95–96; conflict in Iraq and, 142–143; humanitarian intervention and, 142; military speed and, 215–216, 219, 222–224; military technology and, 268; participation in NATO operations, 72; peacekeeping missions and, 153; PNA doctrine and, 193; taxation in, 30–31

United Nations Charter, 12–13, 109; humanitarian intervention and, 141; non-intervention norm and, 12–13, 138–140; perception of war and, 165–166; PNA doctrine and, 193

United Nations Security Council (UNSC), 138–140; China and, 196, 198; Darfur and, 144–145; humanitarian intervention and, 141; Iraq and, 139, 155; Libya and, 145–146; norms of intervention and, 138–141; peacekeeping operations (PKOs) of, 140, 150, 152, 191; perception of war and, 165–166. *See also* United Nations Charter

United Provinces (Netherlands), 38

United States: 2016 presidential election in, 169–170, 181n51; Afghanistan War and, 61, 116–117, 123, 125–129, 137n68; "America First" policy of, 110; China and, 243–244; civilian casualties and, 119–122, 133n22, 134n26; Civil War in, 30–33, 45; CVE operations and, 137nn65–66; cyber attacks on, 172–173; Djibouti and, 192; gray zone conflict and, 162; humanitarian intervention and, 142–143; information technology and, 230; Iran and, 25, 139–140; Iraq and, 117, 142–144, 164 (*See also* Gulf War); Libya and, 71; military speed and, 213–214, 219, 235–246; military technology and, 46–47, 197, 262–266; NATO and, 12, 23, 67, 85–86, 88, 92–94, 102n20, 295;

North Korea and, 25; peacekeeping missions and, 153; PNA doctrine and, 193; small-scale military ventures and, 29–30; Syria and, 142, 146, 199; threshold of war and, 167; Vietnam War and, 34–35, 45–46, 48; war financing in, 30–37; "War on Terror" and, 63, 139, 167, 180n36; wars fought by (*See* individual wars)

Unrestricted Warfare (1999), 171

Ven Bruusgaard, Kristin, 256

Vennesson, Pascal, 296, 300

Vespucci, Amerigo, 292

Vietnam War, 34–35, 45–46, 48

Wade, James, 47

Waldhauser, Thomas, 192

Wang Xiangsui, 171

Warden, John, 46–47

war financing, 26–29, 38–39, 295–296, 299–300; debt and, 28, 37–39; early history (prior to 1850), 26, 27–29; extractive state and, 26–27; following World War II, 34–37; limited war and, 27; modern financial technologies, 29; taxation and, 27–37. *See also* taxation

"War on Terror," 63, 139, 167, 180n36

warrior spirit, 287, 289n1, 297

wartime paradigms, 10–11, 208

Watling, Jack, 242

Weber, Max, 294

Weigill, Rob, 71

Western concept of war, 10, 163–168, 175; contrasted with China, 170–173; contrasted with Russia, 168–170

Western military power, 1, 4–7, 11, 19, 296; Chinese challenges to, 13, 171, 197, 263; gray zone conflict and, 161–162, 164, 173; Russian challenges to, 13, 168; temporality and, 3, 5–7, 275, 292, 295

Wheeler, Nicholas, 266

Whiskey Rebellion (USA), 30
Williams, Heather, 293–294, 297, 300
World Summit (2005), 143–144, 146, 151, 155
World War I, 45, 48, 51, 296; funding of, 30–32
World War II, 25, 35, 45, 51–52; funding of, 30, 32

Xi Jinping, 185
Xinjiang, 150

Yoo, John, 271
Yugoslavia, 140, 166. *See also* Kosovo; Serbia

Zakaria, Fareed, 37
Zheng He, 292
Zimbabwe, 146
Zuckerberg, Mark, 266